COMPUTER SIMULATION OF COMPETITIVE MARKET RESPONSE

Arnold E. Amstutz

The M.I.T. Press
Massachusetts Institute of Technology
Cambridge, Massachusetts, and London, England

This book is respectfully dedicated to the memory of

Ross M. Cunningham

PREFACE

Since publication of the first edition of *Computer Simulation of Competitive Market Response* in 1967, microanalytic behavioral simulations have been applied in many fields. The technique has been used in developing models of markets for consumer products and services including food and beverages, appliances, automobiles, cosmetics, clothing, financial services and transportation. It has been used to simulate markets for industrial products and services including electronic devices, chemicals, computers, metals, training aids, and heavy equipment. In addition, applications of the technique are being made in nonbusiness situations in which management must assess and interact with complex environments that are strongly influenced by human response. The United States government, for example, is using the technique to develop models of complex environments in which it is attempting to establish uniform policy. The government of a major U.S. city is exploring the use of microanalytic simulation in the development of a health services planning and control system.

The experience gained in developing and implementing microanalytic behavioral simulations in these diverse areas has led to a refinement of the four-phase approach to system development described in Chapter 15. The design process has been simplified by dividing the macro specification development into three independent project steps. In the first of the three new phases, a detailed project plan is developed. Preliminary statements of planning and operating goals are established and the focus of the system development effort is defined. Alternative criteria for evaluating project progress and the implemented system are also determined during Phase I.

The second new project phase is devoted to describing in detail the environment on which the system will focus. Major elements of the environment are identified and the significant interactions among these elements are described. Measures to monitor the important interactions are also established.

The third phase of the refined macro specification process focuses on the establishment of explicit management-oriented system specifications. Planning and decision procedures to be supported by the computer are established as well as the environment to be monitored, models and measures to be used, and the functions to be performed by the system.

The previous micro specification phase has been redefined as the "Computer-oriented Systems Specification" phase. This phase continues to be concerned with detailed system specification for development and implementation of the model by programmers and system analysts. The documentation produced in this phase provides a master plan for the control of all programming, testing, and implementation activities. The final two phases, programming and testing, and evaluation and implementation, remain unaltered.

The experience with the technique that has been gained since the original publication of the book in 1967 has served to emphasize the concern for management involvement in the system design process. The importance of human and organizational factors which influence the interaction between manager and system analyst, and the requirement that management understand the conceptual structure underlying the simulation models, have been frequently demonstrated in the various applications.

It is becoming evident that the simulation process and the use of simulation-based systems can have a major impact on the management process. The system design activity places new management emphasis on broader policy problems that are approached with increased effectiveness due to the availability of more meaningful data and a better (model-based) understanding of the environment. Top managers can devote more time to problem definition and the broader planning functions which are often given low priority on the executive agenda in view of current operating problems. Managers spend more time attempting to understand the environment in which their companies operate and formulating assumptions about planning and communication processes. Substantial time is given to explicating, testing, and validating new or alternative hypotheses on the nature of the market environment and the impact of their company on it.

A recent survey of managers of major U.S. corporations revealed that a majority became interested in microanalytic behavioral simulations after obtaining experience with an operating information system. This phenomenon may be attributed to two factors. First, experience with an information system illustrates the importance of models in providing a framework within which system output may be linked to management understanding of significant events occurring in the environment. Second, there is a natural evolution from simple to more complex system structures. A manager's first models tend to be simple and narrowly focused on limited aspects of his environment. As he gains experience with models, the need for a more complete representation and an integrated structure arises. At this point, the manager begins to move toward a simulation-based system.

It is noteworthy that several of the most interesting developments in microanalytic behavioral simulation are occurring outside the United States. What is, perhaps, the most advanced behavioral simulation in commercial use was developed by an international drug company. Managers in many countries have developed simulation-based systems and are experimenting with highly imaginative approaches in an attempt to structure and solve their management problems.

Arnold E. Amstutz

Cambridge, Massachusetts
April 1970

ACKNOWLEDGMENTS

I wish to take this opportunity to acknowledge the assistance of individuals who have contributed to the development of this book and the research on which it is based.

Professors Gerald B. Tallman, William F. Massy, and Peter S. King devoted many hours to the discussion of assumptions, formulations, and research procedures during the formative stages of microanalytic simulation research at the Massachusetts Institute of Technology Sloan School of Management. E. P. Brooks, Dean Emeritus of the Sloan School of Management provided support and encouragement for these early stages of research.

Professor Henry J. Claycamp of Stanford University and Arthur Traub of Decision Technology, Inc., have contributed greatly to the application of models described in this book and to the refinement of conceptual structure. Christopher R. Sprague of the Sloan School of Management has suggested many useful alternative model formulations and developed techniques for efficiently computerizing models discussed in this book. August P. Hess, now Director of Management Information, Johnson & Johnson, contributed to the conceptual development of the consumer model and made possible much of the early research on which that model is based.

Professor Peer O. Soelberg of the Sloan School of Management devoted much time and effort to detailed reviewing of preliminary drafts. Professor Ithiel de Sola Pool of the M.I.T. Political Science Department, and John D. C. Little of the Sloan School of Management made many helpful suggestions regarding approach and system structure. M.I.T.'s President Howard W. Johnson, then Dean of the Sloan School of Management, encouraged and supported this project through many frustrating periods and took time from his duties to serve as Chairman of the author's doctoral dissertation on which this book is based.

System development and testing were done using the facilities of the M.I.T. Computation Center. Much of the research reported here was supported by grants from the Sloan Research Fund of the M.I.T. Sloan School of Management.

I wish to express my particular appreciation for the efforts of Marilyn A. Fedele who typed many preliminary working papers and drafts and efficiently solved the logistical problems encountered in preparing the final document. I am indebted to Pamela C. Marsters for the layout and execution of figures and exhibits and to Channing Stowell, III, for flow chart design and proofreading. My wife Nancy has been of great help to me in reading proof and in otherwise assisting with the preparation of this work.

The helpful comments and criticisms offered by my colleagues and students at the M.I.T. Sloan School of Management who reacted to this work in its various stages of development are gratefully acknowledged.

My final acknowledgment is to Professor Ross M. Cunningham, who provided the impetus for this work and served as chairman of my dissertation committee until his death. In addition to devoting time and energy to evaluating concepts and research procedures, he created an environment in which these new and unorthodox approaches to marketing management could be examined and evaluated. Without him the work reported here would have been impossible.

ARNOLD E. AMSTUTZ

Cambridge, Massachusetts
October 1966

CONTENTS

chapter 14

EDUCATIONAL APPLICATIONS OF BEHAVIORAL SIMULATION 413

chapter 15

MANAGEMENT APPLICATIONS OF MICROANALYTIC BEHAVIORAL
SIMULATIONS 431

COMPUTER SIMULATION OF COMPETITIVE MARKET RESPONSE

Chapter 1

INTRODUCTION

This book was written to present elements of an organized behavioral theory of market interactions and to suggest an approach to management based on the use of microanalytic computer simulations of interactions within the marketing environment. It focuses on the development and implementation of behavioral models and system configurations designed to provide a formal quantitative structure within which management problems involving the environment external to the firm can be defined and analyzed.

The models and methodology described in the following chapters have been successfully applied in management systems concentrating on consumer and industrial product markets. They have also served as the basis for new approaches to undergraduate, graduate, and executive development courses in marketing management and market-oriented information systems.

Objectives

Material presented in the following chapters has been organized to achieve a series of objectives:

1. Develop a conceptual framework within which salient attributes of a market environment or management problem may be delineated.
2. Define a limited set of elements that may serve as the focus of systematic analysis.
3. Develop a theoretical structure through which the interrelations

between these elements may be described, measured, and analyzed.

4. Express relationships between elements and processes in quantitative and measurable terms.
5. Summarize noted relationships in generalized models consisting of properly dimensioned systems of equations amenable to computer simulation.
6. Evaluate the precision, accuracy, and validity of resulting simulation models.
7. Assess the contribution of simulation-based systems to education, policy planning, and management decision making.

Methodology

The first step in moving toward a realization of the noted objectives is to develop an over-all description of important factors in the marketing environment. This qualitative description serves as the basis for a nonmathematical but orderly structure within which key elements and processes may be defined.

The second step involves the design of gross macroflow models encompassing previously defined elements and processes. These preliminary descriptions define major interaction patterns and, as such, serve as the cornerstones of more complete and detailed subsector models.

The third step encompasses quantification of relevant behavior and development of sector models. The models produced at this stage must provide sufficient scope and refinement so that a representation of the total marketing environment may be synthesized by combining them in a single simulation.

The final step is implementation. Problems of validating simulation performance against data obtained from the actual environment must be considered. Other difficulties inherent in the use of the proposed approach by managers and educators also require evaluation.

Perspective

Before outlining the content of following sections it may be useful to establish a perspective.

A Corporate Management View

Relationships and interactions within the business environment will be considered from the point of view of a producer and marketer of goods or services. From this vantage point, attention will be focused largely on the environment external to the firm in an effort to relate variables manipulated by management to processes beyond their direct control.

The central objective will be to develop a framework within which behavior relevant to the manager may be described. It will be assumed that the manager is concerned with the generation of sales at profitable levels under conditions that permit short-run solvency and long-term capital appreciation in the presence of uncertainty.

This perspective requires that tests of relevancy be pragmatic. In deciding to include or exclude a particular factor from representation, management's ability to influence or control that factor must be given major consideration.

Questions of measurement are particularly important in this context. Because meaningful application of theory or structure is dependent on management's ability to relate model states to conditions in the business world, each variable found within the model structure must be measurable in the actual business environment.

The Consumer as Raison d'Etre

In the current literature, it is generally agreed that management's perspective should be expanded to encompass the world outside the firm. Numerous authors advocate a shift from concentration on internal processes to concern for synthesis of a total marketing system oriented toward the external environment.

Management must think of itself not as producing products but as providing customer-creating value satisfactions. . . . Otherwise, the company will be merely a series of pigeonholed parts, with no consolidating sense of purpose or direction.

In short, the organization must learn to think of itself not as producing goods or services but as buying customers, as doing the things that will make people want to do business with it.[1]

The well-known management writer, Peter Drucker, emphasizes this perspective in his book, *The Practice of Management.*

If we want to know what a business is we have to start with its *purpose.* And its purpose must lie outside of the business itself. In fact, it must lie

[1] T. Levitt, "Marketing Myopia," *Harvard Business Review,* Vol. 38 (July–August 1960), p. 56.

in society since a business enterprise is an organ of society. There is only one valid definition of business purpose: *to create a customer.*[2]

Emphasis on Policy Management

It has been suggested that a focus on aspects of the business environment external to the firm — those aspects often associated with marketing management — is most appropriate for "policy management." In *The Practice of Management* Peter Drucker argues:

Because it is its purpose to create a customer, any business enterprise has two — and only these two — basic functions: marketing and innovation. They are the entrepreneurial functions.

Marketing is the distinguishing, the unique function of the business. A business is set apart from all other human organizations by the fact that it markets a product or a service. Neither Church, nor Army, nor School, nor State does that. Any organization that fulfills itself through marketing a product or a service, is a business. Any organization in which marketing is either absent or incidental is not a business and should never be run as if it were one.[3]

It is difficult to find a functional management area in which the gains that may be realized by effective quantitative structuring are greater than in marketing. The need for a systematic (if not scientific) approach to marketing has been discussed frequently in the literature. The following statement of marketing's problem, originally presented in *Management Science* and often referenced, is representative.

The practice of administration in marketing has been handicapped by a type of cultural lag. In every phase of marketing operations the application of systematic methodology to the management task has trailed by approximately one generation the experience in the field of production.

. . . Progress in the construction of an organized methodology of management techniques and in the generalization of conclusions from observation and experiment in the decades between the two great wars was generally oriented in the factory or used the production process as a take-off point for reaching the general management level.

. . . There has been no revolutionary force in marketing comparable to the introduction of the power driven machine in production. Many

[2] P. F. Drucker, *The Practice of Management* (New York: Harper and Brothers, Publishers, Inc., 1954), p. 37.
[3] *Ibid.*, pp. 37–38.

marketing activities are carried on over extended geographic areas. They lack the simple repetitive characteristics of factory production. They are not easily measured and controlled. To a much greater extent than in production they involve people dealing with people (and it is worth reminding ourselves that even the more limited human element in production has been a continually frustrating factor for management). . . . One dominant influence in the marketing process — the consumer — is outside of management's direct control and is only partially, and until now usually unpredictably, susceptible to manipulation and influence.[4]

Some Implications of the Perspective

The perspective adopted in this study naturally influences criteria of relevancy applied when identifying and structuring pertinent decision areas. Promotion decisions, for example, will be structured in terms of content to be communicated as well as dollar expenditure in media. Communication effectiveness will be evaluated in terms of the extent to which specific product attributes and appeals are associated with the promoting brand in the minds of specific consumers. Promotional impact will be described in terms of changes in consumer behavior as it is directed toward acquisition of the product or service embodying promoted characteristics.

Distributors and wholesalers will be viewed as transfer agents conveying product and information to the consumer. Salesmen will be seen as order and information transfer channels.

The government may be perceived as a constraint, limiting activity within the marketing system. Competitive considerations will focus on the prediction of probable competitor actions and responses.

Research may be viewed as a process through which information of varying relevancy about the environment is collected, structured, and communicated with varying degrees of accuracy. The usefulness of research information will be evaluated in terms of management's ability to assimilate and use research results to refine the usually implicit models against which they test alternatives when making decisions. The research value of particular models or systems will be measured by their effect in focusing research or providing structure through which research findings may be related to decisions.

The ultimate focus of this study is the consumer or industrial purchaser. In describing, modeling, and analyzing processes and interac-

[4] M. Anshen, "Management Science in Marketing: Status and Prospects," *Management Science,* Vol. 2 (April 1956), pp. 222–223.

tions within the marketing system, the final objective is to relate all elements and interactions in terms of effect on purchase decisions.

An Interdisciplinary Approach

The business environment may be viewed from a management perspective; however, approaches to problems, frameworks of analysis, and hypotheses regarding behavior and interactions within the business environment will be drawn from many disciplines. Economists, political scientists, sociologists, anthropologists, and psychologists have all suggested methodology, concepts, and theory relevant to the problems discussed in later chapters.

In light of the range of problems considered by the market-oriented corporate executive, meaningful management-oriented behavioral theory must draw from the social and behavioral sciences, the physical sciences, and various areas of business administration and economics.[5] Those concerned with the development of theory in marketing consistently reference "the literature of several intellectual disciplines." [6]

Marketing, political science, and economics have been described as the "policy sciences" by Hans Thorelli, who notes the following common base:

Policy sciences are normative, not in the sense of being inherently biased by one set of values or another, but rather in that they invariably postulate the existence of *some* kind of value structure in terms of which the relative merits of alternative actions may be gauged. These sciences are not limited to studying the process of policy formation in public and private institutions. They are also concerned with specifying decision rules for managerial action.[7]

The perceptive manager shares the psychologists' interest in understanding human behavior and responses.[8] The work of both the cultural

[5] See, for example, W. Lazer and E. Kelley, "Interdisciplinary Horizons in Marketing," *Journal of Marketing,* Vol. 24 (October 1960), pp. 24–30.

[6] W. Alderson and R. Cox, "Toward the Theory of Marketing," *Journal of Marketing,* Vol. 12 (October 1948), p. 142.

[7] H. B. Thorelli, "Political Science and Marketing," in R. Cox, W. Alderson, and S. J. Shapiro (eds.), *Theory in Marketing* (Homewood, Ill.: Richard D. Irwin, Inc., 1964), pp. 125–136.

[8] Aspects of psychological theory and approach applicable in the field of marketing are effectively summarized by R. Ferber and H. G. Wales in *Motivation and Market Behavior* (Homewood, Ill.: R. D. Irwin, Inc., 1958). A more limited

anthropologist and the market researcher is based on a common concern for man in his cultural setting.[9] In a similar vein the common interests of marketers and sociologists have been much discussed.[10]

The common focus of manager and economist on the mechanisms of the market place provides still another basis for an interdisciplinary approach. "Microeconomics"[11] provides a useful framework within which to consider certain aspects of the behavior of a firm in a price-oriented competitive market. Concepts relating to the handling of uncertainty, utility, indifference, substitutability, complementarity, and income effects are particularly worthy of comment and will be discussed in later chapters.

The macroeconomist's concern with aggregate population statistics such as national income and gross national product is shared by business planners. Research directed toward gaining an understanding of consumer allocation of funds to expenditures and savings constitutes still another area of mutual interest.[12]

In view of the benefits to be gained from the insights of those associated with these diverse disciplines, there is much to recommend an eclectic approach based on what might be described as "cultural ecology." In discussing bases for a normative theory of marketing systems Wroe Alderson suggested that

. . . Pending the more comprehensive formulation of a general science of human behavior, the available starting points for the marketing theorist include economics and cultural ecology. Economics and ecology are two ways of looking at the relations between living things and the resources

---

but representative discussion of the contribution of psychologists to understanding of one aspect of consumer behavior is provided by Walter A. Woods, "Psychological Dimensions of Consumer Decision," *Journal of Marketing,* Vol. 24 (January 1960), pp. 15–19.

[9] See J. Gillin, "The Application of Anthropological Knowledge to Modern Mass Society," *Human Organization,* Vol. 15 (Winter 1957), pp. 24–29. See also C. Winick, "Anthropology's Contribution to Marketing," *Journal of Marketing,* Vol. 25 (July 1961), pp. 53–60.

[10] C. H. Johannson, "Contributions of Sociology to Marketing," *Journal of Marketing,* Vol. 24 (October 1959), pp. 29–34, and R. Bartels, "Sociologists and Marketologists," *Journal of Marketing,* Vol. 24 (October 1959), pp. 37–40.

[11] See, for example, P. A. Samuelson, *Economics: An Introductory Analysis* (New York: McGraw-Hill Book Company, Inc., 1955).

[12] H. J. Claycamp, "Characteristics of Owners of Thrift Deposits in Commercial Banks and Savings and Loan Associations," *Journal of Marketing Research,* Vol. 2 (May 1965), pp. 163–170.

which sustain their activities. Marketing as a field of study does not rest comfortably under the label of applied economics. There is an overlap between the tools and concepts of general economics and the analytical needs of the marketing specialist, but far from a perfect fit. The broader framework of ecology holds greater promise for the development of marketing science in both descriptive and normative terms.[13]

Presentation Structure

The following comments are intended as a brief introduction to the organization of material in later chapters. References to "sections" refer to logical segments into which material may be divided for purposes of analysis and do not necessarily denote physical chapters.

Qualitative Description of the Environment

The first section focuses on qualitative description of the environment external to the firm in terms of factors emphasized by contemporary marketing texts. Characteristics derived from this source provide the basis for development of a qualitative analytic structure.

Definition of Macrosectors

The second section is concerned largely with specification and definition. Problems of defining and quantifying elements suggested by the qualitative structure are examined. Previously developed qualitative specifications are refined and an explicit macrostructure is proposed.

Macromodel Development

Development in the third section is based on the proposed macrostructure. Macromodels of processes within the marketing environment are formulated in terms of concepts introduced in the preceding section. Models are categorized in terms of processes affecting (1) the formation, distribution, and consumption of physical product; (2) information generation, communication, and associated response processes; and (3) capital transformation and value flow.

Quantification

The fourth section focuses on the process of quantification with consideration given to measurement techniques, analytic structures, and functional relationships used in developing microanalytic behavioral

[13] W. Alderson, "A Normative Theory of Marketing Systems," in R. Cox, W. Alderson, and S. J. Shapiro, *Theory in Marketing* (Homewood, Ill.: Richard D. Irwin, Inc., 1964), pp. 92–93.

models. Alternative approaches are discussed and solutions to problems inherent in attempts to quantify human interactions are proposed.

Synthesis

The fifth section is devoted to review of the previously developed structure and to organization of a framework within which detailed sector models may be combined. Interactions summarized in the macromodels of product, information, and capital flow are re-examined in terms of processes occurring within and between sectors of the market.

Management decisions are examined in terms of their effect on interactions between the manufacturing level and other sectors of the marketing environment. Relationships are summarized in inputs and outputs through which the decision maker monitors and attempts to influence conditions within the market place.

Micromodel Development

The sixth section encompasses the formulation of detailed behavioral models representing actions and responses within and between specific sectors of the environment. The first model represents consumer actions and responses. Activities in the retailer sector are considered in the second model. The role of the distributor in a national marketing system is summarized in the third model, while the fourth focuses on salesman behavior. Consideration is also given to the representation of behavior associated with the marketing research function and government agencies.

Implementation

The seventh section introduces problems of implementing simulation models in operating business situations. The use of data to provide function estimates and exogenous input is discussed. Relationships between real and simulated circumstances in particular product situations are examined and processes followed in validating key model sectors are discussed.

Applications

A final section is devoted to a discussion of applications of microanalytic simulation in education and management. The use of a simulated marketing environment at undergraduate, graduate, and executive development levels is described. The potential contribution of simulation to management decision making is examined with reference to operating simulation-based decision support systems.

Chapter 2

QUALITATIVE DESCRIPTION OF THE MARKET ENVIRONMENT

In this chapter, traditional conceptions of the market environment will be considered. Representative texts used in college marketing courses will be examined to establish commonly agreed-upon attributes of the environment external to the firm. Once defining characteristics have been identified, a qualitative framework within which these factors may be structured will be proposed.

Common Elements in Contemporary Texts

The Principles Texts

Marketing texts often expound "principles and methods" underlying the "discipline." It is customary to begin with a definition of "the role of marketing."

It is the role of marketing to move goods and the title to them from manufacturers, farmers, mine operators, and others who create them to consumers.[1]

"The nature of marketing" is then discussed. It

. . . includes all the activities necessary to place tangible goods in the hands of household consumers and industrial users, excluding only such activities as involve a significant change in the form of goods.[2]

[1] C. F. Phillips and D. J. Duncan, *Marketing Principles and Methods* (Homewood, Ill.: Richard D. Irwin, Inc., 1960), p. 3.
[2] *Ibid.,* p. 3.

10

The authors of one widely used text suggest three alternative approaches to the study of marketing based on "(1) commodities, such as wheat, dresses, sheet steel, or gasoline; (2) functions, or services performed, such as storage, transportation, or selling; and (3) institutions handling the various commodities and performing the functions such as wholesalers, mill-supply firms, or department stores." [3] After considering the pros and cons of each approach, they conclude that ". . . the nature of marketing is such that it can best be understood if all three of these approaches are used in covering various aspects of the subject." Principles texts normally discuss marketing functions and institutions in terms of concepts such as transfer of title, demand generation, physical distribution, characteristics of agent middlemen, and channels of distribution.

One or more chapters will usually be devoted to discussion of consumer buying behavior and demography. Retail outlets ranging from vending machines and small independent retailers to large department stores, discount houses, mail-order companies, and consumer cooperatives are frequently compared. Characteristics and functions of various types of wholesalers and observable trends in wholesaling are similarly discussed.

Most of the texts differentiate approaches to markets for industrial goods, including raw materials, from those applicable to consumer product markets. For example, Phillips and Duncan discuss "the market for industrial goods, marketing manufactured industrial goods, marketing raw materials, the commodity exchange as a marketing agency, and cooperative marketing by farmers" in this context.

Discussions of market-oriented management policy traditionally focus on functional descriptions of marketing activities undertaken at various levels in a corporate organization. These include market research, merchandising, selection of channels of distribution, buying procedures, transportation, methods of selling, competition in areas other than pricing, and pricing. Management's social and ethical responsibilities are frequently considered in combination with a historical review of pertinent legislation limiting alternatives available to management.

The various texts propounding "Principles of Marketing" introduce the student to terminology and tradition. They provide convenient categorizations. One learns of the differences between the independent general store, the small, independent, limited-line store in a small

[3] *Ibid.*, p. 8.

town, in the neighborhood areas of a city, in the downtown areas, and in outlying shopping districts; chain stores; supermarkets; department stores; discount houses; and retail mail-order houses. They provide background material sufficient to enable a student to answer questions such as "explain briefly three major limitations of marketing research," [4] "explain the types of information the salesman needs to do an effective selling job," [5] and "in view of the fact that many service wholesalers publish annual catalogues, how do you explain the declining importance of the mail order wholesaler?" [6] In short, this approach is effective in introducing the student to the institutions and functions associated historically with the environment external to the firm.

While the Principles texts may identify relevant aspects of the environment, they do not provide an effective basis for improved understanding of the nature of interactions within the market place or guidelines for the development of more effective means of dealing with the problems faced by management. While introducing institutions and describing functions performed at various levels in the market, they largely fail to provide a means of synthesis. The reader may be left with the feeling that marketing is a conglomeration of unassociated institutions and that management decision making consists of classifying a problem properly and applying appropriate principles.

The Analytical Texts

A new type of marketing text has recently appeared to vie with the traditional Principles texts for the college market. The new entries emphasize structure, analysis, integration, and synthesis. A representative text of this type is heralded by its publishers as building "a conceptual view of marketing as a process that is completely integrated with all business activities." [7] This text begins with the question, "What is marketing?" and turns to the American Marketing Association Committee on Definitions and to the President of General Foods Corporation for answers. The authors then consider the relationship of marketing to business in general, the economy, and the free enterprise system. As in the Principles books previously noted, consumer actions

---

[4] *Ibid.,* p. 516.
[5] *Ibid.,* p. 636.
[6] *Ibid.,* p. 312.
[7] W. J. Taylor and R. T. Shaw, *Marketing, An Integrated Analytical Approach* (Cincinnati, Ohio: Southwestern Publishing Company, 1961).

and responses are described in terms of patterns of consumption, buying behavior, the effect of promotion, and demographic statistics. Market functions are defined as pricing, selling, advertising, transportation, storage, financing, and risk taking.

Agricultural and industrial markets, wholesaling, and retailing are examined in the last sections of this book in terms of the flow of goods. "Government, international marketing, and contemporary trends" also receive comment.

In addition to covering the standard functional and institutional material, one of the most popular analytical texts provides a visual structure based on "product, place, promotion, and price." [8]

It may be helpful to think of the four variables which marketing managers can use as the four "P's." [Figure 2.1] emphasizes their interrelationship and focus on consumers (C).

The diagram showing the four P's focusing upon the consumer emphasizes the variables which marketing managers can control. But since marketing

Figure 2.1. The four "P's."

does not exist in a vacuum, certain outside forces must be considered. These — indirectly at least — limit the marketing manager. He must work with or around them. All of these factors can be placed in the following categories:

1. Cultural and social environment — changes very slowly.
2. Political and legal environment — changes slowly.
3. Economic environment — may change fairly quickly.
4. Existing business structure — always changing, dynamic.
5. Resources and objectives of the firm — stable in short run.

All of these factors except the last one, are related to the final, or immediate consumer. Being out of the control of the marketing executive, they will be

[8] E. J. McCarthy, *Basic Marketing, A Managerial Approach* (Homewood, Ill.: Richard D. Irwin, Inc., 1960).

placed in an outer ring in the diagram. But because they are in the outer ring does not mean that they can be or are ignored [Figure 2.2].[9]

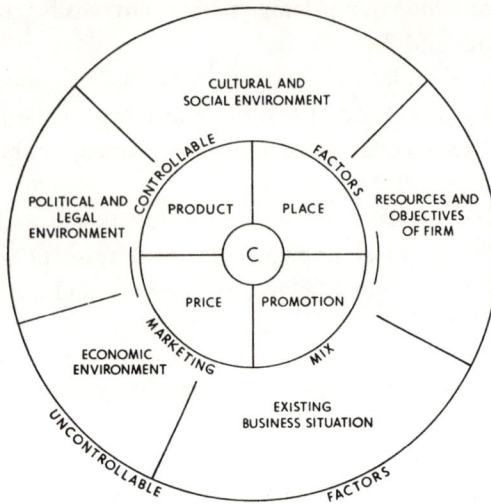

Figure 2.2. The marketing manager's variables.

This visual structure provides a basis for synthesis of institutions and functions within an orderly, albeit macro- and qualitative, framework. Organization of material is an important step in the direction of ultimate integration. It suggests a relationship between manipulatory parts and the marketing environment as a whole and as such provides a basis for more meaningful analysis of end-means relations.[10]

Consumer Content

Substantial space could be devoted to the many marketing texts published in recent years. However, the basic content noted in previously cited examples is encountered consistently.[11] The authors agree that

[9] *Ibid.*, pp. 45, 48–49.

[10] A more complex, but similar, conceptual scheme is discussed by E. J. Kelley and William Lazer, *Managerial Marketing: Perspectives and Viewpoints* (Homewood, Ill.: Richard D. Irwin, Inc., 1958), pp. 478–86.

[11] Texts reviewed in reaching this conclusion include John A. Howard, *Marketing Management: Analysis and Planning* (Homewood, Ill.: Richard D. Irwin, Inc., 1963).

K. R. Davis, *Marketing Management* (New York: The Ronald Press Company, 1961).

J. H. Westing and G. Albaum, *Modern Marketing Thought* (New York: The Macmillan Company, 1964).

the consumer or industrial purchaser, retailer, distributor or wholesaler, and manufacturer are the major institutions of importance to marketing. From a functional standpoint they are concerned with pricing, advertising, selling, product design, and research. All note the impact of government regulation and discuss the effect of governmental control on decision making.

Requirements of a Conceptual Framework

Systematic integration of concepts discussed in contemporary marketing texts must begin with a conceptual framework, a skeletal structure to which the elements of a marketing simulation may be attached. The four "P's" provide a basis for one such framework. While useful for exposition, this structure does not provide adequate support for the development of a representation of the environment external to a firm as a system of interactive parts. A conceptual framework designed to serve this function must

1. Delineate a set of elements that, while common to a broad range of management problems, are defined in sufficient detail to permit differentiation between relevant states of the environment.
2. Serve as a basis for description of processes as well as of elements — provide a means of describing interactions between elements.
3. Be based on measurable entities amenable to quantitative description and validation.

S. F. Otteson, W. G. Panschar, J. M. Patterson, *Marketing: The Firm's Viewpoint* (New York: The Macmillan Company, 1964).

H. Lazo and A. Corbin, *Management in Marketing: Text and Cases* (New York: McGraw-Hill Book Company, Inc., 1961).

E. Cundiff and R. Still, *Basic Marketing: Concepts, Environment, and Decisions* (Englewood Cliffs, N. J.: Prentice-Hall, Inc., 1964).

R. Buskirk, *Principles of Marketing* (New York: Holt, Rinehart, and Winston, Inc., 1961).

P. D. Converse, H. W. Huegy, and R. V. Mitchell, *Elements of Marketing* (6th ed.; Englewood Cliffs, N. J.: Prentice-Hall, Inc., 1958).

H. L. Hansen, *Marketing* (Homewood, Ill.: Richard D. Irwin, Inc., 1961).

R. D. Tousley, E. Clark, and F. E. Clark, *Principles of Marketing* (New York: The Macmillian Company, 1962).

S. H. Britt and H. Boyd, Jr., *Marketing Management and Administrative Actions* (New York: McGraw-Hill Book Company, Inc., 1963).

P. Holmes, R. Brownlee, and R. Bartels, *Text, Readings in Marketing* (Columbus, Ohio: Charles E. Merrill Books, Inc., 1963).

S. Walters, M. Snider, and M. Sweet, *Readings in Marketing* (Cincinnati, Ohio: Southwestern Publishing Company, 1963).

Experience and the literature support the conclusion that markets can be described in diverse ways and depicted in conflicting word pictures. Despite divergent perceptions, there is a common underlying reality to which managers and academicians alike attempt to relate. Whether one listens to a brand manager describe a product line that is not moving or to a marketing professor discussing a theoretical salesman allocation procedure, certain common elements may be noted. These are the elements that must be encompassed by a qualitative framework if it is to support a systematic analysis of marketing phenomena.

A Proposed Conceptual Framework

After experimenting with alternative conceptual frameworks the author has concluded that the desired properties noted previously are efficiently achieved in a qualitative structure consisting of actors, observable actions, and implied actions defined as follows:

1. *Actors.* The actors within the market environment are manufacturers, distribution agents, selling agents, research agents, government, and consumer or industrial purchasers.
2. *Observable Actions.* Observable actions comprise all events that may be directly verified by observation. These include actions associated with the distribution of physical goods, communication of information, implementation of pricing policies, generation of orders, and product or service consumption.
3. *Implied Actions.* Implied actions refer to processes that, although not directly observable, are assumed to underlie and support observable actions. Representation of implied processes involves intermediate variables that must be defined and measured if the existence of implied actions is to be verified empirically. Implied actions include exposure and response to advertising, establishment of effective motivation for sales forces, and the development of and change in knowledge and attitude.

The proposed structure facilitates graphic representation of interactions between market sectors as illustrated in Figure 2.3, which provides a macroview of product and information flow from producer to consumer. Dashed lines represent the flow of information (1) from manufacturer to consumers, retailers, and distributors; (2) from manufacturer through sales force to retailers and distributors; and (3) from

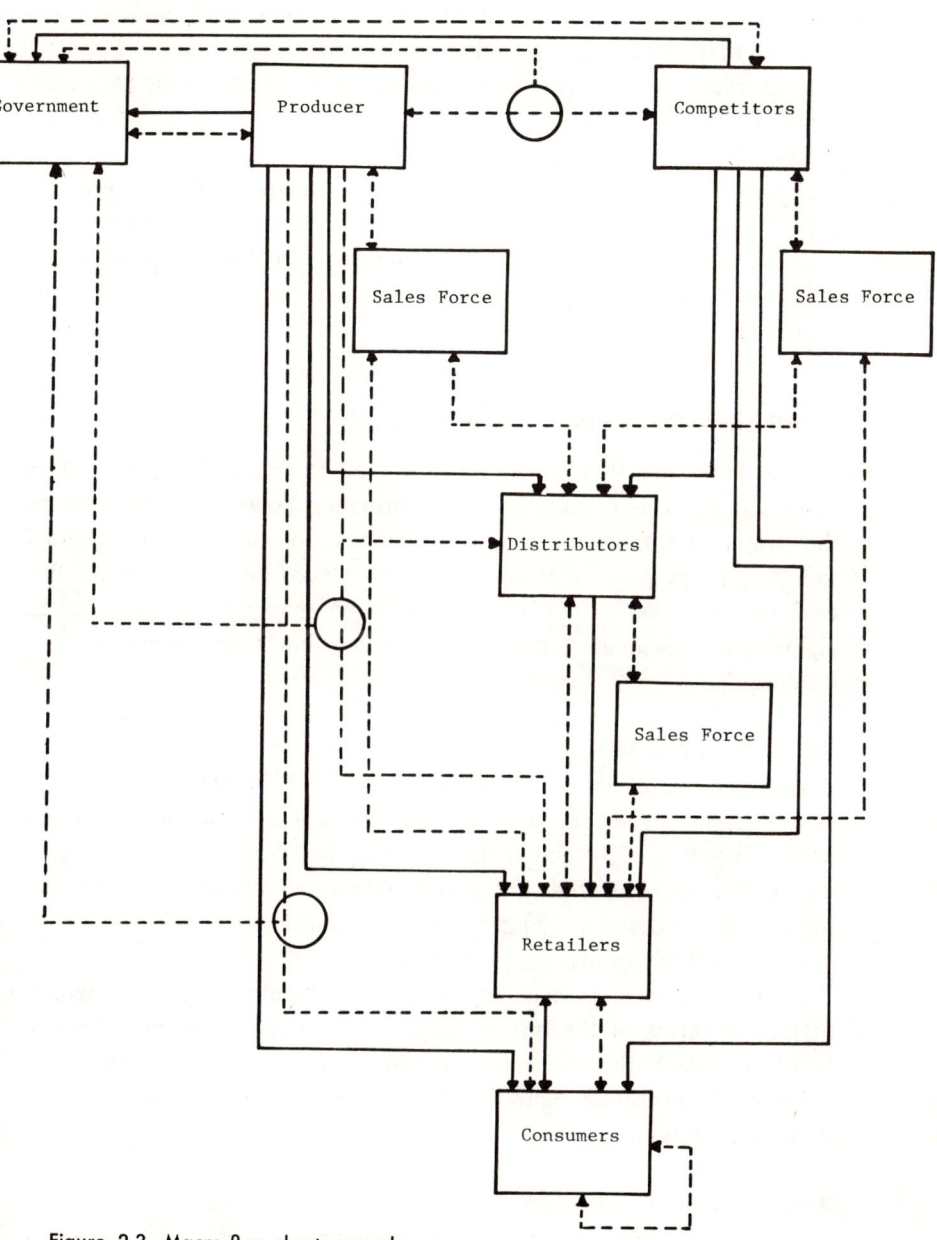

Figure 2.3. Macro flow chart example.

distributor through sales force to retailers. Solid lines indicate that product may flow directly from producer to consumers or indirectly through retailers and distributors. Government concern with producer-competitor communication, advertising, and product produced is also illustrated.

Figure 2.3 is not to be construed as a statement of structural attributes. It is merely an example designed to illustrate that interactions between elements in the marketing system may be easily expressed and rapidly assimilated in graphic form using a framework of the type proposed.

Qualitative Definition of a Framework

The discussion thus far has focused on interactions among actors described in terms of product and information flows. Expanded use of the proposed framework requires refinement of the structure beyond the gross proportions in which it was introduced. Working toward this end, the proposed system structure may be reformulated in terms of eight "active elements," three "elements of flow," and three "passive elements."

Eight Active Elements

Active elements in the marketing system are human and, as such, can originate signals as well as react to signals generated by other active elements. Eight active elements may be identified as (1) a producer, (2) his competitors, (3) distributors and wholesalers, (4) selling agents — salesmen, (5) retailers, (6) consumers, (7) government, and (8) research agents.

Each active element may be described by its characteristic functions defined in terms of the inputs the element receives, the variations in inputs to which the element is sensitive, the outputs the element is capable of generating, and the correlations, if any, between specific inputs and outputs.

Three Elements of Flow

Elements of flow are the vehicles of interaction between active elements. These are the factors which a successful management is able to manipulate to achieve desired objectives. Elements of flow are unable either to initiate or to respond to signals. They are the media through which signals are transmitted, the means of energy transfer analogous to the electrons that flow in an electronic network. The elements of flow are defined as (1) product, (2) information, and (3) capital.

Three Passive Elements

Passive elements may be described as characteristics of the channel through which elements of flow move between active elements. While passive elements affect the signals (elements of flow) moving in the channel with which they are associated, they cannot originate signals or affect active elements directly.

Three types of passive elements are defined. These are (1) time delays that affect the movement of elements of flow between active elements, (2) dissipators that reduce the magnitude of elements of flow transmitted between active elements, and (3) storage elements that accumulate backlogs of elements of flow.

The Market Viewed as a Network

Given the perspective of a company producing and marketing a consumer or industrial product or service, the market may be thought of as a network from which management attempts to obtain particular responses. The manager is able to manipulate passive elements within the network and to control the entry of elements of flow that provide signals to which active elements may respond. He may obtain some information about the state and response of particular elements directly; however, most information relating to the effect of interactions within the system and to total system response must be imputed from analysis of output generated by the system in response to given inputs.

Summary

The proposed qualitative organization of the marketing system may be summarized for a consumer marketing case with reference to the previously introduced Figure 2.3.

Active Elements

Seven of the eight active elements (research agents are excluded) are represented in this figure. As indicated by the dashed lines representing flow of information, each generates and responds to signals (information) from other active elements.

Elements of Flow

Two of the three elements of flow are represented in Figure 2.3. These are product (represented by a solid line) and information (represented by a dashed line). The flow of capital is not included. As illustrated, channels carrying elements of flow originate and terminate at active elements.

Passive Elements

While not explicitly represented in Figure 2.3, the functions of passive elements may be illustrated by a brief description of product flow from producer to distributor as pictured in the flow chart.

The effect of a time delay on the flow of goods from producer to distributor is obvious. Time delays are encountered in producer processing of distributor orders, transferring product from warehouse to channel, transporting product to the distributor, and handling product at the distributor level.

The second passive element, dissipation, is of less importance in the context of product flow than when dealing with information flow. In the case of product flow, dissipation occurs if product is lost, spoiled, or damaged while in transit or inventory.

The concept of a storage element is easily illustrated with reference to producer-distributor product flow. Product is stored in inventory by the producer, it is stored in transit while being transferred from producer to distributor and, once it reaches the distributor, it is stored in inventory until shipped to the retailer.

The Impact of Structure on Description

The impact of even qualitative structure on the description of processes within the marketing environment may be illustrated using Figure 2.3. Consider, for example, producer promotion directed to the consumer. In context of this structure, the problem is formulated in terms of information flow rather than in dollar expenditure alternatives.

Some information is transmitted directly from producer to consumer; other messages reach the consumer only after being filtered (delayed and perhaps partially dissipated) through the distributor. In the first instance, the consumer responds to signals received directly from the producer. In the second, the distributor and his sales force may modify or delete the producer's message before it reaches the consumer.

Description of promotion in context of this structure therefore focuses on transfer functions describing the response and the transfer characteristic of each active element to information inputs from every other active element within a given system.

DEFINITION OF SYSTEM ELEMENTS

In this chapter the qualitative structure introduced in Chapter 2 will be refined. Specifications for active elements, elements of flow, and passive elements will be defined to provide an explicit macrostructure for the later development of microanalytic simulations. Explicit definitions and boundary conditions — the prerequisites of systematic quantitative analysis — will be established. General definitions for each class of system elements will be followed by specific definitions for each item within the class. Graphic representation of characteristic processes will also be considered.

Elements of Flow

Elements of flow are entities that flow in the channels of the marketing system. The three classes of elements of flow delineated in Chapter 2 were product, information, and capital.

The movement of elements of flow is described in terms of a rate of flow over a given time period and measured in units per time period. Processes involving elements of flow may be observed at the point of origin where the element of flow enters a channel, within the channel as the element moves through it, and at the terminal where the element leaves the channel.

The names given the elements of flow are familiar and generally meaningful; however, in order to avoid later ambiguity, specific definitions must be established for product, information, and capital.

The Element of Flow Called "Product"

Two classifications of product flow are of importance within the marketing system. At the manufacturing level, raw material is sequentially converted through work in process to finished goods. Outside the manufacturing sector, product flow involves only finished goods.

Raw Material

Because this study is concerned primarily with the marketing activities of the firm, only limited consideration will be given to subclassifications within the raw material product category. In the present context, raw material is of importance to the extent that it affects product attributes, product cost, and (through scarcity) the firm's ability to supply finished goods.

Finished Goods

Beyond the manufacturing sector, and throughout the distribution system, three types of finished goods are encountered. First are the salable items intended for ultimate consumption that constitute the major portion of product flow. The second classification of finished goods is samples — product distributed at less than normal prices to the trade for display and promotional purposes and product distributed free to potential consumers as part of introductory promotional programs. The third finished goods classification is returns — product returned to the retailer, distributor, or manufacturer, whether for repair or replacement. Differentiating characteristics noted within each finished goods subdivision include distinctions based on brand, model, and product or package size and color.

Product Specification

In summary, the term "product" refers to raw materials or finished goods. Raw material is considered homogeneous, and only one attribute of raw material, degree of scarcity, is recognized. Three categories of finished goods, salable items, samples, and returns, are specified. Within each classification, differentiation on the basis of brand, model, and size is recognized. In order to handle certain product cases, it is necessary to define "model" narrowly with differentiating product characteristics or options considered to constitute a separate model.

This specification of product as an element of flow is summarized in outline form in Specification 3.1.

Specification 3.1. Product as an Element of Flow

I. Classification
   A. Raw Materials
   B. Finished Goods
      1. Salable Items
      2. Samples
      3. Returns
II. Attributes
   A. Raw Material Attributes
      1. Scarcity of Material
      2. Price Elasticity of Supply
   B. Finished Goods Attributes
      1. Brand
      2. Model
      3. Size

The Element of Flow Called "Information"

The flow of information within the marketing system may be specified in terms of three classifications of communication — promotion, operating information, and word-of-mouth communication.

Promotion may originate at the producer or retailer level and is communicated through formal media channels to all or to a segment of the population distinguished by its exposure to specific media. Operating information may originate at the producer, distributor, salesman, or retailer level and is transmitted formally but privately between elements in the distribution system. Word-of-mouth communication is originated by, and transmitted informally to, consumers.

Promotion

The term promotion is intended to encompass all communication relating to product characteristics and/or product-associated appeals directed through media or trade channels to the population at large or selected segments of that population. It may be useful to distinguish between three subcategories of promotion.

1. *Media advertising* encompasses all formal media communication whether through radio, television, direct mail, outdoor, or print.
2. *Point-of-sale* promotion includes all formal information flow to the consumer through brochures, broadsides, placards, and displays at point of sale.
3. *Selling presentations* include all person-to-person information flow from those interested in the sale of a product to potential purchasers.

Operating Information

Three classes of operating information are defined.
1. *Orders and confirmations* include purchase orders, notifications of order receipt, back orders, invoices, and other product-related forms and correspondence.
2. *Policy communiqués* encompass communication from one active element to another in which the first element specifies an action desired of the second element.
3. *Reports* include all information flow between elements specifying present or past conditions existing in the environment.

Word-of-Mouth

The word-of-mouth classification encompasses all product-related communication between consumers. The content of this information flow is specified in terms analogous to promotional information flow. However, word-of-mouth communication is originated by individual consumers and transmitted from person to person; therefore, different response mechanisms are involved, and it must be distinguished from more formal types of information flow.

Communication Content

Complete specification of information flow requires description of communication content — the intelligence conveyed by the flow of information. In later chapters, detailed models of communication generation, transmission, and response will be developed. For purposes of definition, types of promotional and word-of-mouth communication content should be noted. These relate to

1. Product-associated appeals.

2. Product characteristics.
3. Brand name identifications.

Two classes of operating communication content require specification:

1. Orders and confirmation as well as some reports relate to finished goods and, as such, their content is described in terms of the attributes of finished goods specified earlier — brand, model, and size.
2. Content of policy communiqués and reports relating to nonproduct information is specified in terms of price, margins, allowances, direct compensation, or conditions of distribution.

Information Specification

For summary purposes, the classification structure for information as an element of flow is outlined in Specification 3.2.

Specification 3.2. Information as an Element of Flow
  I. Classifications
     A. Promotion
        1. Media Advertising
        2. Point-of-Sale Advertising
        3. Sales Presentations
     B. Operating
        1. Orders and Confirmations
        2. Policy Communiqués
        3. Reports
     C. Word of Mouth
 II. Specification of Content
     A. Content of Orders, Confirmations, and Some Reports
        1. Brand
        2. Model
        3. Size
        4. Quantity
     B. Content of Policy Communiqués and Some Reports
        1. Price
        2. Margins and Allowances
        3. Direct Compensation
        4. Conditions of Distribution

   C. Content of Promotion and Word of Mouth
     1. Product-Related Appeals
     2. Product Characteristics
     3. Brand Name Associations

The Element of Flow Called "Capital"

In a complete representation of corporate activity, capital flow is categorized into numerous subclassifications required for financial analysis. In context of this market-oriented system, a narrowly defined concept of capital will be adopted. Interactions within the environment external to the firm may be described using only two classifications of capital:

1. *Cash* payments for goods received, advertising allowances and other promotional expenditures, and direct compensation in the form of salaries, commissions, or push money.
2. *Discountable paper* which appears primarily in conjunction with accounts receivable and orders.

Orders as Capital

Orders appear as subclassifications of two elements of flow — operating information and capital. An order conveys information regarding demand for a quantity of a particular brand-model-size of product at a given place in the marketing system. It also indicates value to be received and, as such, enters the financial equation. While this distinction may appear pedantic, the importance of separating these two aspects of an order becomes apparent when process representations involving information and capital are developed.

Content of Capital Flow

Two content specifications serve to describe capital flow. These are dollars and dollar value, which are applicable to cash and discountable paper flows, respectively.

Capital Specification

Characteristics of capital as an element of flow are summarized in Specification 3.3.

Specification 3.3. Capital as an Element of Flow
   I. Classifications
     A. Cash

B. Discountable Paper
   1. Orders
   2. Accounts Receivable
II. Specification of Content
  A. Dollars
  B. Dollar Value

Graphic Representation of Elements of Flow

In discussing relationships involving elements of flow, graphic representation often proves more explicit and efficient than verbal description. Unambiguous notation representing each system element discussed in this chapter has therefore been developed.

Conventions for Representation

Graphic representation of elements of flow involves three conventions:

1. Lines are used to indicate channels through which elements of flow are transmitted. A solid line indicates a channel of product or capital flow, while a dotted line represents a channel in which information is the element of flow. The *solid line* thus illustrates a channel in which the element of flow is *tangible* (product or paper) while a *dotted line* illustrates a channel containing *intangible* content (information).
2. Arrows indicate the direction in which elements of flow move through a channel.
3. An oval connected to an arrow may be used to specify channel content.

Sample Representations

Figure 3.1 illustrates these conventions. The solid line on the left of this figure represents a channel of product or capital flow. The dotted line indicates a channel in which information is the element of flow.

The solid line, arrow, and oval in the center of Figure 3.1 illustrate a channel through which capital flow associated with orders for brand b is transmitted. The solid line indicates capital or product flow. The oval identifies a channel transmitting orders for brand b. The element of flow is capital rather than product because Specifications 3.1 and 3.3 establish orders as a subdivision of capital and not of product flow.

The far right of Figure 3.1 illustrates information flow in the form

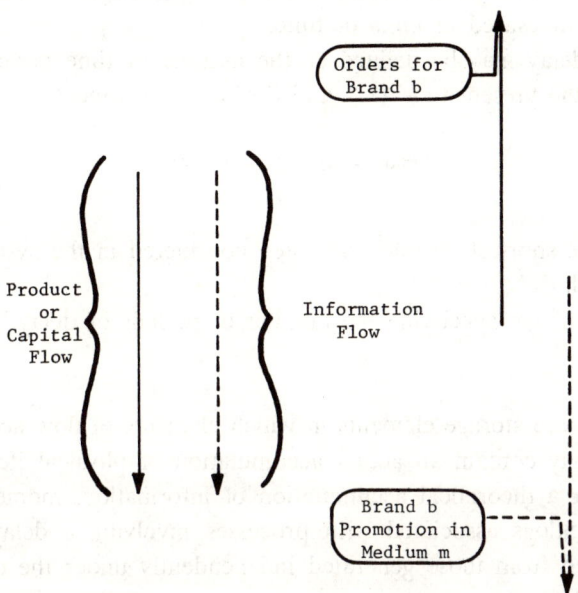

Figure 3.1. Graphic representation of elements of flow.

of promotion through medium m regarding brand b. The dotted line indicates a flow of information, while the oval specifies the type of information. The content of this communication is not known, because the appeals, product characteristics, or brand associations being transmitted are not specified.

Passive Elements

In developing specifications for passive elements, it will be necessary to consider three phenomena and the conditions associated with them.

Definition of Passive Elements

The three passive elements, time delays, backlogs, and dissipators involve concepts frequently used in describing electromechanical systems.

Time Delays

Delays refer to the time lapse between points in a process. They may, for example, be associated with the time required for an element of flow to move through a channel from point of origin to termination. Delays are measured in units of time.

A time delay may be defined as the number of time periods (DT) separating the present time (t_0) and the reference time (t_r).

$$\text{Delay} \equiv t_0 - t_r \equiv D \cdot DT$$

where

DT is the shortest discrete time step considered in the system being examined.

D is an integer specifying the number of periods of delay.[1]

Backlogs

Backlogs are storage elements in which elements of flow accumulate. Backlogs may contain an actual accumulation of physical items (e.g., product) or a theoretical accumulation of information, momentum, or energy. Backlogs associated with processes involving a delay will be differentiated from those generated independently under the control of an active element.

1. *Implicit (Delay-Associated) Backlogs* are inherent in a process involving time delays. Consider, for example, the process by which goods are transferred through a transportation system. The accumulation of goods within the transportation system is represented by a backlog associated with the transportation delay. The extent of this backlog at any point in time is a function of the time delay associated with the transfer process and the inputs to the process.
2. *Explicit (Independently Controlled) Backlogs* are controlled by one or more active elements. For example, a backlog of accumulated cash may be completely depleted by a controlling active element at one point in time regardless of associated processes. The size of the backlog is determined by the active element.

The magnitude of a backlog is measured in units. When physical items are involved, measurement of backlog content is a simple matter of counting items. Information backlogs are mathematically identical to

---

[1] Process delays will, in all instances, be greater than DT. Because of mathematical considerations referenced later, they will normally be equal to or greater than six DT.

physical inventories; however, measurement of information backlog content (e.g., knowledge or attitudes existing in a population) involves something more than counting boxes. Process descriptions involving information backlogs may be conceptually useful but are extremely difficult to verify with reference to real world data.

The magnitude of a backlog may be expressed as the cumulative difference between input rates into and output rates from the backlog over time. Because the backlog is measured in units, its formulation involves the conversion of rates that are measured in units-per-time to units through multiplication by the time period base (DT).

$$\text{Backlog}(t) \equiv \text{Backlog}(t-1) + \left[\sum_{n=1}^{N} \text{Input}(n, t-1) - \sum_{m=1}^{M} \text{Output}(m, t-1)\right] \cdot \text{DT}$$

where

$\text{Backlog}(t) \equiv$ Value of backlog at the present time, t
$\text{Backlog}(t-1) \equiv$ Value of backlog at beginning of immediately preceding time period $t-1$.

$t - 1 \equiv t - \text{DT}$

$\text{Input}(n, t-1) \equiv$ Value of nth input rate during immediately preceding time period.
$\text{Output}(m, t-1) \equiv$ Value of mth output rate during immediately preceding time period.

Dissipators

Dissipators account for the loss of units of elements of flow within the system. When a process is nonconservative — when element of flow is lost between the beginning and end of a process — that which is lost must be accounted for by a dissipation flow out of the system.

As in the backlog case, dissipators are encountered in two mathematically comparable but operationally different contexts.

1. *Implicit (Delay-Associated) Dissipators* are facts of life that the active element must accept with little or no choice.
2. *Explicit (Independently Controlled) Dissipators* are under the control of an active element.

Dissipation is measured as the rate of flow of element of flow (units per time period).

The dissipator can be defined in equation form as follows:

$$\text{Dissipation(t)} \equiv \sum_{n=1}^{N} \text{Input(n, t)} - \sum_{m=1}^{M} \text{Output(m, t)}$$
$$+ \frac{[\text{Backlog(t)} - \text{Backlog(t + 1)}]}{DT},$$

where

$$\sum_{n=1}^{N} \text{Input(n, t)} \geq \sum_{m=1}^{M} \text{Output(m, t)} - \frac{[\text{Backlog(t)} - \text{Backlog(t + 1)}]}{DT}.$$

The dissipation at time t is a rate expressed in units per time period. Thus the equation is dimensionally correct with respect to the input and output rate; however, the backlog factor must be corrected by dividing the unit backlog terms by a time period term to obtain the required units-per-time-period dimension.

Graphic Representation of Passive Elements

The three passive elements will be represented graphically using conventions summarized in Figure 3.2.

Conventions for Representation

Graphic representation of passive elements involves five conventions:

1. Rates of flow into and out of a given channel are indicated by diamond-shaped inserts at the beginning and end of the channel.
2. Delays are represented by an angular wedge intersecting a channel of flow.
3. Backlogs are indicated by a rectangle.
4. Backlogs associated with a delay are appended to the wedge representing the delay.
5. Independent backlogs intersect the channel of flow with which they are associated.

Sample Representations

Figure 3.2 illustrates the application of these conventions. The four elements at the top of this figure represent a conservative channel consisting of an input, a delay with associated backlog, and an output. The channel is conservative in that the element of flow in that channel is conserved — everything entering the channel as input eventually flows out as output.

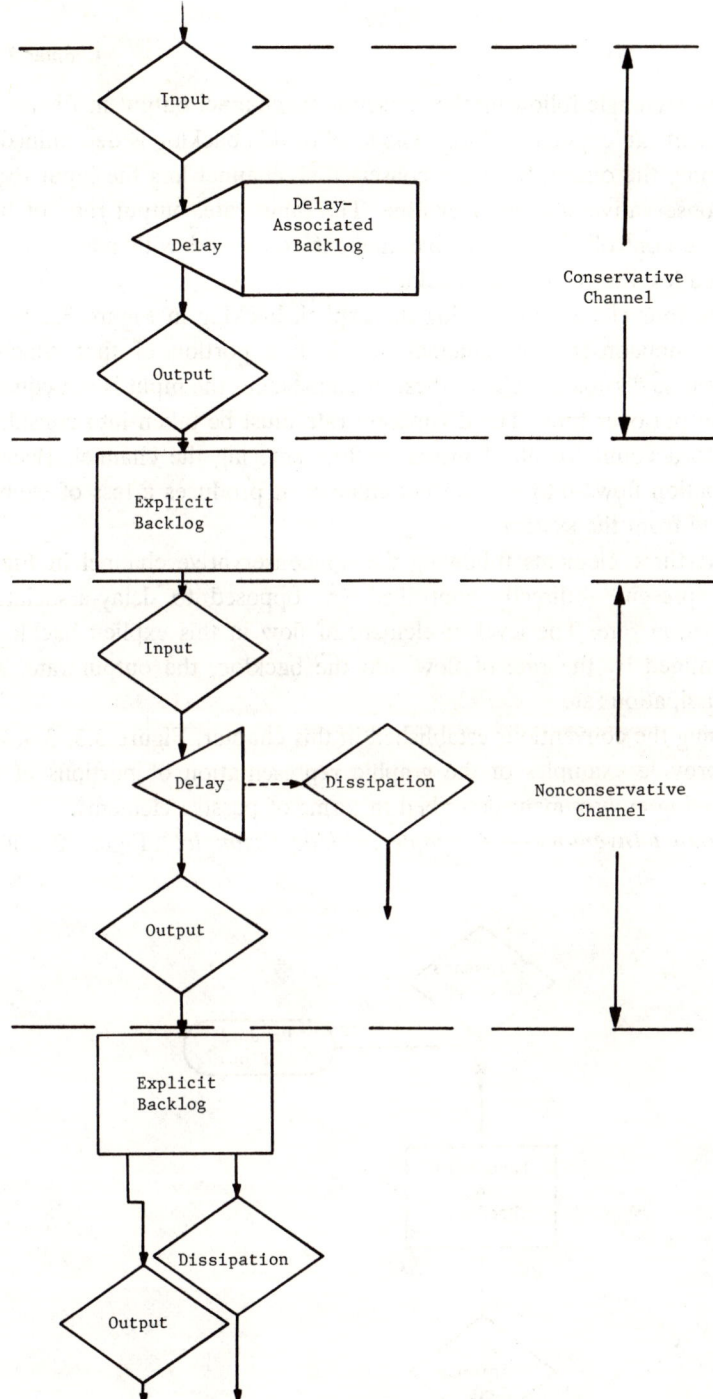

Figure 3.2. General form of representation for elements of flow.

The rectangle following the conservative channel output in Figure 3.2 represents an explicit backlog. The level of this backlog is determined by summing the output from the conservative channel less the input to the nonconservative channel over time. The input rate, output rate, or both may be controlled by an active element concerned with maintaining a desired level in the explicit backlog.

The four elements following the explicit backlog in Figure 3.2 represent a nonconservative channel in which a portion of that which is delayed is dissipated. Under these circumstances the input is not equal to the output over time. The dissipation rate must be taken into consideration to account for all elements of flow entering the channel. Because dissipation flows into an *external* channel, it produces a loss of element of flow from the system.

The three elements following the nonconservative channel in Figure 3.2 represent a directly controlled (as opposed to delay-associated) dissipation rate. The level of element of flow in this explicit backlog is determined by the rate of flow into the backlog, the output rate, and the dissipation rate.

Using the conventions established in this chapter, Figure 3.3, 3.4, and 3.5 provide examples of the graphic representation of portions of the marketing environment described in terms of passive elements.

Product Inventory — A Simple Backlog Example.   Figure 3.3 illus-

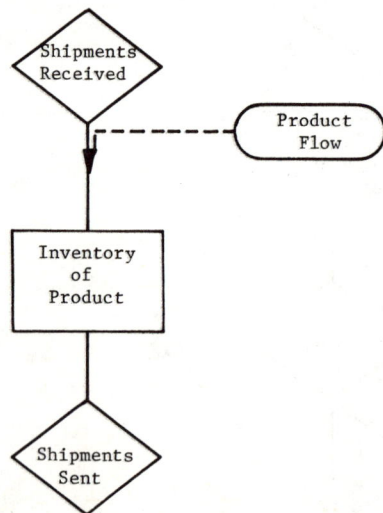

Figure 3.3. Inventory of product. Example of explicitly controlled backlog.

trates an explicitly controlled product inventory backlog. The active element (manufacturer, distributor, or retailer) controls the inventory level by maintaining the desired rate of product flow through manipulation of shipments received and sent.

Shipments in Transit — A Simple Conservative System.   Figure 3.4 illustrates the function of a backlog as part of a conservative channel relating to shipments in transit. Shipments are received by the channel at a "shipments sent" rate and are delayed in channel for a period specified by the transportation delay. Shipments leave the channel at the "shipments received" rate. Product in the channel is part of the implicit backlog, "goods in transit."

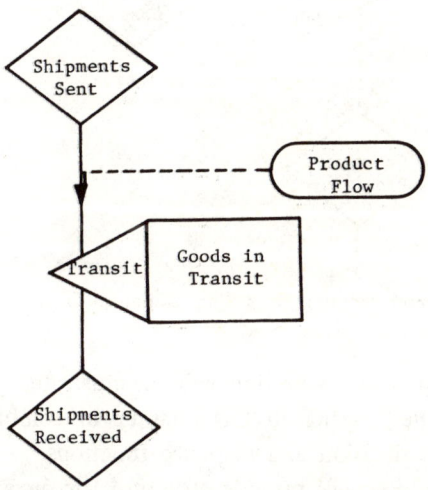

Figure 3.4. Shipments in transit. Example of backlog as part of conservative system.

Salesman Communication — A Simple Nonconservative System. Figure 3.5 illustrates a nonconservative system relating to the salesman's transfer of selling appeals. Information enters this channel at a "promotional material receipt" rate and leaves the channel at a "promotion to customers" rate. In this example, an assimilation delay and loss (dissipation) of information during the time required to assimilate new appeals have been assumed.

Active Elements

Definition of the eight active elements will begin with an examination of common attributes that distinguish active elements as a class. Cen-

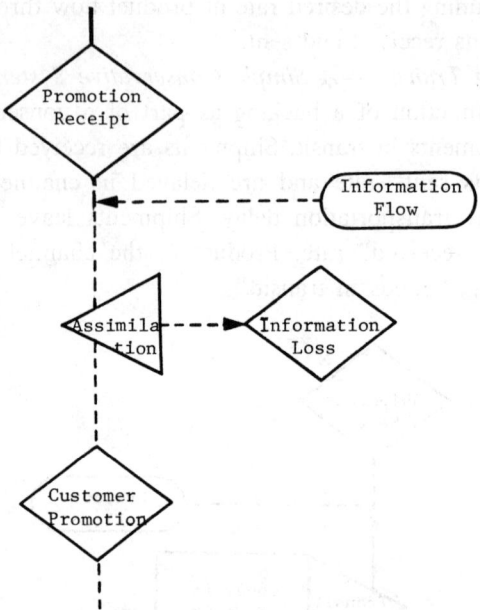

Figure 3.5. Salesman transfer of selling appeals. Example of nonconservative system.

tral aspects of this class definition will be illustrated graphically, using conventions adopted earlier in this chapter in combination with new representations of decision and response functions.

The class definition will provide structure for an analysis of unique characteristics of each active element. As element definitions are established they will be summarized in specifications comparable to those developed for elements of flow and passive elements.

Active Elements — A General Definition

The eight active elements are human. They respond to the actions and communications of other active elements while taking actions and originating communications to which other active elements respond in an iterative sequence.

The concepts and structure introduced in Chapter 2 establish boundary conditions that limit present considerations. The previously proposed qualitative framework constrains active elements to a limited number of action and response alternatives. They are able to

1. Control rates of flow through channels.
2. Control the size of backlogs.
3. Control the extent of delays.
4. Respond to channel content originated by other active elements.
5. Modify existing content in some channels.
6. Originate new content as input to certain channels.

Graphic Representation of an Active Element

Figure 3.6 illustrates this general definition of an active element. The six-sided enclosures in this figure represent decision or response functions through which the active element responds to information or makes a decision affecting processes within the system.

The decision function in the upper left channel in Figure 3.6 combines information regarding an input rate, an output rate, and the level of an implicit backlog to determine the extent of an associated process delay. This decision function controlling a delay corresponds to point 3 of the preceding general definition.

The second decision function associated with the left channel combines information relating to an output, an explicit backlog, and the flow out of the explicit backlog to establish a rate of flow into an explicit backlog. This decision, which controls a rate of flow, corresponds to point 1 of the general definition of an active element.

The second decision function also controls the content of any explicit backlog. The active element varies the input to achieve a desired backlog level. This decision function embodies characteristics of point 2 of the general definition.

The upper right channel illustrates response and decision functions involving information flow. The first function located to the left of the channel determines the active element's response to the content and extent of information flow in the channel. As such, it is an example of point 4 of the general definition.

The output of the response function serves as input to two decision functions. The first decision function, which controls a filter modifying the content of the channel, represents activity of the type associated with point 5 of the general definition. The second decision function controls an assimilation delay, which in turn determines the rate of dissipation in a nonconservative channel, providing another example of behavior of the type indicated by point 3 of the general definition.

The second decision function provides input to a third function deter-

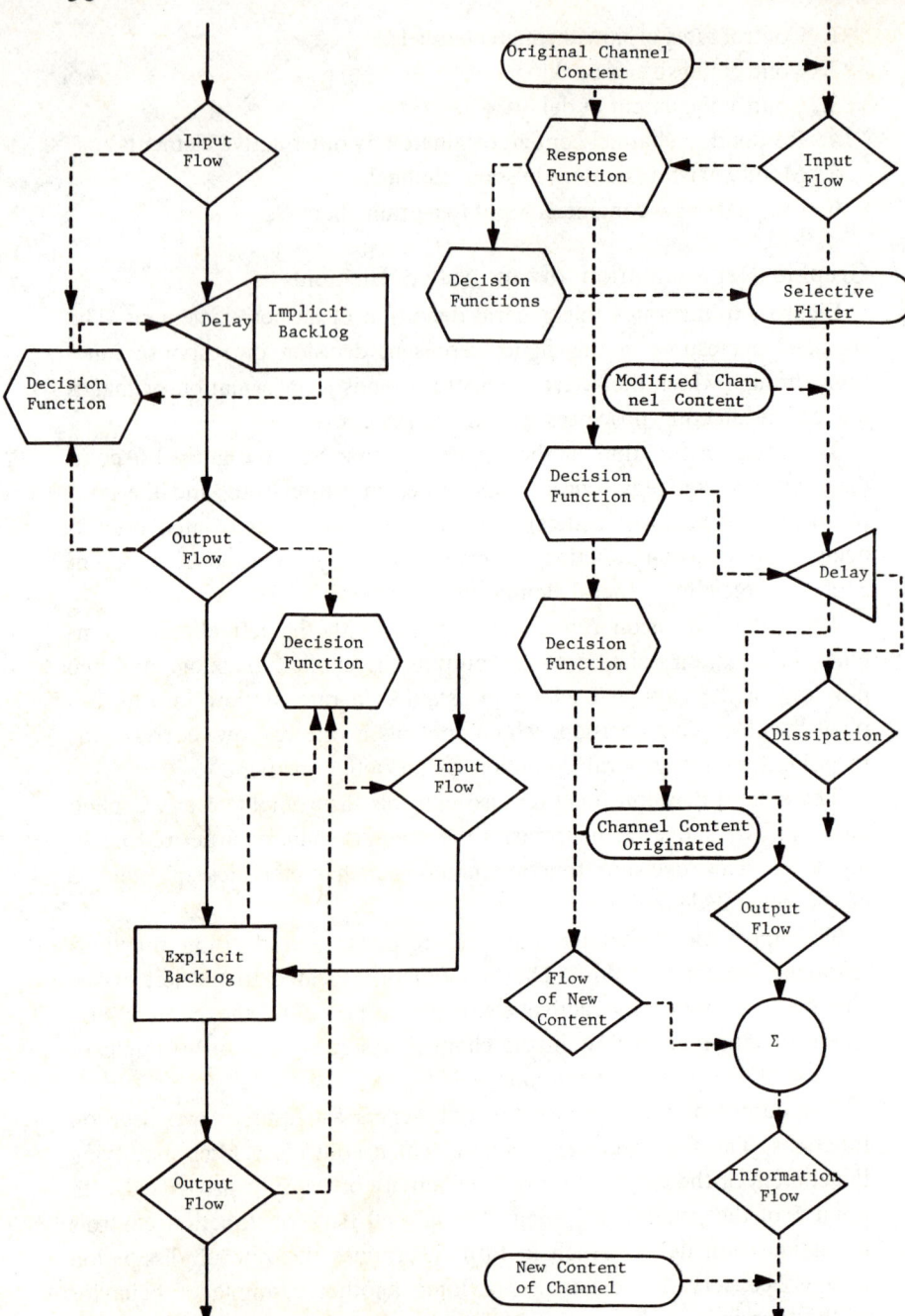

Figure 3.6. Generalized form of representation.

mining the flow rate and content for an information channel. The third decision function is thus representative of point 6 of the general definition.

In the lower portion of the right channel, new and modified content are combined to establish the rate and content of information flow transmitted to other active elements in the system.

Figure 3.6 does not represent a particular active element nor does it encompass all combinations of behavior covered by the basic definition. It merely illustrates one combination of decision and response functions by using previously established conventions.

Specific Definitions for Eight Active Elements

The general definition of active elements specifies characteristic types of behavior. Each element within the class must now be described in terms of its unique defining attributes. The producer, distributor or wholesaler, salesman, retailer, consumer, government, and research agent will be considered in that order. Definitions established for individual elements will provide a basis for description of interactions between elements and establish a macrostructure for specific sector models developed in later chapters.

The Producer (*Marketing Decision Maker*)

Definition of the producer or marketing decision maker requires refinement of the general definition to account for specific actions and responses unique to this active element. It is first necessary to decide which rates of flow controlled by the producer are of sufficient importance to be included in a specific definition. Similar decisions must then be made for backlogs, delays, responses to channel content, content modification, and content origination.

Control of Rates of Flow. Three production-related flows controlled by the producer provide sufficient description of the manufacturing process. These are (1) the flow of orders for raw materials from the producer to his suppliers, (2) the flow of payments for raw materials received, and (3) the flow of raw materials into and the flow of finished goods out of production.

The rate of product flow to distribution channels is determined by the producer who controls shipments to the distributor and/or retailers based on orders received from these sectors. Capital and information channels associated with invoicing and billing parallel the physical distribution channel.

The producer controls information flow in formal promotional channels and communicates (1) to the consumer directly through advertising, (2) to the consumer indirectly through trade channels, and (3) to active elements engaged in distribution and selling activities (the trade).

Control of Backlogs. Backlogs controlled by the producer are related to the flows discussed in the preceding paragraphs. Production-related backlogs include raw material inventory, finished goods inventory, and goods in process. The flow of payments to suppliers is a function of backlogs of cash and accounts payable, controlled by the producer. Although other financial backlogs (e.g., accounts receivable) are associated with the manufacturing sector, the producer cannot exercise direct control over either the inputs or outputs that determine the level of these backlogs. Orders from distributors and/or retailers accumulate in backlogs of orders in process and back orders. Allocation of funds to promotional campaigns produces backlogs of advertising work in process.

Control of Delays. The producer controls delays associated with production scheduling and the manufacturing process. Scheduling delays affect the sensitivity of production to changes in demand, while manufacturing, shipping, and order-handling delays reflect the over-all efficiency of associated processes. Delays associated with communication scheduling are analogous to those involved in the production process. Billing-process delays influence the aging of accounts receivable. Response-associated delays determine the speed of producer response to information regarding the state of the external environment.

Response to Communication. The producer responds to information received directly and indirectly from competitors, the trade, and consumers. Communication regarding competitive actions may relate to five areas of competitive activity: (1) sales, (2) promotional activities, (3) product features, (4) pricing policies, and (5) distribution policies. Information content relating to distribution policies includes choice of distributors, margins and allowances, the use of direct compensation (including "push money"), and missionary selling activities. The terms "pricing policy" and "promotion" should be interpreted in a similarly broad manner.

Producer response to communication from the distribution channel can be categorized in terms of information regarding sales and orders, pricing action, selling effort, inventory levels, and handling of competitive products.

Information from the consumer sector to which the producer responds may relate to product characteristic preferences, purchase patterns, or consumer responses to promotion. Consumer product characteristic preferences should be interpreted broadly to include expected product life and price as well as physical product attributes.

Origination of Communication. The producer originates content for channels of communication to all active elements within the marketing system. Trade-directed communications relate to ordering procedures, pricing policy, selling procedures, margins and allowances, and other characteristics or requirements of the producer's desired distribution system. In a similar manner, the producer originates communication intended to select, allocate, and motivate a selling force in a manner consistent with his sales policies.

Communication from the producer to the distributor, retailer, and sales force regarding compensation (salaries, commissions, and push money) constitutes a further classification of content. Finally, the producer provides content for promotional communication as noted in the earlier discussion of rates of flow.

Communication Content. Specification of promotional content will be given substantial consideration in later chapters. For the moment, promotional content will be arbitrarily classified in terms of product-related appeals, product characteristics, and brand identifiers. The producer is responsible for originating content for all national promotion and, through newspaper mats and prepared content for other media, much local promotion as well.

Content Modification. Within the scope of this system, the producer does not act to modify existing content in any channels that go beyond the confines of his immediate operations. Therefore no actions will be specified under the fifth point in the general definition of active elements.

Producer Specification. Relevant producer activities within each category specified by the general definition of an active element have been noted in the course of the preceding discussion. In combination, these activities define the producer as a unique active element controlling particular flows, backlogs, and delays, responding to specified channel content and originating content for certain channels. This definition is summarized in Specification 3.4.

Specification 3.4. The Producer

   I. Flows Controlled
- A. Orders for Raw Materials
- B. Payments for Raw Materials
- C. Finished Goods Production
- D. Finished Goods Shipments to Distributor and/or Retailer
- E. Invoicing and Billing Distribution Channel
- F. Promotional Communication
  - 1. Direct to Consumer
  - 2. To Consumer via Trade Channels
  - 3. To Trade

  II. Backlogs Controlled
- A. Raw Material Inventory
- B. Finished Goods Inventory
- C. Goods in Process
- D. Cash
- E. Accounts Payable
- F. Orders in Process
- G. Back Orders
- H. Advertising Work in Process

 III. Delays Controlled
- A. Production Scheduling
- B. Manufacturing Process
- C. Order Handling
- D. Shipping
- E. Communication Scheduling
- F. Billing
- G. Response Associated

 IV. Responses to Channel Content
- A. Relating to Competitive Actions
  - 1. Sales
  - 2. Promotion
  - 3. Product Features
  - 4. Pricing Policies
  - 5. Distribution Policies
- B. Relating to Distribution Channels
  - 1. Sales and Orders
  - 2. Pricing

        3. Selling Effort
        4. Inventory Positions
        5. Competitive Product Handling
    C. Relating to Consumers
        1. Product Characteristic Preferences
        2. Purchases
        3. Responses to Promotion
  V. Channel Content Modified — None
 VI. Channel Content Originated
    A. Pricing Policy
    B. Distribution Policy
    C. Sales Force Policy
    D. Ordering Policy
    E. Direct Compensation
    F. Promotion

The Distributor or Wholesaler

Characteristics that define the distributor or wholesaler as a unique actor in the marketing environment may be specified using the previously developed structure.

Control of Rates of Flow. Distributors and wholesalers will be viewed as subsets of a single active element having the primary function of expediting physical goods flow from producer to retailer and/or consumer. The distributor also stands between the producer and the retailer or consumer in the line of communication facilitated by personal contact. The producer who wishes to communicate through trade channels must accept the delays, dissipation, and noise introduced by the distributor. Although it is possible for the distributor to transmit information received from the producer directly to the retailer or consumer without substantial modification, the observed incidence of such occurrences is small. The distributor also controls the flow of promotional communication transmitted through him.

The distributor as a link in the chain of funds flow paralleling product flow controls flows of invoices to retailers and payments to producers.

Whether serving as agent of the producer without taking physical possession of the goods, receiving goods on consignment, or purchasing and maintaining inventories of goods for resale, the distributor controls the flow of value and order-related information.

Control of Backlogs. Three classes of backlogs are controlled by the distributor in the course of maintaining information, product, and value. There are (1) backlogs of product in the form of finished goods inventory, (2) backlogs of orders in process at the distributor level, and (3) backlogs of unfilled orders awaiting action.

Control of Delays. The distributor's handling of physical product and paper work establishes the extent of time delays associated with filling orders and shipping product. In controlling the flow of funds through his organization, he determines the extent of delays associated with billing and payments. When serving as an information transfer agent, he may introduce delays while responding to channel content. As in the case of physical product, delays associated with responses to communication content are largely a function of administrative structure.

Responses to Communication. Distributor responses may be conveniently categorized by source of channel content. The first class of channel content is originated by the producer and includes policy information related to pricing, distribution, credit, and ordering.

A second class of information content generated by the producer relates to promotion. This includes information transmitted to the distributor exclusively, to the distributor and retailer, and to the distributor as well as the consumer population.

A third class of distributor response relates to retailer-generated channel content including orders, existing inventories, prevailing prices, enthusiasm for the product, selling effort, and payments against invoices.

Modification of Channel Content. In addition to introducing delays and dissipation, the distributor may modify existing channel content. He is not apt to emphasize policy information perceived as contrary to his best interests and may modify pricing, credit, or ordering policy directives, changing content or indicating to the recipient that such communications are not to be taken seriously.

The distributor may also modify the content of formal communication channels through selective transmission of certain promotional pieces. As an example of this type of selectivity, large and bulky point-of-sale displays are less apt to reach the retailer than small, easily carried units.

Origination of Communication. The distributor originates content for several channels of communication. Although promotional content may be generated by the distributor, content produced at this level is more apt to be policy oriented. The distributor may, for example, generate content relating to the allocation, composition, and motivation of his sales force, or special pricing designed to encourage the retailer to order more of a particular product.

Distributor Specification. The preceding paragraphs have described the wholesaler or distributor in terms of his control of the flows, backlogs, and delays, his responses to channel content, modification of existing channel content, and origination of new channel content. These identifying attributes are summarized in Specification 3.5.

Specification 3.5. The Distributor

I. Flows Controlled
   A. Finished Goods Shipments to Retailers
   B. Promotional Communication to Retailers
   C. Invoicing to Retailers
   D. Payments to Producer

II. Backlogs Controlled
   A. Finished Goods Inventory
   B. Orders in Process
   C. Back Orders — Unfilled Orders

III. Delays Controlled
   A. Filling Orders
   B. Shipping
   C. Billing
   D. Payment
   E. Ordering
   F. Response Functions (as in IV)

IV. Responses to Channel Content
   A. From Producers
      1. Pricing Policy
      2. Promotional Content
      3. Credit Policy
      4. Distribution Policies
      5. Ordering Policies
   B. From Retailers
      1. Sales — Orders
      2. Pricing Actions
      3. Selling Effort
      4. Payments
      5. Inventory Policies

   V. Channel Content Modified, From Producer Regarding
      A. Pricing
      B. Promotional Content
      C. Credit Policy
      D. Ordering Policy
  VI. Channel Content Originated
      A. Allocation of Sales Force
      B. Direct Compensation Schedule
      C. Desired Composition of Selling Force
      D. Special Incentives to Increase Order Levels

The Salesman

The role of the salesman in the employ of a manufacturer or distributor will be considered in this section. The distributor or manufacturer salesman will be distinguished from the retail salesman dealing with the consumer. Specifications developed in this section are not applicable to the latter.

Control of Flows. The salesman controls the flow of orders. He may also control the flow of certain promotional communications; however, for the salesman working at the distributor or manufacturer level this is of secondary importance.

Control of Backlogs. In line with the flows controlled, the salesman controls backlogs of unprocessed orders, promotional material, and, to the extent that the product with which he is dealing is sampled, backlogs of samples.

Controls of Delays. As in other situations considered, delays may be associated with the salesman's maintenance of backlogs. The salesman also controls delays associated with response functions.

Responses to Communication. The salesman in the employ of a distributor responds to:

1. Policy and promotional channel content generated by the distributor for whom he is working.
2. Responses of the retailer he is attempting to sell.
3. Promotion and compensation from associated producers.

The salesman working directly for the manufacturer responds to:

1. Policy as well as promotional and compensation-related communication generated by his employer, and
2. The reactions of distributors and/or retailers to whom he sells.

The salesman, whether working for the distributor or manufacturer, is also a consumer and, as such, responds to promotional content generated by the producer.

Modification of Information Flow.   Because the salesman communicates with the retailer, previous comments regarding policy modification at the distributor level are also applicable to the salesman. Both distributor and salesman have the potential to modify channel content directed to the retailer. A salesman may hesitate to transmit unfavorable information to his employer and modify communication content regarding unfavorable conditions at the retail level.

Content Origination.   Although presented in the preceding section as a modification of channel content, the salesman's selective transfer of information might be expressed as content origination.

The Industrial Salesman.   Characteristics discussed in this section may be reasonably attributed to either an industrial or a consumer product salesman. The industrial salesman selling to purchasing agents may exhibit additional characteristics of the type attributed to the retailer in a later section of this chapter.

Salesman Specification.   Defining attributes of a distributor or manufacturer salesman are summarized in Specification 3.6.

Specification 3.6. The Salesman

  I. Flows Controlled
      A. Orders
      B. Promotional Communication
 II. Backlogs Controlled
      A. Unprocessed Orders
      B. Samples, Promotional Material
III. Delays Controlled
      A. Order Processing
      B. Response Related
 IV. Responses to Channel Content
      A. From Producer
          1. Promotional Content
          2. Direct Compensation Schedule (if applicable)
          3. Ordering Policy (if applicable)
      B. From Distributor
          1. Promotional Content
          2. Direct Compensation Schedule (if applicable)

        3. Ordering Policy (if applicable)

    C. From Retailer

        1. Sales

        2. Inventory

        3. Selling Effort

  V. Channel Content Modified

    A. From the Manufacturer or Distributor to the Retailer

        1. Ordering Policies

        2. Promotion

    B. From the Retailer to the Manufacturer or Distributor

        1. Selling Effort

        2. Inventory and Sales Conditions

 VI. Channel Content Originated

    A. Retail Inventory and Sales Conditions

    B. Competitive Conditions

    C. Selling Effort

The Retailer

In developing specifications for the distributor, administrative and selling functions were isolated — the distributor was explicitly differentiated from the salesman working for him. In the retailer definition, administrative and selling functions will be combined in a single active element, "the retailer," best exemplified by the one-man proprietorship in which a single owner-businessman-salesman takes orders, maintains inventory, handles promotion, and does the selling. This example is not directly representative of actual behavior in larger stores in which administration, buying, promotion, and selling are handled by different people in wholly separate departments. However, at this level of specification, it is appropriate to specify functions performed without being particularly concerned about who does what within the outlet.

Control of Flows. The retailer controls four types of flow: (1) the rate at which goods are shipped to consumers, (2) the order rate to the distributor or manufacturer from whom he purchases, (3) the rate of payment to distributor or manufacturer for product received, and (4) the rate of consumer-oriented communication generated through his outlet.

Retailer-controlled promotional communication is of three types. The first is transferred through personal contact with the consumer at the retail level. The second involves point-of-sale communication controlled by the retailer who determines point-of-sale display placement in his store. The third is local advertising.

Control of Backlogs. The retailer controls two backlogs that markedly influence manufacturer and distributor expectations and performance. These are the inventory of physical product and the backlog of orders.

Control of Delays. Three classes of delays are controlled by the retailer. These are associated with (1) processing and handling orders, (2) making payments for goods received, and (3) response to communication and experience.

Response to Communication. The retailer's response to information from the producer and/or distributor relates to promotion, pricing, ordering, credit, and compensation policies. The retailer may respond to salesman-generated promotion as well as to the salesman's presentation of existing ordering and pricing policies.

Retailer response to consumer interactions involves three additional types of information content. These are (1) consumer preferences, (2) consumer purchases, and (3) consumer reports on responses to promotion.

Modification of Communication. The retailer is the final transfer agent for all consumer promotion at point of purchase. He is therefore in a position to modify some channel content generated by the producer, the distributor, and the salesman.

Origination of Communication. The retailer may originate channel content directed toward the consumer and other actors in the environment. The majority of consumer-oriented communication is based on materials supplied by the manufacturer and takes the form either of point-of-purchase display or of local media promotion. The retailer may generate original consumer-oriented communication content related to a particular product or directed toward establishing an image for his outlet.

The content of retailer communication directed to other sectors of the marketing environment is most apt to relate to the state of his operations. Such communication may involve formal reports, such as orders or requests to return merchandise, or informal reactions to competitive conditions and appraisal of the business climate.

Retailer Specification. Characteristics of the retailer may be summarized in terms of the six classes of behavior adopted as a structure of analysis. Parallels between the functions of retailer, distributor, and salesman will be evident from a comparison of Specifications 3.5 and 3.6 with 3.7.

Specification 3.7. The Retailer

I. Flows Controlled
   A. Shipments to Consumers
   B. Promotional Communication to Consumer
     1. Through Salesman Contact
     2. Through Point-of-Sale
     3. Through Media Promotion
   C. Payments to Producer or Distributor
   D. Orders to Producer or Distributor

II. Backlogs Controlled
   A. Inventory of Product
   B. Back Orders

III. Delays Controlled
   A. Payment
   B. Ordering
   C. Response Associated

IV. Responses to Channel Content
   A. From Producer
     1. Promotional Content
     2. Pricing Policy (if applicable)
     3. Ordering Policy (if applicable)
     4. Credit Policy (if applicable)
     5. Direct Compensation (if applicable)
   B. From Distributor
     1. Promotional Content
     2. Pricing Policy (if applicable)
     3. Ordering Policy (if applicable)
     4. Credit Policy (if applicable)
     5. Direct Compensation (if applicable)

V. Channel Content Modified
   A. From Producer
   B. From Distributor
   C. From Salesman

VI. Channel Content Originated
   A. Directed to Consumer

      1. Based on Manufacturer or Distributor Supplied Material
      2. Based on Own Generation
   B. Directed to Trade
      1. Formal-Order, Inventory or Sales Based
      2. Informal — Response Based

The Consumer

The consumer controls only one rate of flow, one related backlog, and one delay relevant to management.

Control of Flows. The single flow controlled by the consumer is the rate of physical product flow out of retail outlets. The consumer controls the rates of purchase and consumption.

Control of Backlogs. The single backlog controlled by the consumer is the inventory of product that he maintains. In the case of certain regularly consumed items, this inventory may be equivalent to several weeks of consumption. In the case of capital goods, inventory becomes an almost meaningless concept because the total "inventory" consists of one item used and maintained over a period of years.

Control of Delays. The delay controlled by the consumer is that associated with the purchase process. This is the time lapse between purchases, which may range from a few days to several years. This delay may be viewed in the frequency rather than the time domain as the consumer's frequency of purchase.

Response to Communication. The consumer responds to channel content originated by the producer, the retailer, and other consumers.

The producer and retailer transmit promotional communications that may be described in terms of product characteristic and appeals content. Communication with other consumers — word-of-mouth communication — may be considered analogous to media communication insofar as product characteristics and appeals content is concerned. The consumer may also report personal responses and experience that add additional dimensions to content.

Origination of Communication. In addition to the generation of word-of-mouth communication the consumer may transmit information to retailers with whom he has in-store contact. Through participation in market research he may also transmit information to the manufacturer.

Consumer Specification. Attributes of the consumer are summarized in Specification 3.8. The relative brevity of this specification is somewhat deceptive. The consumer may be the most complex actor represented when modeling market interactions. This macrostructure only defines boundaries within which behavior must be described.

Specification 3.8. The Consumer

  I. Flow Controlled Purchases

  II. Backlog Controlled, Product at Point of Consumption

  III. Delays Controlled Associated with Purchase Process

  IV. Responses to Channel Content

    A. From Producer

      1. Media Promotion

      2. Packaging

      3. Point-of-Sale Promotion

    B. From Retailer

      1. Local Media Promotion

      2. Personal Selling

    C. From Other Consumers

      1. Relating to Product Characteristics and Appeals

      2. Relating to Experiences and Responses

  V. Channel Content Modified

    A. From Producer

    B. From Retailer

    C. From Other Consumers

  VI. Channel Content Originated

    A. Product Characteristics

    B. Product Appeals

    C. Responses to Product and Communication

The Government

As suggested in Chapter 1, the government may be viewed as a constraint on the operation of the marketing system. Actions of this element may be summarized in terms of the extent to which it limits alternatives available to decision makers operating within the system.

Control of Flows. The government controls the flow of certain information, raw materials, and finished goods. The extent of involvement ranges from absolute determination in the case of certain strategic raw materials, drugs, and food products, to intermittent monitoring in the case of other commodities, goods, and services. Government interest in information flow ranges from concern with the content of intercorporate policy communiqués to determination of the appropriateness of specific promotional claims.

Control of Backlogs. In conjunction with control of raw material and product flow, government may control the extent of related inventories.

Control of Delays. The government may effectively control or substantially influence the extent of delays relating to production, order processing, and information transfer as a result of its control of flows just noted.

Communication Modification. The government may be viewed as modifying the content of channels of communication through its effect on pricing and distribution policies, competitive strategies, advertising content, and certain forms of direct compensation.

Boundary Effects. The impact of government may be manifest implicitly through boundary conditions imposed on the actions of other active elements.

Government Specification. The explicit role of government can be summarized within the structure used to describe other active elements as indicated in Specification 3.9.

Specification 3.9. The Government
   I. Flows Controlled
      A. Certain Raw Materials
      B. Finished Goods Production of Certain Goods (e.g., Foods, Drugs)
      C. Distribution of Certain Products (e.g., Foods, Strategic Materials)
      D. Certain Information Content
   II. Backlogs Controlled
      A. Raw Materials
      B. Finished Goods
   III. Delays Controlled
      A. Production Scheduling
      B. Filling Orders — Releasing Certain Drugs, etc.
      C. Information Transfer
   IV. Channel Content Modified
      A. Pricing Policy
      B. Distribution Policy
      C. Advertising Content Regarding Certain Products

The Research Agent

The activities of the research agent are differentiated from those of the manufacturer in order to distinguish interactions and processes occurring within the marketing environment from the flow of information about such events generated through the process of research. The research sector may be viewed as encompassing the activities of an individual or group performing the research function. For purposes of specification, the research function will be defined in terms of the control or modification of information flow between other active elements.

Control of Flows. The research agent controls the flow of information from consumers, distributors, salesmen, retailers, and competitive companies to the manufacturer. The content of this information may relate to any action taken by the active element.

Control of Backlogs. Information backlogs controlled by the research agent may be maintained in order to accumulate information over time or to aggregate information across categories. For example, the research agent accumulating sales over time develops a backlog of sales values. Information regarding the extent of this backlog may be transmitted to the producer as a cumulative or smoothed function of monitored sales. The research agent may similarly accumulate backlogs of information regarding sales by store type and size. In the first case, aggregation is over time and in the second, over store type. In both instances the backlog is used to summarize detailed data — to accumulate numerical information.

Control of Delays. The creation of information backlogs at the research level may involve substantial delays of two types. The first is encountered when transferring information from one point within the system to another. The second is inherent in the process of aggregation over time.

Response to Communication. Research agents may respond to (1) policy channel content, (2) expectations communicated by those for whom they are working, (3) the content of promotional channels, and (4) the content of the very information channels they are researching.

Modification of Communication. Research agents may modify the content of the channel of information flow that they are monitoring. Such modification may take the form of interviewer bias, sampling bias, or faulty analysis or interpretation.

Organization of Communication. In addition to channel content modification that may occur as noted, research agents are often called upon to originate content relating to the nature of implied actions. In such situations they must deduce from intermediate indicators the nature of responses and attitudes throughout the marketing system. In developing these estimates, they originate content that may or may not be related to or consistent with actual behavior occurring in the market.

Research Agent Specification. These characteristics of the research agent or research function are summarized in Specification 3.1.

Specification 3.10. The Research Agent

I. Controls Flow of Information to Producer From
   A. Consumer
   B. Distributor
   C. Retailer
   D. Salesmen
   E. Competitors
II. Backlogs Controlled
   A. Accumulating Information Over Time
   B. Accumulating Information Across Categories
III. Delays Controlled
   A. In Transferring Information
   B. In Accumulating Information
IV. Responses to Communication
   A. Regarding Policy
   B. Regarding Expectations
   C. In Promotional Channels
   D. In Channels Being "Researched"
V. Communication Channel Content Modified
   A. In Extracting from Channel
   B. In Performing Analysis
VI. Communication Channel Content Originated
   A. Based on Analysis
   B. Based on Responses

Summary

This chapter has focused on the development of specifications defining Elements of Flow, Passive Elements, and Active Elements. Specific definitions and conventions for graphic representation have been established. A vocabulary and macrostructure with which activity within the marketing environment may be concisely described have been established. The chapters that follow are devoted to the application of this structure to the analysis and simulation of relevant behavior.

Chapter 4

PROCESS FLOW MODELS

Specifications established in Chapter 3 focus model development on a limited number of interactions within the marketing environment. This chapter will examine product, information, and capital-based processes as they occur within the boundaries prescribed by these definitions.

The three process classes are of course interrelated. The flow of information (orders, for example) clearly influences the flow of product (shipments). Consideration of interactions between processes and relationships between channels that contain different elements of flow will be deferred to later chapters where detailed sector models are formulated.

Product Flow Based Processes

When compared with processes involving information and capital, those in which product is the major element of flow appear comparatively simple and concise. Considerations of product are limited by specification to finished goods and raw material. Definition of raw material as a homogeneous element removes the otherwise complex problem of raw material transformation into finished goods and effectively precludes examination of processes associated with manufacture or fabrication. In addition, product is a substantive, directly observable, and measurable element of flow. There is little opportunity for disagreement over the nature of physical product, and the processes associated with its distribution are well defined and widely recognized.

57

Emphasis on Common Processes

Given the objective of developing generalized models applicable to a large class of products, processes deriving from unique characteristics of specialized products will be excluded from consideration. Processes relating, for example, to the requirement of professional approval prior to purchase, as in the case of prescription drugs, will not be considered. Emphasis will be placed on describing processes common to the marketing of products and/or services mass produced for distribution to and consumption by sizable population segments.

A Macroview of Product Flow

Specifications developed in Chapter 3 indicate that five active elements — the manufacturer, his competitors, distributors, retailers, and consumers — exercise direct control over product flow. Because comments applicable to the manufacturer may be extended to cover his competitors, it is necessary to examine product flow within and between four distinct sectors of the market environment.

The research agent who is concerned primarily with the flow of information does not directly determine flow of product at any point within the system. The salesman transmits orders that influence the flow of product; however, supplying information that affects another active element's control does not meet the requirements of direct control.

Graphic Representation of Macro Product Flow

Figure 4.1 summarizes gross characteristics of product flow between the four active elements with which this chapter is concerned. As illustrated, product flow is originated by the manufacturer and terminated by the consumer. Channels may go directly from the manufacturer to the consumer or may include the distributor and/or retailer as intermediaries. This representation ignores physical product flow out of the system through spoilage as well as differential rates of flow, delays, and backlogs of product at various points within the system.

The rectangles in Figure 4.1 identify sectors associated with particular active elements. The objective of this chapter is to describe processes occurring within each sector in sufficient detail to permit delineation of product flow associated process attributes relevant for inclusion in later models of active element behavior.

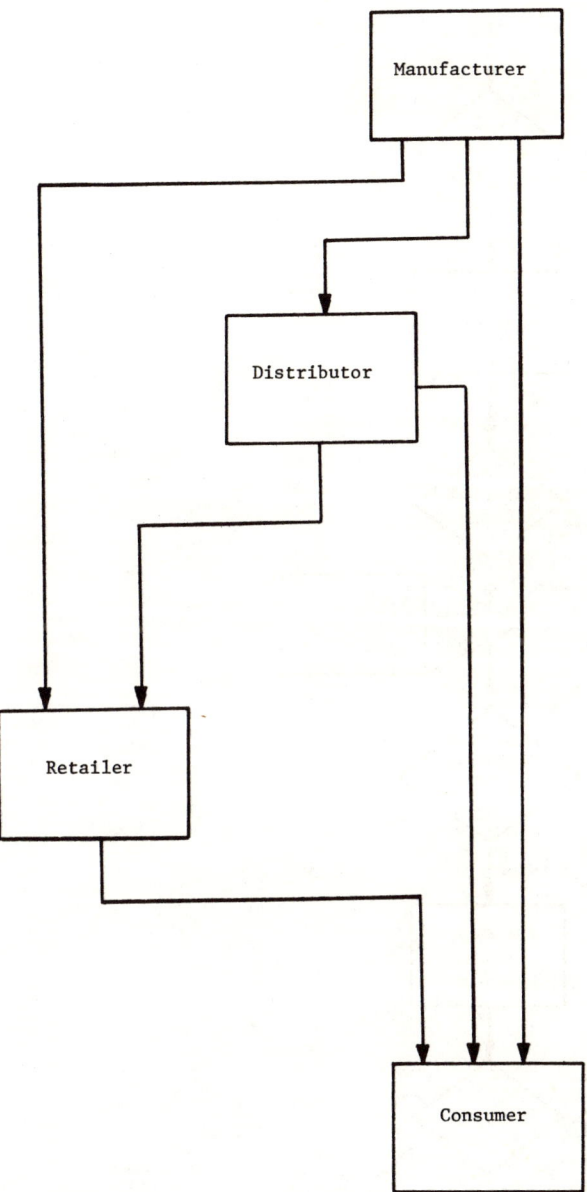

Figure 4.1. Product flow channels. A macroview.

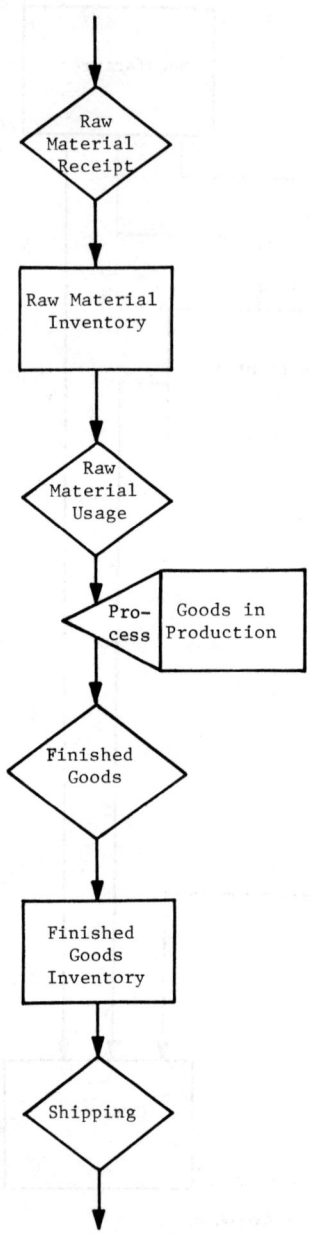

Figure 4.2. Product flow in manufacturer sector.

Product Flow Within the Manufacturer Sector

Figure 4.2 summarizes major attributes of product flow within the manufacturer sector. The three product flow based processes at this level are sequentially related to (1) the receipt and storage of raw material, (2) the conversion of raw material to finished goods, and (3) the storage and shipment of finished goods.

At the present level of aggregation, the receipt of raw materials may be summarized in a single rate of raw material receipt through a channel of flow leading into the manufacturer's inventory of raw material. Raw material for use in the production process flows out of this materials inventory at the rate required to support the existing level of production. The production process delays flow in the channel and creates a backlog of raw material and partially finished goods.

In context of this macroview, the production process produces a flow of finished goods into finished goods inventory from which shipments are made to other market sectors.

Product Flow Within the Retailer and Distributor Sectors

If the distributor and retailer are considered solely in terms of their control of product flow, the processes involving these two active elements are equivalent.

Figure 4.3 summarizes basic characteristics of product flow in the retailer or distributor sector. The supplying sector[1] is linked to the retailer or distributor by the shipping rate illustrated at the top of this figure. Once shipped, finished goods are delayed in transit and may be thought of as stored in a goods in transit inventory during the transfer period. The transportation or pipeline delay responsible for the transit backlog is inserted in the channel into which goods flow at a shipping rate to X to emerge at a rate of receipt of goods at X.

In addition to controlled product flow out of the sector in the form of shipments a spoilage rate may be encountered. The spoilage rate is a flow of finished goods *out of* the system, while the shipping rate is between elements *within* the system. Viewed from the perspective of the retailer or distributor, both are rates of flow out of that sector; but from the standpoint of the system as a whole, shipping is a transfer

---

[1] In the case of the distributor, the manufacturer is the supplying sector, while the retailer may be supplied by either the manufacturer or a distributor.

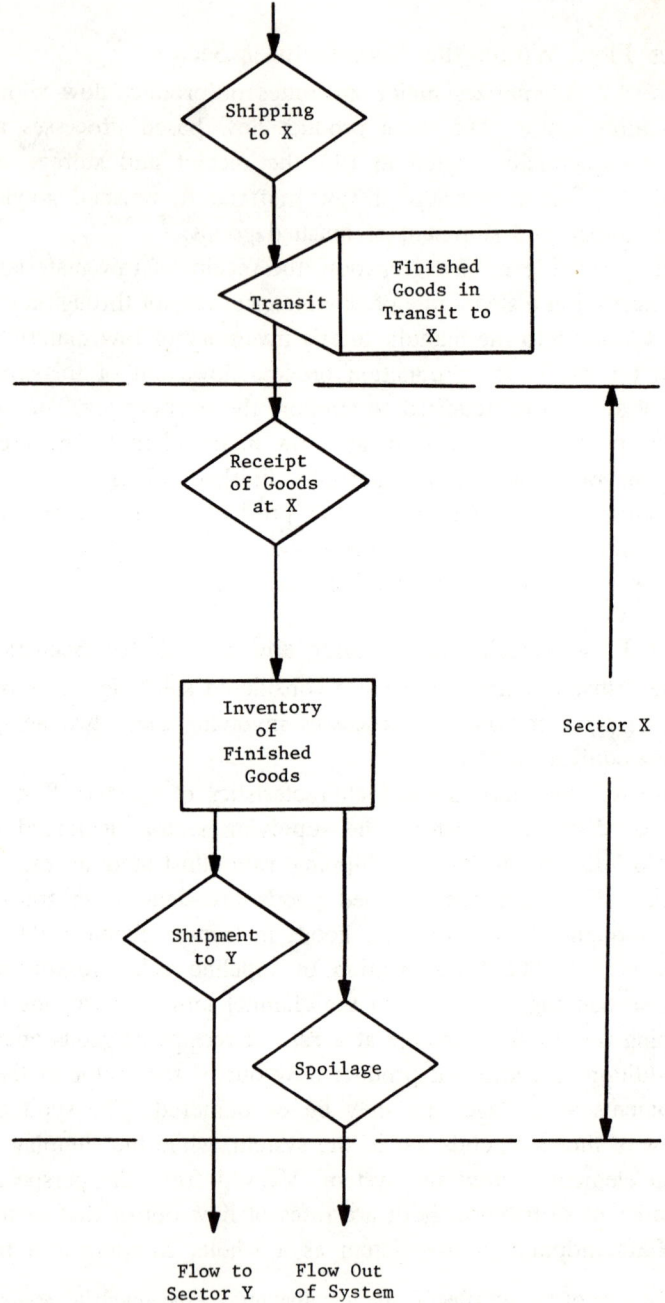

Figure 4.3. Product flow in retailer or distributor sector.

rate, while spoilage constitutes dissipation — loss to the system as a whole.

Product Flow Within the Consumer Sector

Figure 4.4 follows the product flow started in the distributor or retail sector as it enters the consumer sector. The rate of transfer from the distribution system to the consumer sector is established by consumer purchases, which determine the rate of product flow into consumer inventories. Depletion of the consumer inventory is established by a usage rate reflecting product consumption or depreciation. As in the case of distributor and retailer inventories, some depletion of consumer inventories may occur through spoilage, as illustrated in Figure 4.4.

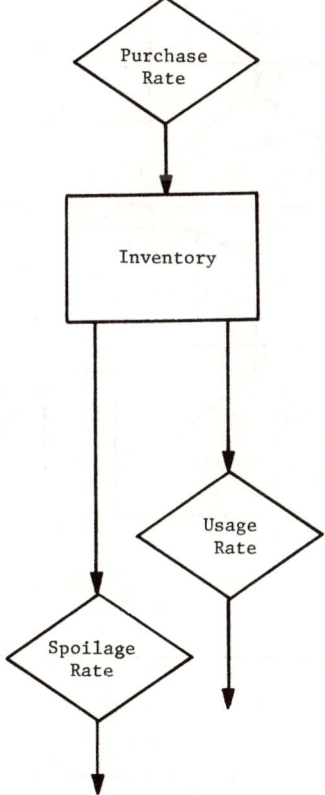

Figure 4.4. Product flow in consumer sector.

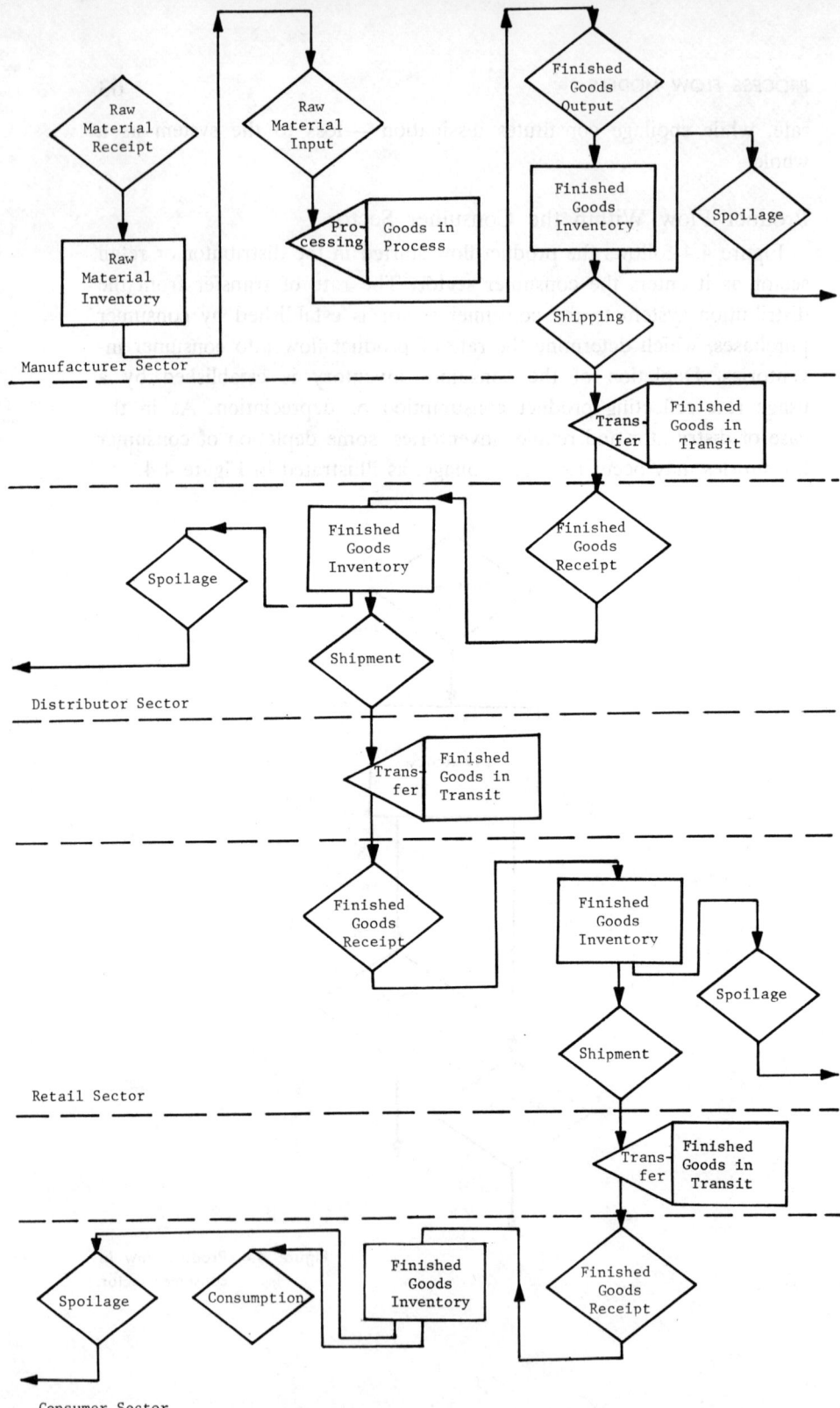

Figure 4.5. Summary of product flow based processes.

Multisector Product Flow

Product-based interactions within the marketing environment may be summarized by combining the microrepresentation of flow within each sector illustrated in Figures 4.2 through 4.4 with the interactions between sectors summarized in Figure 4.1. The addition of channel delays and backlogs to the flow chart of product flow between sectors yields a representation of the type illustrated in Figure 4.5.

Information Flow Based Processes

This section is concerned with processes relating to flows of the three classifications of information specified in Chapter 3: promotion, operating data, and word of mouth.

A Macroview of Information Flow

Figure 4.6 illustrates major channels of communication between active elements with the direction of information flow within channels indicated by arrows. Channels of unilateral flow generally involve formal media, while bilateral communication is most apt to involve personal interaction. If both unilateral and bilateral flows occur in a single channel, the bilateral representation is used (e.g., the association between producer and distributor that may involve both personal and media communication).

Interactions illustrated in Figure 4.6 may be described as follows. Formal media channels link the producer and his competitor to the distributor, retailer, and consumer. Communication between producer and distributor may involve the producer's sales force, while contact between producer and retailer may involve the producer's sales force, the distributor, and the distributor's sales force. Similar conditions affect the relationship of competitors with distributors and retailers.

The government and research agents are viewed as monitors. Channels reviewed by the government are indicated by a circle enclosing the letter "G," while those monitored by the research function are intersected by a circled letter "R." Figure 4.6 illustrates only the research function performed by the producer. Comparable activities of competitors are not represented. The bilateral flow linking distributor, retailer, and consumer to research illustrates information flow generation by research agents through inquiries.

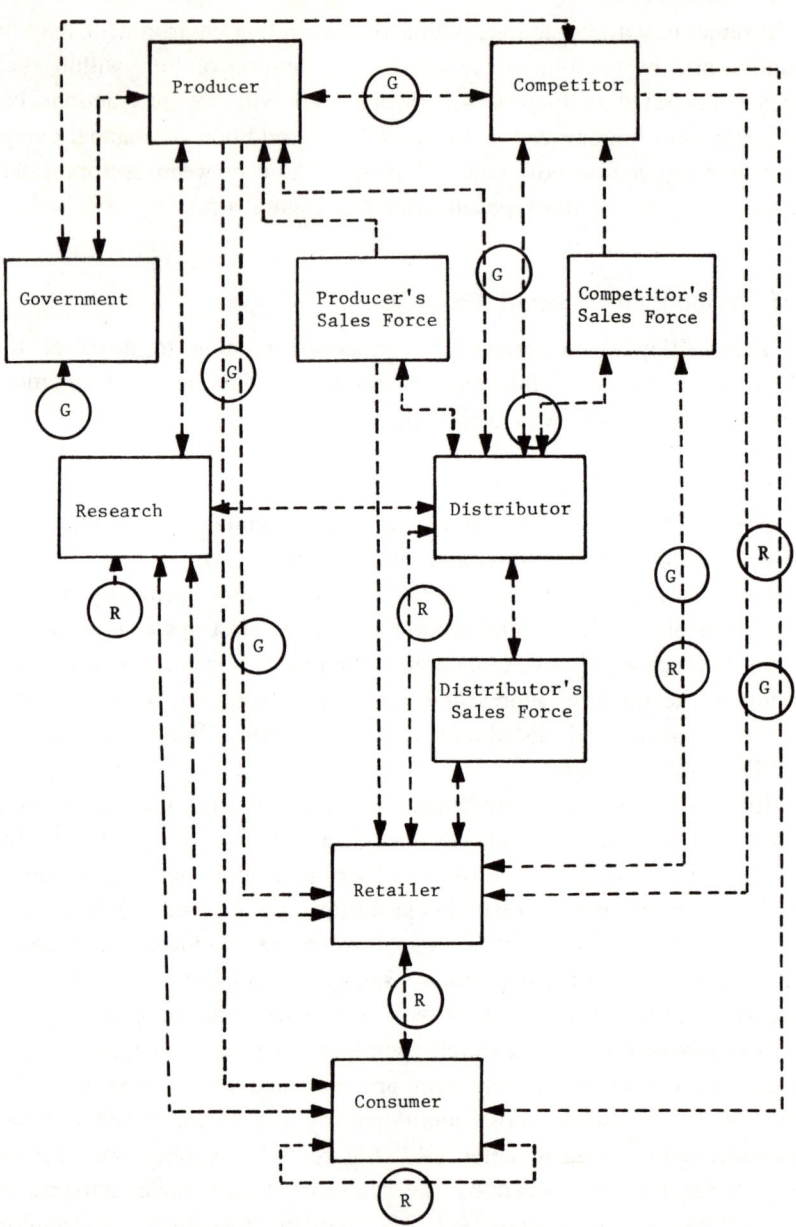

Figure 4.6. Information flow. A macroview.

Figure 4.6 does not specify channel content. In this macroillustration a single channel may contain promotional, operating, or word-of-mouth information, or any combination of these.

The Flow of Promotional Information

Information specifications developed in Chapter 3 establish three subcategories of information as an element of flow: (1) media advertising, (2) point-of-sale advertising, and (3) sales presentations. The first two types of flow are unilateral while the third subclass may be bilateral.

Characteristics of the two unilateral flows are illustrated in Figure 4.7. The left channel represents the flow of media advertising, while the right channel illustrates point-of-sale promotion. Advertising scheduling decisions have been ignored — an established rate of scheduled promotion is assumed as input.

Media Promotion

The flow of media promotion illustrated on the left of Figure 4.7 begins with an initial rate of promotion scheduling. The development of an advertising program is represented by a process delay and backlog of promotion in process. As production is completed, finished mechanicals (plates, mats, master tapes, or films) are released from production at a rate of promotion placement.

Advertising time or space is reserved at a rate of promotion scheduling and transferred to the advertising medium at a rate of promotion placement. Delays associated with media channel processing are summarized in a single media delay with associated backlog of unreleased promotion. Advertisements are published, mailed, or broadcast at a rate of promotion release.

In this flow chart, the potential existence of significant communication delays is recognized through the insertion of a delay with associated backlog for promotion in channels. Following this communication delay, promotion is either seen by the potential audience at a rate of exposure to promotion or wasted at a rate of promotion dissipation.

Three aggregate sectors are designated in the left channel in Figure 4.7. These are (1) the manufacturer sector, (2) the media sector, and (3) the audience sector. The manufacturer sector is that discussed in context of product flow. In addition to transfer delays and backlogs

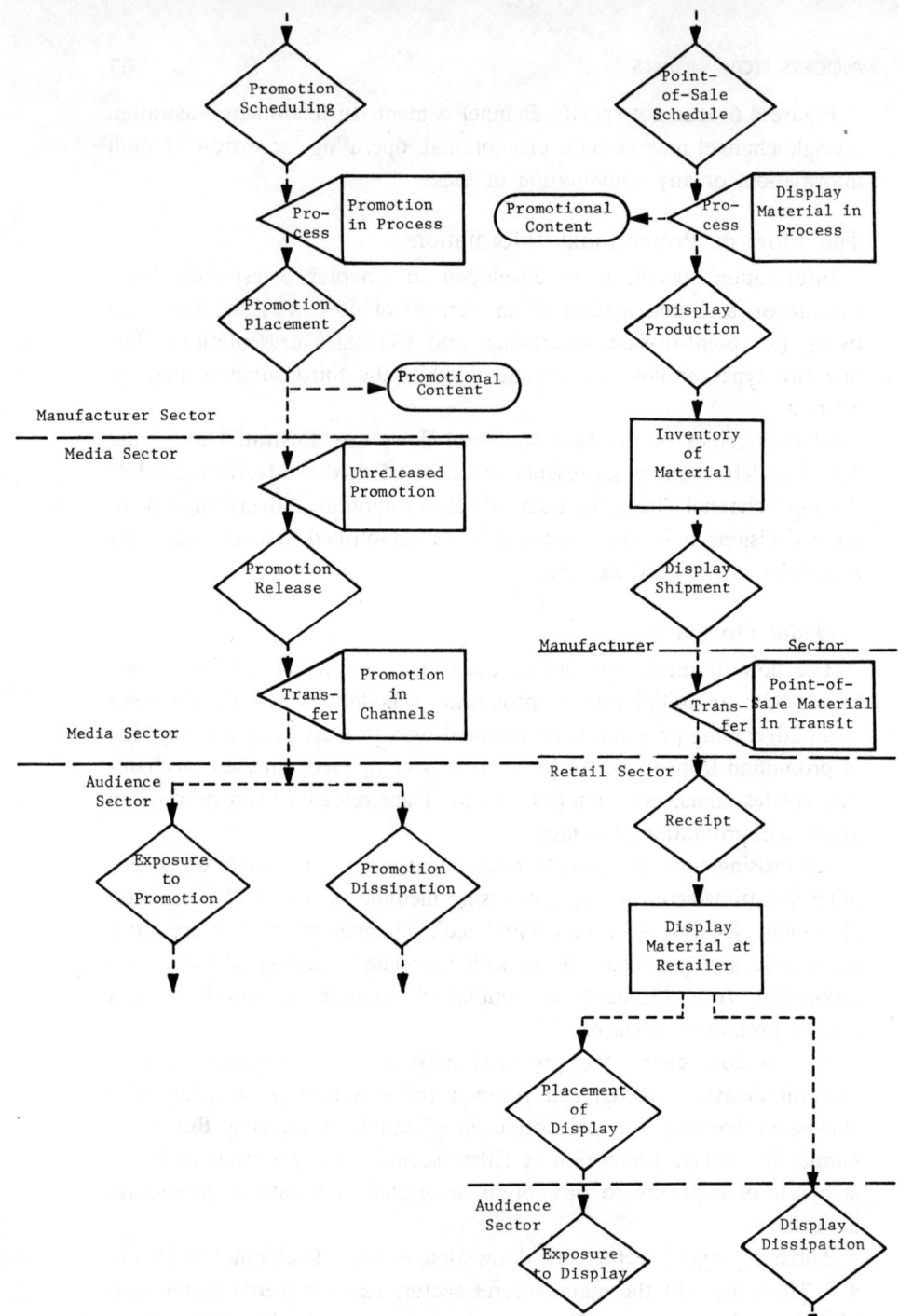

Figure 4.7. Two formal communication channels.

comparable to those in Figure 4.5, the product transportation channel, the media sector encompasses processes within the radio station, television network, newspaper, magazine, or direct mail house through which an advertisement is transmitted to its intended audience.

The audience sector is associated with the active element or elements comprising the audience for the promotion transmitted through the channel of information flow associated with the media sector. Trade advertising media largely exclude consumers as potential audience and claim an audience sector consisting entirely of distributors and/or retailers. Promotion directed to the general public through broadcast or general interest media may reach consumers, distributors, and retailers alike.

The rate of dissipation of promotion, associated with information transfer from the media sector to the audience sector, reflects the inefficiencies inherent in the media process. Although this rate is shown within the audience sector, it might be placed more appropriately in a no-man's-land outside of all sectors.

Point-of-Sale Promotion

The right channel in Figure 4.7 illustrates the flow of point-of-sale promotion beginning with a rate of point-of-sale scheduling. A backlog of display material in process is generated as a result of processing delays associated with the development and production of point-of-sale material. At the conclusion of the production process, content is finalized as indicated by the content oval inserted following the process delay. Display material is completed at a rate of display production and then inventoried.

Figure 4.7 assumes that inventories are maintained at the manufacturer level with shipments made directly to the retailer. Material might alternatively be distributed to retailers by salesmen or distributors who would be expected to expedite display placement in retail stores. However, for purposes of illustration, material is shipped from inventory at a rate of display shipment, delayed in channel for a time period specified by the transit delay, and received in the retailer sector at a rate of receipt. Displays may be backlogged at the retailer until they are installed at a rate of placement of display or discarded at a rate of dissipation of display. Given placement, audience exposure may occur at a rate of exposure to display.

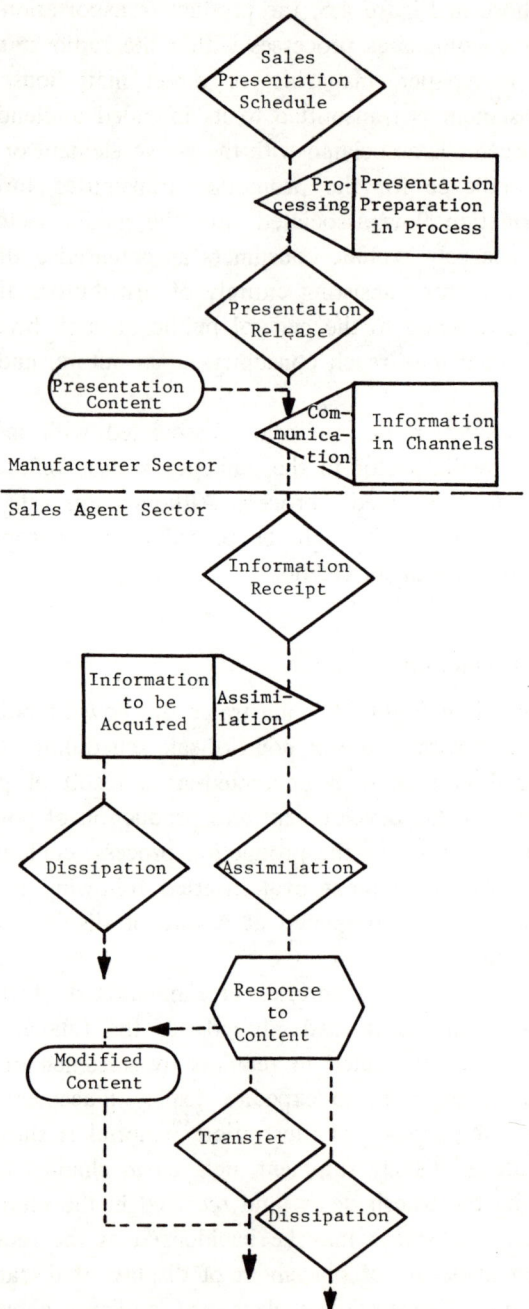

Figure 4.8. Transfer of sales presentation.

Sales Presentations

In moving from point-of-sale displays to sales presentations, additional barriers to efficient information transfer emerge. The communication content of point-of-sale material is established when the display is produced, and, assuming that the material is transferred through the system to the point of ultimate display, the message will remain intact. Communication content is not modified as the display moves through the channel. In the case of sales presentations, active elements influence the content as well as the presence or absence of communication.

Figure 4.8 illustrates the generation and transfer of a sales presentation through a single sales agent. Beginning with a rate of sales presentation scheduling, a process delay reflects presentation preparation prior to release. Presentation content has been established at this point as indicated by the oval in Figure 4.8. A communication delay is incurred while the presentation is backlogged in channel during transfer to the sales agent sector.

Receipt of the presentation plan does not guarantee presentation. A delay is inherent in the information assimilation process, and information backlogged for assimilation may actually be dissipated. Given assimilation, the sales agent responds to presentation content and may modify or reject original channel content. Resultant content, which may differ markedly from that originally prepared by the manufacturer, is transferred to the audience sector by the sales agent. If the sales agent rejects proposed content, the information flow is dispersed at a rate of dissipation.

Response to Communication

Figure 4.9 portrays a communication response process that begins with a rate of exposure to specific information channel content. Exposure to a formal media channel may be determined by media availability, while exposure to personally communicated information (e.g., sales presentations or word-of-mouth communication) may be a function of the extent of interaction between potential respondent and communicator.

Assuming that exposure occurs (communication is available to the potential respondent), it is necessary to determine whether or not the respondent will assimilate the communication. Assimilation is defined

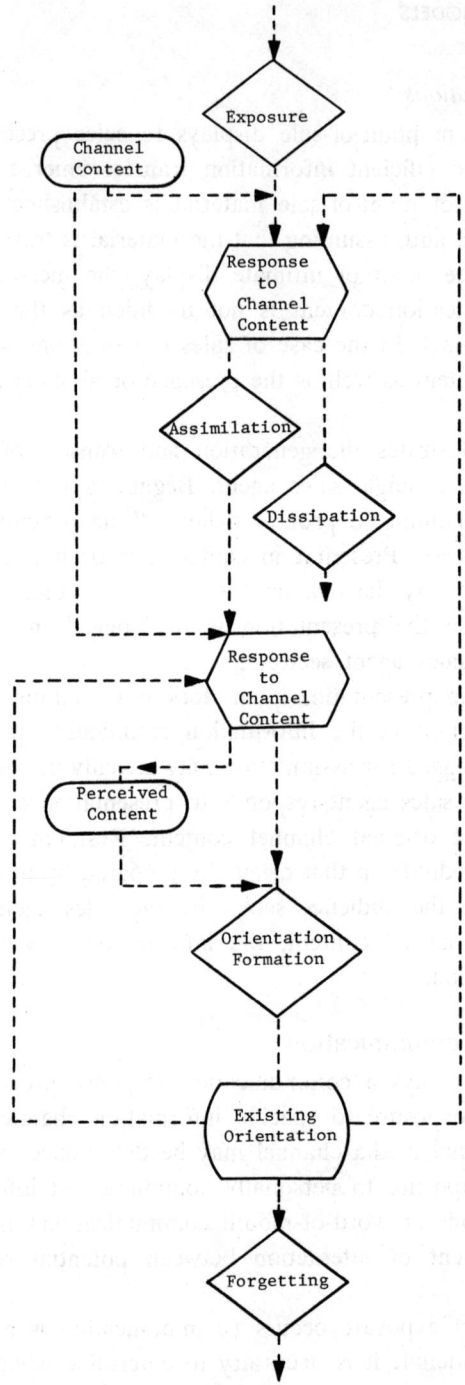

Figure 4.9. Macro flow chart of response to communication.

as achieving a level of conscious recognition sufficient for later unaided recall of communication content. If the communication is not assimilated, its content may be considered totally dissipated.

The perceived content concept provides a useful mechanism for considering the effect of an assimilated communication on the respondent. Evidence discussed in later chapters suggests that, rather than perceiving communication content objectively, the respondent apperceives new content in context of previous experience and prevailing biases summarized in an existing orientation.[2] A second response function incorporating channel content and prior orientation represents this process in the Figure 4.9 flow chart. The output of this response function determines the rate of orientation formation, an input to the existing orientation backlog. The modification of orientation through forgetting is represented as dissipation indicated by a forgetting rate.

The Flow of Operating Information

Three classes of operating information, (1) orders and confirmations, (2) policy communiqués, and (3) reports, were specified in Chapter 3. Processes associated with each type of information flow will be considered separately.

Orders and Confirmations

Processes associated with the flow of orders and confirmations are largely duplicated within each sector of the marketing system. The manufacturer schedules production rather than making an ordering decision of the type effected by the distributor or retailer; however, data processing and demand estimation procedures are not fundamentally different from comparable processes encountered at the retail or distributor level.

Major attributes of these processes are summarized graphically in Figure 4.10 with sufficient generality to be applied to the producer, distributor, or retailer sector. The producer's *rate of finished goods receipt* is actually his rate of production. With this exception, the characteristics summarized in Figure 4.10 are largely equivalent within the three sectors.

Orders flow into the sector at a rate of order receipt. Clerical delays are involved in processing orders, and a backlog of orders to be proc-

---

[2] For a detailed discussion of this process with appropriate references, see "The Process of Information Assimilation" in Chapter 8, pp. 193–194.

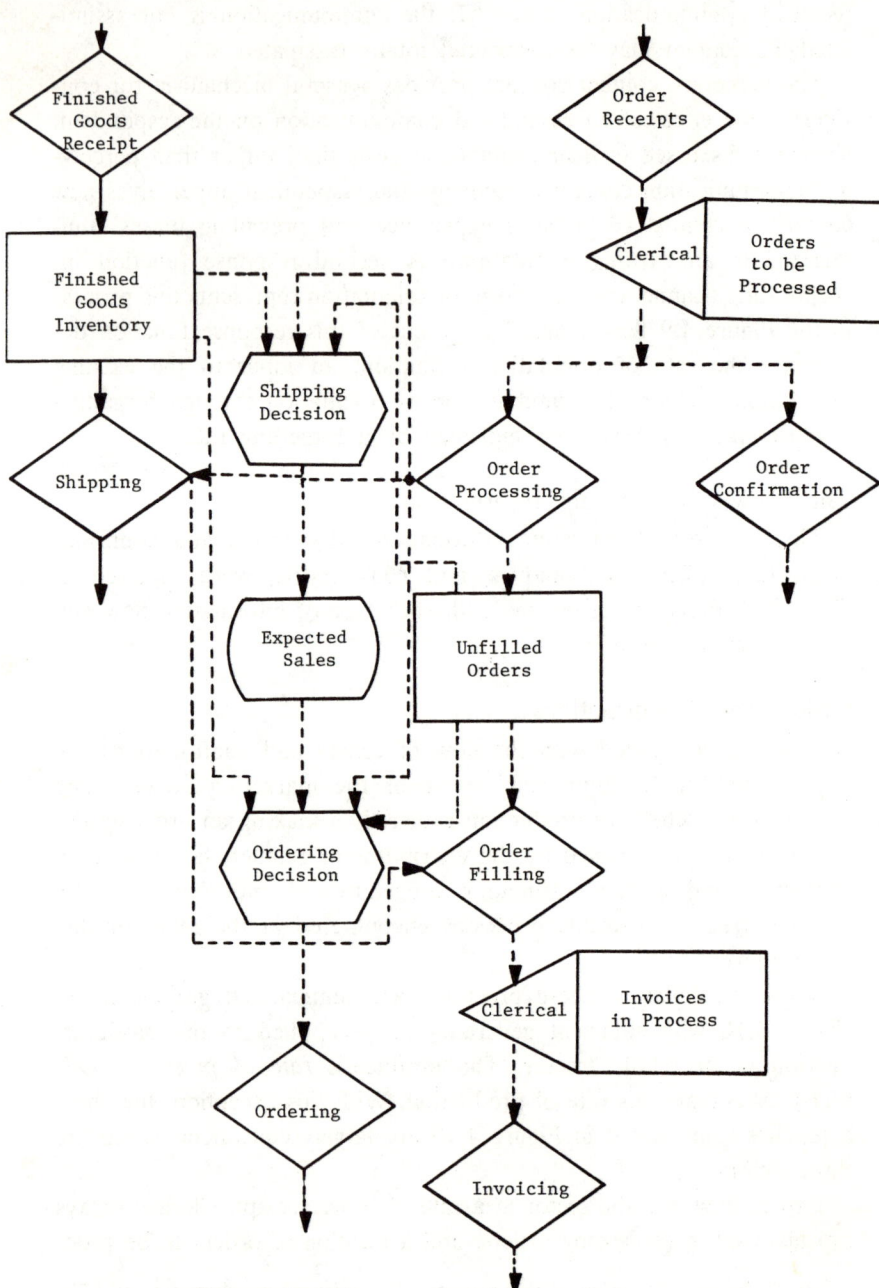

Figure 4.10. Macro flow chart of orders and conformations.

essed is maintained. As orders are processed, confirmations are sent to the ordering sector at a corresponding rate of order confirmation. Once processed, the orders become part of an unfilled orders backlog, which is reduced as orders are filled at a rate established by the shipping decision. Clerical delays are associated with the preparation of invoices that are mailed to the orderer at a rate of invoicing.

The rate of order processing is an input to several decision functions. First, in combination with information regarding the level of unfilled orders and finished goods inventory, it enters the shipping decision as a determinant of what will be shipped to whom. Second, the rate of order processing serves as the basis for the formulation of an expected sales function summarizing expectations regarding the seasonality and trend of demand. Finally, the rate of order processing in combination with the level of unfilled orders, the level of finished goods inventory, and expected sales affects the ordering decision that determines the rate at which orders will be sent to suppliers.

Addition of information flow to a portion of the Figure 4.3 product flow representation illustrates the interaction between information and physical product flows. As indicated in the upper left of Figure 4.10, a shipping decision based on information regarding the state of relevant elements within the sector governs the rate at which physical product is shipped.

Policy Communiqués

For purposes of this discussion, information channels transmitting policy communiqués can, with one exception, be viewed as paralleling channels of order and product flow. The exception is introduced by the government sector, which, although not normally involved in product flow, may provide policy communiqués.

Reports

Information channels containing reports parallel those through which policy communiqués are transmitted; however, the flow of reports is in the opposite direction, beginning with the retailer and returning through other active elements to the producer.

Response to Policy Communication

The previous discussion of response processes is applicable to operating information. Response functions may be inserted in series with shipping and ordering decision to indicate that information is apperceived rather than objectively assimilated.

Word-of-Mouth Communication

Description of word-of-mouth communication processes focuses on the individual consumer and on those factors that cause him to generate specific information content relating to a brand of product at a particular time or to respond to the communication of others.

Generation of Word-of-Mouth Communication

The Chapter 3 specifications of consumer actions establish two bases for brand specific consumer experience: the consumer can respond to the content of assimilated communication or to product usage.

Figure 4.11 provides a first approximation representation of processes associated with consumer generation of word-of-mouth communication based on experience. The two rates of flow appearing at the top of this figure indicate the individual's rate of communication assimilation and rate of product usage. The response function and rates of assimilation, brand image formation, orientation change, and forgetting represented in the left channel correspond to similar functions illustrated in Figure 4.9. The orientation concept is refined in this representation by the inclusion of a perceived brand image updated at a rate of brand image formation (analogous to the rate of orientation change discussed earlier) and diminished by forgetting. The perceived brand image is a specific orientation — the individual's attitude toward and perception of particular brand-models of product.

The right channel in Figure 4.11 relates to the individual's rate of product usage and response to such usage. The response function associated with product is affected by the individual's preusage orientation and experienced product characteristics. The use of a circle to represent product characteristics indicates that this factor is supplied as an input to the model rather than generated endogenously within the model. The response function influences orientation change and brand image formation.

Outputs from response functions associated with communication assimilation and product usage affect product awareness that diminishes with time through forgetting.[3]

[3] The concept of awareness is developed in terms of specific measurement techniques in Chapter 5, pp. 94–97, and formulated as part of a detailed response model in Chapter 8, pp. 194–202.

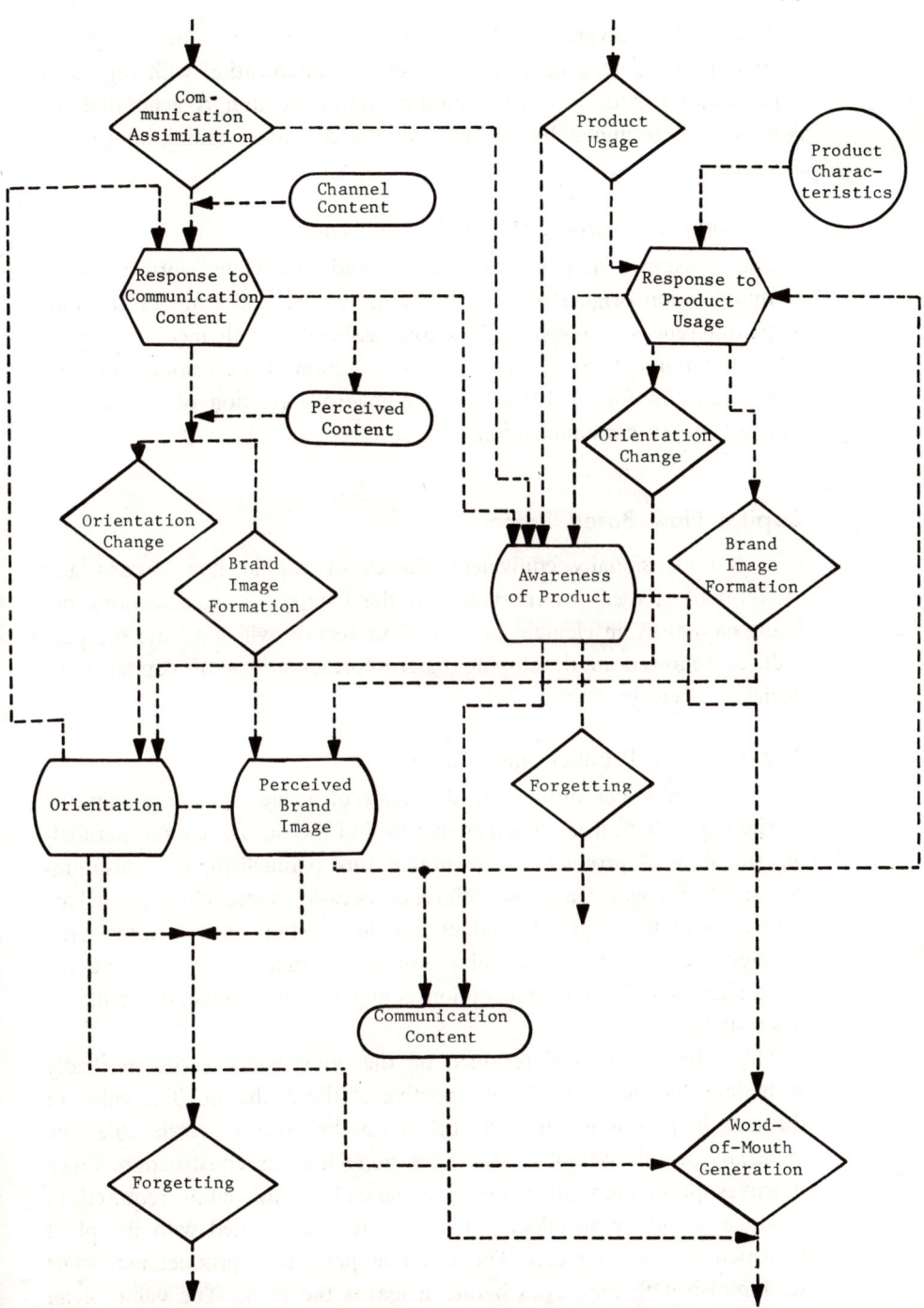

Figure 4.11. Macro flow chart of word-of-mouth generation.

The level of awareness and perceived brand image determine the probability of generating word-of-mouth communication with regard to a particular brand. If word-of-mouth communication is generated, its content is determined by the individual's perceived brand image and awareness.

Response to Word-of-Mouth Communication

The consumer may be exposed to and assimilate word-of-mouth communication originated by another individual. Ignoring for the moment differences in response functions associated with media and personal communication, the general representation of the response process summarized in Figure 4.9 provides a macrodescription of response to word-of-mouth communication.

Capital Flow Based Processes

Two dimensionally equivalent classes of capital flow — cash and discountable paper — were noted in the Chapter 3 specifications defining capital as an element of flow. This section will illustrate the procedures followed in developing macrorepresentations of capital-based decision processes.

The Flow of Product and Value

Because physical product is the basis of value transfer within the marketing system, it is not surprising to find the flow of capital paralleling the flow of product. While noting this parallelism, it is also important to recognize a basic difference between these channels. Characteristics of the physical product remain constant as it is transferred through the system. A particular unit of product continues to be the same size, model, color, and option configuration throughout its life — it is a stable entity.

The value of physical product, on the other hand, varies markedly with time, location, and the perspective of the evaluator. The value of the unit in production may be based on the costs of retrievable raw materials or subassemblies that have gone into its construction. Once it leaves production, its value is enhanced by the labor required to produce it and by an allocation of overhead associated with the plant in which it was produced. The value of perishable product may start to diminish with time even before it leaves the plant. The value of an inventoried item reflected on the books of the company may be affected by pricing policies and fluctuations in costs over time.

As product is transported, stored, displayed, demonstrated, promoted, taxed, sold, and consumed, its value is constantly changing. Yet the flow of value, however unstable, is inextricably intertwined with the flow of physical product. The macrodescription of product flow summarized in Figure 4.1 is therefore applicable to value flow.

Because previously specified capital flow related functions of the government, research agent, and salesman are of marginal importance, this section will focus on the role of manufacturer, distributor, retailer, and consumer in processes in which capital or value is the central element of flow.

Capital Flow Within the Manufacturer Sector

Capital-related decisions within the manufacturing sector may be summarized under two headings: allocation procedures and pricing procedures.

Allocation Procedures

In discussing allocation procedures, we will assume that criteria for the allocation of resources have been devised. Such criteria might be based on marginal return, percentage of net revenue, or fixed dollar allocations.

Given a criterion of evaluation, the allocation process is easily described, as illustrated in Figure 4.12. The rate of income flow into the manufacturer sector produces a backlog of revenues that must be allocated to (1) raw material, (2) sales maintenance, (3) promotion, (4) research and development, and (5) addition to surplus. For purposes of this macrodiscussion, capital investment may be assumed to come from retained earnings. Net plant, which determines the manufacturer's capacity to produce, may be assumed to increase as a result of investment from the capital or surplus account and decrease through depreciation.

Each allocation of funds establishes a flow of dollars to support a process discussed earlier in this chapter. Allocation of dollars to raw material acquisition supports a raw material ordering rate. Allocation of funds to sales force maintenance provides salesman compensation. Allocations to promotion influence advertising and point-of-sale scheduling decisions. Funds allocated to research and development determine

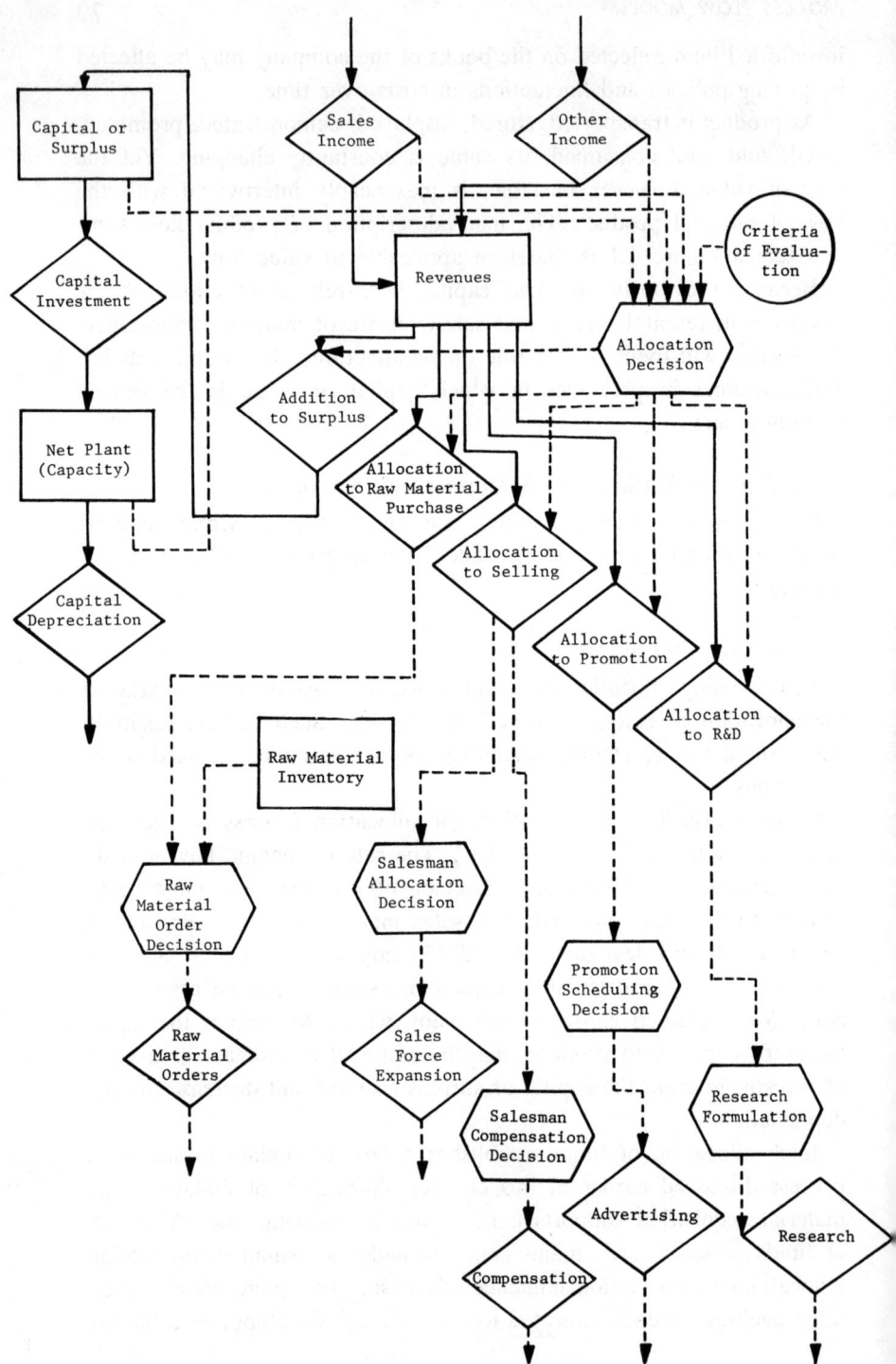

Figure 4.12. A macroview of the producer's allocation process.

the rate at which research and new product development efforts will be scheduled.

The assumption that capital and retained earnings are to be used only for investment requires that funds allocated to noncapital expenditures come from cash flows generated by the company with existing revenues imposing an upper limit on total expenditures. This representation of the allocation process ignores cost of capital and alternative sources of funds. In context of this simplified view, income is the sole revenue source, and the manufacturer must either expend funds in the operating areas or retain them in a surplus account from which capital investment is made.

This representation of the allocation process implies that the manufacturer controls the extent of retained earnings. He may determine the closing profit-and-loss statement at a particular point in time by deciding on a desired rate of return and making allocations to achieve that rate. This procedure can obviously not be followed for an extended period of time.

Financial Reports as a Description of Process. Analysis of a firm is often based on corporate records indicating allocations made and return realized. Such reports (e.g., profit-and-loss statements) are of little use when developing actual models based on a structure of the type illustrated in Figure 4.12. The level of aggregation over time and decision areas normally precludes analysis of operations at a point in time. Given consistency in reporting, some insight into process relationships may be gained by examining such reports over time and noting trends and variations indicative of successive allocations.

Pricing Procedures

In theory, pricing procedures may be described with reference to (1) empirically derived or assumed attributes of the price elasticity of demand or (2) the cost structure of the firm. Cost-based approaches imply that the price elasticity of demand is sufficiently small so that the firm may establish price on the basis of its cost structure without adversely affecting demand or that appropriate allocations to promotion can shift the demand curve to a position compatible with the desired pricing structure.

Demand-Based Pricing. A pricing decision based on price elasticity of demand projects expected sales at a hypothetical price and under certain expected demand conditions. The final market price is established at a level that maximizes profits, subject to the constraint that established demand must not exceed the manufacturer's capacity to produce. This approach either ignores competitive interactions or assumes that the market effect of competitor policies is represented by the demand curve.

Cost-Based Pricing. The cost-based pricing approach begins with an expected sales volume, unit cost, total investment, desired margin, and desired rate of return on investment. Given these parameters, the price is established at a level that permits a desired return to be realized. If the expected sales volume is not realized at the established price, the decision is reconsidered in light of corrected unit cost figures.

A Combined Representation. Macrocharacteristics of both market- and cost-based pricing processes may be combined in a single pricing function based on the concept of expected rate of return. This procedure begins with the formulation of an expected sales level derived from hypothetical price and demand conditions. Expected unit cost and investment estimates are then developed. The expected sales and hypothetical price yield expected revenues that, in combination with expected investment and unit costs, produce an expected rate of return. The expected rate of return associated with alternative prices is then evaluated using the producer's criteria.

Given an existing price and established sales and income rates, this process may be formulated in terms of the incremental investment required to achieve a desired rate of return as illustrated in Figure 4.13.

Pricing in Practice. In practice, this theoretical procedure may be discarded in favor of "realistic" approaches. Detailed consideration gives way to aggregate rules of thumb, standard markups, and meet-all-reasonable-competition policies. Pricing is often based on roundoff formulas[4] rather than estimated demand curves, and allocation decisions are expressed in fixed percentage budgets rather than evaluations of potential return.

When pressed to rationalize prevailing practice, most businessmen pay homage to basic tenets of the decision structure outlined, indicating that procedures followed either optimize, satisfy, or at least do not wholly pervert either demand or profit concepts.

[4] See R. M. Cyert, J. G. March, and C. G. Moore, "A Model of Retail Ordering and Pricing by a Department Store," Frank et al., *Quantitative Techniques in Marketing Analysis* (Homewood, Ill.: Richard D. Irwin, Inc., 1962), pp. 502–522.

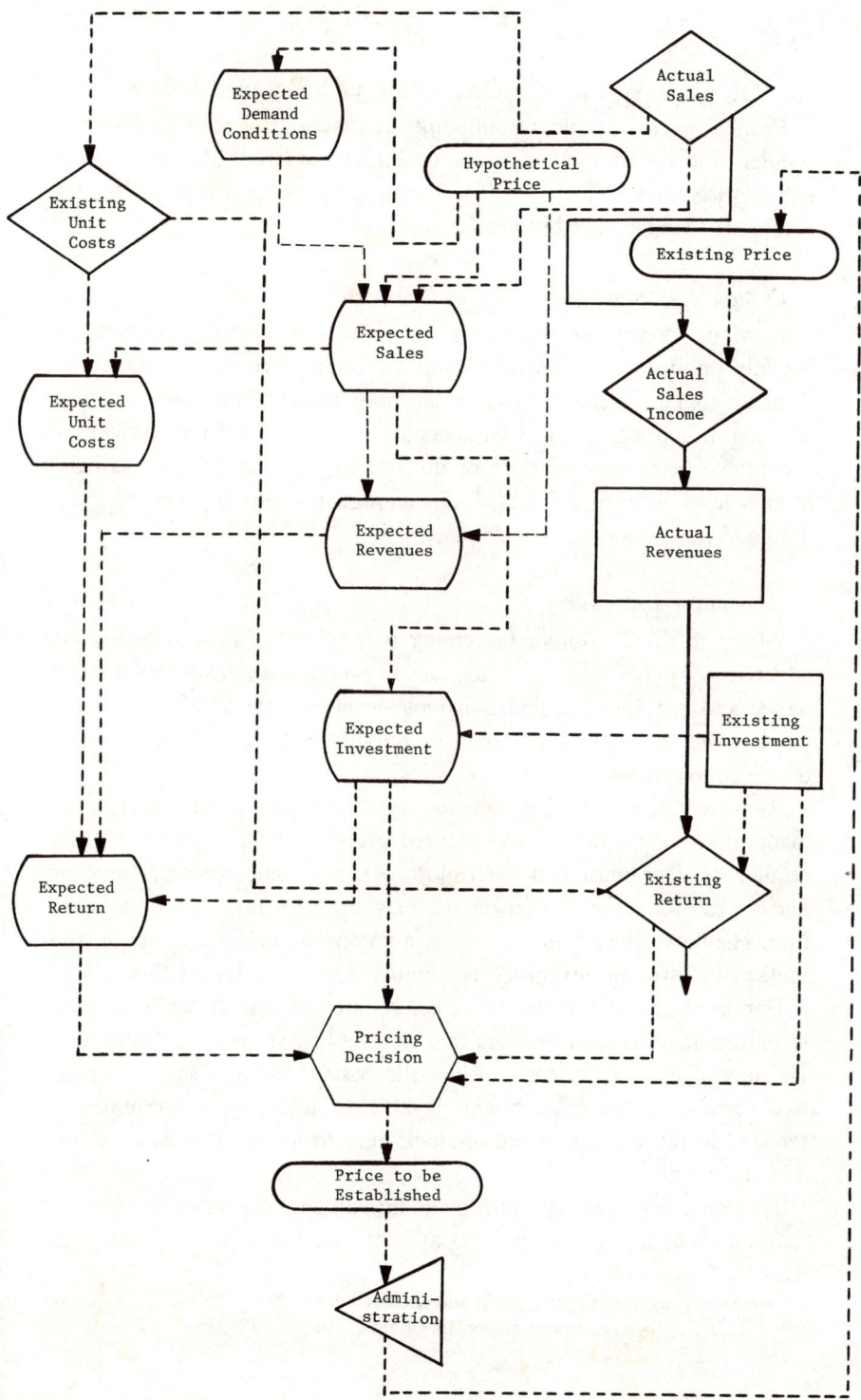

Figure 4.13. A macroview of the producer's pricing process.

Capital Flow Within the Distributor and Retailer Sectors

From a macro cash flow standpoint the functions of the manufacturer, retailer, and distributor are not substantially different. All must establish a price for which they will sell their products and allocate existing resources to operating business functions.

Pricing Procedures

Previous comments regarding manufacturer pricing policies are broadly applicable to the distributor or retailer. In each instance the decision maker attempts to consider both market and cost factors in arriving at a price that will be accepted by the market and provide an acceptable percentage markup or dollar margin. Such analysis as exists at this level is normally based on average markup or relative dollar volume.[5]

Allocation Procedures

Although the distributor or retailer may allocate funds to selling and advertising, the major allocation activity relates to inventory maintenance and ordering decisions. In most instances, the retailer's stock of goods is his greatest capital asset or liability and, as such, is the focus of allocation considerations.

Representative capital flow based relationships between sales, costs, inventories, and orders are structured graphically in Figure 4.14. The retailer or distributor can determine his actual sales income, revenue, and/or rate of return based on the existing sales rate and price structure. His "investment" in a brand is a composite of costs of space, promotional effort, and inventory as summarized on the left of Figure 4.14.

For purposes of this example, the retailer or distributor is assumed to extrapolate his existing sales rate to establish an expected sales level. He may in some instances consider the cost of losing a sale — a negative "cost" for the retailer who is able to trade up a consumer interested in purchasing an out-of-stock item to an in-stock item offering a higher profit.

Expected sales, rate of return on investment, and cost of lost sales may all be considered in arriving at a desired inventory that enters the

---

[5] Retailer pricing decisions are modeled in Chapter 9, pp. 253–258, while distributor pricing behavior is discussed in Chapter 10, pp. 313–315.

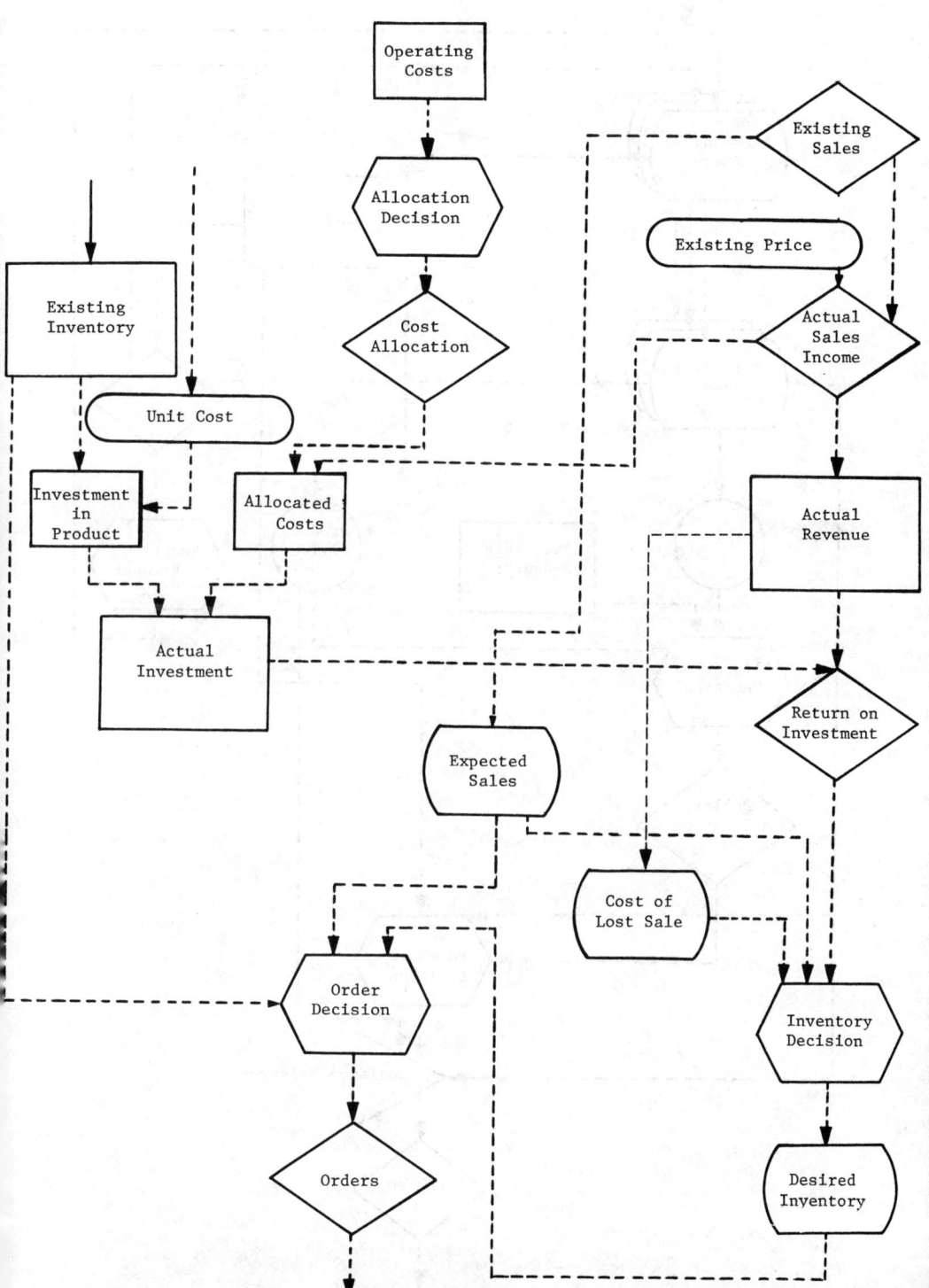

Figure 4.14. Capital flow and the ordering decision.

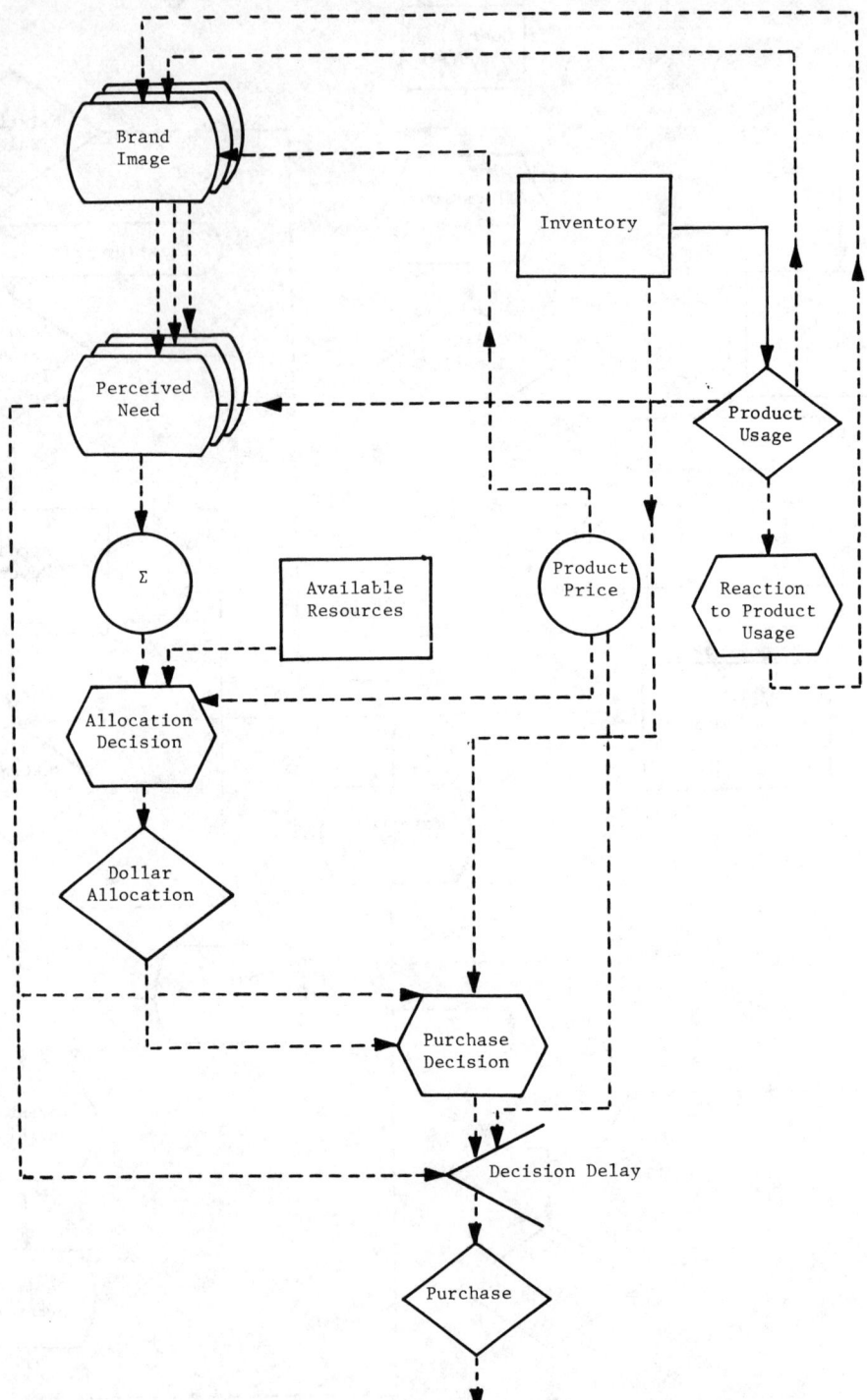

Figure 4.15. Price and the consumer purchase decision.

order decision in combination with expected sales and existing inventory. This process is discussed in detail in later chapters.[6]

Capital Flow Within the Consumer Sector

Consumer purchase behavior may be viewed as an allocation process through which the consumer considers his needs and allocates available resources to products that he believes will satisfy these needs. The consumer attempts to match his concept of value based on perceived need with the market's evaluation of worth reflected in price.

The concept of perceived brand image was introduced earlier to describe a consumer's perception of brand attributes. The perceived need concept extends to the value that a consumer places on obtaining product attributes corresponding to a particular perceived brand image.

Representation of the Purchase Decision

The perceived brand image and perceived need constructs provide a basis for structuring the purchase decision as an allocation process. As illustrated in Figure 4.15, this process begins with a set of brand images and perceived needs associated with specific brands within relevant product classes. Price enters the brand image as a product characteristic.

The cumulative impact of all perceived needs is evaluated in the light of available resources and existing alternatives in an allocation decision that yields a rate of resource allocation to a purchase decision based on existing inventory and level of perceived need.

The delay in effective purchase is represented as a function of price and of perceived need, suggesting that time spent in making a purchase decision is a function of associated costs and potential benefits. Following the decision delay, funds are expended at a rate of purchase.

Summary

Representative processes associated with the three elements of flow have been structured in this chapter as illustrations of micro process description. Product flow associated processes were related to interactions between the manufacturer, distributor, retailer, and consumer. Factors

---

[6] Retailer ordering decisions are discussed in Chapter 9, pp. 278–283. Distributor order decision formulations appear in Chapter 10, pp. 318–324.

influencing the extent of physical product flow rates, backlogs, and process delays were discussed.

Information-associated processes were examined with reference to three classifications of information flow. Consideration of promotional information flow focused on media and point-of-sale advertising as examples of formal and unilateral information flow. Sales presentations were noted as examples of formal bilateral information-based process. Processes involving operating information were found to parallel and interact with the product flow channels discussed previously. Interactions between information and product in processes associated with order generation provided an example of information impact on decisions controlling the flow of other elements. Discussion of informal bilateral information flow focused on word-of-mouth generation and response.

Processes in which capital or value is the major element of flow were categorized as relating to pricing or allocation decisions. Pricing decisions based on market and cost viewpoints were examined. Allocation decisions at the manufacturing level were discussed in terms of control of functional operations. At the distributor and retailer level, the allocation process discussion focused on ordering and inventory decisions.

The consumer purchase decision was structured as an allocation of consumer resources to the satisfaction of existing needs as perceived by the consumer. Price, in addition to determining the extent of required resource allocation, was assumed to affect product image, consumption rate and time required to effect a purchase decision.

Chapter 5

QUANTIFICATION OF MARKETING PROCESSES

Models discussed in later chapters have been developed to describe complex interactions. They are designed to provide a structure within which the implications of factors influencing complex management decisions may be analyzed.

These models approach complexity by structuring existing knowledge and assumptions in a series of explicit, quantitative, and testable assertions. The alternative is to be content with "intuitive" decision processes based on internalized models that cannot be communicated or evaluated because they have never been made explicit.

The objective when making explicit the internalized models of managers and observers of the business environment is to structure the insights of informed individuals so that they may be communicated with a minimum of ambiguity. Quantification produces a usable model — a model on which operations can be performed in lieu of operation in the actual physical environment, a model that may be objectively verified or rejected with reference to data from the real world.[1]

---

[1] The following quantitatively oriented texts were reviewed in compiling the sections of this study relating to quantitative methods and specific model approaches. While not quoted specifically, they have contributed to the development of ideas presented in this and following chapters.

R. L. Day, *Marketing Models: Quantitative and Behavioral* (Scranton, Pa.: International Textbook Company, 1964).

P. Langhoff (ed.), *Models, Measurement, and Marketing* (Englewood Cliffs, N. J.: Prentice-Hall, Inc., 1965).

R. Cox, W. Alderson, and S. Shapiro, *Theory in Marketing* (New York: American Marketing Association, 1964).

R. D. Buzzell, *Mathematical Models and Marketing Management* (Boston:

Problems of Being Explicit

Abstraction is inherent in the modeling process. The individual who develops a model must impose structure on a situation. He must specify what is relevant.

Whether or not the decision maker develops an explicit model, the information considered in reaching a decision is determined by his perception of the decision environment. We are all familiar with the observation ". . . it seems to me that this is basically a matter of . . . ," which frequently precedes presentation of highly abstract verbal models. Subjective evaluation is present whether or not an explicit model is established. However, as a model is made explicit, the level of abstraction — the extent to which the model builder has reduced the situation to a limited and manageable number of factors — becomes more obvious.

The perceptiveness of the individual who has the ability to "separate the wheat from the chaff" and "get to the nub of the problem" is often lauded. Yet, when this same perception is applied to the structuring of an explicit decision model through exclusion of other than the most relevant factors, the results may appear appallingly "simple minded" and be dismissed as "naïve" or "sophomoric."

Seasoned managers may become unnerved when asked to summarize factors considered in arriving at a decision and to make explicit the assumptions underlying their choice of factors. The resultant "model" is usually a simple one, and the manager is seldom happy with it. It is disturbing to recognize that a decision affecting an expenditure of tens of millions of dollars in a complex environment is made on the basis of a model that takes into account only two or three gross descriptors. It is even more distasteful to admit that a direct relationship has been assumed between ill-defined descriptors and a complex outcome. It is far more satisfying to retain the aura of understanding that flows from ambiguous general discussion than to face the frustrations inherent in being specific. For this reason, underlying models are seldom made explicit or, in the rare instances when a model is proposed, it is accompanied by a dis-

Division of Research, Graduate School of Business Administration, Harvard University, 1964).

F. M. Bass, et al., *Mathematical Models and Methods in Marketing* (Homewood, Ill.: Richard D. Irwin, Inc., 1961).

R. E. Frank, A. A. Kuehn, and W. F. Massy, *Quantitative Techniques in Marketing Analysis* (Homewood, Ill.: Richard D. Irwin, Inc., 1962).

claimer that "this is only to highlight a few of the more important factors considered in this situation." "Obviously many other things must be considered before reaching a final decision."

It is generally possible to obtain agreement from practicing marketing men on the contents of the annotated lists with which marketing texts abound. These compilations of factors to be considered in a particular decision context and their counterparts in "principles of marketing" are sufficiently ambiguous to gain acceptance from people who have substantially different views of the situation under discussion.[2] When lists and principles are replaced by explicit and testable statements, differences of opinion will be encountered. It might be suggested, in fact, that if differences of opinion are not encountered the model is probably not explicit enough. If explicit formulation achieves no other objective, it should provide an unequivocal statement of knowledge or assumptions. The men who examine such a formulation should be able to focus their attention on specific points of disagreement.

Types of Models

The appropriateness of a model can be evaluated only when the functions that it is to serve are known. The characteristics discussed here are selected because of their relevance to the particular problem at hand. They do not constitute an exhaustive list nor are they necessarily mutually exclusive. They are simply dimensions along which the acceptability of a model may be evaluated in the context of present objectives.

Dimensions of a Model

Models may be described in terms of those functions which they are to serve, the occupations of the people who develop them, the contexts in which they are used, or the techniques through which they are implemented. The following dimensions are relevant in the present context:

1. Implicit — explicit
2. Qualitative — quantitative
3. Macro — micro
4. Simple — complex

[2] Simon has suggested that, in a perverse adaption of laws of physics, for every "principle" of management there is an equal and opposite counter "principle." See H. Simon, *Administrative Behavior* (New York: The Macmillan Company, 1948), p. 20.

    5. Static — dynamic
    6. State change — process
    7. Deterministic — probabilistic
    8. Theoretical — empirical
    9. Correlation based — behavioral
  10. Descriptive — predictive
  11. Descriptive — normative
  12. Manual — computerized
  13. Operations research — econometric

The discussion thus far has focused on the first two dimensions, emphasizing the desirability of explicit and quantitative as opposed to implicit or qualitative models.

Chapter 4 established macrocharacteristics of the environment to be modeled. To go beyond this level of aggregation it is necessary to move toward the microend of the third dimension — to develop models based on detailed analyses of actions and responses.

Specification in terms of the fourth dimension can be misleading. While the total system may be complex, individual model segments may be simple. It is precisely this characteristic that makes quantification of complex processes feasible. By describing microbehavior in terms of simple, verifiable functions, it is possible to achieve description of the complex whole through simulation-based synthesis.

To describe processes occurring over time, models must be dynamic and represent processes rather than single changes of state.

Because the situations to be described involve probabilistic rather than deterministic causality (i.e., it is not normally possible to abstract from all contingencies), models developed in later chapters will be probabilistic rather than deterministic. Stochastic elements will take account of the existence of conditions that, while necessary for the realization of a particular outcome, are not in and of themselves sufficient to guarantee that outcome.[3]

While models formulated in later chapters are initially theoretical rather than empirical, they are stated in a manner that permits empirical verification. Because description of behavior within the market environment is a basic objective of this work, the models developed must be

---

[3] For a more complete discussion of this problem, see R. L. Ackoff, *Scientific Method: Optimizing Applied Decisions* (New York: John Wiley & Sons, Inc., 1962), pp. 14–19.

behavioral rather than merely functional. They must describe a process rather than simply correlate outputs and inputs.[4]

To be applicable in the business environment as a representation of the real world, models should portray *that which is* rather than *that which should be*. The models developed are therefore descriptive rather than normative. However, if these models are to be used to predict probable outcomes under specified conditions, the function of the final system must be predictive rather than merely descriptive.

In view of the detail and scope to be encompassed by the system, the models must be amenable to computer solution.

Distinctions between operations research and econometric models often appear to be a matter of semantics. Econometric models are often viewed as having ". . . the primary objective of *predicting* what the future values of a set of certain *variables* . . . will be." Operations research or "programming" models, on the other hand, have as their objective ". . . maximizing (or minimizing) *some functional element* such as profits or costs by determining what the future values of certain variables (over which one has some control) *should* be. . . ."[5] Within the context of these definitions, our objective is the development of econometric models to be applied to achieve operations research objectives. The models to be developed will be designed to predict probable outcomes under specified conditions, not to generate a maximizing strategy for use in these circumstances. They may be used, however, to examine implications of alternative strategies and, as such, provide the basis for external maximization according to an objective function (criterion) specified by management.

Desired Model Characteristics

Conclusions reached in the preceding discussion may be summarized in two sentences. Models to be developed will be complex, computerized, microanalytic simulations of dynamic processes based on empirically verifiable behavioral theory. Resulting models are to be used to provide predictions of probable outcomes under specified competitive market conditions and to evaluate implications of alternative marketing strategies.

The words "complex computerized microanalytic simulation" reflect

[4] A lucid consideration of this distinction is provided in Buzzell, *op. cit.*, Footnote 1, pp. 206–209.

[5] E. G. Bennion, "Econometrics for Management," *Harvard Business Review,* Vol. 39 (March–April 1961), p. 105.

a concern with complex individual behavior rather than aggregate statistics and with the use of the computer simulation technique.

The term "dynamic process" indicates a focus on the time paths of relevant variables, the process of feedback through which changes in one variable affect the state of another, and the processes through which the system moves from one state to another.

The reference to "empirically verifiable behavioral theory" emphasizes the importance of understanding actions and responses underlying observable phenomena, expressing knowledge and assumptions explicitly, and formulating concepts in terms of measurable quantities.

The allusion to "predictions of probable outcomes under specified . . . conditions" indicates that models are to be stochastic, to be used to generate outputs in response to alternative inputs, and to focus on competitive interactions within the marketplace.

References to "evaluation of alternative strategies" indicate that the models must encompass relevant variables controlled by management, provide outputs in terms of meaningful measures of management performance, and represent the effect of company actions on behavior within the market.

Questions of Measurement

Development of models based on explicitly defined variables related through empirically verifiable functions requires careful attention to questions of measurement.

Variable Specification

If functions included in a model are to be empirically verifiable, variables must be specified in a manner that permits objective measurement in the real world environment. The dimension of each variable and the compatibility of units within functions must be considered. Probable limits as well as expected values must be established for each variable.

Types of Measurement

Some measurements are appropriately made using an ordinal scale. Others require an interval or ratio scale.

An ordinal scale is useful when ranking entities in terms of a particular attribute without concern for differences between ranks. For example, salesman allocation requires ranking of salesmen by productivity. Ordinal ranking indicates that the top salesman on the list is more productive than the second salesman but does not specify the extent of his superiority.

Interval scales are particularly useful when measuring psychological dispositions. Attitudes, for example, may be measured using an interval scale that combines ranking with a constant unit of measure. By using this scale, it is possible to compare attitude changes of different individuals, but it is not possible to say that one individual's attitude is "X times greater" than another's.

The majority of the variables used in later models are measured on a ratio scale that permits comparisons of extent as well as differences and rank. For example, in using a percentage scale to measure the probability of an event, it is correct to say that an event with a probability of .20 is twice as likely to occur as one with a probability of .10.[6]

Unit Compatibility

In addition to maintaining compatible dimensions for interacting variables, the developer of a simulation model must maintain compatible time references. Because rates of flow are measured in units per time, while backlogs are expressed in units, manipulation using the simulation time step is required to maintain dimensional compatibility. This consideration may be ignored when a unitary time step (for example, one day) is employed and all rates are measured in units per time step. The potential problem should be recognized, however, because the use of other than a unitary time step is frequently desirable.[7]

When using discrete approximations to continuous functions, certain assumptions regarding the order in which the steps of a process occur must be made. The value of a time-dependent variable in the *preceding time period* must be used to establish *current period* values for a function of that variable.[8]

An additional class of problems relating to the size of time steps employed in models using third-order exponential delays should be

[6] For a more complete discussion of this topic, see S. S. Stevens, "Measurement, Psychophysics, and Utility," in C. W. Churchman and P. Ratoosh, *Measurement: Definitions and Theories* (New York: John Wiley & Sons, Inc., 1959), pp. 24–26.

[7] For a complete discussion of the implications of these considerations, see J. W. Forrester, *Industrial Dynamics* (Cambridge, Mass.: The M.I.T. Press and John Wiley & Sons, Inc., 1961), pp. 75–77.

[8] *Ibid.*, pp. 73–75 and 396–401.

noted by those seriously concerned with the structure of simulation models.[9]

Use of Intermediate Variables

Models of implied processes involve behavior that cannot be directly observed and must be measured through intermediate variables. The attitude and awareness variables employed in the generalized response model developed in Chapter 8 are examples of this class of measurement.[10]

An Awareness Measure

Awareness is a binary variable measuring a top-of-mind association between product class and brand name. The consumer's awareness of a particular brand in a product line is established through the following interview procedure.

I am going to mention a number of different products and would like you to tell me the brand names which come to mind. Just name the first brand that comes to your mind. Now if I say soap, what brand do you think of? . . . milk? . . . bread? . . . toothpaste? . . . etc.

When measuring individual response, the single brand mentioned is assigned an awareness value of 1 and all other brands are given an awareness value of 0. In measuring the awareness of a population, the percentage of respondents mentioning a brand is defined as that brand's awareness score.

An Attitude Measure

While awareness is used to measure the extent of association between product and brand name, the attitude measure is employed to establish how a respondent feels about a particular brand. Attitude is measured by showing the respondent a 11-point scale of the type proposed by Osgood as illustrated below.[11]

[9] For a discussion of this problem see A. L. Pugh III, *Dynamo User's Manual,* (2nd ed.; Cambridge, Mass.: The M.I.T. Press, 1963), pp. 42–43.

[10] The use of attitude and awareness as intermediate variables grew out of work done by Eric Marder, President of Eric Marder Associates, Inc., New York, communicated to the author through unpublished manuscripts and discussions with Dr. Marder.

[11] C. E. Osgood, G. J. Suci, and P. H. Tannenbaum, *The Measurement of Meaning* (Urbana, Ill.: University of Illinois Press, 1957), Chapter V.

TABLE 5.1.   The Attitude Scale

$$
\left.\begin{array}{r}
+5 \,\text{—} \\
+4 \,\text{—} \\
+3 \,\text{—} \\
+2 \,\text{—} \\
+1 \,\text{—}
\end{array}\right\} \text{Like}
$$

$$
\quad\; 0 \,\text{—} \quad \text{Indifferent}
$$

$$
\left.\begin{array}{r}
-1 \,\text{—} \\
-2 \,\text{—} \\
-3 \,\text{—} \\
-4 \,\text{—} \\
-5 \,\text{—}
\end{array}\right\} \text{Dislike}
$$

The individual's attitude toward a brand is established using this scale in an interview procedure in which the respondent is told:

This scale is used to measure how different people feel about different things. If you like something you should give it one of these plus numbers. The more you like it, the bigger the plus number you should give it. If you like it very much you might want to give it a +5. If you like it a little bit, you might want to give it a +1. On the other hand, if you dislike something you should give it one of these minus numbers. The more you dislike it, the bigger the minus number you should give it. If you dislike it very much, you might want to give it a −5, while if you dislike it only slightly you might want to give it a −1. If you have no particular feeling about something you would give it a 0 indicating that you neither like nor dislike it. Now, what number would you give toothaches, baseball, apple pie, Ivory Soap, Ford Falcon automobiles, etc.?

In the individual case, the number given a brand is defined as the respondent's attitude toward that brand. In developing population measures, the average of the ratings given a brand is defined as the population's attitude toward that brand.[12]

The Effect of Computers on Quantification

Models developed in the following chapters are designed to be compatible with a total market simulation programmed for operation on an electronic data processing machine. Characteristics of the computers

---

[12] For a discussion of alternative techniques of attitude measurement, see B. S. Greene, "Attitude Measurement," in Lindzey (ed.), *Handbook of Social Psychology*, Vol. I (Cambridge, Mass.: Addison-Wesley Publishing Company, Inc., 1954), pp. 335–369.

(hardware) and programming languages (software) to be used therefore influence the structure and design of these models.

The Impact of Computer Hardware

In developing a system of the scope and complexity achieved when the models described in the following chapters are synthesized into an operating simulation, one becomes unavoidably concerned with characteristics of the computer on which the system is to run. Three classes of hardware characteristics are particularly relevant to the model builder. The first relates to the speed and capacity of the machine, the second concerns the structure of available storage, and the third is the binary or decimal organization of the computer's memory.

Computer Speed

The operation of a large-scale simulation involves lengthy iterative loops. As an example, consider a model of the type described in Chapter 8 in which each member of an artificial consumer population must have the potential to be exposed to all advertisements appearing in several media during a simulated time period. This may involve testing for exposure to as many as 4,000 insertions during a simulated year. When the model encompasses a reasonable variety of consumer characteristics, the requisite size of the simulated consumer population can become quite large. Runs of the Chapter 8 model have been made using a simulated population of 10,000 consumers. With a population of this size, between 20 and 40 million exposure tests are made during a simulated year. Using an IBM 7094-Mod II computer with a 2-microsecond cycle time, approximately 12 minutes are required to perform requisite exposure comparisons for advertisements generated by major competitors during one simulated year. Considering that the commercial rate for the 7094-Mod II is approximately $600 an hour, the economic implications of this time requirement are significant.

Computer Capacity

The impact of computer storage capacity is similar to that of speed in that it limits the practical scope of models. Given a finite random access memory, the amount of information accessible at high speed is limited. The capacity problem is complicated by the existence of various classes of storage ranging from magnetic cores through disc and drum storage to magnetic tape. (When dealing with systems of the size being discussed, it is unreasonable to consider punched cards or paper tape for other than initial input.) Types of storage as well as capacity available vary from machine to machine. It is possible to design a system that operates very efficiently on a particular computer installation. However, transfer of that system to another computer of the same make and model but with a different storage complement may result in extreme inefficiency. From a design standpoint, the problem is one of using available storage in such a way as to minimize cumulative access time — the time required for the computer to retrieve and store all data with which it must work in processing a model or series of models during a given run. This involves both "packing" information into high-speed storage to make the most efficient possible use of this valuable asset and developing look-ahead procedures to insure that data stored in slower access memories will be sought out and brought into fast access memories prior to the time it is needed.

Capacity constraints may eventually become insignificant. The emergence of large-capacity systems encompassing millions of words of relatively fast access storage suggests that the importance of these considerations will be substantially reduced in the future.

Sequential versus Random Access

Solution of the capacity problem normally requires that the system designer become involved with various sequential storage devices. When using high-speed, random access memory, the model builder is concerned only with capacity constraints related to the storage medium. All data in the random access medium are equally accessible.

When the capacity of core is exceeded and it becomes necessary to use a sequential storage medium (magnetic tape being the most common), questions of data organization may become controlling. The designer must consider the location of data stored on magnetic tape and the speed with which the system can access this information at different points in the operation. Proper organization of the magnetic tape storage medium can mean the difference between a practical operating system and complete infeasibility.

Binary versus Decimal Machines

Economical data packing and efficient logical manipulation of information as well as processing efficiencies favor the use of a binary (scientific) computer rather than a decimal (business) computer for simulation. Although the computers available in many companies are decimal machines and it is possible to implement reasonably complex models using these computers, the effective operation of a large-scale simulation is greatly facilitated by using techniques that take advantage of the unique characteristics of a binary machine.

The Impact of Computer Software

The choice of computer language can be among the most important decisions made by the designer of a simulation system. In this section, assemblers, compilers, and specialized simulation languages are briefly discussed together with the choice of language used to implement the models described in later chapters.

Assembler Languages

The use of machine language or an assembler such as the FORTRAN assembly program (FAP) [13] enables the sophisticated system designer to make the fullest use of the capacity and capabilities of the machine with which he is working. Portions of a memory word may be efficiently accessed. Specialized instructions may be employed to save valuable cycles or to perform manipulations. Programs can be organized to conserve core storage. Input and output timing can be greatly refined.

There is only one real disadvantage to the use of an assembler language. Only system designers and/or programmers can figure out what is going on. Although to some individuals intent upon making themselves indispensable this may appear to be a real advantage, from management's point of view it is a distinct liability. Effective development and utilization of a simulation is dependent upon effective communication of the system structure and the ability to modify that structure easily so as to take account of new concepts and alternative formulations. The use of assembler languages restricts prohibitively the group capable of working intelligently with models in the form in which they are processed on the computer.

It is frequently argued that it is not necessary for those concerned with the conceptual structure of a system to understand the program through which these concepts are communicated to the computer. Although continual review may not be required, it is highly desirable for those

[13] For a description of compatible machine language and assembler languages for the IBM 7090, see *Reference Manual: 7090 Data Processing System* (New York: International Business Machines Corp., 1961), and *FORTRAN Assembly Program (FAP) for the IBM 709/7090* (New York: International Business Machines Corp., 1961).

concerned with conceptual development to be in a position to review programs when it becomes evident that the programmer's understanding and the designer's concepts are incongruent.

Compiler Languages

The most evident advantage of a generalized compiler language such as FORTRAN [14] or COBOL is in the communications sphere. Due to their use of general algebraic conventions, these languages are comprehensible to persons who have had no experience with computers.

The disadvantages of compilers relate to their inefficiency in the use of core capacity (it is particularly difficult to pack data in core when using a compiler), the limitations imposed by conventions that must be followed when using the compiler, and lack of access to the more sophisticated capabilities of the hardware (e.g., bit manipulation is prohibitively time-consuming).

In addition, despite extensive testing and use, even the widely used IBM FORTRAN system (FORTRAN II-Mod 26) contains errors that cause it to compile incorrectly programs that comply with all conventions of the language.[15] Although these compiler errors are not encountered frequently the results can be devastating when they do occur. The situation is particularly traumatic if the programmer and system designer do not have the ability to check the machine language program prepared by the compiler to determine the nature of the compiler-generated error.

Simulation Languages

Several specialized compilers have been developed specifically for use in simulation. These include DYNAMO, SIMSCRIPT, and GPSS.[16]

[14] For a description of a compiler language compatible with the previously referenced assembler see *Reference Manual: 709/7090 FORTRAN Programming System* (New York: International Business Machines Corp., 1961).

[15] For example, the FORTRAN II-Mod 26 compiler may fail to load appropriate index registers prior to execution of index modified instructions when such instructions are reached by transfer from another section of the program even though the transfer compiles with all conventions of the language.

[16] For a discussion of the DYNAMO language, see A. L. Pugh III, *DYNAMO User's Manual* (2nd ed.; Cambridge, Mass.: The M.I.T. Press, 1963). The SIMSCRIPT language is described in H. M. Markowitz, B. Hausner, and H. W. Karr, *SIMSCRIPT: A Simulation Programming Language* (Englewood Cliffs, N.J.: Prentice-Hall, Inc., 1963). The GPSS compiler is described in R. Efron and G. Gordon, "A General Purpose Digital Simulator and Examples of Its Application," *IBM Systems Journal*, Vol. 3, No. 1 (1964), pp. 22–34.

The use of a "cell" model rather than a "backlog" structure precluded the use of DYNAMO or GPSS in this study, while SIMSCRIPT was relatively untested at the time this model development was initiated.

Languages Used in This Study

To achieve the communication advantage just noted, the sector models described in later chapters were programmed in the FORTRAN language. Use of this language permitted direct programming from equation sets with the conversion of summations to "DO loops," the translation of specialized expressions (i.e., maxima, minima, exponentials, and absolute values) into appropriate FORTRAN functions, and the modification of index and control variables to comply with FORTRAN conventions regarding integer expressions.

The use of the FORTRAN compiler has facilitated communication and idea exchange between the system designer, businessmen, academicians, and programmers. Communication difficulties between programmers and those concerned with conceptual development have been minimized and, when necessary, it has been possible for all concerned to consider alternative formulations in the language in which they are communicated to the computer.

The majority of input/output processing; data packing, unpacking, storage, and retrieval; functional routines; and all supervisory and control programs were written using the FAP assembler language. By applying the assembler selectively in these contexts, it has been possible to obtain near-optimal use of machine capabilities in the very areas in which the compiler language is weakest while maintaining the communication advantage of the compiler in those applications where the assembler offers little advantage over the compiler.

Because equations in later chapters are structured in compliance with conventions of the FORTRAN language, comment regarding this form of representation may reduce confusion for those unfamiliar with the language.

Conventions Employed in Model Formulations

The form of representation employed in the FORTRAN language is analogous to that of noncomputer mathematics.

Variable Identification

Letters used for variable identification are chosen to be mnemonic and equations are annotated with variable definitions. As an example, the awareness measure defined in the preceding section appears in the FORTRAN compatible representation as follows:

> AWARE(c,b)   AWAREness of brand b by consumer c
> $= 1.0$, if consumer aware,
> $= 0.0$, if consumer unaware.

Array and Matrix Notation

Because it is impossible to use normal subscript or superscript notation when preparing a computer program, elements in an array or matrix are specified through the use of parentheses following the variable. Thus, in the example above, the letters c,b following the variable name AWARE indicate an element in a C by B matrix. In a similar fashion, the expression SALES(t,b,r) represents the sales at time t of brand b by retailer r.

Function Representation

If the last letter of the variable name preceding the parentheses is an F, the variable is a function and the contents of the parentheses are the arguments of the function rather than dimensions. Thus the variable name RANNOF(x) refers to a random number generating Function for which x is an argument.

Exponentiation

Functions of e (the base of the natural system of logarithms, 2.718) will be expressed as ENXPF(...). Thus the expression ENXPF(x) is equivalent to e^x.

Arithmetic Expressions

The familiar plus sign $(+)$, minus sign $(-)$, and slash $(/)$ represent addition, subtraction, and division in the FORTRAN compatible equation statements. The asterisk $(*)$ specifies multiplication.

Logical Expressions

Due to specialized conventions relating to FORTRAN representation of logical expressions, logical AND, OR, and NOT operators will be specified in words when required and translated as part of programming.

Summary of Functions

Much of the model development discussed in later chapters will be concerned with the selection of appropriate functions to provide logical or mathematical representation of concepts that are first expressed verbally or graphically. This section summarizes characteristics of functions referenced in later models and identifies specialized conventions.

Logical Functions

As indicated earlier, logical expressions, when required, will be expressed in English. Therefore symbolic representation of logical expressions can be ignored. It is assumed, however, that the reader is familiar with the basic concepts associated with the four logical operators: AND, OR, NOT, and EXCLUSIVE OR.[17]

Mathematical Functions

Four classes of functions encompass all mathematical representation employed in the following chapters. These are linear, quadratic, exponential, and logistic relationships.

Linear Relationships

If changes in one variable (Y) are directly proportional to changes in another variable (X), the relationship between Y and X can be expressed as $Y = MX + B$. This relationship is summarized graphically in Figure 5.1.

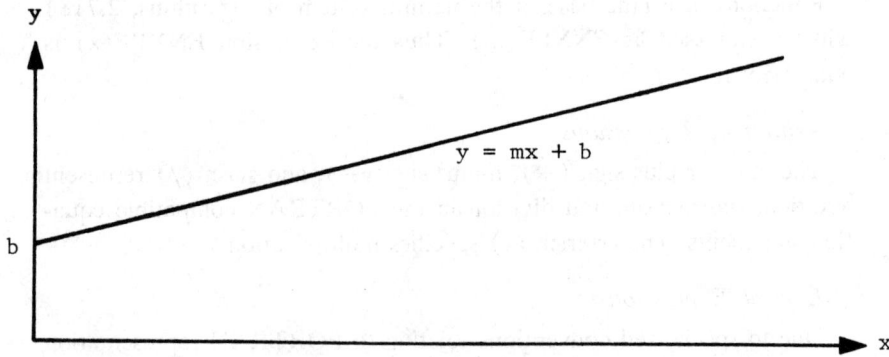

Figure 5.1. A linear function.

[17] Those unfamiliar with logical expressions or interested in reviewing this topic may find S. Langer, *An Introduction to Symbolic Logic* (New York: Dover Press, 1953) a useful reference.

Quadratic Relationships

Data on which certain functions are based are appropriately summarized through a quadratic relationship of the type illustrated in Figure 5.2.

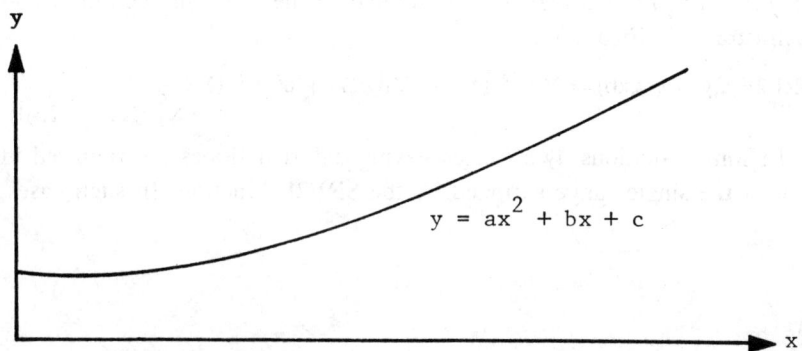

Figure 5.2. A quadratic function.

Exponential Relationships

The characteristics of the exponential functions illustrated in Figure 5.3 make them particularly appropriate as representations of learning and response relationships.

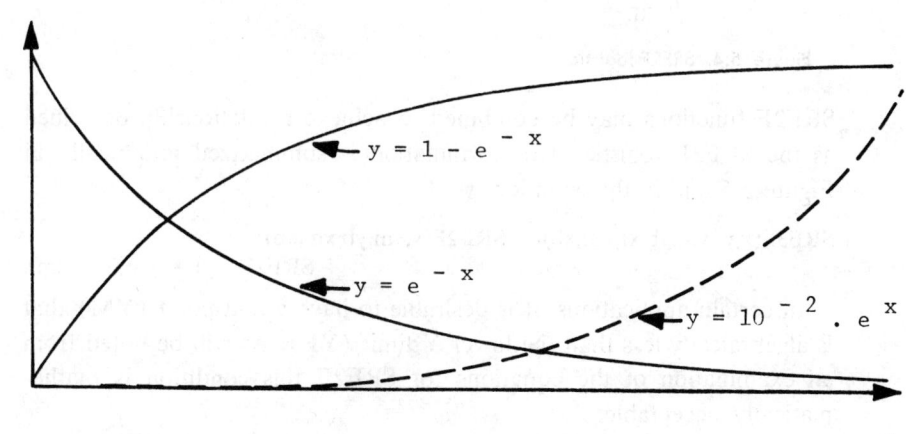

Figure 5.3. Exponential functions.

Logistic Functions

At times there is a need for a continuous relationship that is approximately linear in a specified range and constant outside the limits of that range. A logistic function has been developed to provide this type of representation.[18] In the models that follow it is referred to as SRF2F (x,yt,yb,xt,xb). This logistic is described in the following equation and is illustrated in Figure 5.4.

$$SRF2F(x,yt,yb,xt,xb) = YB + (YT - YB)/(1. + e[[2. * (XT + XB)$$
$$- 4. * X]/(XT - XB)]).$$

In some situations, two ranges having different slopes are required in lieu of the single range supplied by the SRF2F function. In such cases,

SRF2

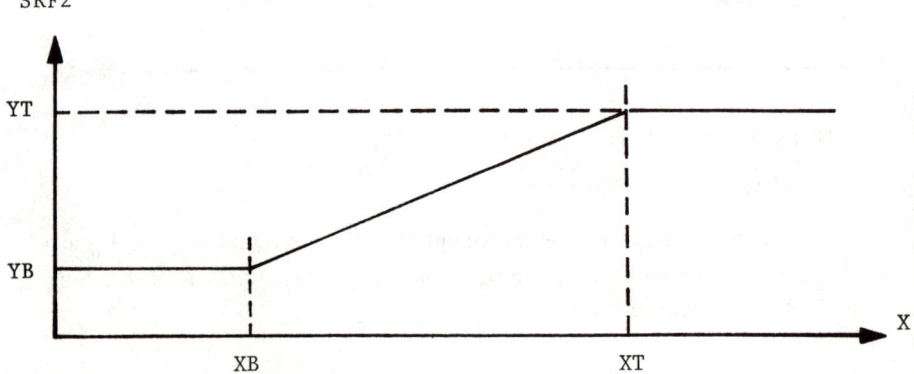

Figure 5.4. SRF2F logistic.

SRF2F functions may be combined to achieve a relationship described as the SRF3F logistic. This formulation is summarized graphically in Figure 5.5 and in the equation

$$SRF3F(x,yt,ym,yb,xt,xm,xb) = SRF2F(x,ym,yb,xm,xb)$$
$$+ SRF2F(x,yt - ym,0.,xt,xm).$$

In certain applications, it is desirable to have a mid-point (YM) that is algebraically less than the lower Y limit (YB). As will be noted from an examination of the equations for SRF2F this condition is mathematically acceptable.

[18] The SRF2F and 3 logistics were developed and programmed by C. R. Sprague of the M.I.T. Sloan School of Management to whom the author is indebted for these highly useful formulations.

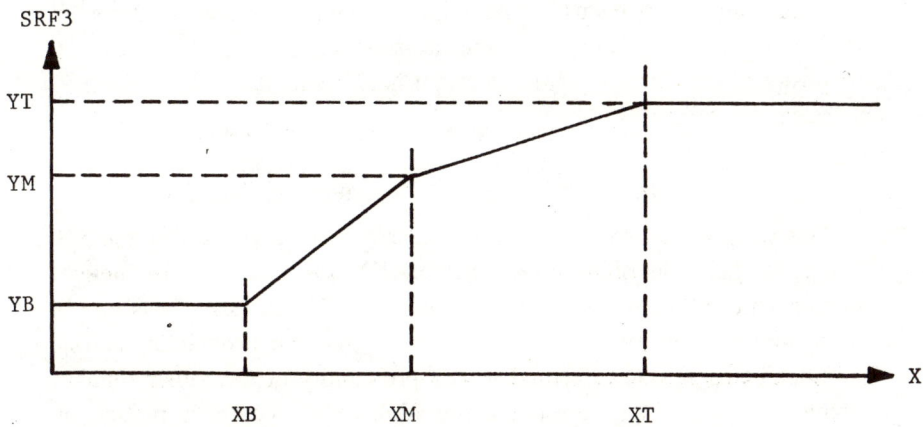

Figure 5.5. SRF3F logistic.

Stochastic Decision Processes

Decision functions formulated in later chapters indicate the probabilities of occurrence for alternative decision outcomes. It is therefore necessary to establish a mechanism for determining whether or not an event will occur, given the probability of its occurrence.

Use of a Random Number Generator

The procedure followed in such situations makes use of a random number generator accessed through the RANNO function.

The function RANNOF(x) is used to draw a number randomly from a rectangular distribution of range 0 to 1.0. This "random number" then becomes the value of RANNOF(x).

Consider, for example, an equation of the form

$$A = B - RANNOF(x),$$

which indicates that the value of A is determined by subtracting from the value of B a number randomly generated from a rectangular distribution having a range of 0 to 1.0. In the decision formulation context, B is the probability that a particular event will occur. Let us say, for example, that B has the value of .7 — the chances are 7 out of 10 that the event referenced by B will occur.

Simulation of a Probabilistic Event

In simulating the occurrence of the event having a probability of occurrence B, the value of A based on the probability B and the RANNO function output can be used to obtain a binary — yes, no — decision. If A is negative, the outcome of the decision is negative; while if A is 0 or positive, the outcome of the decision is affirmative.

Decision Outcome	Value of A	Relationship
Negative	<0	B $<$ RANNOF(x)
Positive	≥ 0	B $\geq$ RANNOF(x)

This relationship is represented graphically in Figures 5.6 through 5.8. The rectangular distribution on which RANNO is based may be thought of as a set of all numbers between 0 and 1. RANNOF(x) selects one of these numbers by a process which insures that the probability of one number being selected is equal to the probability of any other number being selected. In Figure 5.6 the probability of selection is plotted on the vertical axis and the numbers from 0 to 1 are indicated on the horizontal axis.

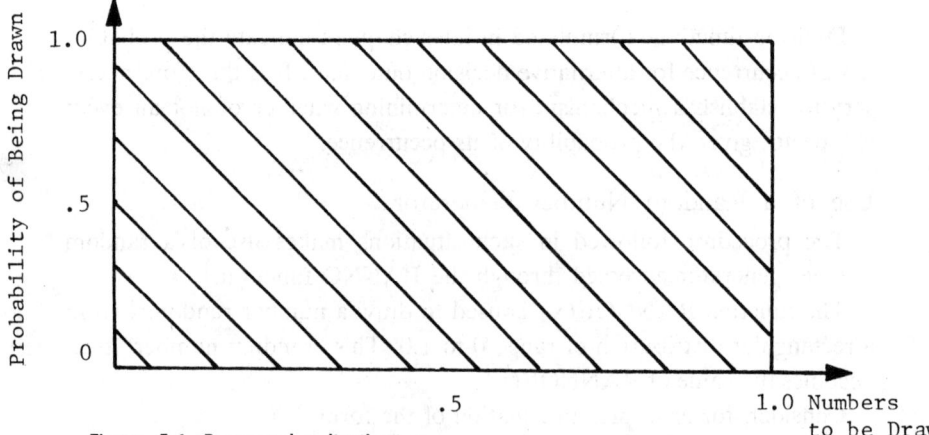

Figure 5.6. Rectangular distribution.

In the context of this illustration, the probability specified by the value of B defines a portion of the distribution that will constitute a positive outcome. Given a binary situation in which the answer is either yes or no, once the positive portion of the distribution has been defined, the remainder of the distribution must represent negative answers. The previous example in which B represented a probability of .7 is illustrated in Figure 5.7.

In this situation, the number .363 drawn from the distribution yields a positive outcome — .363 is in the range defined by B as representing positive outcomes. On the other hand, the number .827 yields a negative

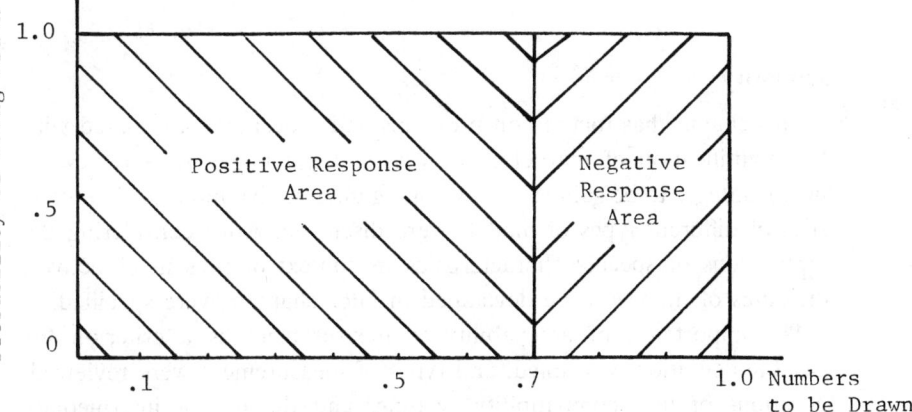

Figure 5.7. Illustration of probability limit of .7.

outcome — .827 is in the range defined by B as constituting negative outcomes.

It should now be evident that the expression

$$B - RANNOF(x)$$

is simply a mathematical notation for comparison of a random number with a limit value specified by the probability. If the value of this expression is positive, the random number drawn is from the set of values that represent positive outcomes — yes answers. If the value of the expression is negative, the randomly selected value represents a negative outcome — a no answer.

Flow chart representation of this type of decision outcome determination will take the form illustrated in Figure 5.8.

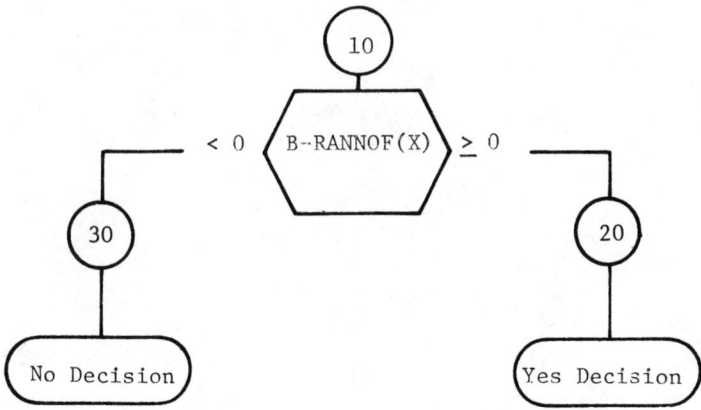

Figure 5.8. Flow chart representation of probabilistic decision.

Summary

This chapter has focused on problems and procedures associated with the quantification of marketing processes. Beginning with a review of the advantages to be gained by developing quantitative models, characteristics of different types of models were discussed. After considering the implications of specific characteristics in context of present objectives, attributes of models to be developed in later chapters were specified.

The importance of amenability to measurement as a criterion for variable definition was noted, and types of measurement were reviewed. Questions of unit compatibility, scaling, and the use of intermediate variables were then considered.

The effect of computer characteristics on the design and implementation of simulation models was discussed briefly with reference to the impact of computer hardware and software. Characteristics of functions employed in later models were summarized in the final section of this chapter.

Chapter 6

ORGANIZATION OF A TOTAL MARKET SIMULATION

The following chapters are devoted to microanalytic simulations of the behavior of active elements defined in earlier chapters. These models are designed for inclusion in a total market simulation that will facilitate management examination of alternative policies and strategies under specified competitive conditions.

Micro- versus Macrosimulation

The simulation developed is designed to encompass behavior common to a broad range of product markets. It is a special type of microanalytic simulation that differs from other "simulations" in several important respects.

A Definition of "Simulation"

It is difficult to accept that models of vastly different scope, complexity, and exactness can be properly described as "simulations." C. West Churchman offers the following formal definition of simulation.

[The statement that] . . . "X simulates Y" is true only if X is a formalized system with appropriate (non-error-free) rules. X enables one to predict Y within certain limits, and Y describes reality. According to the systematic theory, Y itself must be a system, i.e., the system of reality. Hence for this theory, the assertion that X simulates Y must mean that X is an approximation to Y. In other words a realistic simulator is a system that comes as near to the real system as we can get. But we already have names like "model" and "theory" for these approximations. As far as I can see, therefore, the purpose for keeping the name "simulation" is to identify a certain kind of formal system, namely, one in which the rules of validation require a sampling of the relevant entities. . . . Hence, "X simulates Y" is true if and only if (A) X and Y are formal systems, (B) Y is taken to be the real system, (C) X is taken to be an approximation to the real system, and (D) the rules of validity in X are non-error-free.[1]

Viewing this problem from a slightly different perspective, John Harling has suggested that simulation be defined as ". . . a last resort." [2]

Characteristics of a Macrosimulation

It is possible to develop a "simulation" that is little more than two or three effectiveness functions relating dollar inputs to an output expressed as unit or dollar sales. Such a model is usually based on the analysis of historical correlations between certain input variables (i.e., dollars of advertising, number of salesmen, number of products, number of competitors, etc.) and the single output, sales.[3] This kind of model simulates an observed historical condition but says nothing about the underlying market dynamics which produced that condition. It can provide information about the apparent historical correlation between variables that management can manipulate and sales.[4] However, it cannot lead to an understanding of the process through which these variables influence sales. Such models do not contain behavioral representations that are subject to validation or rejection.

Characteristics of a Microsimulation

In contrast to these aggregate models, a microanalytic simulation provides an integrated statement of that which is known and assumed about actions, reactions, and responses within the environment being

[1] C. W. Churchman, working paper No. 34, Center for Research in Management Science, University of California, Berkeley, July 1961.

[2] J. Harling, "Simulation Techniques in Operations Research — A Review," *Operations Research*, Vol. 6 (May–June 1958), p. 313.

[3] See, for example, the model relating advertising expenditures to sales described in M. Vidale and H. Wolfe, "An Operations Research Study of Sales Response to Advertising," *Operations Research*, Vol. 5 (June 1957), pp. 370–381.

[4] See, for example, R. S. Weinberg, "Multiple Factor Break-Even Analysis: The Application of Operations Research Techniques to a Basic Problem of Management Planning and Control," *Operations Research*, Vol. 4 (April 1956), pp. 152–186.

simulated.[5] An example of this type of simulation is the system developed by Balderston and Hoggatt in their study of trading patterns and business operations of lumber manufacturers, wholesalers, and retailers on the Pacific Coast of the United States. Their monograph, which focuses specifically on "the operation of markets in which information is limited and costly to obtain and transmit," demonstrates the value of computerized simulation as a technique for describing and analyzing basic market processes.[6]

Selection of a Microsimulation Structure

Although a microanalytic simulation made up of numerous sector models is more complicated than an aggregate econometric model, it has the potential to provide a wealth of information that the macromodel is incapable of supplying. A microanalytic simulation can be designed to encompass all behavior that management considers relevant and, as such, can provide structure for the solution of a wide range of consumer and industrial product marketing problems.[7]

The advantages of a microanalytic simulation are largely a function of its behavioral content. By encompassing knowledge and assumptions regarding behavior within the market, it provides a means of relating management actions to purchase behavior. While an aggregate model may generate correct answers at a point in time, it provides little or no insight into the reasons for these answers. The microanalytic simulation has the potential to provide the right answers for the right reasons. It is this consideration above all others that recommends it for use in the present situation.

[5] Further development of the characteristics of a microsimulation is provided by A. Kuehn, "Complex Interactive Models," Frank, Kuehn, and Massy, *Quantitative Techniques in Marketing Analysis* (Homewood, Ill.: Richard D. Irwin, 1962), pp. 106–123.

[6] F. E. Balderston and A. C. Hoggatt, *Simulation of Market Processes* (Berkeley: University of California, Institute of Business and Economic Research, 1962).

[7] The use of microsimulations has been proposed in other contexts for reasons similar to those presented here. See, for example, G. Orcutt, "Views on Simulation and Models of Social Systems" in Balderston and Hoggatt, *Symposium on Simulation Models* (Cincinnati, Ohio: South-Western Publishing Co., 1963), pp. 221–236.

System Structure

Each of the preceding chapters has contributed to the synthesis of a framework within which models developed in later chapters may be structured. The following summary of this development is designed to set the stage for formulation of detailed models.

Summary of Interactions

Figure 6.1 summarizes interactions among the five major active elements modeled in the following chapters. In keeping with previously developed conventions, dashed lines are used to represent the flow of information and/or capital, while solid lines illustrate product flow.

As illustrated in Figure 6.1, the manufacturer may potentially interact with salesmen, distributors, retailers, and consumers. Manufacturer salesmen may communicate with retailers or distributors as well as with the manufacturer. Their interactions may involve transfers of policy and promotional information, compensation, and orders. Distributor-manufacturer exchanges may also involve the bilateral flow of policy and promotion communication, orders, payments, and, disregarding returned units, product flow from the manufacturer to the distributor. Potential manufacturer-retailer interactions parallel those between manufacturer and distributor. If the manufacturer sells directly to the consumer, he may provide promotion and product and receive orders and payments. The manufacturer may, alternatively, advertise to the consumer and distribute product (and additional promotion) through trade channels.

The distributor transfers promotion and policy information received from the manufacturer to his salesmen and/or retailers, compensates his salesmen and ships product to retailers. He receives orders from salesmen and/or retailers and payment from retailers.

The distributor salesman receives promotional information and compensation from the distributor and provides information to the retailer from whom he receives orders that are then transmitted to the distributor.

The retailer may receive policy and promotional communications from and place orders with the manufacturer, manufacturer's salesmen, distributor, or distributor's salesmen. He receives product from and makes payment either to the manufacturer or to the distributor and may transfer promotional communication and product to the consumer, from whom he receives word-of-mouth communication and payment.

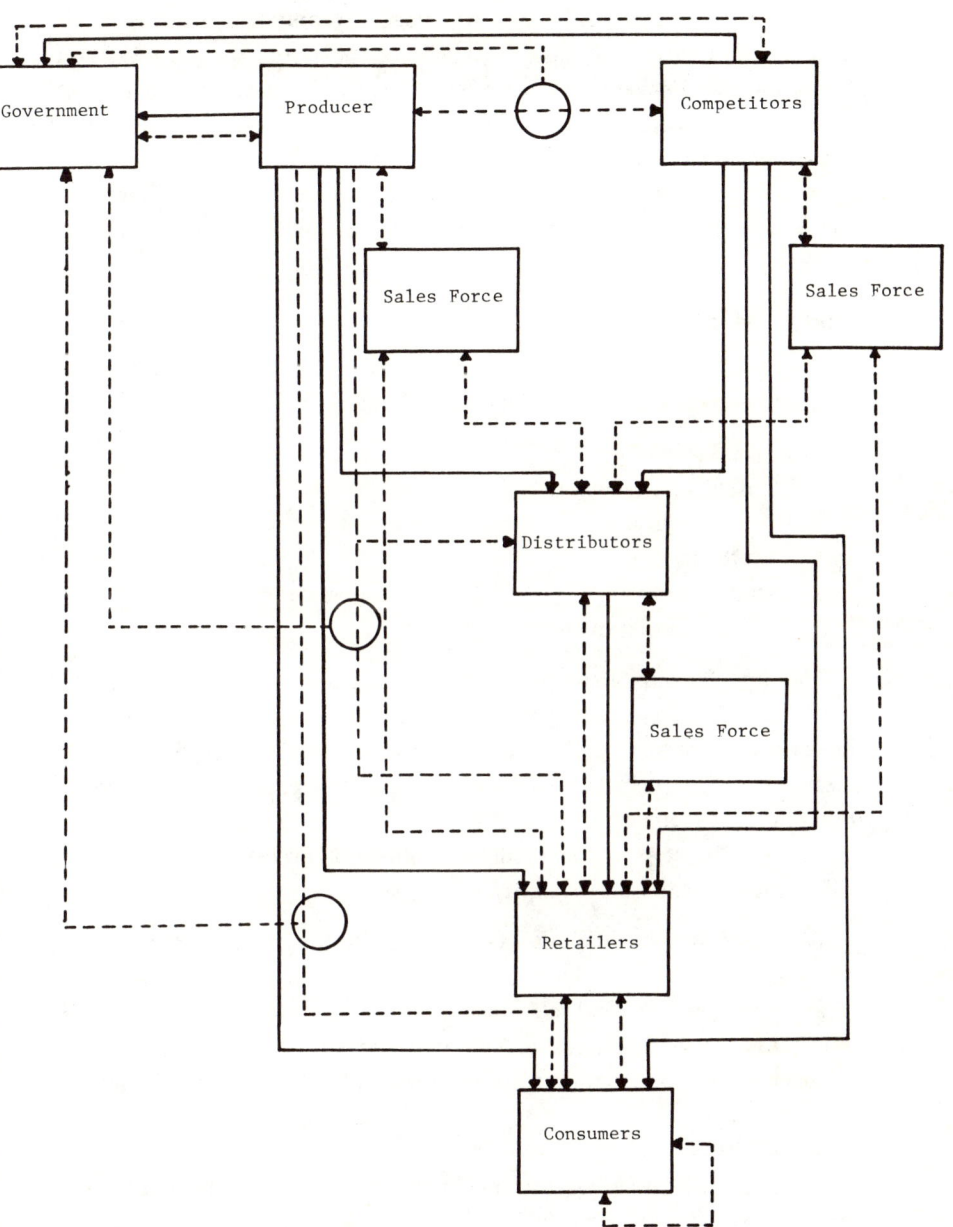

Figure 6.1. Macro flow system structure.

The consumer may receive promotional information from either the manufacturer or the retailer and will normally obtain product from the retailer although he may also receive shipments from the manufacturer. The consumer makes payment to the source from which he receives product and engages in word-of-mouth communication with the retailer and other consumers.

In macroflow terms, this is the system structure within which detailed sector models simulating active element behavior are to be formulated.

Model Development

A well-known operations research text describes the process of model development in terms of the following six steps:[8]

1. Formulate the problem.
2. Construct a model.
3. Derive a solution.
4. Test the model.
5. Establish control.
6. Put the solution to work.

The first eleven chapters of this book are largely concerned with steps 1 and 2 of this procedure. Steps 3 and 4 are discussed in Chapter 13 in context of system performance validation, while steps 5 and 6 are discussed in Chapters 14 and 15 with reference to applications in education and management.

The second step in the model development process may be further subdivided into these procedures:

1. Establish specifications determining the scope and structure of a model.
2. Describe functional relationships.
3. Develop mathematical or logical expressions.
4. Generate data required to initialize, validate, and run the system.

Specification

Macrospecifications establishing boundary definitions for each sector model have already been defined in Chapter 3. Microspecifications will be developed in later chapters devoted to appropriate market sectors.

[8] C. Churchman, R. Ackoff, and E. Arnoff, *Introduction to Operations Research* (New York: John Wiley & Sons, Inc., 1957), p. 18.

Population Description

The extent of differentiation among population subsegments is established by the number of differentiating characteristics specified within the model structure and the size of the simulated population — the number of cells simulated. Population specifications will be delineated for each sector model by descriptors that establish the dimensions along which individual cells within the sector may be described. Model structures will be flexible with respect to population size.

Model Structure

Model structure is largely determined by the inputs and outputs associated with each sector model as specified at a macrolevel in Chapter 4 and summarized in the preceding section.

Functional Description

Preliminary descriptions of functional relationships summarize salient process attributes. These are refined to achieve detailed microspecifications. Alternative micromodels are then evaluated and a single representation is chosen prior to final quantification.

Formal Representation

The final step in the description process is to develop formal mathematical or logical expressions of interactions among factors. At the completion of function formulation, each sector model is expressed in equations compatible with computer solution, using the FORTRAN conventions discussed in Chapter 5.

Data Generation

Some sector models require inputs generated in other sectors or supplied from outside of the system. Endogenous values supplied from other functions within the sector or system are generated during normal operation of the system. Exogenously generated values require special consideration simply because they must be developed externally and supplied to the system prior to operation.

Input requirements may be considered in two contexts. First, it is useful to distinguish data for system initialization from those required as operating input. Second, it is helpful to differentiate between parameter values, population distributions, and environmental conditions.

Data for Initialization

It is generally necessary to initialize parameter values and population distributions with starting values derived from past data and management "priors." Initialization based on historical data may establish starting conditions based on measurements made at a particular point in time. A system might, for example, be initialized on the basis of conditions that existed during January 1961.

In the absence of past data or in situations in which the circumstances to be modeled are substantially different from those historically encountered, initialization can only be based on the estimates of knowledgeable observers. The best-informed observers are often the management and staff of a company operating in the market to be simulated. These individuals are frequently too involved in the process being modeled to be objective observers. However, one may attempt to refine their estimates by obtaining from several sources maximum, minimum, and average values for desired parameters.

Operating Data

Population distributions may change significantly over time, requiring respecification of population characteristics; however, the majority of operating inputs relate to market actions and environmental conditions.

Data specifying actual or assumed actions taken by competing companies constitute an important class of operating input. Such inputs may describe historical conditions for purposes of validation or represent alternative courses of action contemplated by management and expected competitor responses.

Expected environmental conditions are described through inputs detailing population growth, expected changes in population distributions, economic conditions, introduction of supplemental or substitute products, entry or withdrawal of competitive companies, and other changes created by factors outside the system boundaries.

The Modeling Process

Subsequent chapters describe the process followed in developing quantitative models of behavior within major sectors of the market environment. Simulations of the manufacturer, consumer, retailer, distributor, and salesman are presented in Chapters 7 through 11. Government and research agents are considered jointly in Chapter 12.

Summary

This chapter has focused on the organization of a total market simulation. Characteristics of micro- versus macrosimulation were reviewed. Attributes of the system being developed were summarized with reference to interaction characteristics described in Chapter 4.

The process of model development was described in terms of specification, formulation, and data acquisition. Specifications procedures noted included delineation of boundaries, definition of population characteristics, and representation of functional relationships. Model formulation was described as a multistage process, beginning with a conceptual structure and ending with mathematical or logical representations. Data inputs required for system initialization and operation were noted.

Chapter 7

THE MANUFACTURER: MARKETING DECISION MAKER

The objectives and perspective established in Chapter 1 dictate that interactions within the market environment are to be considered from the point of view of the manufacturer. The major focus of this study is thus the behavior observed by the manufacturer rather than the behavior he exhibits. In this chapter, manufacturer actions will be structured in terms of decision outcomes communicated to the environment external to the firm.

Perspectives on the Firm

Activity within the firm may be viewed from three perspectives that will be examined in this section to establish a frame of reference for later analysis of specific decisions.

The Firm as an Organization

The focus of management effort, priorities assigned to specific decisions, values placed on alternative allocations of resources, decision procedures, and criteria applied to the evaluation of decision outcomes may all be influenced by company organization. It is therefore appropriate to consider organization structure as one basis for analyzing decision processes within the firm.

David Moore has suggested that management is at present in transition

120

from an old to a new model of managerial organization.[1] It is his contention that the old model was characterized by ". . . concern with system and internal process, . . . emphasis on functional skill rather than on the whole man . . . (and) . . . concern with the job within the system rather than the overall result — there is a tendency to become lost in the system and to forget what the system was set up to accomplish."

In his opinion, this old set of management organizational values is being supplanted by a new model characterized by ". . . concern with external ends — the business is viewed basically as a problem of relationship among various claimant groups with varying interests which must be integrated and re-integrated in a dynamic changing world . . . (and) . . . subordination of system to overall results — the organization is viewed as an ad hoc arrangement which can always be adjusted and changed if need be."

The use of microanalytic simulation as a decision aid is oriented toward the new model organization. This approach assumes a management focus on external ends rather than internal processes. It emphasizes the importance of considering alternative strategies geared to the prevailing situation instead of blindly following habitual practices. It directs management attention to a broad system of interactions and away from limited functions.

The Firm as a Behavior System

Among the proponents of a behavioral perspective on actions within the manufacturer sector is Wroe Alderson who proposes that the firm be viewed as "an organized behavior system." [2] In context of this perspective, the major objective of management is survival in an environment that confronts the organization with problems and opportunities. Given this orientation, the manager's view of interactions within the marketing environment can be likened to that of other organisms operating in terms of a principle of self-interest.[3]

[1] D. G. Moore, "Marketing Orientation and Emerging Patterns of Management and Organization", in F. M. Bass (ed.), *The Frontiers of Marketing Thought and Science* (Chicago: American Marketing Association, 1957), pp. 102–109.

[2] For a discussion of the attributes of the behavioral system as conceived by Alderson, see W. Alderson, *Marketing Behavior and Executive Action* (Homewood, Ill.: Richard D. Irwin, Inc., 1957), pp. 29–97.

[3] W. Alderson, "Survival and Adjustment in Organized Behavior Systems," in R. Cox and W. Alderson (eds.), *Theory in Marketing* (Homewood, Ill.: Richard D. Irwin, Inc., 1950), pp. 65–87.

Richard Cyert and James March suggest that "in order to understand contemporary economic decision-making, we need to supplement the study of market factors with an examination of the internal operation of the firm — to study the effects of organizational structure and conventional practice on the development of goals, the formation of expectations, and the execution of choices." [4]

Cyert and March express dissatisfaction with existing theory of the firm because of its motivational and cognitive assumptions (specifically the drive to maximize profit and the assumption of perfect knowledge) and its failure to encompass much of the "richness" of the actual business environment. Their efforts are directed toward constructing ". . . a theory that takes (1) the firm as its basic unit, (2) the prediction of firm behavior with respect to such decisions as price, output, and resource allocation as its objective, and (3) an explicit emphasis on the actual process of organizational decision making as its basic research commitment." [5]

Representation of behavior within the firm through models formulated in terms of the variables that affect "organizational goals, . . . organizational expectations, . . . and organizational choice" is proposed by these authors.[6] The business decision-making process encompassed by these models is described in terms of four "relational concepts . . . (1) quasi resolution of conflict, (2) uncertainty avoidance, (3) problemistic search, and (4) organizational learning." [7]

Through the process described as "organizational choice" the coalition which is the firm is viewed as adopting or learning a "set of behavior rules — the standard operating procedures." The firm operating as an adaptive system is seen to follow three basic principles that provide the necessary guidelines for the choice process. These are (1) avoid uncertainty, (2) maintain the rules, and (3) use simple rules. The rules that are maintained constitute a set of specific standard operating procedures that provide stability for the coalition members within the firm (and insure that simulation output stays on a reasonably scaled chart). The value of a model based on this concept of organizational

---

[4] R. M. Cyert and J. G. March, *A Behavioral Theory of the Firm* (Englewood Cliffs, N.J.: Prentice-Hall, 1963), p. 1.

[5] *Ibid.*, p. 19.

[6] *Ibid.*, p. 21.

[7] For a discussion of these concepts see Cyert and March, *Ibid.*, pp. 116–125.

choice has been effectively illustrated through the application of a duopoly formulation to data from the can industry.[8]

The Firm as Input Generator

In the context of this study, the firm may be described by the inputs that it provides to the external environment. Its interactions with external sectors are limited to the transfer of product, information, and capital by the system specifications established earlier. Subject to this constraint, the firm may generate a wide range of inputs to specified sectors and respond to outputs received from these sectors.

Structuring the Management Decision Process

As indicated in earlier chapters, this book is concerned with models of market behavior and an approach to management based on the use of these models. The manager's theory — his model of behavior within the market — is a major determinant of his decision procedure. This relationship between the manager's theory and his practice of management involves what C. W. Churchman has described as "the fascinating notion that knowledge is a way of doing, . . . a certain kind of management of affairs."

To say that knowledge is a type of management is to imply that the validity of our ideas can only be tested in the context of decision making. If the decision making is uniformly good, then the principles relating to the decisions are valid, i.e., known.

Now, "theory" and "fact" are aspects of knowledge; they represent some of the things that are known well or badly. If we regard knowing to be a type of management, then we will feel impelled to regard "theory" itself as a certain kind of management activity.

In other words, to discuss a "theory of marketing" is to discuss a mode of managing marketing functions.[9]

Because management decisions involve choices between alternatives under uncertainty, the decision process may be described in terms

---

[8] *Ibid.*, pp. 83–113.

[9] C. W. Churchman, "Marketing Theory as Marketing Management," in Cox, Alderson, and Chapiro (eds.), *Theory in Marketing* (Homewood, Ill.: Richard D. Irwin, Inc., 1964), pp. 313–321, p. 313.

of probable outcomes associated with alternative courses of action. Bayesian decision theory provides an orderly structure based on this view of the decision process.[10]

A Bayesian Structure

The Bayesian approach to management decision making may be summarized in terms of the following steps.[11]

1. Identify all reasonable possibilities in the given situation — specify all facts or strategies which might be followed.
2. Enumerate the states of nature — indicate for each act or strategy the possible outcomes or states of nature governing the effect of the decision.
3. Explore further possibilities and outcomes — continue with additional rounds of actions and outcomes until the chain of effects and reactions that would result from a given decision course have been explored.
4. Estimate the payoffs for each decision point in each chain of decisions. Although the payoff is normally measured in monetary terms, it may involve other consequences of a decision (e.g., increase in market share).
5. Assess probabilities — assign probabilities to each outcome under each possible decision.
6. Compute expected payoffs and choose the optimal decision within the structure of the problem provided by the decision chain. Combining the estimated payoffs established in step 4 with the probability of that payoff occurring as established in step 5, actual computation of expected payoffs is a simple matter of multiplication.

Under this procedure, the optimal decision set is that which produces the highest expected payoff.

It may be argued that practical application of this approach is limited by management's ability to estimate the probabilities required in step 5.

---

[10] A thorough development of the Bayesian point of view is provided by R. Schlaifer, *Probability and Statistics for Business Decisions* (New York: McGraw-Hill Book Company, Inc., 1959).

[11] This procedural description is based on R. D. Buzzell and C. C. Slater, "Decision Theory and Marketing Management," *Journal of Marketing,* Vol. 26 (July 1962), pp. 7–16.

Raising this objection introduces the question of available alternatives. What will management do in lieu of this procedure? Is management uncertainty revealed or created by the approach? Recognition of uncertainty and even gross assessment of probabilities moves management in the direction of more systematic analysis. An orderly procedure, however crude, may aid management in structuring the problem situation, focusing on key aspects of the decision process, and selecting research activities that contribute effectively to the decision.[12]

The decision theorists' approach to management decision making provides a structure that facilitates segmentation of complex problems into manageable parts for explicit analysis.

. . . the principal advantage of formal decision theory over informal executive judgment is implied by the word "formal." The type of analysis illustrated here requires the decision maker to *formalize* his thinking regarding a problem — to structure his judgment and to "put it down in black and white." That this is likely to improve the quality of executive judgment seems self-evident. Whenever a decision must be made and its outcome is not known with certainty some informal equivalent of the decision theory must be employed.[13]

The Bayesian approach requires management assessment of the probability of occurrence of certain events within the time period covered by the decision. The usefulness of this procedure is thus contingent upon management ability to generate meaningful short-term forecasts — the procedure is applicable only when decision periods are sufficiently short to render management forecasts meaningful. Beyond this time horizon, management cannot make meaningful decisions between alternatives. They may, however, formulate contingent plans.

Commenting on this distinction between long-range planning and short-term forecasting, Peter Drucker notes that planning

. . . is not masterminding the future. Any attempt to do so is foolish; human beings can neither predict nor control the future. . . .

To try to mastermind [the future] is therefore childish, we can only discredit what we are doing by attempting it. We must start out with the conclusion that forecasting is not respectable and not worthwhile beyond

---

[12] Application of the Bayesian decision theory approach to the formulation of research objectives is discussed in Chapter 12.

[13] *Loc. cit.,* Buzzell and Slater, Footnote 11.

the shortest of periods. *Long range planning is necessary precisely because we cannot forecast.*[14]

The Contribution of Simulation

A simulation encompassing detailed behavioral models of the type developed in the following chapters may contribute to steps 2, 3, and 4 of the decision process outlined earlier in this chapter. Through simulation, management is able to give more thorough consideration to a greater number of alternatives — to develop estimates of the payoffs associated with numerous strategies. However, the worth of alternative payoffs remains to be evaluated. Management must, for example, assess the relative value of increased market share as opposed to greater profitability on a reduced market share.

This is not to suggest that the contribution of simulation to management decision making is limited to short-term forecasting. On the contrary, it may be argued that its greatest potential is in the area of planning.[15] Application of an orderly decision process in planning, however, requires dramatic changes in traditional planning techniques, which largely ignore the presence of risks in the planning process. Management is in the habit of expressing long-term outcomes in certainty equivalent terms rather than as a range of probabilities.

Little or no attempt is made to consider even low order interactions of the courses of action being evaluated. . . . Little or no attempt is made to test the sensitivity of the outcomes of the study to departures in the basic assumptions. . . . [and] . . . few formal devices are used to incorporate feedback data from the field, such as market surveys or early sales results. . . .

The deficiencies of traditional techniques might be grouped conveniently under two classes: (*a*) the lack of a suitable conceptual framework within which the characteristics of planning problems can be viewed; and (*b*) a lack of a means to implement this conceptual framework from a computational standpoint. [16]

Because of the dependence of planning outcomes on processes occurring through time, simulation may contribute significantly to an

[14] P. F. Drucker, "Long-Range Planning," *Management Science,* Vol. 5 (April 1959), p. 238.

[15] This question is discussed in Chapter 14.

[16] P. E. Green, "Decisions Involving High Risk," *Advanced Management — Office Executive,* Vol. 1 (October 1962), pp. 18–23.

understanding of processes that affect the development and implementation of plans. The primary need is for structure, for a systematic methodology through which the implications of complex interactions may be studied. In the words of Peter Drucker, ". . . At least we need to know enough to organize our ignorance." [17]

Functional Decision Areas

Market-oriented decisions of the manufacturer may be categorized conveniently in terms of seven functional areas in which action must be taken when developing and implementing a marketing plan. These are product policy, production, distribution, promotion, pricing, sales force maintenance, and research management.

Product Policy Decisions

Product policy decisions may relate to specifications for a new product or modification of existing product characteristics. In both cases, management must assess the probable responses of relevant market sectors to the introduction of an item having the proposed characteristics.

Factors Affecting Product Contribution

Product policy literature frequently focuses on the evaluation of product contribution to the firm. The following excerpts from Joel Dean's discussion of product-line policy in the *Journal of Business* are representative.

> Three important problems encountered by top management in formulating policy on adding new products are: (1) scouting out potential product additions, (2) appraising these proposals and making the product selection, and (3) launching each new product venture in a way that gives it a maximum chance of success.

> . . . The pivotal test for the addition of a new product is its profitability. If profit maximization were the sole goal of the enterprise, this test would encompass all others, but pluralistic motivation makes the other goals

[17] Drucker, *op. cit.,* Footnote 14, p. 249.

relevant as well. The relevant concept of profits is incremental returns over the appropriate time period. . . .[18]

Admonitions to evaluate a new product in terms of its contribution to profit are meaningless unless management is able to assess responses within each sector of the market to the introduction of a new or modified product. Will the trade be interested in carrying this product? What consumer subsegments will buy, and how much will they buy at various prices? Will competitors respond with increased promotion of existing product lines, additional competitive products, or indifference? Models developed in later chapters simulate behavior, determining the answers to some of these questions. While specific competitor action models will not be presented in this chapter, past competitor behavior and assumptions regarding probable future competitor responses have been summarized in explicit models that incorporate variables defined here.[19]

Product Decision Outputs

The final output of product policy considerations is a product exhibiting specific attributes. The product decision establishes product characteristics for a new or modified product. Product characteristics as used in this context refer to product attributes such as size, color, weight, horsepower, etc., and functional capabilities such as speed, cleaning power, analgesic effect, etc. — the measurable attributes of the product.[20]

The Brand-Model. For purposes of formulation, each differentiable model produced by a manufacturer is designated as a "brand." Ford Thunderbirds, Ford Falcon Sedans, and Ford Falcon Convertibles with "Super Sport" options constitute three distinct brands under this

---

[18] J. Dean, "Product-Line Policy," *Journal of Business,* Vol. 22 (October 1950), pp. 248, 251.

[19] Simulations describing behavior within the manufacturer sector are described by Cyert and March, *op. cit.,* Footnote 4. See particularly Chapter 5, "Organizational Choice," Chapter 7, "A Specific Price and Output Model," Chapter 8, "A General Model of Price and Output Determination," and Chapter 9, "A Model of Rational Managerial Behavior."

[20] This is not to suggest that measurable product characteristics determine product perceptions in other sectors of the environment. The question of subjective apperception of objectively defined characteristics is considered in later chapters. See particularly the discussion of "Perceived Brand Image" in Chapter 8, pp. 224–226.

form of representation. Confusion may be avoided if "brand" is read as "brand-model."

Product Characteristic Specification. Because each brand exhibits a variety of product characteristics, a matrix indicating the presence or absence of each of NP product characteristics for each of B brands may be used to describe the brand population. The elements of this matrix are defined as

Equation 7.1

PRDCHR(np, b)   PRoDuct CHaRacteristic specifier for characteristic np of brand b. Dimension: a pure number (binary).

= 1, if characteristic np is exhibited by brand b,
= 0, if characteristic np not exhibited by brand b.

Product Decisions

Given a decision to produce a brand exhibiting specific product characteristics, the manufacturer must determine the quantity of product to be produced during specified time periods.

Scheduling and Related Processes

In the context of this system, the production decision is fundamentally a scheduling procedure. It may, however, involve sales estimation and financial analysis. The manufacturer's desire to have enough product to satisfy future demand motivates sales forecasting,[21] while high inventory costs and limited capital lead to analyses of alternative uses of funds.[22]

Production Decision Outputs

The primary output of the production decision is a production rate established by taking into account orders, unfilled orders, product inventory, and available raw material. Figure 7.1 illustrates the relationship between the production decision, orders, shipments, and invoicing using previously established conventions.

---

[21] For a discussion of a proposed procedure for scheduling production on the basis of sales forecasts, see J. Parkany, "A New Approach to Sales Forecasting and Production Scheduling," *Journal of Marketing*, January 1961. A thorough discussion of more traditional forecasting techniques is provided by P. R. Winters, "Forecasting Sales by Exponentially Weighted Moving Averages," *Management Science*, Vol. 6 (April 1960), pp. 324–342.

[22] The production scheduling decision is a specific example of the allocation decision procedure outlined previously in Chapter 5.

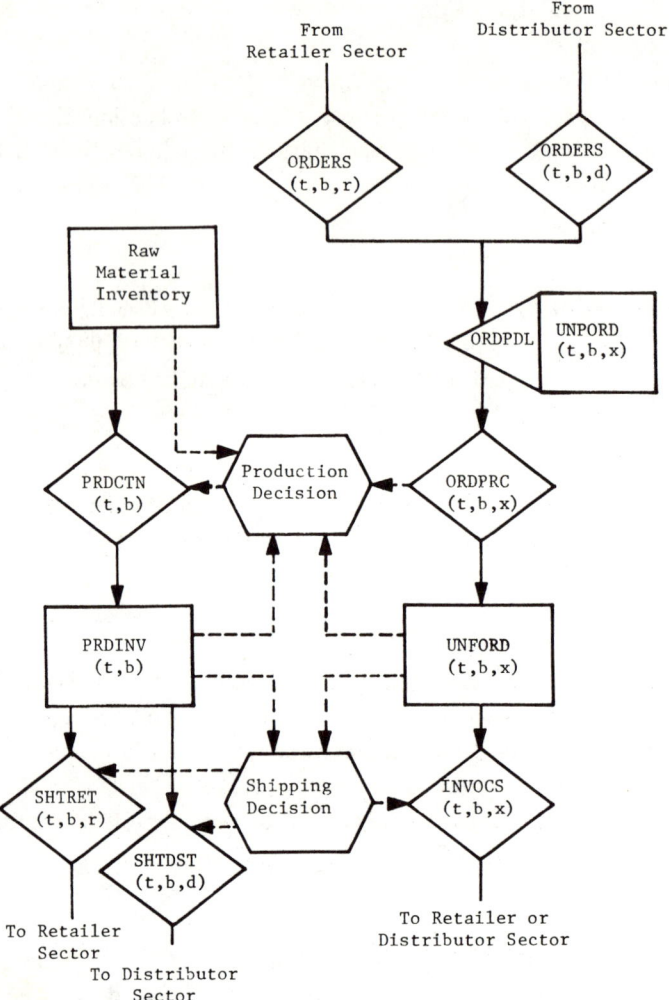

Figure 7.1. Basic production decision process.

The following variables referenced in the Figure 7.1 flow chart require definition.

Equation 7.2

ORDERS(t, b, r)   ORDERS for brand b received from retailer r at time t. Dimension: value units per time period (rate of value flow).

ORDERS(t, b, d)   ORDERS for brand b received from distributor d at time t. Dimension: value units per time period (rate of value flow).

ORDPDL ⟶ ORDer Processing DeLay. Dimension: time units.

UNPORD(t, b, x) ⟶ UNProcessed ORDers for brand b received from sector x (x = r or d), in backlog at time t. Dimension: value units.

ORDPRC(t, b, x) ⟶ ORDers for brand b received from sector x PRoCessed at time t. Dimension: value units per time period (rate of value flow).

UNFORD(t, b, x) ⟶ UNFilled ORDers for brand b received from sector x backlogged at time t. Dimension: value units.

INVOCS(t, b, x) ⟶ INVOiCeS for brand b sent to sector x at time t. Dimension: value units per time period (rate of value flow).

PRDCTN(t, b) ⟶ PRoDuCTioN of brand b at time t. Dimension: product units per time period (rate of product flow).

PRDINV(t, b) ⟶ PRoDuct of brand b in INVentory at time t. Dimension: product units.

SHTRET(t, b, r) ⟶ SHipments of brand b To RETailer r at time t. Dimension: product units per time period (rate of product flow).

SHTDST(t, b, d) ⟶ SHipments of brand b To DiSTributor d at time t. Dimension: product units per time period (rate of product flow).

Distribution Decisions

Distribution policy formulation involves decision subsets relating to (1) distribution structure, (2) outlet selection, and (3) channel maintenance.

Distribution Structure

The first step in distribution system design is the decision to distribute through distributors, wholesalers, or manufacturers' agents, or by direct sale to retailers or consumers. Alternative distribution structures available to the manufacturer were discussed in the Chapter 4 analysis of product flow.

A particular structure may be selected because of contractual or trading considerations or on the basis of logistic or physical characteristics.[23] The manufacturer's channel structure decision determines the

---

[23] For a discussion of the contractual aspects of distribution system structure, see T. L. Berg, "Designing the Distribution Systems," in W. D. Stevens (ed.), *The Social Responsibilities of Marketing* (Chicago: American Marketing Association, 1962), pp. 481–490. For a consideration of logistics see J. F. Magee, "The Logistics of Distribution," *Harvard Business Review,* Vol. 38 (July–August 1960), p. 89.

channel or combination of channels through which the product line is
to be distributed.

Outlet Selection

The second step in distribution system design establishes a complement of outlets within the general channel structure. The manufacturer
must choose between intensive distribution through carefully selected
outlets (often granted exclusive territorial franchises) and extensive
distribution through numerous outlets offering maximum coverage at
the cost of selectivity.

This manufacturer decision is analogous to the distributor's evaluation of retail outlets discussed in Chapter 10.[24]

Channel Maintenance

Channel maintenance decisions relate to the manufacturer's interest
in motivating trade channels to "push" his brand, his need to police
channels to insure maintenance of policies established by the firm, and
his desire to carry sufficient physical inventory and an appropriate
selection to fill the demand generated by the channels.

Motivational aspects of channel maintenance are manifest in pricing
and promotion policy. Pricing policy is formulated with consideration
for margin provided distributors and/or retailers. Advertising allowance may also be used to supply additional margin dollars.

Compensation-based motivation may take the form of direct payment
of X dollars per unit sold (referred to as "push money" by the trade)
or contests in which the winner is chosen on the basis of units sold.

Distribution channel policing centers on distributor or retailer pricing
and use of advertising allowances. The degree of manufacturer concern
with price maintenance ranges from attempts at strict control through
fair-trading to total lack of concern "as long as product keeps moving."
Control of advertising allowances at the retail level normally involves
salesman monitoring of point-of-sale promotion and company review
of "tear sheets" verifying that the retailer has placed advertisements
in local media.

The manufacturer must determine the level and composition of inventory to be maintained at the factory and at points throughout the
distribution system given existing orders, trends over time, and future
expectations.

[24] See "Value of a Retail Outlet" in Chapter 10, p. 325.

Figure 7.2 provides an expanded description of the production decision process and adds the manufacturer's consideration of expected conditions to factors previously discussed in conjunction with Figure 7.1. In this revised representation, a forecasting decision that incorporates planned and historic pricing, promotion, and distribution pol-

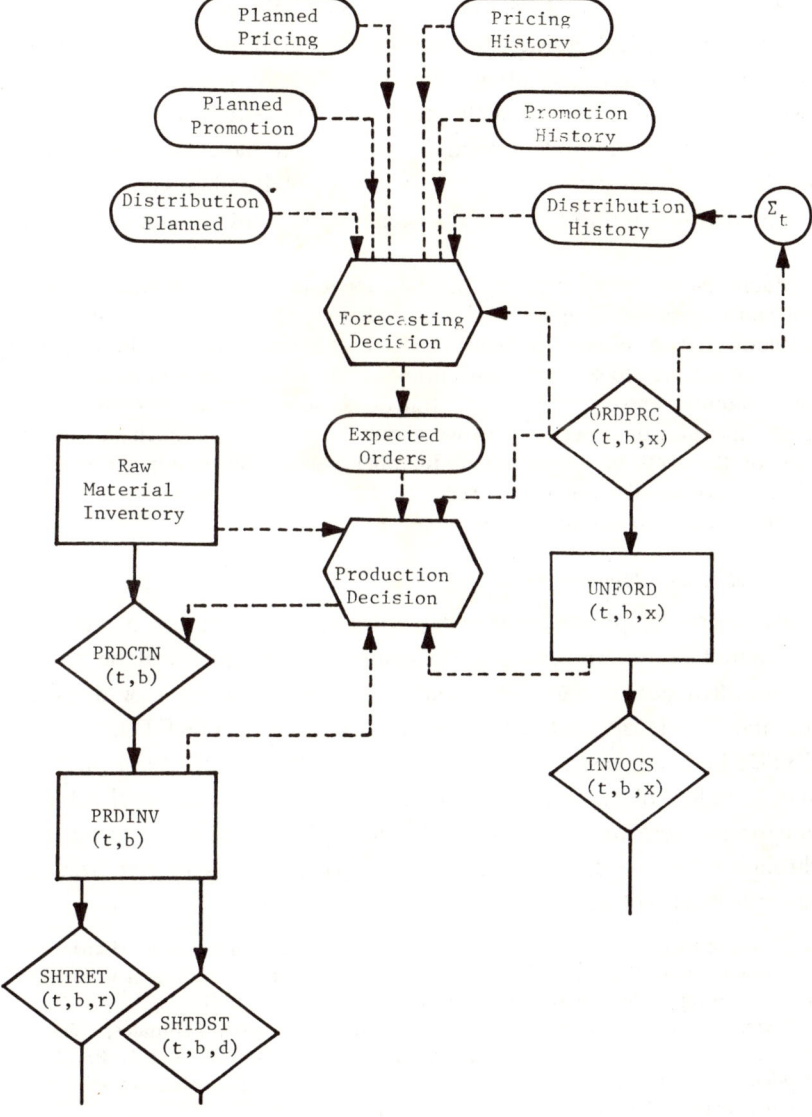

Figure 7.2. Modified production decision.

icies in conjunction with existing and historic order rates yields an expected order rate that enters the production decision along with the factors considered earlier in Figure 7.1. Criteria based on inventory costs and the value of lost sales are applied to this expected order rate to determine a desired inventory and the level of production.[25]

Inventory maintenance models have found wide management acceptance due to two related considerations. First, distribution management works with physical entities that can be measured and controlled easily by using traditional accounting techniques. Second, because of the close association of distribution with production, inventory procedures and scheduling techniques developed in production have been applied to distribution problems as a logical extension of familiar concepts.[26]

The distribution area is also the scene of substantial computerization.

Machines are being used to maintain local inventory balances, forecast near term demand, employ forecasts and inventory balances as inputs in calculating item orders, prepare tentative purchase orders, allocate item balances among stock points, and draw up production schedules and work force requirements. . . . In these functions, the machine systems are interpreting rules or procedures to work out the decisions implicit in them in light of the facts of the situation. In other words, the equipment is doing what we would like intelligent clerks to do: diligently following policy and weighing costs to arrive at day-to-day actions.[27]

Distribution Decision Outputs

By supplying product selectively to certain distributors or retailers, the manufacturer may attempt to insure that product will be carried by specified outlets only. This control is represented by r or d indices for the previously defined shipment variables SHTRET(t,b,r) and SHTDST(t,b,d) respectively. In addition, the manufacturer may instate a policy of exclusive distribution, franchising selected distributors and/or retailers to carry specific brands. This condition is designated through exclusive distribution indicators generated as output from the manufacturer sector.

[25] This process is modeled in Chapter 9 and 10. See particularly, "Expectation Formation" and "The Order Decision" in Chapter 9, and "Expectation Formation" and "Ordering Under the Slow Service Condition" in Chapter 10.

[26] See, for example, R. G. Brown, "Less Risk in Inventory Estimates," *Harvard Business Review,* Vol. 37 (July–August 1959), pp. 104–116, and J. F. Magee, *Production Planning and Inventory Control* (New York: McGraw-Hill Book Company, Inc., 1958).

[27] Magee, "The Logistics of Distribution," *op. cit.,* Footnote 23, p. 95.

Equation 7.3

    EXCLSV(b)   EXCLuSiVe distribution indicator. Dimension: a pure number (binary).

                = 1, if brand b is franchised,
                = 0, if brand b not franchised.

Margin-related outputs from the manufacturer's decision to motivate distributors and/or retailers through particular pricing policies are covered later in this section.

Representation of direct compensation involves simple bookkeeping. A dollar payment is made for each unit sold. Contests and other probability-based motivation schemes create a situation in which each retailer or distributor has a probability of receiving a substantial payoff but may receive nothing. This condition may be represented by using an expected value concept. In a contest for a $10,000 prize involving 1000 retailers, each retailer has 1 chance in 1000 of receiving the $10,000 prize, and the expected value of this contest to each retailer is therefore $10.

In the previous example, the payoff to the retailer was independent of his sales of the brand sponsoring the contest. More accurate representation requires an estimate of the number of units that will be sold and calculation of an expected value based on proportion of sales rather than number of retailers. If, for example, the manufacturer offers a $10,000 prize to be chosen through a drawing with one ticket given to each salesman for each unit sold, a salesman who estimates that approximately 10,000 units might be sold during the period of the contest would calculate an expected value of $1 for each unit sold.

Direct retailer compensation (push money) and contests or other probabilistic incentives are communicated to the retailer and/or distributor sector through direct and probabilistic compensation variables.

Equation 7.4

    DSMCOM(b, x)   Direct SalesMan COMpensation available to salesmen in outlet x selling brand b. Dimension: dollars per product unit.

    PRBINC(b, x)   PRoBabilistic INCentive available to salesmen in outlet x selling brand b. Dimension: value units (dollars) per product unit (expected sales).

    ADVALL(b, x)   ADVertising ALLowances available to outlet x selling brand b. Dimension: value units (dollars) per product unit.

Manufacturer policing of distributor and retailer activities does not result directly in output generation. The internal manifestations of this response process are based on manufacturer monitoring of price and promotional variables defined in Chapters 9 and 10.

Promotion Decisions

The manufacturer promotion decision may be described in four dimensions. These are (1) communication channel to be used, (2) content to be communicated, (3) form of presentation, and (4) extent and frequency of presentation.

Communication Channel Selection

The manufacturer interested in communicating with consumers may make use of TV, radio, magazines, newspapers, outdoor advertising, direct mail, point-of-sale promotion, or personal selling. While these consumer-oriented communication channels may reach the trade, trade magazines and trade newspapers provide more selective media for communicating with this group.

After defining a target group in terms of demographic characteristics or special-interest orientation, the manufacturer attempts to maximize the probability of target group exposure to his message, subject to budgetary constraints. In some instances, the message to be communicated also influences choice of communication channel. If, for example, product demonstration is considered desirable, either personal selling or a dynamic media type such as TV may be preferred over static magazine and newspaper presentation.

Content Description

Three classes of promotional information content were defined in the Chapter 3 specifications for information as an element of flow. The three categories are (1) product-associated appeals, (2) product characteristics, and (3) brand name identifications.[28]

Appeals. Product-associated appeals denote needs that the product is promoted as satisfying — all such are based on alleged benefits of product use. In the case of a food product, appeals might include health, enjoyment, economy, or prestige. Product-related appeals for an ap-

---

[28] For a review of these specifications, see Chapter 3, "Information Specification," p. 26.

pliance might include efficiency, addition to leisure time, ease of task performance, modernity, or status.

Characteristics. Product characteristics are attributes that can be perceived by the five senses. Product characteristics of a food item include package size, product color, salinity, sweetness, and texture. Product characteristics descriptive of an appliance include size, weight, material of construction, and brand features such as high-speed motor or automatic timer.

Brand. Brand name identifications include the company name (Ford), the company logo (IBM), specific brand name (Mustang), brand symbols (the Mustang pony), and the distinctive appearance of the product or its package.

Content Specification

Promotion content will be specified as the proportion of communication devoted to particular appeals, product characteristics, or brand name identifications. Such specification involves quantification of qualitative attributes and therefore requires coding by a human intermediary.

Coding. It is the coder's responsibility to identify product characteristics, appeals, and brand name identifications present in an advertisement and to evaluate the relative importance of each of these elements. In assessing relative importance one might measure the surface area of a magazine insertion or the proportion of a broadcast time segment devoted to each characteristic or appeal. Such an approach, however, ignores the effectiveness of advertising layout and design in transmitting an impression of relative importance to the human observer.

The Prominence Scale. Quantitative expression of the coder's perception of relative importance is achieved by using the relative prominence scale shown in Table 7.1.

TABLE 7.1. *The Relative Prominence Scale*

Level of Prominence	Evaluation Scale
Extremely Prominent — Impossible to Miss	4
Very Prominent — Major Emphasis Given	3
Average Prominence — Normal Identification	2
Present but Not Prominent — Easily Missed	1
Not Present — Impossible to Determine	0

The coder's evaluation of the importance of each product characteristic, product-related appeal, and brand name identification appearing
in a promotion is expressed using this scale. The proportion of that
promotion devoted to each element is then defined as the ratio of that
element's prominence to the sum of the prominences of all elements
present.

Form of Presentation

Form of presentation includes the layout, size, color, and insertion
characteristics of a magazine or newspaper advertisement and the design
and running time of a radio or TV commercial. The effect of design
and layout in focusing the attention of the reader or viewer on particular elements of a promotion is accounted for by the relative prominence formulation discussed in the preceding section. The dimensions
of color and size (number of pages or time period) are specified by
output variables defined below.

Promotion Schedule

The period of time over which a particular advertisement is to be
run and the number of appearances (the frequency of presentation)
are determined by the media schedule, which establishes the presentation of a particular message within specified media.

Allocation Procedures

Given an unlimited budget, the manager's promotional program is
determined by the four decisions outlined earlier. Because unlimited
budgets are seldom available, it is necessary to consider procedures
for determining the dollar allocation to a particular promotional program. The budgetary constraint is often manifest in limitations on the
form of presentation (particularly the number of pages or length of
time available) and the period and/or frequency of presentation.

Five approaches to the problem of planning total advertising expenditures have been identified.[29]

1. The fixed percentage of sales approach establishes budgeted advertising as a percentage of past or expected sales. Although not

---

[29] For a discussion of these alternatives see J. Dean, "How Much to Spend on
Advertising," *Harvard Business Review,* Vol. 29 (January–February 1951), pp.
65–74.

analytically justifiable in most instances, this approach has the advantages of being explicit, competitively stable, and financially appealing because expenditures are geared to dollar inflows.

2. The "all you can afford" approach devotes a predetermined share of profits or available funds to advertising. If the company is operating within the appropriate region of the normally assumed S-shaped response curve and their advertising activities are "effective," this policy results in a substantial "investment" in market development through advertising. Arguments based on corporate income tax laws may also be raised in favor of this procedure.

3. The return on investment approach permits advertising to be viewed as a problem in capital budgeting. This approach has many conceptual advantages. The main problem in practical implementation is to estimate the rate of return on advertising investments and distinguish investments in long-term market position from expenditures required for immediate competitive effects. Appropriate depreciation periods for an advertising investment are also difficult to determine, given presently available data.

4. The objective-and-task approach requires budgeting of an amount considered necessary to attain predetermined objectives. This procedure is most consistent with the management philosophy advocated in this study; however, its practical implementation is limited by the absence of data accurately reflecting the historical cost of achieving specific objectives under given market conditions.

5. The competitive parity approach involves maintaining the company's advertising outlays so that they are in the range of accepted values for the industry. This usually means keeping the company's percentage of total industry advertising at a level consistent with the company market share in that industry. This approach ignores the interaction effects of the firm's advertising and that of its competitor as well as the different role played by promotion in alternative marketing strategies. The major advantage in its use is the relative stability achieved when competitors agree not to compete through advertising expenditure.

Competitive action is frequently the major deterrent to successful evaluation of the worth of advertising expenditures. It is not surprising,

therefore, to find the use of game theory proposed as a means of determining the best alternative to follow under various assumed competitive conditions.[30]

Media Specification

Before defining promotion decision outputs, relevant characteristics
of the previously noted media sector require specification.[31]

Media Identification. In discussing promotional communication, the
index variable "mn" will be used to refer to a particular medium (e.g.,
Time magazine) while the index variable "m" will be used to reference
a specified media type (e.g., weekly news magazines) encompassing MN
media.

Media Coverage. Each media type may be described by its coverage and the dollar expenditure required at saturation — the expenditure required to reach the entire circulation or coverage at the maximum
attainable frequency. This would correspond to the expenditure required
to place an advertisement in every issue of every weekly news magazine
during a particular week or to place a spot television commercial on
all stations in a specified area during each major time segment.[32]

Two media variables are established to provide this information.

Equation 7.5

TOTPOP(m)   TOTal POPulation — unduplicated circulation to which
             media type m is available. Dimension: cell units.

SATADV(m)   SATuration ADVertising — rate of advertising expendi-
             ture required to reach TOTPOP(m) with maximum attain-
             able frequency. Dimension: value units (dollars) per time
             period.

The total population variable is dimensioned in "cell units." When
referencing the consumer sector, this variable indicates the number

---

[30] See, for example, F. D. Robinson, "The Advertising Budget," *The Controller*,
Vol. 26 (August 1958), pp. 368–369, 388–389.

[31] The term "media sector" was used in Chapter 4 to refer to segments of the
marketing environment in which activity related to the transfer of promotional
messages through media was effected. See Chapter 4, p. 66.

[32] "Time segment" as used here refers to the time block differentiated for purposes of spot television time sales (e.g., early morning, midmorning, noon, etc.).
The problem of relating exposure opportunities in different media types cannot be
effectively solved without referencing material developed in later chapters. For
purposes of this development, it may be assumed that management will supply a
subjective evaluation of the relative merit of competing media types based on the
audience to be reached and form of presentation used.

of households in which the media type is available; while in the context of the distributor or retailer sector, it specifies the number of distributors or retailers to whom the media type is available.

Media Circulation and Overlap.   Each medium within a given media type is specified in terms of its circulation or coverage and the extent to which it overlaps other media of the same type.

Equation 7.6

CIRCUL(mn, m)	CIRCULation of medium mn of media type m. Dimension: cell units.
OVRLAP(mn, mn', m)	OVeRLAP between medium mn and medium mn' of media type m. Dimension: cell units.

Promotion Decision Outputs

Outputs generated as a result of the manufacturer's promotion decisions may be summarized in terms of media schedule, form of presentation, and content.

Schedule.   The promotion schedule may be described in terms of information or capital flow. In the first instance, promotional content appearing in identified media over time is summarized. In the latter case, dollars allocated to each medium over time are noted. These two dimensions of promotion scheduling are referenced using the following variables.

Equation 7.7

SCHED(na, mn, t)	SCHEDule for appearance of promotion na in medium mn (of media type m) at time t. Dimension: a pure number (binary).
ADVEXP(m, t)	ADVertising EXPenditure in media type m at time t. Dimension: value units (dollars) per time period.

Size and Color.   Print or broadcast promotion characteristics, other than those associated with content manifestations of layout, may be summarized in terms of the size of print advertisements (or time in minutes and/or seconds for radio and television) and the presence or absence of color. These characteristics are coded using the two variables defined below.

Equation 7.8

ADVSIZ(na)	ADVertisement SIZe (or time measure) as measured for promotion na. Dimension: pure number (ratio).
ADVCLR(na)	ADVertisement CoLoR as measured for promotion na. Dimension: pure number (binary).

Advertisement size is dimensioned as a ratio-indicating measurement against a standard reference (e.g., full page or one minute). The color variable is a binary measure permitting differentiation between black-and-white advertisements and those in which color is present but not between one- or two-color and full color presentations.[33]

Point-of-sale displays also require size specification (the presence of color may be assumed). The appropriate measurement is floor area required for the display, as specified by the following variable.

Equation 7.9

PSDSIZ(na)   Point-of-Sale Display SIZe measured in terms of floor space required by display na. Dimension: square feet.

Content. The content of media and point-of-sale promotion is specified in terms of appeals, product characteristics, and brand name identifications. Variables referencing these content descriptors are defined as follows:

Equation 7.10

EVAPWT(n, na)   EValuation of APpeals WeighTing (relative prominence) for appeal n in promotion na. Dimension: pure number (ratio).

EVPSAW(n, na)   EValuation of Point-of-Sale Appeal Weighting (relative prominence) for appeal n in point-of-sale display na. Dimension: pure number (ratio).

EVPCWT(np, na)   EValuation of Product Characteristic np WeighTing (relative prominence) in promotion na. Dimension: pure number (ratio).

EVPCWP(np, na)   EValuation of Product Characteristic np Weighting (relative prominence) for Point-of-sale display na. Dimension: pure number (ratio).

EVIDPR(b, na)   EValuation of brand b IDentification PRominence in promotion na. Dimension: pure number.

EVPBPS(b, na)   EValuation of Prominence of Brand b in Point-of-Sale display na. Dimension: pure number.

Manufacturer-Generated Retail Promotion. The manufacturer may prepare promotional material for use by retailers and distributors. The

---

[33] While the binary measure is totally adequate for description of television promotions, certain studies of the effect of color in magazine promotion suggest that distinctions based on the number of colors present are significant. See, for example, D. W. Twedt, "A Multiple Factor Analysis of Advertising Readership," *Journal of Applied Psychology,* Vol. 36. (June 1952), pp. 207–215.

most common form is the newspaper mat supplied by the manufacturer with space for retail store name insertion; however, manufacturer-prepared radio and television spots are frequently offered and used.

The content of manufacturer-prepared retail promotion is indicated using the content variables already defined. The manufacturer's decision to prepare and make available such promotion is transmitted to other sectors through an availability indicator defined as follows.

Equation 7.11

> REMATA(b)   REtail MAT Availability for brand b. Dimension: pure number (binary).
>
> > = 1, if manufacturer prepared retail promotion available,
> > = 0, if manufacturer prepared retain promotion not available.

Pricing Decisions

Pricing decisions may be categorized as (1) cost oriented, (2) based on economic theory, or (3) managerial (pricing viewed as part of an over-all marketing strategy).[34]

Decision Procedures

Under the cost-oriented approach, a sales forecast is developed, and expected costs at forecasted levels are computed. A desired or normal markup is then added to obtain the selling price.

The economic theory approach assumes the existence of a demand curve against which the firm's supply curve may be matched to establish the point at which the market is cleared. Because demand, which is more often perceived as a dynamic condition than as a static relationship, is difficult to measure, this approach is seldom used by operating management.

Under the managerial approach, price is established in conjunction with other marketing variables as a compromise between a cost-based and competitive market-determined level.

It is often suggested that pricing strategy should be geared to the relative maturity of a product market. Noting that "pricing in the pioneering stage of the cycle involves difficult problems of projecting potential demand and of guessing the relation of price to sales . . . ,"

[34] For a thorough discussion of this categorization scheme, see C. M. Hewitt, "Pricing — An Area of Increasing Importance," *Business Horizons,* Special Issue, First International Seminar on Marketing Management Vol. 4. (February 1961), pp. 108–111.

one author outlines two diametrically opposed pricing policies that may be followed.

The policy of relatively high prices in the pioneering stage has much to commend it, particularly when sales seem to be comparatively unresponsive to price but quite responsive to educational promotion. On the other hand, the policy of relatively low prices in the pioneering stage, in anticipation of the cost savings resulting from an expanding market, has been strikingly successful under the right conditions. Low prices look to long run rather than short run profits and discourage potential competitors.[35]

Application of a Bayesian approach to pricing offers advantages of the type noted earlier in this chapter.[36]

Traditional techniques rarely consider *alternative* states of nature, let alone assigning prior probabilities to their occurrence. Moreover, traditional market planning techniques seldom provide for testing the sensitivity of the study's outcomes to departures in the basic assumptions.

At the very least, the Bayesian model forces a more rigorous approach to market planning problems and offers a useful device for quickly finding the financial implications of assumptions about the occurrence of alternative states of nature.[37]

Pricing Decision Outputs

Outputs of the pricing decision may be intended for implementation within the manufacturer sector, or at the distributor or retailer level.

Distributor-Oriented Pricing. The manufacturer's selling price to distributors is established within the manufacturer sector as the price at which product is available to the distributor. Because prices may change with time and be used as a selling variable ("the price is going up so you'd better order now"), the manufacturer may communicate a price that will apply at some time in the future as opposed to the presently applicable price. The two distributor-oriented prices are defined as follows:

Equation 7.12

MANFPR(b, t)   MANuFacturer's PRice for brand b at time t. Dimension: value units (dollars) per product unit.

FUDPSP(b)   FUture to Distributor Price SPecification for brand b. Dimension: value units (dollars) per product unit.

[35] J. Dean, "Pricing Policies for New Products," *Harvard Business Review,* Vol. 28 (November–December 1950), p. 53.

[36] See "A Bayesian Structure," p. 124.

[37] P. E. Green, "Bayesian Decision Theory in Pricing Strategy," *Journal of Marketing,* Vol. 27 (January 1963), p. 14.

Retailer-Oriented Pricing. In a similar manner, the manufacturer's present and anticipated future price to retailers may be specified in terms of the following variables:

Equation 7.13

PRTRET(b, r, t) PRice for brand b To RETailer r at time t. Dimension: value units (dollars) per product unit.

FURPSP(b, r) FUture to Retailer r Price SPecification for brand b. Dimension: value units (dollars) per product unit.

Manufacturer direct sale to the consumer will not be modeled in developing this system. However the manufacturer may establish a suggested "list" or retail price (as opposed to price *to* the retailer) which is communicated to the retail sector.

Equation 7.13A

SUGPRC(b) SUGgested retail PRiCe for brand b. Dimension: value units (dollars) per product unit.

Sales Force Maintenance

The manufacturer's handling of sales force maintenance can be described in terms of decisions relating to (1) salesman compensation, (2) salesman allocation, and (3) the selling program.

Salesman Compensation

Salesman compensation normally consists of a salary plus commission. While arguments have been presented in support of every conceivable combination of these components, for present purposes it is sufficient to note that the manufacturer must establish a basis for compensation of salesmen in his employ.[38]

The Allocation Decision

For purposes of this discussion, allocation will be considered to include the hiring and firing of salesmen as well as their assignment to specific accounts. In making an allocation decision in this broad sense, the manufacturer must decide on the number of salesmen to be hired, the desired normal call period (the time lapse between successive calls to an outlet), the number of calls a salesman is to make during

---

[38] A relatively comprehensive approach to the development of a compensation program is provided in H. Tosdal, "How to Design the Salesman's Compensation Plan," *Harvard Business Review,* Vol. 31 (September–October 1953), p. 70.

a call period, and the allocation of specific salesmen to specified outlets. While allocation criteria will not be considered in this chapter, distributor salesman allocation is modeled in Chapter 10.[39]

The Selling Program

Because the salesman may be viewed as a communication channel, the manufacturer must establish information content for transfer by this medium. The previously developed product characteristic, appeal, and brand name identification categories may be employed to represent the content of a salesman's selling presentation as established by the manufacturer.

Sales Force Decision Outputs

Compensation. Salary and commission offered a sales force by a manufacturer will be specified through variables defined as follows:

Equation 7.14

COMMIS(b)   COMMISsion paid salesmen on sales of brand b. Dimension: value units (dollars) per product unit.

SALARY(b)   SALARY paid salesmen selling brand b. Dimension: value units (dollars) per time period.

Allocation. The manufacturer's sales force allocation decision may be summarized in two outputs communicated to the salesman sector: (1) the number of calls per salesman per period and (2) the average call period. The allocation of a given salesman and the decision to hire or fire that salesman will be specified through the elements of a call schedule. (A decision to fire is communicated by a zero call schedule.)

Equation 7.15

NCPSPP(b)   Number of Calls Per Salesman selling brand b Per time Period. Dimension: pure number per time period.

NCALPD(b)   Normal CALl PerioD of salesmen selling brand b. Dimension: time units.

SMCSCH(s, x, b)   SalesMan Call SCHedule indicating that salesmen s selling brand b is to call on distributor or retailer x. Dimension: pure number (binary).

Selling Message. The content of sales presentations designated by the manufacturer is summarized in the relative prominence of product

[39] See "The Salesman Allocation Decision" in Chapter 10, pp. 324–327.

characteristics and product-related appeals. As in media promotion, the relative prominence of brand emphasis may also be recorded.

Equation 7.16

EVSPCW(np, b)   EValuation of Salesman Product Characteristic np Weighting (relative prominence) in presentation spcified for brand b. Dimension: pure number (ratio).

EVSAPW(n, b)   EValuation of Salesman APpeal n Weighting (relative prominence) in presentation specified for brand b. Dimension: pure number (ratio).

Research Decisions

Isolation of the research function in a separate sector limits the manufacturer's research outputs to designation of measurements to be taken and channels of information, product, or value flow to be monitored. This process does not require additional variables definition because desired inputs are defined in terms of the flows or backlogs in other sectors to be monitored.

Integrated Planning

This chapter has focused on the outputs of discrete decisions, ignoring completely questions of over-all planning. Integrated planning may be described as effective allocation of outputs from decision processes to achieve specified business objectives.

The first step in the development of an integrated plan is target market definition. Once this group has been identified, campaign objectives can be stated in terms of desired target market responses. Given objectives, the assets and liabilities of the company and its competitors are evaluated to establish a strategy built upon the company's assets and taking advantage of competitor liabilities. The strategy selected would ideally be the product of careful consideration of alternative approaches — a synthesis of effects produced by each decision output. Plans and schedules for implementation of the selected strategy must be developed along with monitor and review procedures designed to detect discrepancy between planned and realized conditions, unanticipated opportunities, and unexpected problems.

While the planning process has been described sequentially, interactions occur between the various stages. It is, for example, unrealistic to define target markets without considering campaign objectives and corporate capabilities.

Integrated planning requires assessment of each marketing tool's potential contribution to stated objectives. The goal of planning is a program in which all assets are employed with maximum achievable effectiveness. Peter Drucker has described this striving ". . . for the best possible economic results from the resources currently employed or available . . . [as] . . . the first duty — and the continuing responsibility — of the business manager." [40]

An example of this type of alternative evaluation is provided by the experimental design developed by Henderson, Hind, and Brown, ". . . to predict the most efficient promotional alternatives from consumer or trade media advertising, personal selling, point-of-purchase effort, cooperative advertising and premium offers, . . . to determine the place of each in the total promotional effort for a product . . . [and] . . . , holding promotional expenditures relatively constant for each technique tested, [to relate] promotional outlay . . . to sales returns." [41]

The major problem in integrated planning rests on the difficulty of evaluating the relative effectiveness of alternative actions. Peter Drucker refers to this dilemma as ". . . the confusion between effectiveness and efficiency that stands between doing the right things and doing things right. There is surely nothing quite so useless as doing with great efficiency what should not be done at all. What we need is (1) a way to identify the areas of effectiveness (of possible significant results), and (2) a method for concentrating on them." [42]

It is the contention of this study that a validated simulation encompassing management's explicit models of interactions occurring within the market may be used to test the implications of alternative decision output sets. Through this approach, more effective, integrated planning is achieved by enabling management to give more thorough consideration to the implications of a greater number of alternative courses of action.

Summary

This chapter has focused on decision processes within the manufacturer sector. Seven market-oriented decision areas have been examined

[40] P. F. Drucker, "Managing for Business Effectiveness," *Harvard Business Review,* Vol. 41 (May–June 1963), pp. 53–60.

[41] P. L. Henderson, J. F. Hind, and S. E. Brown, "Sales Effects of Two Campaign Themes," *Journal of Advertising Research,* Vol. 1 (December 1961), pp. 2–11.

[42] Drucker, *op. cit.,* Footnote 40, p. 54.

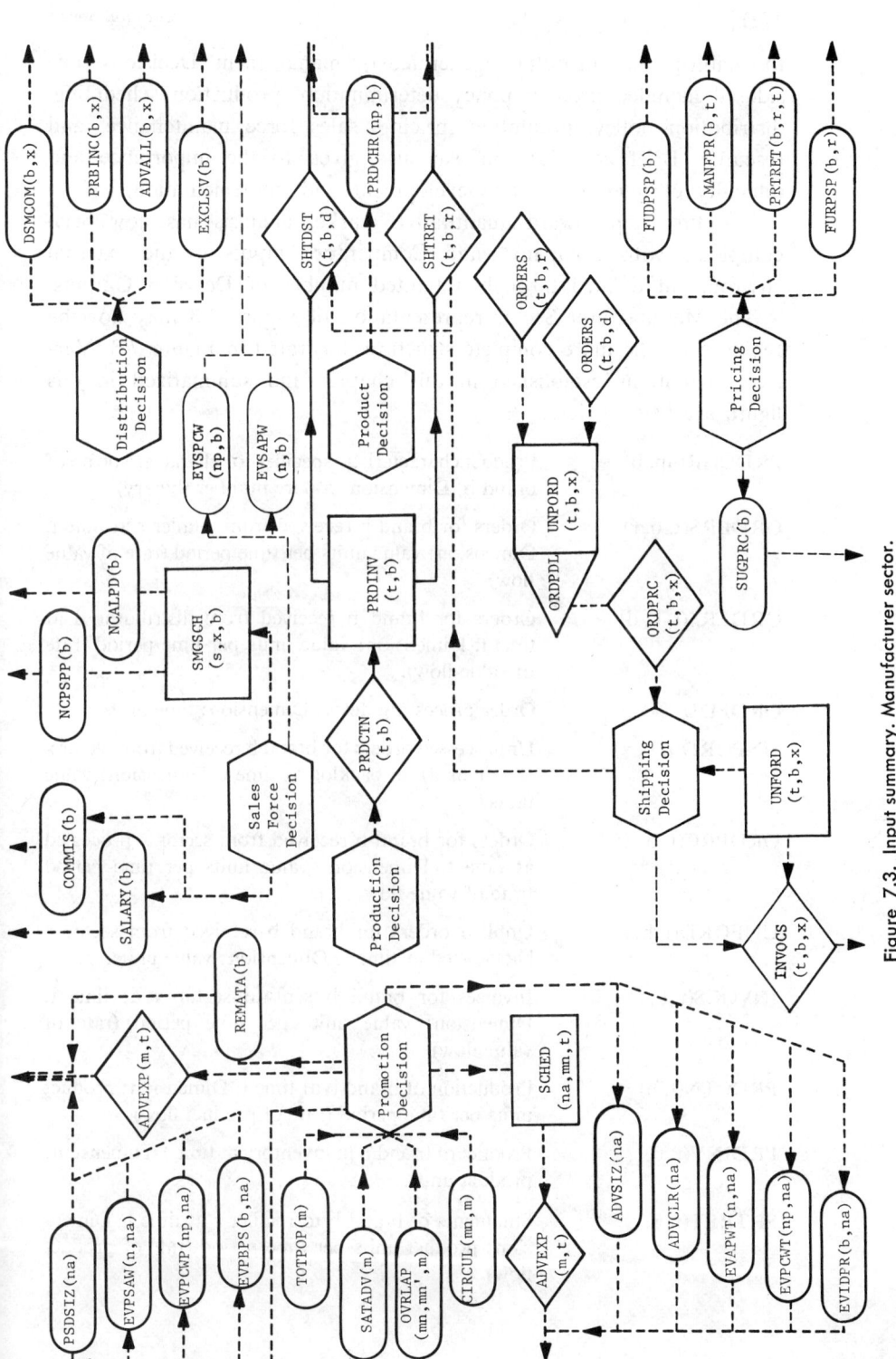

Figure 7.3. Input summary. Manufacturer sector.

to establish relevant outputs generated by management. Decisions considered included product policy determination, production scheduling, distribution policy, promotion, pricing, sales force maintenance, and research. Brief consideration was also given to the importance and difficulty of integrated plan development and implementation.

The first step toward quantitative market analysis has now been completed with Company (and Competitor) inputs to the external environment defined through a limited number of Decision Outputs.

The Manufacturer Sector representation of Figure 2.3 may now be replaced by the more complete structure illustrated in Figure 7.3. Variable definitions established in this chapter and summarized in this figure are listed below:

PRDCHR(np, b)   Product characteristic specifier for characteristic np of brand b. Dimension: a pure number (binary).

ORDERS(t, b, r)   Orders for brand b received from retailer r at time t. Dimension: value units per time period (rate of value flow).

ORDERS(t, b, d)   Orders for brand b received from distributor d at time t. Dimension: value units per time period (rate of value flow).

ORDPDL   Order processing delay. Dimension: time units.

UNPORD(t, b, x)   Unprocessed orders for brand b received from sector x (x = r or d), in backlog at time t. Dimension: value units.

ORDPRC(t, b, x)   Orders for brand b received from sector x processed at time t. Dimension: value units per time period (rate of value flow).

UNFORD(t, b, x)   Unfilled orders for brand b received from sector x backlogged at time t. Dimension: value units.

INVOCS(t, b, x)   Invoices for brand b sent to sector x at time t. Dimension: value units per time period (rate of value flow).

PRDCTN(t, b)   Production of brand b at time t. Dimension: product units per time period (rate of product flow).

PRDINV(t, b)   Product of brand b in inventory at time t. Dimension: product units.

SHTRET(t, b, r)   Shipments of brand b to retailer r at time t. Dimension: product units per time period (rate of product flow).

SHTDST(t, b, d)	Shipments of brand b to distributor d at time t. Dimension: product units per time period (rate of product flow).
EXCLSV(b)	Exclusive distribution indicator. Dimension: a pure number (binary).
DSMCOM(b, x)	Direct salesman compensation available to salesmen in outlet x selling brand b. Dimension: dollars per product unit.
PRBINC(b, x)	Probabilistic incentive available to salesmen in outlet x selling brand b. Dimension: value units (dollars) per product unit (expected sales).
ADVALL(b, x)	Advertising allowances available to outlet x selling brand b. Dimension: value units (dollars) per product unit.
TOTPOP(m)	Total population — unduplicated circulation to which media type m is available. Dimension: cell units.
SATADV(m)	Saturation advertising — rate of advertising expenditure required to reach TOTPOP(m) with maximum attainable frequency. Dimension: value units (dollars) per time period.
CIRCUL(mn, m)	Circulation of medium mn of media type m. Dimension: cell units.
OVRLAP(mn, mn', m)	Overlap between medium mn and medium mn' of media type m. Dimension: cell units.
SCHED(na, mn, t)	Schedule for appearance of promotion na in medium mn (of media type m) at time t. Dimension: a pure number (binary).
ADVEXP(m, t)	Advertising expenditure in media type m at time t. Dimension: value units (dollars) per time period.
ADVSIZ(na)	Advertisement size (or time measure) as measured for promotion na. Dimension: pure number (ratio).
ADVCLR(na)	Advertisement color as measured for promotion na. Dimension: pure number (binary).
PSDSIZ(na)	Point-of-sale display size measured in terms of floor space required by display na. Dimension: square feet.
EVAPWT(n, na)	Evaluation of appeals weighting (relative prominence) for appeal n in promotion na. Dimension: pure number (ratio).
EVPSAW(n, na)	Evaluation of point-of-sale appeal weighting (relative prominence) for appeal n. In point-of-sale display na. Dimension: pure number (ratio).

EVPCWT(np, na)	Evaluation of product characteristic np weighting (relative prominence) in promotion na. Dimension: pure number (ratio).
EVPCWP(np, na)	Evaluation of product characteristic np weighting (relative prominence) for point-of-sale display na. Dimension: pure number (ratio).
EVIDPR(b, na)	Evaluation of brand b identification prominence in promotion na. Dimension: pure number.
EVPBPS(b, na)	Evaluation of prominence of brand b in point-of-sale display na. Dimension: pure number.
REMATA(b)	Retail mat availability for brand b. Dimension: pure number (binary).
MANFPR(b, t)	Manufacturer's price for brand b at time t. Dimension: value units (dollars) per product unit.
FUDPSP(b)	Future to distributor price specification for brand b. Dimension: value units (dollars) per product unit.
PRTRET(b, r, t)	Price for brand b to retailer r at time t. Dimension: value units (dollars) per product unit.
FURPSP(b, r)	Future to retailer r price specification for brand b. Dimension: value units (dollars) per product unit.
SUGPRC(b)	Suggested retail price for brand b. Dimension: value units (dollars) per product unit.
COMMIS(b)	Commission paid salesmen on sales of brand b. Dimension: value units (dollars) per product unit.
SALARY(b)	Salary paid salesmen selling brand b. Dimension: value units (dollars) per time period.
NCPSPP(b)	Number of calls per salesman selling brand b per time period. Dimension: pure number per time period.
NCALPD(b)	Normal call period of salesmen selling brand b. Dimension: time units.
SMCSCH(s, x, b)	Salesman call schedule indicating that salesman s selling brand b is to call on distributor or retailer x. Dimension: pure number (binary).
EVSPCW(np, b)	Evaluation of salesman product characteristic np weighting (relative prominence) in presentation specified for brand b. Dimension: pure number (ratio).
EVSAPW(n, b)	Evaluation of salesman appeal n weighting (relative prominence) in presentation specified for brand b. Dimension: pure number (ratio).

Chapter 8

A MODEL OF CONSUMER BEHAVIOR

This chapter is concerned with the development of a micro-analytic simulation of consumer behavior compatible with the macro-structure specifications.[1]

Model Structure and Function

The model discussed in this chapter is based on a cell structure in which each purchasing unit is represented explicitly by a single logical cell in the computer. The greater the diversity of the consumer population to be examined, the greater the number of differentiating attributes to be encompassed by the model, and the greater the number of cells required within the structure of the model. The individual cell or household is the micro building block of this simulation.

Cell characteristics for the previously noted "Simulmatics Project" population established a maximum of 108 different voter types in a particular simulated state. The developers of the Simulmatics model "assumed that a voter of a given voter type would be identical regardless of the state from which he came. The simulated state therefore consisted of a weighted average of the behaviors of the voter types in that state, the weighting being proportional to the numbers of such persons in that state."[2]

A model is structured to function in a particular context — to achieve

[1] Specifications for the consumer sector are established in Chapter 3. See "The Consumer," p. 51.

[2] I. de Sola Pool and R. Abelson, "The Simulmatics Project," *The Public Opinion Quarterly*, Vol. 24 (Summer 1961), pp. 167–183, p. 175.

certain objectives. The appropriateness of simplifying assumptions that limit the scope or detail of a particular model can be evaluated only in context of the objectives that the model was designed to achieve. Before describing this model, it may therefore be useful to review the criteria that governed its development. The model's major research function was to provide a framework within which the implications of alternative representations of consumer behavior could be examined. Its management applications were to be in studying probable consumer responses to alternative marketing strategies. In the educational context it was to represent interactions within the consumer sector in sufficient detail to permit realistically comprehensive market research. Student managers analyzing developments in the simulated environment of the model were to utilize research tools applicable to the investigation of comparable phenomena in the "real world."

Description of a Consumer

Discussing a nation-wide survey of consumer income and expenditures completed in 1957 under the sponsorship of *Life* magazine, Robert Ferber notes the following implications of manifest trends in the consumer economy.

1. Consumers are becoming increasingly able to act differently from each other, yet in practice they seem to act more like one another. Consumer budgets on the whole are very similar to one another, even when comparisons are made by income levels; the main differences appear to lie in the qualities of the goods and services that are bought rather than in what is bought. . . . Consumers appear to be becoming homogenous in an era when they are being endowed increasingly with the capacity to behave differently.

2. New concepts of market analysis are needed. The growing impact on consumer expenditures of a host of factors other than income means that the past practice of predicting sales by deriving a simple relationship between income and expenditures will yield increasingly inferior results as time goes on.

3. The role of the consumer as a purely passive agent in business fluctuations is a relic of the past. With incomes well above subsistence levels and with enormous reserves of unneeded spending power in the form of verbal assets and unused credit, consumers are much more free to spend as they please. The point is that the consumer has become . . . a potential catalyst in business fluctuations.[3]

[3] R. Ferber, "Our Changing Consumer Market," *Business Horizons,* Vol. 1 (Spring 1958), pp. 49–66.

Development of a representative cell model of a consumer population requires that a selected set of attributes be chosen from the available universe to serve as the basis of differentiation among consumers in the model structure. This model was designed to encompass an artificial consumer population separated into a sufficient number of differentiated areas to permit examination of regional market phenomena. The population has been arbitrarily divided into 30 geographic areas with subclassifications of rural, suburban, and metropolitan residence established within each geographic area.

Within each geographic region and residential subdivision, differentiating characteristics must be established for each consumer cell. Attributes chosen for inclusion in this model may be summarized under the general headings: (1) demographic, (2) socioeconomic, (3) behavioral, and (4) psychological (attitudinal).

Demographic Characteristics

Many demographic attributes in addition to geographic location and city size may influence consumer behavior in a particular product case. Factors considered when formulating specific product models include marital status of head of household, family size, and age and sex distribution of household members. This model, however, will be limited to a representative descriptor set influencing consumer actions associated with a variety of products.

The age of the wage earner in each household will be used as a representative demographic characteristic. This attribute is selected in part as an indicator of the household's position in what has been described as "the family life cycle." [4]

Data obtained from large sample consumer panels facilitates the study of household consumption by market segments defined in terms of selected demographic variables.[5]

---

[4] Several aspects of consumer behavior, including broad categories of consumption activity, may be explained by analysis of the economic implications of family life cycle. See, for example, J. A. Fisher, "Family Life Cycle Analysis in Research on Consumer Behavior," L. H. Clark (ed.), *Consumer Behavior,* Vol. II, *The Life Cycle and Consumer Behavior* (New York: New York University Press, 1955), pp. 28–35.

[5] For a discussion of the effect of family life cycle on purchase behavior based on data from the consumer panel maintained by the Market Research Corporation of America, see S. G. Barton, "The Life Cycle and Buying Patterns," *ibid.,* pp. 53–57.

Socioeconomic Characteristics

Weber distinguishes between three orders of socioeconomic stratification defined as "class, status, and party." [6] "Class" refers to an individual's economic opportunities in the labor or commodity markets (the individual's opportunities for worldly success or "life chance"). Weber notes a lack of identification between classes because they do not share "community." "Status groups," on the other hand, are normally communities. They have a specific "style of life" associated with the behavior of those belonging to the status group. Classes are stratified according to the members' activities in relation to production and acquisition of goods, whereas "status groups" are stratified by the principles of consumption according to which group members consume.

Social class has been suggested as a determinant of purchase behavior. A study of the social and psychological values of the wife of a blue collar worker, *Working Man's Wife,* suggests, for example, that attitudes, needs, behavior, and responses are a product of the environment in which the blue-collar worker and his wife live and their selective perception and interpretation of aspects of that environment.[7] Others have argued that, due to the dynamic nature of social stratification in the U.S. national market and interactions between social class and income, social class has limited value as a basis for market segmentation.[8]

J. A. Kahl defines six socioeconomic variables that he maintains may be "operationally defined":[9]

1. Personal prestige — deference — studied by asking people about their attitudes and respect towards others and by watching their behavior.

2. Occupation — referring to a social role that describes the major work of a person. In Kahl's opinion, because we are people

[6] M. Weber, *The Theory of Social and Economic Organization,* Translated by A. M. Henderson and T. Parsons (eds.) (New York: Oxford University Press, 1950).

[7] L. Rainwater, R. P. Coleman, and G. Handel, *Working Man's Wife* (New York: Oceana Publications, Inc., 1959).

[8] R. P. Coleman, "The Significance of Social Stratification in Selling," in M. L. Bell (ed.), Proceedings of the 43rd National Conference of the American Marketing Association, December 1960, pp. 171–184.

[9] J. A. Kahl, *The American Class Structure* (New York: Rinehart and Company, Inc., 1957).

devoted primarily to business, we give highest prestige to successful business and professional men.

3. Possessions — this factor is income related because higher-income families can afford an elegant style of life and consumption behavior and can multiply their incomes.
4. Interaction — patterns of differential contact — the "who invites whom to dinner" based measure.
5. Class consciousness — the degree to which people at a given stratification level are explicitly aware themselves of the distinctive social groupings.
6. Value orientation — the things considered good, important, and beautiful. This orientation defines the ends of life and the approved means of approaching them.

Income has frequently been proposed as a surrogate for the occupation and possessions variable. Due to its availability as a population descriptor, it has been adopted as the single index of socioeconomic position in some models. This use as sole population descriptor has been attacked on the grounds that "consumption patterns operate as prestige symbols to define class membership, which is a more significant determinant of economic behavior than mere income."

Income has always been the marketer's handiest index to family consumption standards. But it is a far from accurate index. For instance, the bulk of the population in a metropolitan market today will fall in the middle-income ranges. This will comprise not only the traditional white collar worker, but the unionized craftsman and the semi-skilled worker with their tremendous income gains of the past decade. Income-wise they may be in the same category. But their buying behavior, their tastes, their spending-saving aspirations can be poles apart. Social-class position and mobility-stability dimensions will reflect in much greater depth each individual's style of life.[10]

Level of education will be adopted as a second socioeconomic index for members of the artificial population in this model. Education is a determinant of "value orientation" and interacts with income to influence "personal prestige" and "interaction." Kahl suggests a correlation between class and education in that the upper and upper-middle classes are college graduates, the lower-middle class are high-school graduates with little additional training, the working class are graduates of gram-

[10] P. Martineau, "Social Classes and Spending Behavior," *Journal of Marketing,* Vol. 23 (October 1958), pp. 121–130.

mar school with some high-school training, and the lower class have little education beyond grammar school, if that.

While income and education of the head of household will be used as first-order indices of socioeconomic position for purposes of this model, specific product models have encompassed other socioeconomic characteristics including the value or size of the residence occupied, profession or occupation of head of household, religion, ethnic background, ownership of certain products, asset holdings, and leisure time pursuits.

Behavioral Characteristics

Behavioral attributes of the consumer population include measures affecting the frequency and extent of participation in activities creating a recognition of, need for, or opportunity to use the product. The population of this model will be described in terms of three representative behavioral characteristics: (1) present product (brand) ownership, (2) media availability (potential for exposure) of 36 media, and (3) retail store preference — the frequency with which the household shops in various outlets.

Psychological (Attitudinal) Characteristics

Psychological characteristics include population descriptors describing the consumer's knowledge of brand characteristics and his feelings about (attitude toward) those attributes. The attitude and awareness measures introduced earlier will be used to differentiate among consumers along this dimension.[11] These variables, serving as intermediaries linking response to product and information to the purchase decision, are "operational." They are (1) easily measured using simple objective tests, (2) provide verifiable evidence of consumer response to product and information exposure, and (3) have been empirically linked to the consumer's probability of purchase.

The use of an attitude scale measure is controversial and has been questioned on the grounds that it is unreasonable to expect consumers to reveal their actual feelings about products through a direct measurement technique. One author proposing the use of projective techniques in the measurement of attitude has attacked the use of ". . . simple

---

[11] The attitude and awareness variables used in this model are defined in Chapter 5, see pp. 96–97. Validation of portions of the model employing these variables is discussed in Chapter 13.

scales and . . . direct questioning, because they deal only with manifest verbal content and fail to reach into the more comprehensive aspects of the personality. The person who is asked point-blank to express his feelings on a subject about which he is reticent for one reason or another may well evade the issue by providing an answer which conforms with the views of the investigator or which is sufficiently neutral to protect his psychological security." [12] On the other hand, verbal attitude scores have been used as a basis for evaluating projective techniques.[13]

In this model, the attitude and awareness variables are related to product characteristics, brands, and retail outlets.[14] This approach has been successfully applied to the analysis of markets for a wide range of products including foods, appliances, automobiles, special industrial training products, and drugs. Other personality variables have been found to be highly correlated with the use of certain products. In a study of antacid-analgesics, for example, significant relationships were established between "attitudes toward health," "compulsiveness," and "punitiveness," and product usage.[15]

Some researchers have suggested that personality profile data may be used to relate personality traits to consumption.[16] Available tests are, however, difficult to administer and validate. Improved procedures for acquiring such data must be developed if these measures are to become operational, in the sense just discussed, for attitude and awareness.

Structure of a Consumer Cell

Because this model is to be formulated for a digital computer, the attributes of each consumer cell (household) must be represented in the

[12] I. R. Weschler and R. E. Bernberg, "Projective Techniques in Attitude Measurement," in Ferber and Wales, *Motivation and Market Behavior* (Homewood, Illinois: Richard D. Irwin, Inc., 1958), pp. 103–122, p. 105.

[13] See S. Dubin, "Verbal Attitudes Scores from Responses Obtained in the Projective Technique," *Sociometry,* Vol. 3 (January 1940), pp. 24–48.

[14] For an example of alternative model formulations based on these concepts, see A. E. Amstutz and B. C. Hood, *Interim Report on Marketing Systems Research* (Working Paper), (Cambridge, Mass.: Sloan School of Management, 1960).

[15] M. J. Gottlieb, "Segmentation by Personality Types," L. H. Stockman (ed.), *Advancing Marketing Efficiency* (Chicago: American Marketing Association, 1959), pp. 148–158.

[16] An example of the use of the Gordon Personal Profile is provided by W. T. Tucker and J. J. Painter, "Personality and Product Use," *Journal of Applied Psychology,* Vol. 45 (1961), pp. 325–329.

computer's memory. Table 8.1 summarizes variable definitions, forms of representation, and storage requirements. Consumer attributes are described under the heading CHARACTERISTIC. The alphabetic code representing this characteristic in the computer model, the variable

TABLE 8.1. Variable Definition and Storage Allocation

Characteristic	Variable	Gradations	Bits Required
Geographic Location	—*	—*	—*
Rural, Urban, Suburban			
Classification	RUSID(c)	3	2
Age of Wage Earner	AGEID(c)	4	2
Income of Consumer Unit	INCOM(c)	6	3
Education of Consumer Unit	EDUCA(c)	4	2
Brand of Product Owned	PROWN(b, c)	1	B
Retail Store Preference	RETPR(r, c)	1	R
Media Availability (subscription)	MEDAV(m, c)	1	M
Attitude Toward PC			
Product Characteristics	ATITD(pc, c)	7	3*PC
Attitude Toward AP			
Product-Associated Appeal	ATITD(ap, c)	7	3*AP
Attitude Toward B Brands			
of Product	ATTBR(b, c)	7	3*B
Attitude Toward R Retail			
Outlets	ATTRET(r, c)	7	3*R
Awareness of B Brands of			
Product	AWARE(b, c)	1	B

* Geographic location specified at a level higher than the consumer unit is implicit in the consumer cell location. Explicit representation of this characteristic at the cell level is redundant.

definition, is indicated under the heading VARIABLE.[17] The column headed GRADATIONS specifies the number of differentiated categories used in scaling the variable. The column headed BITS REQUIRED indicates the number of binary bits of computer core memory utilized in storing the variable value for one consumer unit.

Sequence of Model Development

The model developed in this chapter is to represent interactions between a consumer c described in terms of the characteristics summarized in Table 8.1, producers of B brands of product, R retail outlets,

[17] Variable representation in a FORTRAN-like computer program is discussed in Chapter 5.

and C-1 other consumers. The model is adapted to a specific geographic region by setting model population parameters to comply with population statistics in the region to be simulated.

Simulation of behavior defined by the Chapter 3 consumer specifications will begin with the decision to shop. This will be followed by representation of the decision to purchase, and determination of the extent and content of word-of-mouth communication. Reaction models establishing probabilities of exposure and response to communication and product will then be developed. The chapter concludes with process models representing forgetting and conflict resolution.

The Consumer Decision to Shop

Consumer c may go to a store to examine a brand or product line. This decision to shop constitutes a specific commitment to obtain product information and is quite different from accidental exposure to product in the course of "shopping" in the more conventional sense of the word. Accidental exposure to products will be considered separately as a distinct process.

The explicit shopping decision will be formulated in terms of consumer c's probability of shopping PRSHP(c) described in terms of his perceived need for product, PRNED(c), and income, INCOM(c).

The Perceived Need Construct

Verbal descriptions of the consumer purchase decision often reference a hierarchy of needs assumed to reflect the relative priority attached to the satisfaction of various needs. Relevant motives or needs may generally be categorized as (1) visceral drives: hunger, thirst, air-getting, temperature regulation, effectuality, etc., (2) activity drives: exercise, rest, perseverance, rhythm, novelty, exploration, etc., (3) aesthetic drives: color, tone, specific qualities of taste, smell, and touch, rhythm, etc., (4) emotions: fear, rage, disgust, shame, etc.[18] It is also useful to distinguish physiological needs such as hunger and sex from acquired or learned needs, which are less easily defined.[19] In the present context we are

[18] G. Murphy, L. B. Murphy, and T. M. Newcomb, *Experimental Social Psychology* (rev. ed.; New York: Harper and Brothers, 1937), pp. 98–99.

[19] For an example of one vehicle developed in an attempt to measure acquired needs, see A. L. Edwards, *Edwards' Personal Preference Schedule* (rev. ed.; New York: Psychological Corporation, 1959). For a discussion of an application of this test in evaluating the needs of Chevrolet and Ford owners living in Park

concerned with the consumer's perception of his need hierarchy. The term perception is used here to encompass a wide range of assimilative processes in the manner of the social psychologists who, ". . . by defining perception in a very broad manner . . . have been able to tie it up heuristically with a wide range of collective phenomena." [20]

The concept of "perceived need" is introduced to suggest that (1) the individual's frame of reference changes with time as new information is received and assimilated so that the same individual will not necessarily have the same orientation or come to the same conclusion at different points in time, (2) that the individual's private conception of the world as revealed in his attitudes is an important determinant of behavior and response.[21]

In simplest terms, one shops for items that are "needed." A shopping list may therefore be viewed as a formal manifestation of a consumer's proposed means of satisfying needs existing at a point in time. Both needs and the means of satisfying them are subjectively structured by the consumer. Only in the exceptional case can either be established by the objective observer. Qualification of the concept of need therefore involves representation of the processes through which a consumer orders needs and alternative means of satisfying them.

The Perceived Need Function

Wroe Alderson has made use of a formulation based on need in developing a model of consumer search behavior. He proposes that consumer search activity be thought of as ". . . taking place in a multidimensional product space. Every point in this space represents a unique combination of qualities, each quality being scaled along one of the dimensions of the product space."

The purpose of consumer search is to find the point in product space which provides the best match for the need in question. . . . The searcher's quest for information is gathered in each step by subjective probabilities

---

Forest, Illinois, see F. B. Evans, "Psychological and Objective Factors in the Prediction of Brand Choice: Ford vs. Chevrolet," *The Journal of Business,* Vol. 32 (1959), pp. 340–369.

[20] F. H. Allport, *Theories of Perception and the Concept of Structure* (New York: John Wiley & Sons, Inc., 1955), p. 365.

[21] This point of view is supported in J. S. Bruner, "Social Psychology and Perception," in E. E. Maccoby, T. M. Newcomb, and E. L. Hartley (eds.) *Readings in Social Psychology* (3rd ed.; New York: Holt, Rinehart, and Winston, Inc., 1958), pp. 85–94.

based on the partial information he already has. He is not interested in a representative measure of some aspect of the universe but in finding a unique point within the universe.[22]

Consumer knowledge of a particular product line influences the perceived importance of that product. The consumer cannot attach significance to a product line about which he knows nothing. The previously introduced awareness measure provides a first approximation measure of the level of brand-specific knowledge.

Consumer attitude toward, or satisfaction with, appeals, product characteristics, and brands also affects the importance attributed to a product. Stronger feelings produce greater attributed importance. The consumer's subjective satisfaction (experienced or anticipated) will be expressed using the Attitude Scale introduced earlier.[23]

This concept of perception assumes that a consumer's orientation toward his environment manifest in his attitudes and awareness influences his perception of that environment — attitude and awareness influence response to stimuli and hence that which is "perceived." [24] Perceived need for a product line containing a brand of which the consumer is "Aware" will be greater than that for a product line in which no brands are familiar. "Perceived Need" will increase with increasing attitude — the better the perceived product image (the higher the attitude toward brands within the line), the greater the perceived need for the product and, conversely, the lower the attitude the lower the perceived need.

Empirical findings indicate that high positive or negative attitudes motivate significantly more action than relatively neutral attitudes. Data describing the relationship between attitude and perceived need approximate the exponentially weighted function illustrated in Figure 8.1, which also includes the effect of alternate awareness states.

[22] W. Alderson, *Marketing Behavior and Executive Action* (Homewood, Ill.: Richard D. Irwin, Inc., 1957).

[23] The general concepts of need and awareness have been referenced in other simulations of consumer behavior; however, neither concept has been defined in terms of measurable attributes of consumer populations. Forrester, for example, has referred to ". . . a pool of 'prospective customers' who are aware of their impending need to buy a product but who have not yet purchased it." J. W. Forrester, "Advertising: A Problem in Industrial Dynamics," *Harvard Business Review*, Vol. 37 (March–April 1959), p. 104.

[24] This assumption is not entirely consistent with present psychological thinking on the subject of perception, which is in itself not entirely consistent. This aspect of psychological thinking is discussed in F. H. Allport, *op. cit.* Footnote 20, pp. 362–364.

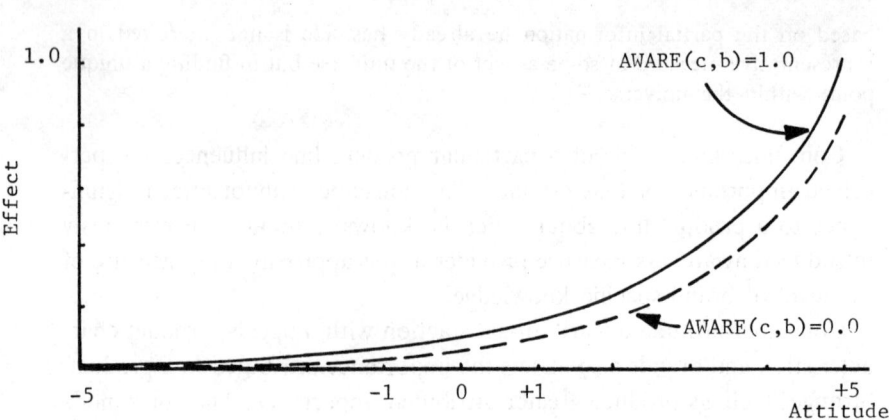

Figure 8.1. Effect of attitude on perceived need.

Use Opportunity

The consumer's opportunity to use a product may be expressed in terms of a *use opportunity coefficient,* indicating the probability that the consumer will have an opportunity to make use of the product during a specified period of time. In practice, this coefficient is defined in terms of consumer descriptors determining use opportunity for the product being studied. In a model depicting the market for certain alcoholic beverages, for example, the coefficient is based on the consumer's geographic and urban-rural location, income, frequency of entertaining, and occupation.

For purposes of generalizable formulation, a linear function will

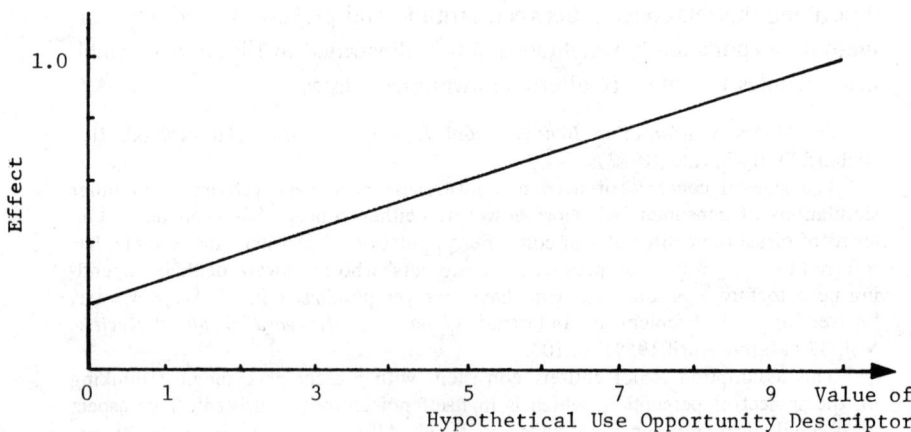

Figure 8.2. Effect of consumer use opportunity on perceived need.

reflect the normally encountered condition that perceived need increases in proportion to the opportunity for product use as illustrated in Figure 8.2.

Product Ownership

Because the consumer who has recently purchased product has temporarily satisfied the need that motivated purchase, product ownership influences perceived need. The extent of satisfaction may be expressed as a function of time since purchase and product life. Product life varies from a few days in the case of perishable foodstuffs to many years for an appliance. The effect of product ownership on perceived need may normally be formulated as an exponentially increasing function of time since purchase and average product life as summarized in Figure 8.3.

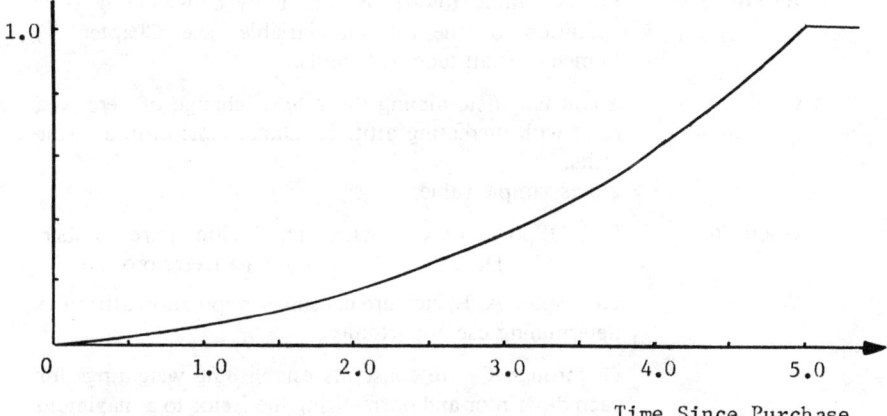

Figure 8.3. Effect of time since purchase on perceived need.

Formulation of Perceived Need

The Perceived Need construct based on attitude, awareness, use opportunity, and product ownership may be summarized in equation form for a particular brand as follows:

Equation 8.1

PRNED(c, b)   PeRceived NEeD of consumer c for product of brand b. Dimension: pure number.

$$= \left[C_1 + \frac{AWARE(c, b)}{C_2} \right] * ENXPF \left(- \frac{5.0 - ATTBR(c, b)}{C_4} \right)$$
$$* USOPC(c) * PROWC(c).$$

C_1 constant specifying the base value of perceived need in the absence of awareness. Dimension: pure number.

= .8 as sample value.

AWARE(c, b) a binary measure of the awareness of consumer c with respect to brand b. (For definition of the awareness variable, see Chapter 5.) Dimension: awareness scale units (binary).

= 1, if aware.

= 0, if unaware.

C_2 a constant establishing the proportionate increase in perceived need added to the base level specified by C_1 as a result of nonzero awareness of brand b for which the perceived need is being formed. Dimension: awareness scale units.

= 5.0 as sample value.

ATTBR(c, b) the ATTitude toward BRand b by consumer c. (For definition of the attitude variable, see Chapter 5.) Dimension: attitude scale units.

C_4 a constant determining the rate of change of perceived need with increasing attitude. Dimension: attitude scale units.

= 2.0 as sample value.

USOPC(c) USe OPportunity Coefficient. Dimension: pure number.

= $(C_5 + C_6 * \text{Descriptor A}) * (C_7 + C_8 * \text{Descriptor B})$.

Where: Descriptor A, B, etc., are consumer population attributes determining use opportunity.

C_5 through C_8 are constants establishing weightings for each descriptor and normalizing the factor to a maximum value of 1.0.

PROWC(c) PRoduct OWnership Coefficient. Dimension: pure number.

= 1, if no ownership.

= $.1 * \left[\text{ENXPF} \left[-\dfrac{t - t\ \text{purchase}}{C_9} \right] - 1.0 \right]$, if ownership.

≤ 1.0, by constraint.

t present time period. Dimension: time units.

t purchase time period in which purchase was made. Dimension: time units.

C_9 a constant based on average product life determining the sensitivity of the product ownership coefficient to the passage of time. Dimension: time units.

Equation 8.1 (Figures 8.1 through 8.3) indicates that (1) increasing attitude toward a brand increases the perceived need for that brand, (2) perceived need increases with time since purchase, and (3) limited use opportunity reduces perceived need.

The Effect of Ability to Purchase

The decision to shop is also influenced by the consumer's ability to purchase, which, for purposes of this model, is manifest in consumer income.

The effect of income on ability to purchase is a function of product cost. As extreme examples, one might contrast the effect of income on ability to purchase the evening paper as opposed to an encyclopedia, a scooter and a Cadillac, a row boat and a yacht. In each instance, the relevant income range and gradations (the relevant step size within the range) are determined by product cost.

The income function is normally expressed as a table specifying the income breaks applicable to the product under consideration. The discrete income function provided as an example in Equation 8.2 was applicable to a specific product (a small appliance) in a particular market area and might be wholly inappropriate for other product classes or markets.

Equation 8.2

INCOM(c) INCOMe of consumer unit c. Dimension: income units.

$= 1$ for consumer unit income > 0 but $< 2,000$
$= 2$ for consumer unit income > 2 but $< 4,000$
$= 3$ for consumer unit income > 4 but $< 6,000$
$= 4$ for consumer unit income > 6 but $< 8,000$
$= 5$ for consumer unit income > 8 but $< 10,000$
$= 6$ for consumer unit income > 10 but $< 15,000$
$= 7$ for consumer unit income $\geq 15,000$

Formulation of the Shopping Decision

The shopping decision may now be formulated as a function of perceived need and income. The probability of consumer c shopping for brand b, given his perceived need for that brand and income level, may be expressed as follows:

Equation 8.3

PRSHP(c, b) PRobability that consumer c will SHoP for brand b. Dimension: pure number (probability).

$= \text{PRNED}(c, b) * (C_{10} + C_{11} * \text{INCOM}(c)).$

C_{10} a constant (in most instances negative) specifying the threshold point above which a nonzero probability of shopping for a particular brand will exist given a specified level of consumer income. Dimension: pure number.

= .5, as sample value.

C_{11} a constant determining the rate at which the probability of shopping increases with increasing income level. Dimension: units per income unit.

= .25, as sample value.

$$0 \le PRSHP(c,b) \le 1.0, \text{ by constraint.}$$

The constraint in equation (8.3) introduces a "clipping function" to ensure that the probability of shopping will not go below zero or above one. The clipping function produces discontinuities that could be avoided by using an exponential asymptotically approaching zero and one at its limits. The simple constraint is more efficient in use of computer time, and the impact of discontinuities is not serious in this instance.

The probability that consumer c will shop for brand b is summarized in the family of curves shown in Figure 8.4.

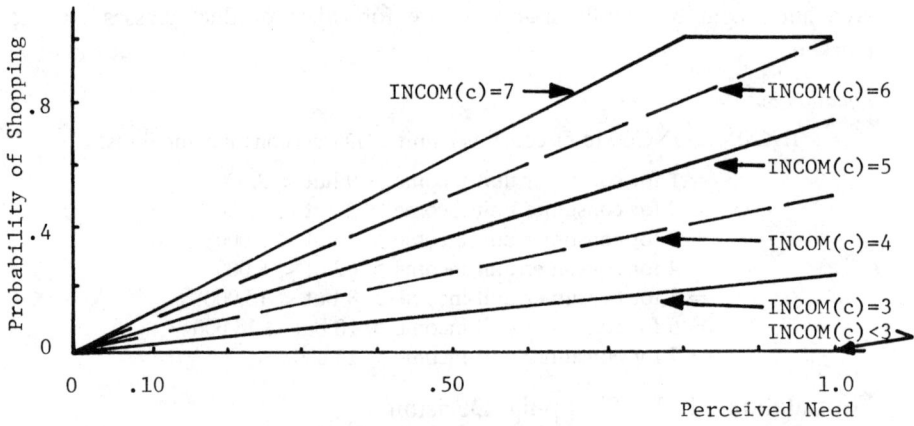

Figure 8.4. Probability of shopping as function of perceived need and income.

Equation 8.3 establishes that consumer c is most apt to shop for that brand for which he has the highest perceived need. His probability of shopping for a product of the type considered is his probability of shopping for *any* brand within that line and may be represented as follows:

Equation 8.3A

PRSHP(c)   PRobability of consumer c SHoPping for product line (implied). Dimension: pure number (ratio).

$$= \sum_{b=1}^{B} \text{PRSHP}(c, b).$$

It is sometimes argued that the consumer who decides not to shop for the brand for which his perceived need is highest will under no circumstance decide to shop for a lower priority brand. If this reasoning is accepted, a single calculation based on the highest priority brand establishes the probability of shopping for the product. Implementing this assumption, Equation 8.3 becomes

Equation 8.3B

$\text{PRSHP}(c) = \text{PRSHP}(c, b_m).$

b_m brand b for which $\text{PRNED}(c, b)$ is maximum.

From Shopping to Purchase

The previously developed formulations indicate only the probability that consumer c will start on his way toward a shopping experience. They specify nothing about the store he will visit or his probability of encountering displays, salesmen, or particular brands of product.

Following the outline established earlier, the next process to be modeled is that associated with the purchase decision. In proceeding in this sequence, there is no intention to imply that the decision to purchase follows immediately the decision to shop. Events in the chain linking the decisions to shop and purchase will be explored in detail later in this chapter. For the moment, it will be assumed that all intervening events have occurred, and the consumer has reached the point of deciding whether or not to purchase a particular brand.

The Consumer Decision to Purchase

An Economist's View

To the economist, the consumer purchase decision is a choice between alternatives in which the principle of diminishing marginal utility determines the outcome. Given a fixed income and a constant utility function, each unit of a product purchased during a specified time interval has decreasing utility for the consumer. In the context of this type of model, it is possible to speak of optimal allocation of income among alternative products so as to achieve a utility from the last unit of each product purchased that is proportional to the relative price paid to acquire that unit.

Although some economists have attempted to take account of changing consumer preferences, the normal microeconomic treatment assumes constant utility functions.[25] This model assumes that the consumer does not respond to experience. His perceived need cannot change in response to information acquired through communication or use.

The possible effects of consumer interaction must be ignored by the microeconomist because his model requires that individual utility functions be independent and market demand derivable as a summation over individual demand functions.[26]

Microeconomic theory largely ignores consumer choice between brands. It is most apt to focus on the choice among assumed homogeneous product classes, with interclass effects characterized in terms of extent of product substitutability or complementarity. Description of class interaction is normally confined to examinations of the cross elasticity with respect to price.

Behavioral Perspectives

Wroe Alderson suggests that the consumer in a purchase situation is uncertain as to which of several available courses of action is most appropriate. In context of this hypothesis, purchase behavior is viewed as an effort ". . . to reduce uncertainty to the point where a course of action can be adopted with some confidence . . . the problem solver is trying to see the essential structure in a complicated situation and trying to make the best gamble in being prepared for future requirements which are subject to chance variations." [27]

Consideration of motives leads to additional complexities. One author has suggested that ". . . many purchasing decisions are made not in order to acquire but in order to destroy, in order to gratify hostility

[25] For a discussion of the implications of changing consumer preferences see: R. L. Basmann, "A Theory of Demand with Variable Consumer Preferences," *Econometrica,* Vol. 20 (January 1955), pp. 47–58.

[26] The implications of this constraint are noted in O. Morgenstern, "Demand Theory Reconsidered," *The Quarterly Journal of Economics,* 62 (1947–1948), p. 175.

[27] W. Alderson, *op. cit.,* Footnote 22, p. 167.

rather than to attain comfort or enjoyment. These purchasing decisions can be judged to be symptomatic because they do not facilitate living but make it more burdensome for the purchaser and his associates. . . . A recognition of the destructive purposes of purchasing decisions . . . suggests a source of customer motivation of considerable effectiveness, the exploitation of which, however, would be incompatible with the traditional value system of our culture." [28]

Observers of purchase behavior often emphasize those aspects of consumer behavior that are explained by apparently rational factors such as price or distribution coverage. This focus may ignore factors responsible for the majority of behavior. In one study, "cognitive behavior" was noted as responsible for about 20 percent of the observed market activity.[29]

The Effect of Past Experience

Experiences affect the consumer's orientation toward and knowledge of product characteristics, appeals, and brand name identifications. In this model structure, the orientation variables, attitude and awareness serve as intermediaries linking experiences in the environment to the ultimate decision to buy or reject a given brand of product. In this sense, attitude and awareness represent the *net* effect of consumer responses through a point in time.

The Impact of Experience at Point of Sale

Consumer point-of-sale experience may include exposure to promotional material, product displays, and salesman presentations. The impact of these aspects of point-of-sale experience will be described through a generalized response model developed later in this chapter. The potential effects of product availability, salesman emphasis on a particular brand, and the price at which brands are offered require separate consideration.

Product availability can be dispensed with by limiting purchase decision alternatives to brands available in the store in which the decision is made. This constraint ensures that the simulated consumer's purchase decision will encompass only brands stocked by this simulated retailer.

---

[28] O. Pollak, "Symptomatic Factors in Consumer Behavior," in Cox, Alderson, and Shapiro, *Theory in Marketing* (Homewood, Ill.: Richard D. Irwin, Inc., 1964), pp. 281–288, from 282.

[29] B. Gedalecia, "The Communicators: An All Media Study," Third Annual Advertising Research Foundation Conference, November 14, 1957.

Selective positive emphasis on one brand by the retail salesman, regardless of accompanying communication content, serves to pressure the customer to take action favoring the emphasized brand. Consumer response to such pressure will be considered later in this section. Because retail salesman "push" is not present within some retail environments (e.g., supermarkets), models oriented toward products sold through such outlets ignore this factor.

The Price-Quality Syndrome

The meaning of price changes from consumer to consumer. That which is acceptable to one consumer is wholly unrealistic in the eyes of another. Price must be considered in light of the orientation of the consumer who perceives it as but one attribute of a product having many characteristics.

While price is a brand attribute in the same sense as color, size, or operating characteristics, the importance of price may be greater than that of most product characteristics. In addition to the previously noted relationship between price, income, and willingness to consider purchase, one encounters an important class of consumer expectations founded on the assumption that quality costs more. In the words of a leading coffee producer's television commercial, "As John Arbuckle would say, you get what you pay for."

It is not necessary to enter the exotic realm of precious stone markets to encounter evidence of this price expectation phenomenon. In the industrial market for an electronic computer trainer, a product that at $85 was viewed as an "expensive toy" became a respectable "scientific-educational-device" when the price was raised to $235. Consumers had basic expectations regarding computers. Regardless of production costs or visible simplicity, a product associated with this technology had to cost hundreds of dollars. If it did not, it could not be legitimate.

If a consumer's price expectations are exceeded at either end of the price scale, he becomes suspicious and his probability of purchase is reduced. At the same time, he may assume a correlation between price and quality. This assumption is manifest in the behavior exhibited when the consumer in search of a wedding present is shown a $7 glass bowl and indicates, "I'd like something a little nicer, don't you have anything in the $10 to $12 range." The customer seeking a product of given value accepts price as a basis for evaluation. She does not want a "cheap" product but, on the other hand, does not want to "splurge." A higher-priced product is more effective in satisfying the consumer's need for the display of status symbols than one of lower price.[30]

Roger Brown notes an interesting aspect of the price-quality syndrome in his discussion of persuasion, expression, and propaganda in *Words and Things*.

The best way to get a product accepted as a symbol of high status is to charge a high price for it but, in that case, it probably will in truth be associated with people of high status and so its advertising does not lie and people get what they pay for.[31]

Formulation of the Purchase Decision

The consumer purchase decision may be described in terms of the interaction between price, attitude and awareness (summarizing the net effect of other environmental influences) and salesman selling effort.

Price Effects

Two effects of price on probability of purchase have been noted. The first parallels the income-dependent effect on probability of shopping. The second applies within comparable brand groups where the probability of purchase increases as price decreases. Exceptions to this rule involve the price-quality syndrome.

The Income-Dependent Price Effect.   The income-dependent price effect varies with product classes. The range and sensitivity of a function appropriate for automobile purchase is simply not applicable to the glass bowl purchasing situation noted earlier. A representative formulation of the price effect based on appliance data will be presented as an example.

Figure 8.5 illustrates the basic characteristics of the income-dependent price effect. Acceptable price levels are higher for upper-income groups than for lower-level population segments. In addition, the upper-income groups are hesitant to purchase a product priced substantially below an expected range.

For purposes of illustration, a step function and table formulation are used to illustrate the income-dependent effect of price on purchase. In practice, the table function in Equation 8.4, p. 178, would be replaced by a logistic to eliminate discontinuities and associated conceptual problems.

[30] For a discussion of the status value of price, see T. Veblen, *The Theory of the Leisure Class* (New York: Modern Library, Inc., 1934), pp. 68–101.
[31] R. Brown, *Words and Things* (Glencoe, Illinois, Free Press, 1958), p. 337.

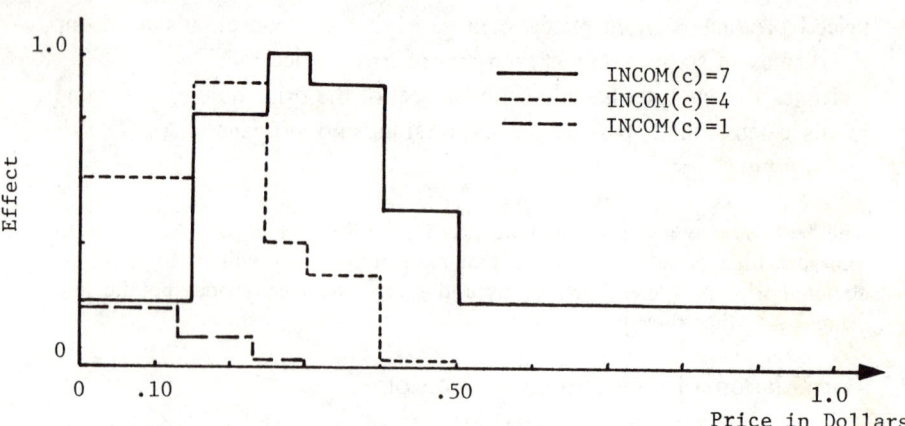

Figure 8.5. Income-dependent price effect on probability of purchase.

The discrete price step formulation is based on the observation that consumers perceive prices as falling within a range, that prices within a given range are viewed as approximately equivalent, and that definite barriers are encountered when the price moves from one range to another. For example, the illustration plotted in Figure 8.5 indicates a major price break at $40. The consumer perceives prices between $30 and $40 as substantially different from those between $40 and $50. This price break concept is the basis of much retail pricing.[32]

The Relative Price Effect.   Within comparable brand sets, the probability of brand purchase increases as the price difference favoring a brand increases. If the consumer considers two brands within the same income-sensitive price range to be equivalent in terms of product characteristics and appeals, he is more apt to purchase the lower priced brand.

The relative price effect has been verified against price deviations within normally encountered ranges (e.g., 29¢ to 36¢ on a food product package size normally retailing for 33¢). While it is possible to imagine more extreme deviations, cost considerations largely constrain real-world behavior except in the case of unusual price leader or dumping promotions involving small quantities of merchandise.

Within normally encountered ranges, the relative price effect is linear

---

[32] See, for example, "A Specific Price and Output Model," in R. M. Cyert and J. G. March, *A Behavioral Theory of the Firm* (Englewood Cliffs, N.J.: Prentice-Hall, Inc., 1963), pp. 128–148.

as illustrated in Figure 8.6, subject to the constraints specified in Equation 8.4.

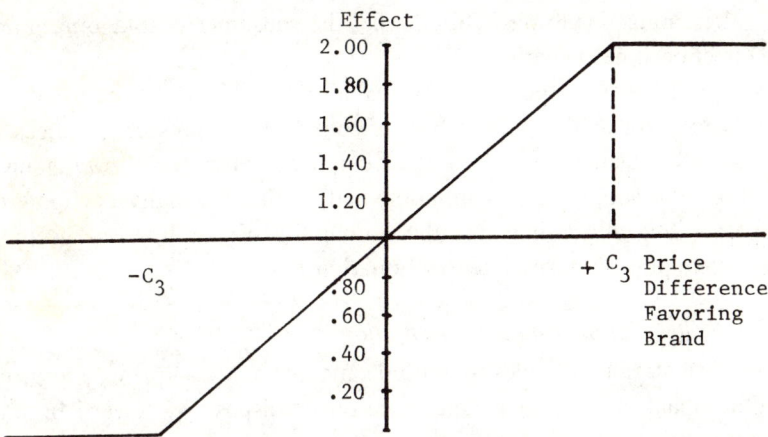

Figure 8.6. Relative price effect.

The Effect of Selling Effort

The effect of retail salesman selling effort or "push" on consumer purchase is positive in most instances; within the normally encountered range of selling pressure, this activity increases the probability of purchase. The effect may generally be assumed proportional to the effort expended by the salesman as illustrated by the solid line in Figure 8.7.

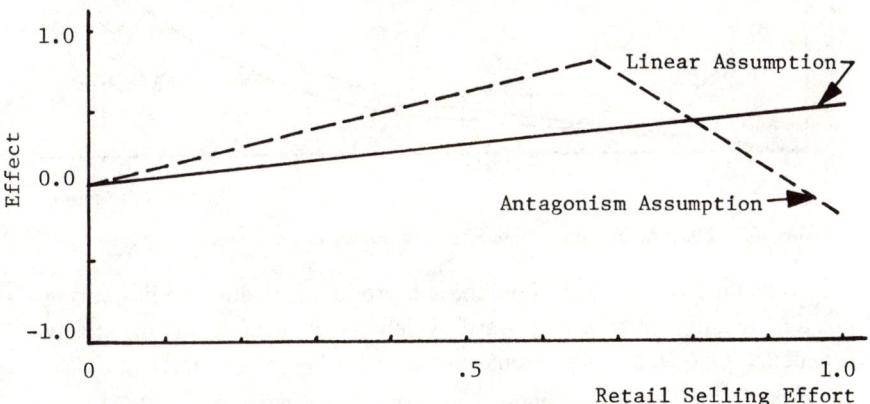

Figure 8.7. Effect of retailer selling effort on probability of purchase.

In some instances, extreme salesman selling effort antagonizes the consumer and produces a negative effect deterring rather than encouraging purchase. The dotted line on Figure 8.7 illustrates this negative effect of extreme selling effort. Selling effort is effective up to a point, but as the salesman begins to push "too hard," the consumer is antagonized and the effect becomes negative.

While the negative effect is observable, it is difficult to determine the transition point — the point where effective selling pressure changes to antagonistic push. In the absence of empirical bases for an antagonism function, the simplifying assumption that, within normally encountered ranges, selling effort increases the probability of purchase is accepted. This assumption is formulated in Equation 8.4.

The Effect of Consumer Orientation

The orientation variables — attitude and awareness —provide a record of the impact of consumer experience on predisposition toward brands. In this context, attitudes are part of the organism's cognitive approach to its environment as ". . . enduring predispositions for or against . . . objects, people, or events." [33]

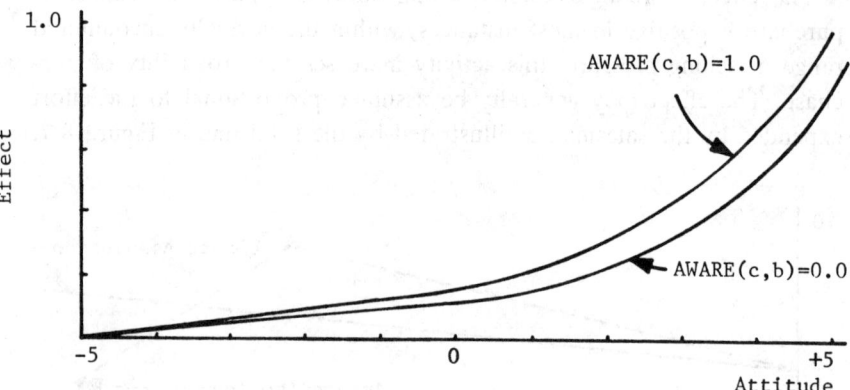

Figure 8.8. Effect of consumer attitude on probability of purchase.

A consumer is more apt to purchase a product for which he has strong positive feelings than one toward which he is neutral or negatively oriented.[34] One would not ordinarily expect to find a consumer purchas-

[33] D. Krech and R. S. Crutchfield, *Theory and Problems of Social Psychology* (New York: McGraw-Hill Book Company, Inc., 1948), p. 64.

[34] The one exception to this condition encountered in research relating the attitude variable to purchase activity concerns the housewife who may buy certain products for other family members despite her own dislike of the product. This phenomenon is particularly prevalent in the purchase of specialty foods.

ing a product that he regards negatively. In most instances, the probability of purchase increases as attitude increases. Figure 8.8 summarizes the observed phenomenon that very high attitudes are more apt to produce action than medium attitudes. As in the shopping case, awareness has been found to amplify the effect of attitude on purchase.

The attitude variable employed in this formulation is a narrowly defined measure of orientation toward specific brands. George Katona of the Survey Research Center, University of Michigan, has made use of a broader but conceptually similar measure of changes in consumer attitudes toward durable goods as a class. The "index of consumer attitudes" described as a measure of "psychological propensities" focuses on general outlook rather than attitude toward specific products, brands, or product characteristics.[35]

The Index of Consumer Attitudes is an average of eight attitudes: recent change in own financial situation, expected change in own financial situation, one-year business outlook, five-year business outlook, evaluations of buying conditions for household goods, price expectations, plans to buy home, plans to buy automobile.[36]

The Nature of Factor Interaction

Given definition of the three factors influencing the probability of purchase, it is necessary to consider the form of interaction between them.

If product is not available, the consumer cannot purchase it. Therefore product availability enters the formulation as a multiplier that, when zero (indicating absence of product), totally negates the effect of other factors.

In the limiting case where salesman push is absent, other factors remain unchanged. On the other hand, extremely high salesman push would be expected to produce a substantial effect (negative or positive depending upon the function adopted) on other factors. The effect of salesman push is therefore additive.

The interaction between price and other determinants of the purchase decision outcome parallels that already noted for product availability. If product is given away, the consumer will not refuse unless the price-

[35] G. Katona and E. Mueller, *Consumer Expectations,* Survey Research Center, Ann Arbor, Michigan, 1956.

[36] G. Katona, "Consumer Buying Habits: Analysis of Ten-Year-Study," *The Integrated Approach to Product Planning,* Marketing Series No. 101 (New York: American Management Association, 1957), p. 60.

quality syndrome is manifest in a suspicion that "there must be a gimmick." On the other hand, if the product is greatly overpriced, the consumer will not purchase regardless of other factor values. The price effect is thus multiplicative.

The impact of the orientation variable is similarly multiplicative. An unusually high or low attitude biases the purchase decision outcome in a manner represented by a geometric weighting.

These interactions between price, salesman push, consumer attitude and awareness, and product availability are expressed in Equation 8.4:

Equation 8.4

PRPCH(c, b, r)	PRobability that consumer c will PurCHase brand b in retail outlet r. Dimension: pure number (probability).

$$= \text{EFPPU}(c, b) * \text{EFSMPP}(r, b) * \text{EATBP}(c, b) * \text{CARRY}(b, r).$$

$$0 \le \text{PRPCH}(c, b, r) \le 1.0, \text{ by constraint.}$$

EFPPU(c, b)   EFfect of Price of brand b on Probability of consumer c PUrchase. Dimension: pure number.

$$= \text{PRICIN}(c, b) + \left[1 - \frac{\text{PRICE}(b, r) - \text{AVPRIC}(r)}{C_3 * \text{AVPRIC}(r)} \right]$$

$$0 \le \text{EFPPU}(c, b) \le 2.0, \text{ by constraint.}$$

PRICE(b, r)   PRICE charged for brand b by retailer r.
= Output of Retailer Model. See Equation 9.8.

AVPRIC(r)   AVerage PRICe charged for brands in product line carried by retailer r.

$$= \frac{\sum_{b'=1}^{Br} \text{PRICE}(b', r)}{Br}.$$

Br   total number of brands carried by retailer r.
= output of retailer model. See Equation 9.3A.

C_3 a constant determining the effect of relative price differentials. Dimension: pure number.
= .10 as sample value.

PRICIN(c, b)   PRICe INcome effect on probability of consumer c purchasing brand b. Dimension: pure number.
= a table function based on INCOM(c) specifying a value for the price coefficient for each discrete price level.

EFSMPP   EFfect of SalesMan Push in retail outlet r on the probability of Purchase of brand b in that outlet. Dimension: pure number.
$= 1 + C_{12} * \text{RETSLE}(r, b).$

C_{12} a constant specifying the effect of salesman's push on the probability of purchase — the slope of the effectiveness curve. Dimension: units per units of selling effort.
= .5 as sample value.

RETSLE(r, b) RETail SeLling Effort in favor of brand b in retail outlet r. Dimension: units of selling effort (proportion of time).
= a function of elements of the model of retailer behavior formulated and discussed in Chapter 11 (Range: 0 to 1.0).

EATBP(c, b) Effect of consumer c's Attitude Toward brand b on probability of Purchase. Dimension: pure number.

If $ATTBR(c, b) \geq 0.0$,
$$= (C_1 + AWARE(c, b)/C_2)$$
$$* ENXPF\left[-\frac{C_{13} - ATTBR(c, b)}{C_{14}}\right].$$

If $ATTBR(c, b) < 0.0$,
$$= (C_1 + AWARE(c, b)/C_2) * \frac{(C_{15} + ATTBR(c, b))}{C_{16}}.$$

C_{13} and C_{15} constants specifying the limiting value of the attitude effect in the case of positive and negative attitude, respectively. Dimension: attitude scale units.
= 5.0 as sample values.

ATTBR(c, b) ATtitude of consumer c Toward BRand b. Dimension: attitude scale units.
= see Equation 8.42, p. 226.

C_{14} and C_{16} constants indicating the rate of change in the effectiveness function as a result of changes in the positive or negative attitude, respectively. Dimension: attitude scale units.
= 2.5 and 37. as sample values, respectively.

CARRY(b, r) specification of brands CARRied by retailer r. Dimension: pure number (binary).
= 0.0, if b not carried, or 1.0, if b carried, as function of retailer model discussed in Chapter 9.

Probabilistic formulation of the purchase decision process avoids many of the problems encountered by those who attempt to make exact yes-no predictions and are forced to conclude that consumers are "inconsistent and unpredictable" when black-white predictions are not validated.

Even though a housewife may truly prefer one product sample to another, she cannot be expected to be perfectly accurate in recognizing the one she prefers. Being neither an automaton nor a laboratory technician, she may be influenced in her choice by factors other than the actual differences between two samples. Thus it is reasonable to think of her ability to recognize the sample she prefers in probabilistic terms. If her preferences are strong and the differences in product are great, she will have a high probability of selecting the one she truly prefers. But if differences are slight and her preferences are weak, the probability that the housewife will recognize the item she prefers may be little better than .5.[37]

Experience After Purchase

If the consumer purchases a brand, his probability of continuing to shop is substantially reduced by the time-since-purchase effect of the probability of shopping function. If no purchase is made, he may continue to shop in the same or in other stores. Following purchase, the consumer may respond to use experience — be satisfied or dissatisfied with brand performance evaluated in terms of expectations formed prior to purchase. Consideration of response to product usage will be delayed until the discussion of response models in a later section.

The Consumer's Decision to Talk about a Brand

Product experience after purchase may motivate the consumer to talk about the brand purchased — to generate word-of-mouth communication. This section is devoted to a discussion of factors determining the probability that consumer c will generate word-of-mouth communication regarding brand b.

Effect of Time Since Purchase

Because the importance of a purchase decision diminishes over time, it is not surprising to find the probability of word-of-mouth generation based on purchase decreasing with time since purchase.

The Effect of Consumer Orientation

The previously defined orientation variables offer a conceptually sound and mathematically simple solution to the problem of representing the basis for differential probabilities of word-of-mouth generation. Empirical findings indicate that consumers talk about products of which

[37] A. A. Kuehn and R. L. Day, "A Probabilistic Approach to Consumer Behavior," in Cox, Alderson, and Shapiro (eds.), *Theory in Marketing* (Homewood, Ill.: Richard D. Irwin, Inc., 1964), p. 390.

they are "aware" and are more apt to discuss a product about which they have strong feelings either positive or negative; people with high positive or negative attitudes are more apt to talk than those with low or neutral attitudes.

The Probability of Word-of-Mouth Generation

The time-since-purchase effect establishes that a consumer is most apt to be aware of and/or have a strong attitude about a product immediately following response and before forgetting has occurred.[38] The attitude and awareness effect yields an increased probability of word-of-mouth generation by the consumer who forms strong opinions as a result of use after purchase. The combined effects provide for continued generation by the consumer who continues to maintain awareness of and high attitudes without regard to his position in the purchase time cycle.

These concepts are summarized in Figure 8.9 and Equation 8.5.

Equation 8.5

PRWMG(c, b)   PRobability that consumer c will Generate Word-of-Mouth communication regarding brand b. Dimension: pure number.

$$= \left[1 - \text{ENXPF} \left(-\left| \frac{\text{ATTBR(c, b)}}{C_{17}} \right| \right) \right] * \text{AWARE(c, b)}.$$

ATTBR(c, b)   the ATTitude of consumer c toward BRand b. (It should be noted that the absolute magnitude of the attitude variable is used in this formulation.) Dimension: attitude scale units.

$= -5$ to $+5$ per Equation 8.42, p. 226.

C_{17} a constant determining the rate of change in the probability of word-of-mouth generation as a result of a one-unit change in the value of the attitude variable. Dimension: attitude scale units.

$= 2.0$ as sample value.

AWARE(c, b)   the value of the AWAREness variable for consumer c with reference to brand b. Dimension: pure number (binary).

$= 1.0$, if aware per formulations developed later in this chapter.

$= 0.0$, if unaware per formulations developed later in this chapter.

---

[38] The attitude and awareness formation processes are discussed in a later section of this chapter. See "Brand Attitude Formation" on page 224.

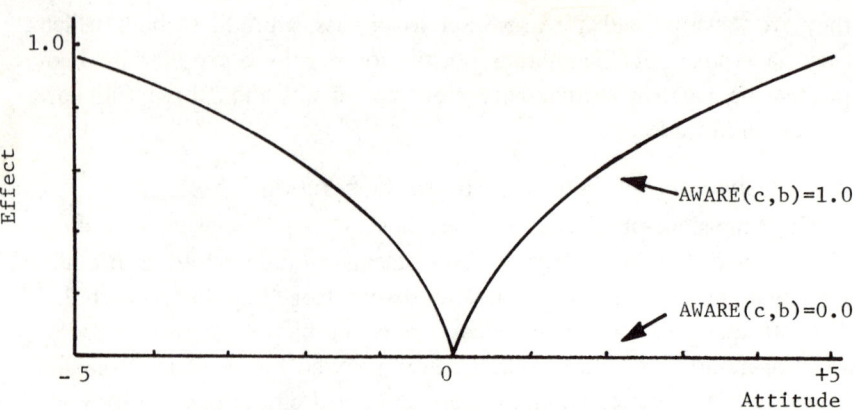

Figure 8.9. Effect of attitude and awareness on probability of word-of-mouth generation.

Content of Word-of-Mouth Communication

If the consumer talks about a brand, what will he say? What will be the "content of word-of-mouth communication" generated? This is the question to be answered in this section.

The Impact of Attitude

The content of consumer communication is determined in part by the attitudes of the communicating consumer. Representation of this effect involves the previously discussed assumptions that (1) a product can be described in terms of NP product characteristics and AP appeals, and (2) consumers have attitudes toward product characteristics and appeals. If the consumer's attitudes toward characteristics associated with a brand are predominantly negative, the consumer's response to the brand is negatively biased. Conversely, strong positive attitudes toward characteristics of a brand produce positively biased responses. In the case of a neutral attitude, the related attribute is assumed to be unimportant to the consumer.

The Brand Image Concept

Implications of this model of consumer brand orientation are discussed in conjunction with response function formulation later in this chapter. For purposes of this discussion it is sufficient to note that a consumer's attitude toward characteristics weighted by the relative prominence of each characteristic in accumulated perceived communication will define that consumer's "perceived brand image."

Equation 8.6

> PEBRI(c, n, b) PErceived BRand Image of consumer c with reference to characteristic n of brand b. Dimension: attitude scale units.
> = see Equation 8.41, p. 225.

The consumer's attitude toward product characteristic np is independent of brand. However, unless communication regarding all brands as perceived by the consumer is identical, different characteristics will be associated with each brand and the consumer's perceived image of the brands will be different.

As an example, consider a consumer who abhors product characteristic A. If characteristic A has not been associated with brand 1, the consumer's perceived brand image of brand 1 is not affected by his strong dislike. If, on the other hand, communication received regarding brand 2 has included a strong emphasis on product characteristic A, the consumer, with his strong negative bias against product feature A, will be sensitive to it and his perceived image of brand 2 will be adversely affected.

Formulation of Content Generated

Because consumers talk about the world they perceive, the content of word-of-mouth communication regarding b generated by consumer c may be expressed in terms of his perceived brand image.

Equation 8.7

> CONWMC(c, n, b) CONtent (extent and bias) of Word-of-Mouth Communication regarding characteristic n of brand b generated by consumer c. Dimension: attitude scale units.
> = PEBRI(c, n, b).

> CONWMC(c, b) CONtent (net) of Word-of-Mouth Communication regarding brand b generated by consumer c. Dimension: attitude scale units.

$$= \sum_{n=1}^{N} PEBRI(c, n, b).$$

The prevailing consensus of existing word-of-mouth communication at a population level may be expressed as the summation of the perceived brand images of those generating word-of-mouth communication at that time.

Equation 8.7A

CONWMC(n, b)   CONtent (consensus) of Word-of-Mouth Communica-
                 tion regarding characteristic n of brand b. Dimension:
                 attitude scale units.

$$= \sum_{c=1}^{\text{NWMG}} \text{PEBRI}(c, np, b).$$

NWMG   Number of consumer Word-of-Mouth Generators
                               talking about brand b.

Equation 8.7A should be interpreted as a selective summation over the NWMG consumers who are talking about brand b.

A Review of Three Consumer Decisions

Factors discussed in this portion of the chapter are summarized in Figure 8.10, which illustrates the decisions to shop, purchase, and talk about a product.

As indicated by this flow chart, the decision to shop is a function of the consumer's income (an exogenously supplied characteristic of the consumer population indicated by a circle), and the consumer's perceived need for the product.

Perceived need is shown as a function of the derived consumer use opportunity, product ownership, attitude, and awareness. An oval indicates a factor derived endogenously within the model rather than supplied exogenously from outside the model.

The purchase rate, inventory, and usage rate are shown with dotted rather than solid line enclosures to indicate that they are not covered by formulations developed thus far.

The decision to talk, based on consumer attitude and awareness, determines the rate of word-of-mouth generation, while word-of-mouth content is a function of consumer attitudes and the rate and content of assimilated communication. Because the perceived brand image function has not been formulated, it, as well as the communication input, is represented by a dotted enclosure.

Consumer Reactions and Responses

This section will be devoted to the representation of consumer exposure and response to advertising, point-of-sale promotion, salesman communication, word-of-mouth discussions, product exposure, and product usage.

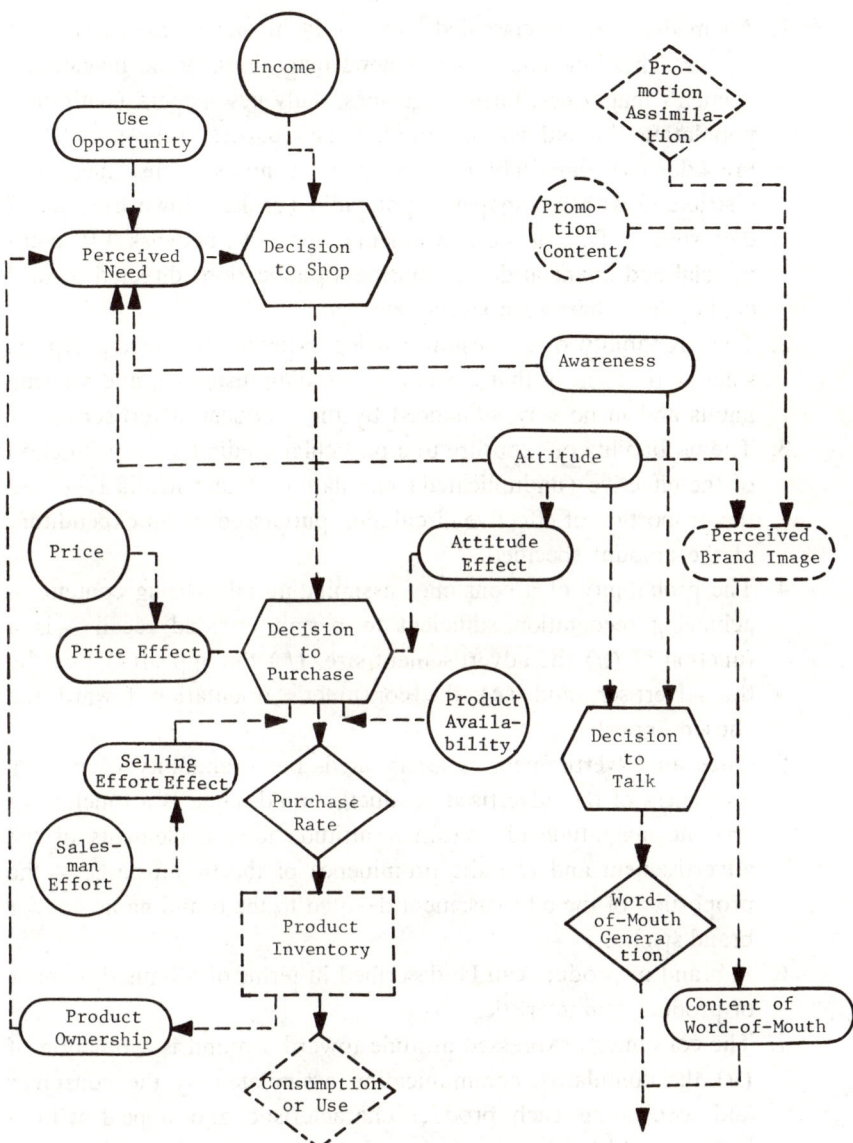

Figure 8.10. Factors influencing three consumer decisions.

Consumer Exposure and Response to Media Communication

The generalized model of consumer response to advertising presented in this section may be summarized in the following assertions regarding information transmitted through formal media channels.

1. All media may be classified exclusively in one of m media type classes. These include: general news magazines, home magazines, women's magazines, farm magazines, daily newspapers (with city-population breakdowns), Sunday newspapers (city-population breakdowns), daily tabloids, newspaper comic sections, magazines distributed with newspapers, spot radio (broken down by time of day, spot, "I.D.", or announcement), spot TV, network TV, commercial and financial dailies, business publications directed toward chain stores, hardware stores, etc.

2. The probability of a consumer being exposed to a media type is solely a function of that consumer's reading, listening, and viewing habits and in no way influenced by the producer-advertiser.

3. The probability of exposure to a particular media type is a function of the effective (unduplicated) circulation of that media type and the proportion of effective circulation purchased by an expenditure of the amount specified.

4. The probability of a consumer assimilating advertising content — achieving recognition sufficient to permit unaided recall — is a function of (a) the advertisement size, (b) the appeal(s) used by the advertiser, and (c) the consumer's orientation toward the chosen appeal.

5. Once an advertisement is assimilated, the probability of gaining awareness of the advertised product's brand name is a function of (a) the magnitude of consumer attitude toward elements of the advertisement and (b) the prominence of the brand name — the proportion of the advertisement devoted to the brand name and/or brand symbols.

6. A brand or product can be described in terms of a limited number of product characteristics.

7. The consumer's expressed attitude toward a brand is a function of (a) the cumulative communication assimilated by the consumer and associating each product characteristic and appeal with a brand and (b) the consumer's attitude toward each product characteristic and appeal component of the assimilated brand image.

Probability of Media Exposure

Each consumer is assumed to have certain media available to him throughout the simulated time period. The probability of consumer c being exposed to media type m is established by the value of a corresponding exposure cell. For purposes of this model, a binary indicator specifies the presence or absence of availability. In more refined models this indicator is expanded to an exposure probability measure.

The media availability characteristic of the consumer cell is defined as

Equation 8.8

> AVMED(c, m)   AVailability of MEDia type m to consumer c.
> = 1, if media available,
> = 0, if media not available.

Probability of Exposure to Media Promotion

Once it is known that media type m is available to consumer c, it is necessary to determine whether or not that consumer will be exposed to the specific combination of media within media type m that a particular advertiser has chosen to use in promoting his brand.

Given Total Expenditure

If only the advertiser's total expenditure in media type m is known, the probability of exposure, given availability of media type m, must be developed as a function of the advertising expenditure in the media type and the applicable saturation level of advertising expenditure — that level at which all consumers having media within media type m available will be reached.

Equation 8.9

> ADVEXP(b, m, t)   ADVertising EXPenditure promoting brand b in media type m at time t. Dimension: value units (dollars) per time period.
> = Input from manufacturer sector. See Equation 7.7.[39]
>
> SATADV(m)   SATuration level of ADVertising expenditure for media type m. Dimension: value units (dollars) per time period.
> = Media descriptor. See Equation 7.5.

The probability of exposing a subscriber to media of type m during time period t with a total advertising expenditure of ADVEXP(b, m, t) may be approximated by the ratio of actual to saturation expenditure as illustrated in Figure 8.11.

Equation 8.10

> PRMTEX(b, m, t)   PRobability of Media type m EXposure regarding brand b during time period t. Dimension: pure number.

$$= 1 - \text{ENXPF}\left[-C_{18} * \frac{\text{ADVEXP}(b, m, t)}{\text{SATADV}(m)}\right].$$

C_{18} a constant determining the rate of change of exposure probability with expenditure. Dimension: pure number.

$= 3.0$, as sample value.

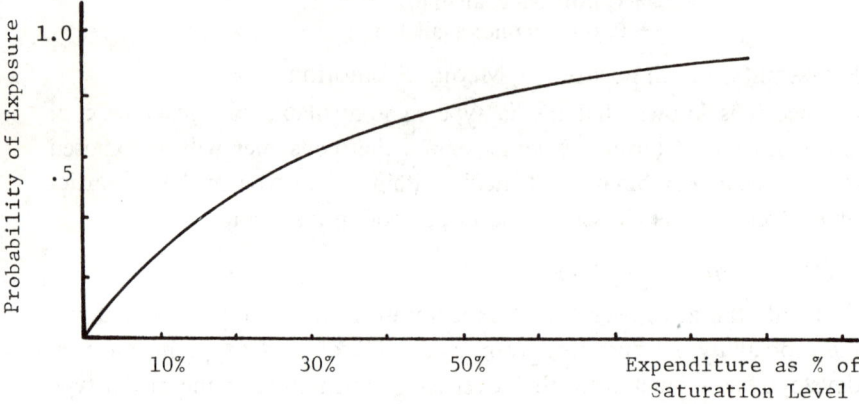

Figure 8.11. Probability of exposure to media type m.

Given Advertisement Cost

In the case of a multitheme campaign it may be important to consider the probability of exposure to a particular advertisement. If more than one advertisement is used in media type m and the allocation of advertising expenditure among advertisements is known, the probability of exposure to advertisement na during time period t may be formulated as

Equation 8.11

PRADEX(na, t)   PRobability of ADvertisement EXposure to advertisement na (promoting brand b in media type m at time t). Dimension: pure number.

$$= 1 - \text{ENXPF}\left[-C_{18} * \frac{\text{ADVEXP}(na, m, t)}{\text{SATADV}(m)}\right].$$

[39] The subscript b identifying the brand to which promotion relates is implicitly identified in the manufacturer sector and does not appear explicitly in the Chapter 7 formulation. It is required in this formulation to account for the availability of promotion from several manufacturers.

Given Media Characteristics

Given media characteristics for medium mn within media type m, the probability of exposure to advertisement na appearing in a combination of media may be explicitly expressed as

Equation 8.11A

PRADEX(na, t)	PRobability of ADvertisement EXposure to advertisement na at time t. Dimension: pure number.

$$= [CIRCUL(1) * AVPGEX(1) * SCHED(1, na, t)$$
$$+ CIRCUL(2) * AVPGEX(2) * SCHED(2, na, t)$$
$$* (1 - OVRLAP(2, 1) * SCHED(1, na, t)) \dots$$
$$+ \dots CIRCUL(mn) * AVPGEX(mn)$$
$$* SCHED(mn, na, t) * (1 - (OVRLAP(mn, 1)$$
$$* SCHED(1, na, t) \dots + \dots OVRLAP(mn, mn - 1)$$
$$* SCHED(mn - 1, na, t)))]/TOTPOP(m).$$

CIRCUL(mn)	CIRCULation — Coverage — of medium mn. Dimension: cell units.
	= media characteristic. See Equation 7.6.
OVRLAP(mn, l)	OVeRLAP in circulation of media l and mn. Dimension: pure number (ratio).
	= media characteristic. See Equation 7.6.
AVPGEX(mn)	AVerage PaGe EXposure probability for advertisement in medium mn.
SCHED(mn, na, t)	SCHEDule of medium mn (of media type m) for advertisement na at time t. Dimension: pure number (binary).
	= input from manufacturer sector. See Equation 7.7.
	= 1, advertisement is scheduled.
	= 0, advertisement is not scheduled.
TOTPOP(m)	TOTal POPulation — unduplicated circulation to which media type m is available. Dimension: cell units.
	= media characteristic. See Equation 7.5.

Consumer Advertisement Exposure

Equation 8.11A expresses the probability that a consumer who has media type m available will be exposed to a *particular advertisement* (na) in one or more media mn of type m. The probability of a particular consumer c being exposed to ad na is advertisement na's exposure probability weighted by consumer c's media availability coefficient.

Equation 8.12

> PRADEX(c, na, t)   PRobability of consumer c being EXposed to ADvertisement na at time t. Dimension: pure number.
> = AVMED(c, m(na)) $*$ PRADEX(na, t).
>
> m(na)   media type in which advertisement na appears.
> = descriptor of advertisement na based on SCHED (mn, na, t).

Probability of Assimilating an Advertisement

Given that consumer c is exposed to advertisement na, his probability of assimilating that advertisement — of achieving a degree of cognizance sufficient to permit later unaided recall of advertising content — has been shown to be affected by ad size and color.[40]

Within the normally encountered range of advertisement sizes, the effect of advertisement size on the probability of recall may be described by the following linear relationship.

Equation 8.13

> EFADSZ(na)   EFfect of ADvertisement SiZe on probability of assimilation of advertisement na. Dimension: pure number.
> = $C_{19} * $ ADVSIZ(na).
>
> ADVSIZ(na)   ADvertisement SIZe measured for advertisement na. Dimension: pure number (ratio).
> = advertisement descriptor. Input from manufacturer sector. See Equation 7.8.
>
> C_{19} a scaling constant determining the change in effect per unit change in size. Dimension: pure number.
> = .43, as sample value.

While the previously footnoted research indicates a more complex relationship, for purposes of this representation the probability of recall will be related to the presence of color as follows:

Equation 8.14

> EFADCL(na)   EFfect of ADvertising in CoLor on probability of assimilation of advertisement na. Dimension: pure number.
> = $C_{20} * $ ADVCLR(na).
>
> ADVCLR(na)   ADVertisement CoLor as measured for promotion na. Dimension: pure number (binary).

---

[40] The representation of the effect of color and page size on probability of exposure adopted for use in this model is based on an analysis of readership recognition reported in D. W. Twedt, "A Multiple Factor Analysis of Advertising Readership," *Journal of Applied Psychology*, Vol. 36 (June 1952), pp. 207–215.

= advertisement descriptor. Input from manufacturer sector. See Equation 7.8.

= 1.0, if color present.

= 0, if black and white.

C_{20} a scaling constant determining the change in effect due to presence of color. Dimension: pure.

= .57 as sample value.

The combined effects of advertisement size and color are summarized in Figure 8.12.

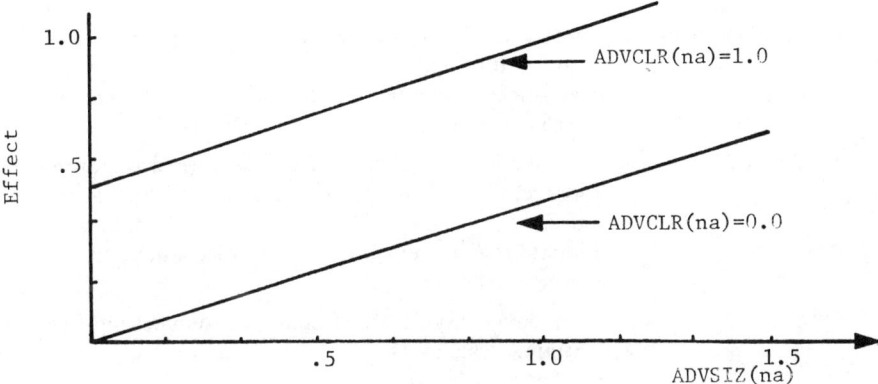

Figure 8.12. Effect of advertisement size and color on content recall.

Appeals presented by an advertisement are normally assumed to influence the probability of that advertisement being assimilated. Advertisers attempt to attract the attention of potential purchasers by associating positive appeals with use of their brand.

There is no toilet soap that will not give the user lovelier skin, nor face cream that will not secure romance and eternal love for the purchaser, and no whiskey that is not milder, smoother, and longer aged than all others on the market.[41]

The effectiveness of such appeals in arousing the interest of the reader, listener, or viewer appears to be a function of the consumer's pre-exposure attitude toward appeals used in the advertisement and the prominence of the appeal presentation. If a linear relationship is adopted, the following equation summarizes the effect of appeals present in

[41] E. Dichter, "A Psychological View of Advertising Effectiveness," *The Journal of Marketing*, Vol. 14 (July 1949), p. 61.

advertisement na on the probability of that advertisement being assimilated.

Equation 8.15

EFADAP(c, na) EFfect of ADvertising APpeals present in advertisement na on probability of consumer c assimilation. Dimension: pure number.

$$= C_{21} + C_{22} * \left[\frac{\sum\limits_{ap=1}^{AP} \left| ATITD(ap, c) \right| * EVAPWT(ap, na)}{\sum\limits_{ap='}^{AP} EVAPWT(ap, na)} \right].$$

ATITD(ap, c) ATtITuDe of consumer c toward appeal ap. Dimension: attitude scale units.
= consumer characteristic. See Table 8.1 (range -5 through $+5$).

EVAPWT(ap, na) EValuation of APpeals WeighTing (relative prominence) for appeal ap. Dimension: pure number (ratio).
= input from manufacturer sector. See Equation 7.10 (range 0 through 1.0).

C_{22} a scaling constant. Dimension: pure number units per attitude scale units.
= 0.2 as sample value.

C_{21} a constant specifying threshold (zero attitude) level for appeals effect. Dimension: pure number.
= 0.5 as sample value.

The Assimilation Function

The probability of consumer c assimilating content of advertisement na in medium mn is the combined probability of his (1) having media type m available, (2) being exposed to advertisement na in medium mn within that media class, (3) reacting to the appeals presented in the advertisement. Given the formulations summarized in Equations 8.12 through 8.15, the probability of consumer c assimilating advertisement na may be expressed as

Equation 8.16

PRASAD(c, na, t) PRobability of consumer c ASsimilating ADvertisement na at time t. Dimension: pure number.
= PRADEX(c, na, t) * [EFADSZ(na) + EFADCL(na)] * EFADAP(c, na).

The Process of Information Assimilation

Once consumer c has assimilated the content of advertisement na, he may respond positively, negatively, or indifferently to that content. The basic question to be answered is, "Does consumer c change his orientation toward the advertised brand as a result of noting advertisement na?" Within this model structure, orientation is defined in terms of attitude and awareness and the question of orientation change reduces to whether or not advertisement na changes consumer c's attitude toward or awareness of brand b.

Quantitative description of consumer responses to promotion is dependent on quantitative specification of communication content. The three content descriptors defined in Chapter 7 provide such a definition.[42]

EVAPWT(ap, na)   EValuation of APpeals WeighTing (relative prominence) for appeal ap in promotion na. Dimension: pure number (ratio).

EVPCWT(np, na)   EValuation of Product Characteristic WeighTing (relative prominence) for attribute np in promotion na. Dimension: pure number (ratio).

EVIDPR(b, na)   EValuation of brand b IDentification PRominence in advertisement na. Dimension: pure number.

As indicated by the subscripts, each variable is specified for each advertisement na. The appeals evaluation is coded for AP appeals, the evaluation of product characteristics is supplied for NP product characteristics, and brand identification prominence may relate to any of B brands.

Wroe Alderson has suggested that it may be useful to conceive of the function of advertising in terms of consumer search activity within the market.

The consumer as buying agent searches the market for products needed to replenish or extend an assortment or inventory of goods. Search can be defined in terms of communication theory as request for information. The word information is used here in the technical sense of embracing all "messages" received which contribute to a final decision. Impressions included under this category are obtained from observation, experience, and conversation with sales clerks and friends. The advertising message is transmitted through various media to the consumer designed to induce purchasing decisions. Advertising, therefore, is part of the network of search activities performed vicariously on behalf of the consumer.[43]

[42] Manufacturer handling of the promotion decision is discussed in Chapter 7, pp. 136–143.

[43] W. Alderson, "A New Approach to Advertising Theory," *Cost and Profit Outlook* (Spring 1961), pp. 1, 2, 608.

Alderson's concept of search implies that the consumer is engaged in a process of information acquisition. "Impressions" are recorded in the consumer's memory as the result of response to product and communication. Response effects a change in the content of the consumer's store of information. Within the structure of this model, two types of change may be observed. The consumer may associate *new* product characteristics or appeals with a particular brand or *existing* associations may be reinforced. Representation of this process of information acquisition is discussed in the following section.

Representation of Response to Communication

If, as suggested earlier, the response process is a function of communication content and consumer predisposition, a model of this process should be applicable to communication in general and not require differentiation based on content source. Within this system content is specified in a similar manner for advertisements, displays, sales messages, and word of mouth. In the absence of evaluations of relative effectiveness, all assimilated information inputs will be considered equivalent and the simulated consumer's memory will be updated through the same process for all information inputs received.

The content of consumer memory would be expected to reflect the number of communications involving specific information content assimilated. The record of retained communication content should also be affected by the relative prominence of each element of content in a particular communication.

Selective Perception

To be meaningful, comunication must relate to something relevant to the person receiving the communication. Communication elements are relevant or important to a person because he has preconceptions (attitudes) regarding them. The consumer will not react equally to all elements of communication content. He will be most responsive to those elements toward which he is most sensitive — toward which he has the strongest (highest magnitude) preassimilation attitudes.[44]

This conception of selective communication perception is consistent

[44] See, for example, T. M. Newcomb, "The Influence of Attitude Climate Upon Some Determinants of Information," *Journal of Abnormal and Social Psychology,* Vol. 69 (July 1964), pp. 291–302.

with empirical evidence. It is substantiated by studies of the effect of attitudes on content remembered from pictorial presentations.[45] Further support is provided by the findings of investigations of the phenomenon of selective perception and recall in terms of learning and forgetting processes.[46]

The assumption that the individual selectively directs his attention to specific aspects of the environment as a result of his attitudes toward elements of that environment has broad support.[47] It is, in fact, reasonable to assume that the *process* of human attitude development is essentially the same, regardless of the frame of reference.[48]

Formulation of the Selective Perception Process

Quantitative representation of the concept of selective perception requires that consumer memory elements associated with the promoted brand be incremented by the content of noted communication weighted by the magnitude of consumer attitude toward that content.

This procedure may be summarized in equation form for the case of consumer c's response to appeals in advertisement na as follows:

Equation 8.17

APPMEM(ap, b, c)   APPeals MEMory entry associating appeal ap with brand b in simulated mind of consumer c. Dimension: pure number.

$$= \text{APPMEM(ap, b, c)} + \text{EVAPWT(ap, na)}$$

$$* \frac{\text{EVIDPR(b, na)}}{4} * [C_{23} + C_{24} * |\text{ATITD(ap, c)}|].$$

(See Footnote 49).

EVAPWT(ap, na)   EValuation of APpeals WeighTing (relative prominence for appeal ap in advertisement na. Dimension: pure number ratio (range 0 to 1.0).

$$= \text{input from manufacturer sector. See Equation 7.10.}$$

[45] V. Seeleman, "The Influence of Attitude Upon the Remembering of Pictorial Material," *Archives of Psychology* (September 1940) 258.

[46] J. M. Levine and G. Murphy, "The Learning and Forgetting of Controversial Material," *Journal of Abnormal and Social Psychology,* Vol. 38 (October 1943), pp. 507–517.

[47] See, for example, D. C. Dearborn and H. A. Simon, "Selective Perception: A Note on the Departmental Identifications of Executives," *Sociometry,* 21 (1958), pp. 140–144.

[48] M. Sherif and H. Cantril, "The Psychology of Attitudes, Part II," *Psychological Review,* Vol. 53 (January 1946), pp. 1–24.

EVIDPR(b, na)   EValuation of IDentification PRominence of brand b in advertisement na. Dimension: pure number (prominence).

= input from manufacturer sector. See Equation 7.10 (range 0 to 4).

ATTITD(ap, c)   ATTITuDe of consumer c toward appeal ap. Dimension: attitude scale units.

= consumer characteristic. See Table 8.1.

C_{23} constant establishing extent of memory update for zero attitude element. Dimension: pure number.

= 1.0, sample value.

C_{24} constant establishing extent of memory update due to each attitude scale unit. Dimension: units per attitude scale units.

= 1.0, sample value.

In a similar manner consumer c's response to product characteristic information contained in advertisement na may be formulated as

Equation 8.18

PCHMEM(np, b, c)   Product CHaracteristics MEMory entry associating product characteristic np with brand b in simulated mind of consumer c. Dimension: pure number.

= PCHMEM(np, b, c) + EVPCWT(np, na)

$$* \frac{EVIDPR(b, na)}{4} * [C_{23} + C_{24} * |ATITD(np, c)|].$$

(See Footnote 49).

EVPCWT(np, na)   EValuation of Product Characteristic WeighTing (relative prominence) for attribute np in advertisement na. Dimension: pure number.

= input from manufacturer sector. See Table 8.1.

ATITD(np, c)   ATtITuDe of consumer c toward product characteristic np. Dimension: attitude scale units.

= consumer characteristic. See Table 8.1.

C_{23}, C_{24}, and EVIDPR(b, na) are as defined in Equation 8.17.

An Illustration

This process is illustrated in Figure 8.13 for two consumers, c and c′, responding to the content of a hypothetical advertisement na. In this illustration, EVIDPR(b, na) = 4.0, C_{23} = 1.0, and C_{24} = 1.0.

---

[49] Those unfamiliar with computer programming may find this equation confusing. The expression $A = A + B$ indicates that the previous value of the variable A (the content of storage location A) is replaced by the value of $A + B$ (the content of storage location A added to the content of storage location B).

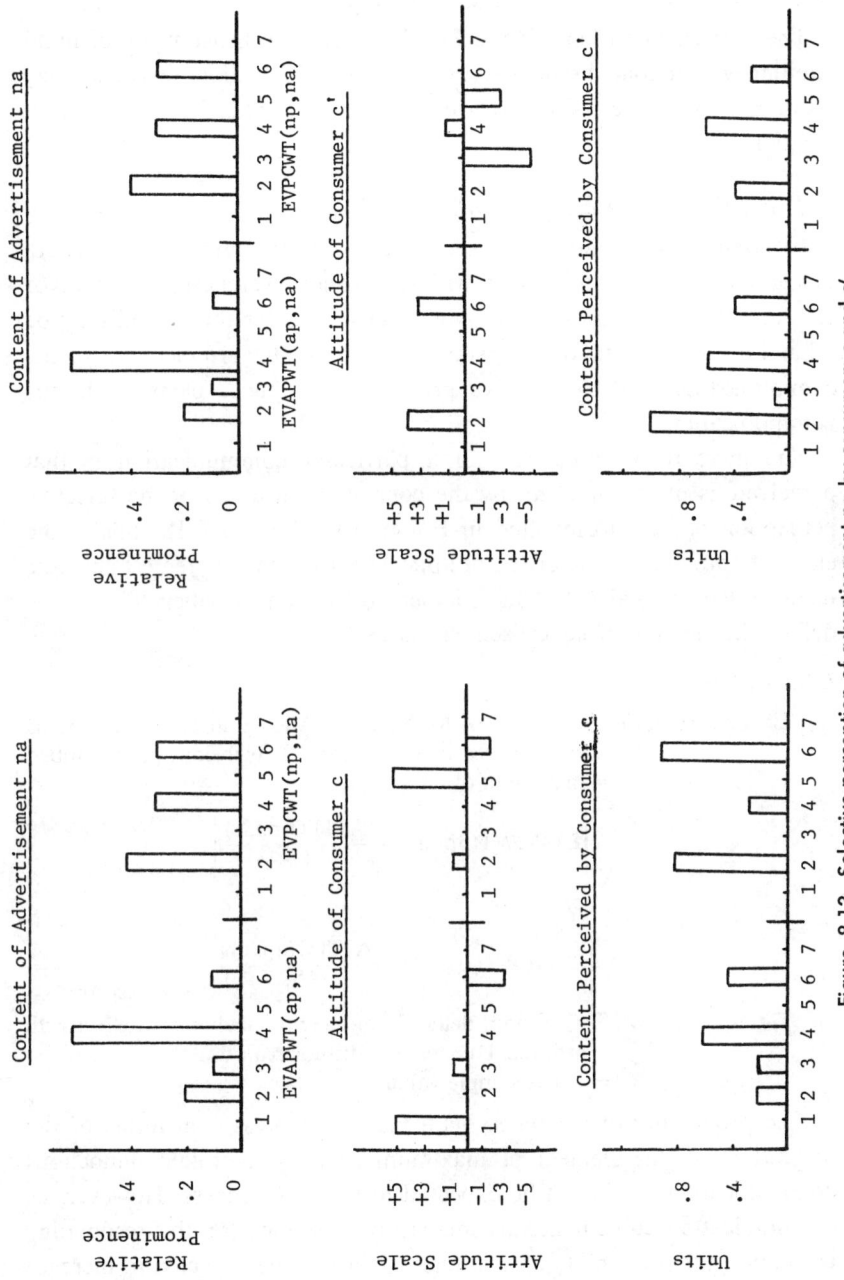

Figure 8.13. Selective perception of advertisement na by consumers c and c'.

Effect of Response on Brand Awareness

The awareness variable is used in this model to measure top-of-mind familiarity with one brand of product. Communication response may produce an awareness shift favoring the brand discussed in the communication.

The Effect of Perceived Content

In context of the attitude-based perception structure just discussed, the probability that consumer c will achieve an awareness gain in favor of brand b as a result of noting advertisement na for that brand may be related to the magnitude of consumer c's attitude toward elements of the communication and the relative prominence of those elements in the communication.

The most relevant element in a particular communication is that perceived as most important by the consumer. In terms of the selective perception process formulated in Equations 8.17 and 8.18, this is the element (product characteristic or appeal) for which the greatest absolute memory gain is realized. This "element of maximum saliency" may be defined in the case of advertisement na as

Equation 8.19

ELMXSA(na, c)   ELement of MaXimum SAliency in advertisement na as perceived by consumer c. Dimension: pure number.
= maximum of

$$\left| \text{EVPCWT(np, na)} * \left| \frac{\text{ATITD(np, c)}}{C_{25}} \right| \right|_{\text{np} = 1 \text{ through NP}}$$

or

$$\left| \text{EVAPWT(ap, na)} * \left| \frac{\text{ATITD(ap, c)}}{C_{25}} \right| \right|_{\text{ap} = 1 \text{ through AP}}.$$

C_{25} a constant determining the rate of change of effect with attitude. Dimension: attitude scale units.
= 1.0 as sample value.

The probability of awareness gain may be expressed in terms of the magnitude of this element of maximum saliency. A totally innocuous communication would not be expected to affect awareness. However, as communication content attains increasing relevance for the responding consumer, the probability of awareness gain may be expected to increase as follows:

Equation 8.20

EFPCAG(na, c)   EFfect of Perceived Content on Awareness Gain
$$= 1 - \text{ENXPF}\,[-\text{ELMXSA(na, c)}].$$

This relationship is illustrated in Figure 8.14.

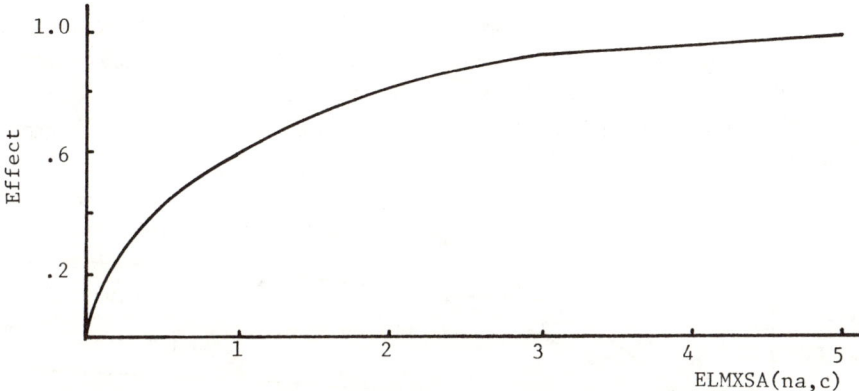

Figure 8.14. Effect of perceived content on probability of awareness gain.

The Effect of Brand Identification

Because awareness is brand specific, the probability of awareness gain is influenced by the prominence of communicated brand identification. Increasing prominence yields an increasing probability of awareness gain, with average prominence (2.0) producing a neutral (=1.0) multiplier effect.

Equation 8.21

EFBPAG(na, b)   EFfect of Brand Prominence on Awareness Gain.

$$= \frac{\text{EVIDPR(na, b)}}{C_{26}}.$$

EVIDPR(na, b)   EValuation of brand b IDentification PRominence in advertisement na. Dimension: pure number (range 0 to 4.0).
                 = input from manufacturer sector. See Equation 7.10.

C_{26} a constant determining the rate of change of effect with brand prominence. Dimension: pure number.
                 = 2.0, as sample value.

The Effect of Existing Awareness

The probability of awareness gain is affected by consumer awareness prior to response because a person is more likely to maintain an existing awareness than to develop awareness of a new brand. It is easier for a communication to reinforce an existing orientation than to create a new one.

The Probability of Awareness Gain

The probability of awareness gain resulting from response to communication content is a combination of the effect of the maximum saliency element, brand awareness, and the prominence of brand identification as summarized for advertisement na in Equation 8.22 and Figure 8.15.

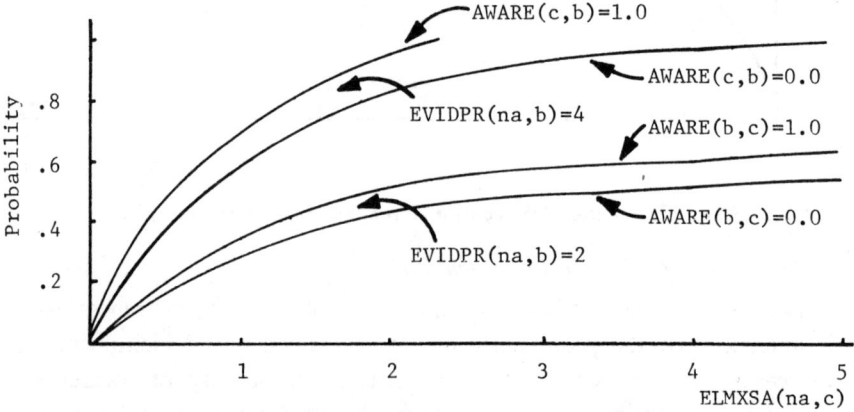

Figure 8.15. Probability of awareness gain due to advertising.

Equation 8.22

PRAGAD(na, b, c)	PRobability of a brand b Awareness Gain by consumer c in response to ADvertisement na. Dimension: pure number.
	$= \text{EFPCAG(na, c)} * \text{EFBPAG(na, b)}$
	$* [1 + C_{27} * \text{AWARE(c, b)}].$
	≤ 1.0 by constraint.
C_{27}	a constant specifying the effect of existing awareness on the probability that awareness will be maintained. Dimension: pure number.
	$= .2$, as sample value.

Interaction Summary

The exposure and response relationships developed in Equations 8.11 through 8.22 are summarized in Figure 8.16.

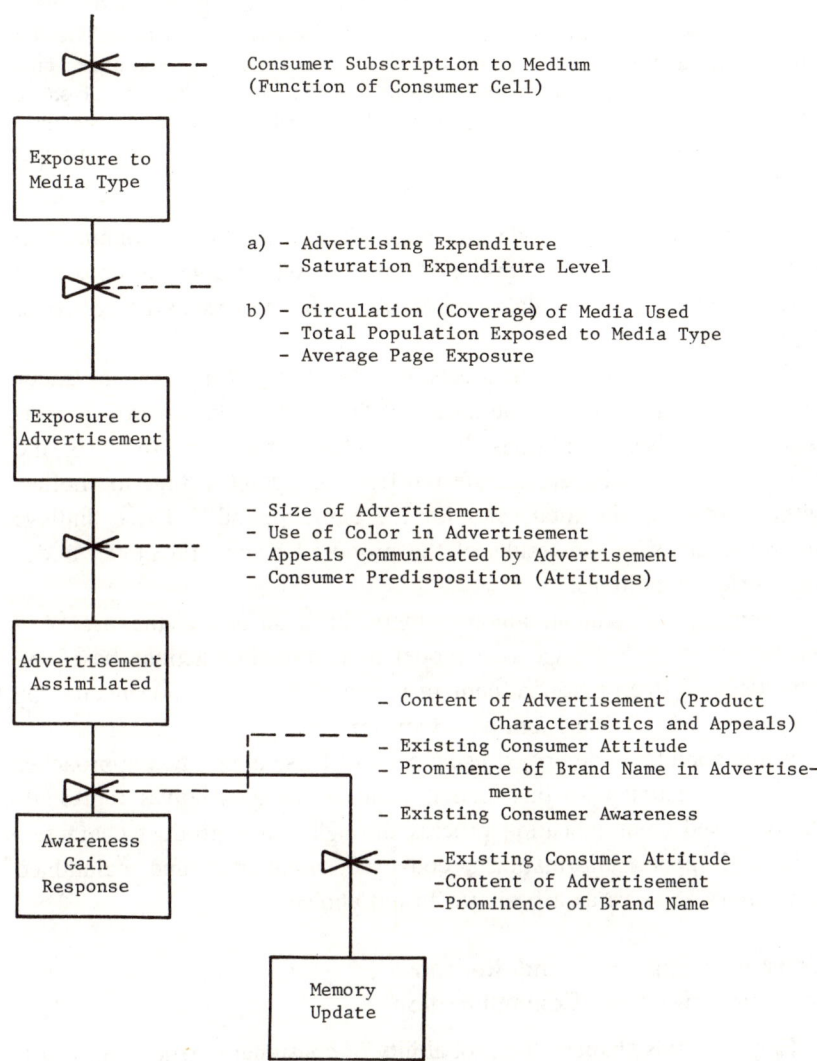

Figure 8.16. Advertising exposure and response processes.

Alternative Models of Communication Effect

In one of the first empirically based studies of advertising response, Vidale and Wolfe hypothesized a model of the response of sales to a promotional campaign "described by three parameters: λ, the exponential sales decay constant, m, the saturation level, and r, the response constant."

A mathematical model of sales response to advertising, based on these parameters, is represented by: $dS/dt = rA(t) (M-S)/M-\lambda s$, where S is the rate of sales at time t and $A(t)$ is the rate of advertising expenditure. This equation has the following interpretation: the increase in the rate of sales, dS/dt, is proportional to the intensity of the advertising effort, A, reaching the fraction of potential customers $(M-S)/M$, less the number of customers that are being lost, λS.[50]

The response of the model developed in this section in combination with forgetting functions developed later in this chapter is consistent with that observed by Vidale and Wolfe under conditions described in their article.

Forrester has analyzed the effects of sudden advertising increase under assumed conditions where the inflow of "prospective customers" is constant. Under these conditions, he concludes that the net result of the campaign is that sales are transferred from one point in time to another without affecting the total sales for the entire period.[51] These findings are consistent with the results of the proposed behavioral model under appropriate conditions.

Weinberg and Kuehn, among others, have suggested the use of a market share or exchange rate model of market interactions based on advertising.[52] If promotional content is assumed to be homogeneous, the proposed model is consistent with their approach.

While conditions described using each of these alternative approaches may be simulated with this model, none of the alternatives represents the observed communication process through which product characteristics and appeals information is conveyed, assimilated, and maintained in memory to serve as a basis for brand choice.

Consumer Exposure and Response to Word-of-Mouth Communication

Earlier in this chapter, the probability of consumer c generating word-of-mouth communication regarding brand b, PRWMG(c,b), was developed along with a representation of the aggregate content of existing

[50] M. L. Vidale and H. B. Wolfe, "An Operations-Research Study of Sales Response to Advertising," *Operations Research,* Vol. 5 (June 1957), p. 377.

[51] J. W. Forrester, "Advertising: A Problem in Industrial Dynamics," *Harvard Business Review,* Vol. 37 (March–April 1959), pp. 100–110.

[52] For an example of the use of this approach see: R. S. Weinberg, "Multiple Factor Break-Even Analysis," *Operations Research,* Vol. 4 (April 1956), pp. 152–186. Implications of this type of formulation are examined in A. A. Kuehn, "How Advertising Performance Depends on Other Marketing Factors," *Journal of Advertising Research,* Vol. 2 (March 1962), pp. 2–10.

word-of-mouth communication — CONWMC(n,b). This measure of word-of-mouth content is, with one exception, comparable to the advertising content descriptors evaluating the product characteristic and appeals content of advertising communication — EVPCWT(np,na) and EVAPWT(ap,na) respectively.

Word-of-Mouth Bias

The difference between word-of-mouth and advertising communication content relates to bias. The bias of advertising communication has been assumed fixed and neutral or positive. In the case of word-of-mouth communication, such an assumption is not justified. Consumers with negative as well as positive attitudes talk. Therefore word-of-mouth communication regarding a brand may be positively or negatively biased.

The perceived brand image, PEBRI(c,b,n), formulated later in this chapter indicates consumer c's perception of attribute n (product characteristic or appeal) of brand b. The magnitude of this variable represents consumer c's perceived importance of attribute n of brand b while the sign reflects his bias toward that product characteristic.

Probability of Exposure to Word-of-Mouth

The probability of word-of-mouth generation for the population and specification of content of word-of-mouth communications provide inputs comparable to those previously established for advertising. Both the availability of information (prevalence of comment) and content of communication generated (what is being said) are known.

The probability that a member of a homogeneous consumer population will be exposed to word-of-mouth discussion regarding brand b may be defined as the average probability that any other consumer whom he might encounter will talk about that brand.

Equation 8.23

PREXWM(b)   PRobability of Exposure to Word-of-Mouth discussion about brand b. Dimension: pure number.

$$= C_{28} * \frac{\sum_{c=1}^{C} PRWMG(c, b)}{C}.$$

C_{28} a constant based on the average number of people to whom a typical consumer talks during a time period. Dimension: cell units.

C   total number of consumers in population being analyzed. Dimension: cell units.

The cell simulation structure permits modeling of interactions between cell units representing individual members of a heterogeneous population. Within this structure it is possible to formulate the probability that consumer c will be exposed to consumer c_t talking about a brand b given interaction between c and c_t.

Equation 8.23A

PREXWM(c, c_t)   PRobability of EXposure to Word-of-Mouth generated by consumer c_t given association between consumers c and c_t. Dimension: pure number.
= PRWMG(c_t, b).

PRWMG(c_t, b)   PRobability that consumer c_t will Generate Word-of-Mouth communication.
= see Equation 8.5.

The Nature of Word-of-Mouth Interaction

A particularly useful description of word-of-mouth interaction is provided by Lazarsfeld, Berelson, and Gaudet's 1940 study of voting behavior in Erie County, Ohio. They observed individuals who, after assimilating mass media communication, passed on what they heard and read to other members of the community for whom they served as "opinion leaders." This process was described as "the two step flow of communication." [53]

Their research findings suggest that word-of-mouth communication between individuals may be more influential than direct communication by mass media although the extent of advantage is not clearly defined. The survey indicated that voters who switched candidates during the campaign or did not choose a candidate until late in the campaign (those having the least predisposition) were most apt to mention personal interaction as a factor influencing their decision.

Further evidence may be cited to substantiate the claim that the importance of word-of-mouth interaction may be substantially increased for the individual who has little or no experience and no firmly established attitudes. These are the circumstances in which the individual is most apt to turn to others as a source of information and evaluation. [54]

[53] P. F. Lazarsfeld, B. R. Berelson, and H. Gaudet, *The People's Choice* (2nd ed.; New York: Columbia University, 1948), p. 151.

[54] See M. Sherif, "Group Influences Upon the Formations of Norms and Attitudes," in E. E. Maccoby, T. M. Newcomb, and E. L. Hartley, *op. cit.,* Footnote 21, pp. 219–232.

Assuming that the self-designated "opinion leaders" in the 1940 study would have been regarded as such by their friends and neighbors, it is reasonable to assume that opinion leaders are more sensitive to — more apt to note — mass communication than others in the population. In terms of this model, those who talk have assimilated more communication.

The study also found opinion leaders in every strata of the population, suggesting that an opinion follower may be more influenced by an opinion leader having a similar background and social position.[55] Later data suggest that those identified as opinion leaders in the Erie County study were themselves influenced by higher-order opinion leaders.[56] These findings suggest that any individual may at one time be an opinion leader and at another a recipient of influential communication.

Other investigations of interpersonal relations provide evidence to support the hypothesis that communication content (the subject being discussed) determines which individuals will be leaders and followers.[57] This conclusion supports the model structure relating probability of word-of-mouth generation to individual attitudes toward content.[58]

Despite tendencies toward topical emphasis within particular population groups, people are most apt to communicate with, influence, and be influenced by others of common background in their immediate environment. There is also evidence to suggest that an individual is more easily able to influence those who are striving to be like him and are attempting to identify with his position.[59]

In final analysis, the effectiveness of an individual in the role of word-of-mouth communicator appears to be a combination of both who he is

[55] P. F. Lazarsfeld, B. Berelson, and H. Gaudet, op. cit., Footnote 53, pp. 150–151.

[56] B. R. Berelson, P. F. Lazarsfeld, and W. N. McPhee, Voting (Chicago: University of Chicago Press, 1954), p. 110.

[57] R. K. Merton, "Patterns of Influence: A Study of Interpersonal Influence and Communications Behavior in a Local Community," in P. F. Lazarsfeld and F. N. Stanton (eds.), Communications Research (New York: Harper and Bros., 1948–1949), pp. 187–188.

[58] This conclusion is further substantiated by the findings of a study of market decision making in Decatur, Illinois. See E. Katz and P. F. Lazarsfeld, Personal Influence: The Part Played by People in the Flow of Mass Communications (Glencoe, Ill.: The Free Press, 1955), pp. 327–334.

[59] See, for example, C. P. Marshall and A. L. Coleman, "Farmers Practice Adoption Rates in Relation to Adoption Rates of Leaders," World of Sociology, Vol. XIX (1954), pp. 180–183.

(his descriptors), whom he knows (his interactions), and what he knows (his memory content).[60]

Assimilation of Word-of-Mouth Communication

The following conclusions summarized by Katz provide a verbal description of response to word of mouth.

Opinion leaders and the people whom they influence are very much alike and typically belong to the same primary groups of family, friends, and co-workers. While the opinion leader may be more interested in the particular sphere in which he is influential, it is highly unlikely that the persons influenced will be very far behind the leader in their level of interest. Influentials and influencees may exchange roles in different spheres of influence.[61]

Consumer assimilation of word-of-mouth communication appears to be a function of the characteristics of the listener and the person generating the communication. The assumption is that a person will tend to assimilate communication generated by an individual who has characteristics similar to those that he possesses or aspires to possess and will tend to reject the communication of one whose characteristics are substantially different. The three previously defined consumer characteristics — income, education, and age — may be used to categorize socio-economic bases for consumer interaction as indicated in the following expression for the probability of noting word-of-mouth communication.

Equation 8.24

$PRNWM(c, c_t)$ PRobability of consumer c Noting Word-of-Mouth communication generated by individual c_t (conditional upon interaction between c and c_t).

$$= PREXWM(c, c_t) * [1 - [INCDFR(c, c_t) + AGEDFR(c, c_t) + EDUDFR(c, c_t)]].$$

$PREXWM(c, c_t)$ see Equation 8.23A.

$INCDFR(c, c_t)$ INCome DiFfeRential between consumers c and c_t.

$$= C_{29} * |INCOM(c_t) - INCOM(c)|,$$
if $INCOM(c_t) < INCOM(c)$.
$$= 0, \text{ if } INCOM(c_t) > INCOM(c).$$

[60] For a summary of the bases of this conclusion see Elihu Katz, "The Two Step Flow of Communication: An Up-to-Date Report on an Hypothesis," *The Public Opinion Quarterly* (Princeton, N.J.: Princeton University Press), Vol. 21 (Spring 1957), pp. 73–78.

[61] *Ibid.*, p. 77.

AGEDFR(c, c_t) AGE DiFfeRential between consumers c and c_t.
= $C_{30} * |\text{AGEID}(c_t) - \text{AGEID}(c)|$.

EDUDFR(c, c_t) EDUcation DiFfeRential between consumers c and c_t.
= $C_{31} * |\text{EDUCA}(c_t) - \text{EDUCA}(c)|$,
if $\text{EDUCA}(c_t) < \text{EDUCA}(c)$.
= 0, if $\text{EDUCA}(c_t) \geq \text{EDUCA}(c)$.

INCOM(c) INCOMe function value of consumer c. Dimension: pure number.
= function of consumer characteristic. See Table 8.1.

AGEID(c) AGE function value of consumer c. Dimension: pure number.
= function of consumer characteristic. See Table 8.1.

EDUCA(c) EDUCAtion function value of consumer c. Dimension: pure number.
= function of consumer characteristic. See Table 8.1.

C_{29}, C_{30}, and C_{31} weighting constants determining relative importance of three descriptors. Dimension: pure numbers.

Equation 8.24 reflects the assumption that the impact of positive and negative differences is not equally undesirable. Positive differences in education and income are interpreted as indicating that the speaker has characteristics toward which the listener aspires. The equation is therefore formulated to take into account the favorable (nonnegative) effect of positive difference.

The probability of word-of-mouth communication being noted is thus 1.0 if the speaker and listener belong to the same reference group — have identical income, education, and age characteristics. As the listener deviates from the word-of-mouth generator in the directions of a higher income or education group or toward either a younger or older age group, the communication decreases at a rate determined by C_{29}, C_{31}, and C_{30} respectively.

Response to Assimilated Word-of-Mouth Communication

Once a word-of-mouth communication has been noted, the process through which the consumer selectively perceives and responds to communication content is identical with that described in the preceding section for advertising response.

Replacing the advertising content descriptors with those for word-of-mouth, the selective memory update process may be represented as follows:[62]

[62] See "Formulation of the Selective Perception Process," pp. 195–200, particularly Equations 8.17 and 8.18.

Equation 8.25

APPMEM(ap, b, c)   APPeals MEMory entry associating appeal ap with brand b in simulated mind of consumer c. Dimension: pure number.

$$= APPMEM(ap, b, c) + CONWMC(ap, b, c_t)$$
$$* [C_{23} + C_{24} * |ATITD(ap, c)|].$$

PCHMEM(np, b, c)   Product CHaracteristic MEMory entry associating product characteristic np with brand b in simulated mind of consumer c. Dimension: pure number.

$$= PCHMEM(np, b, c) + CONWMC (np, b, c_t)$$
$$* [C_{23} + C_{24} * |ATITD(np, c)|].$$

Brand identification prominence is assumed to have a maximum (4.0) value in the case of word-of-mouth communication. With this definition of brand identification, the previous formulation for probability of awareness reduces to the following representation.[63]

Equation 8.26

PRAGWM(c_t, b, c)   PRobability of a brand b Awareness Gain by consumer c in response to noting Word-of-Mouth generated by consumer c_t. Dimension: pure number.

$$= [1 - ENXPF (-ELMXSA(c_t, c))]$$
$$* [1 + C_{27} * AWARE(c, b)].$$

ELMXSA(c_t, c)   ELement of MaXimum SAliency in communication of consumer c_t as perceived by consumer c. Dimension: pure number.

= Maximum of

$$\left\| CONWMC(np, b, c_t) * \left|\frac{ATITD(np, c)}{C_{25}}\right| \right\|_{np = 1 \text{ through NP}}$$

or

$$\left\| CONWMC(ap, b, c_t) * \left|\frac{ATITD(ap, c)}{C_{25}}\right| \right\|_{ap = 1 \text{ through AP}}.$$

Consumer Product Experience

Formulations describing consumer response to advertising and word-of-mouth communication and decisions to shop and purchase have now been completed. Factors affecting response to product and promotion at point of sale and to product use after purchase may now be considered.

[63] For a detailed discussion of this formulation, see "Effect of Response on Brand Awareness," pp. 198–200, particularly Equations 8.19 through 8.22.

Experience at Point of Sale

Consumer experience at point of sale involves alternatives that can best be examined with the aid of a flow chart. Figure 8.17 summarizes the circumstances that may lead to various consumer experiences and responses at point of sale.

The *Explicit Decision to Shop* illustrated at the top of this figure is the consumer's decision to shop based on perceived need developed earlier in this chapter. The consumer who does not decide to shop may be accidentally exposed to a brand in the course of shopping for other products. Such accidental exposure is most apt to occur in a consumer's highest preference retail outlet. Once the consumer's presence at a product display has been established, behavioral differences associated with accidental as opposed to planned shopping are largely irrelevant.

Figure 8.17 indicates that the consumer's perceived need for all brands is established prior to determining whether or not he will make an explicit decision to shop. Given an affirmative decision to shop, the consumer goes first to his first preference retailer, that retailer toward whom he has the highest attitude. It is then necessary to determine whether or not that retailer is carrying the consumer's favored (highest attitude) brand. If the retailer is not carrying the brand of first choice, the consumer may look elsewhere for the desired brand or consider other brands carried by that retailer. The outcome of this decision is based on the consumer's relative preference for (attitude toward) brand and retailer. If attitude toward brand is greater than attitude toward retailer, he will continue to shop. If the converse is true, he will consider other brands.

Once we have established that the consumer is exposed to a brand in a retail outlet, it is necessary to determine whether he will be exposed to point-of-sale promotion in support of that brand. If exposure is achieved, assimilation and response (memory update and awareness gain) is determined. Consumer exposure and response to selling effort generated by the retail salesman is modeled in a similar fashion.

Given product exposure in the retail outlet, the consumer may purchase following procedures formulated earlier in this chapter.[64] If a purchase is made, point-of-sale activity is terminated. However, if no purchase is made, the process continues until potential actions and responses to all brands available in the retail outlet have been considered.

[64] See "The Consumer Decision to Purchase," pp. 169–180.

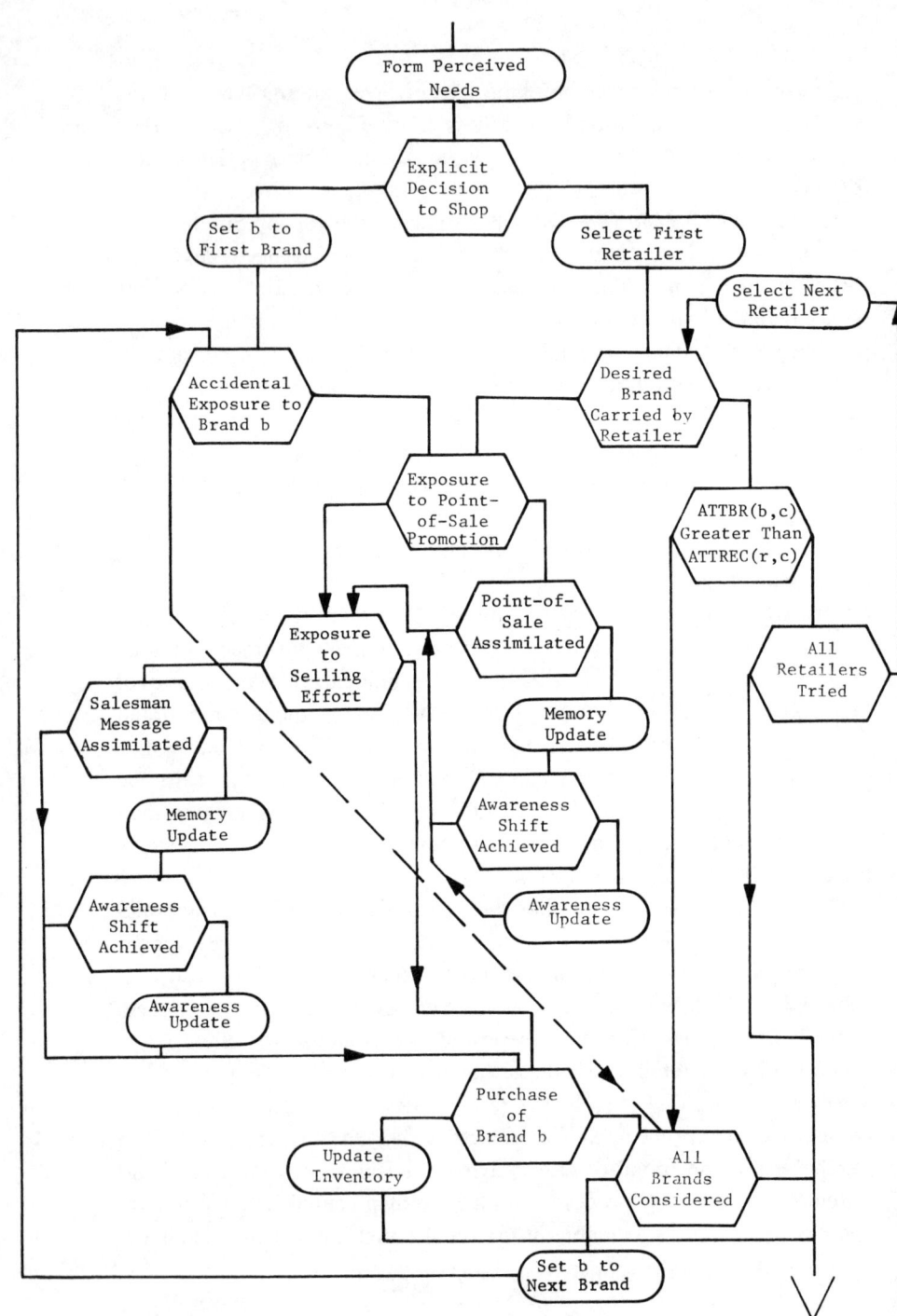

Figure 8.17. Consumer point-of-sale activity.

As noted earlier, the probability of a consumer making an explicit decision to shop has been formulated.[65] Accidental exposure to brand b at point of sale must now be considered.

The Probability of Accidental Exposure to Brand b

Description of accidental exposure to brand b in retail outlet r, first requires determination of whether or not retailer r is carrying brand b. This condition is established by retailer decisions modeled in Chapter 9.

If the brand is in the store, the attention-attracting (as opposed to communication) effect of point-of-sale display is evaluated in terms of the prominence of product display described using the prominence scale developed earlier in this chapter.

The following equation graphed in Figure 8.18 summarizes the probability of *accidental* exposure to brand b in retail outlet r as a function of brand presence and display.

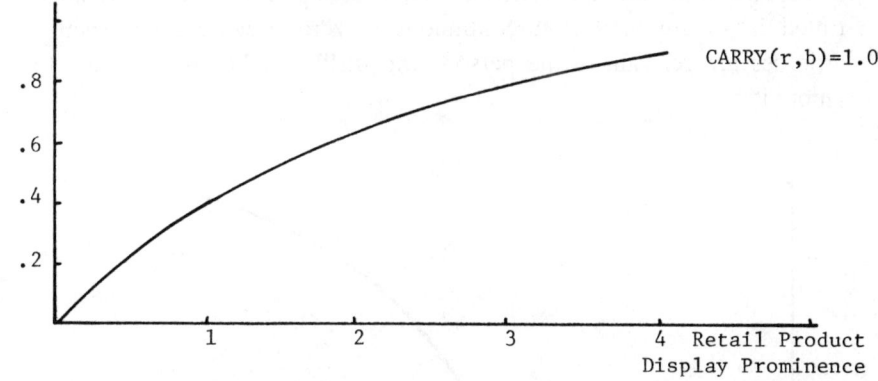

Figure 8.18. Effect of coverage and display prominence on probability exposure.

Equation 8.27

PREXBR(r, b)   PRobability of EXposure to BRand b in store type r.
                Dimension: pure number.
             = CARRY(b, r) $*$ EFPDPR(r).

CARRY(b, r)   brands CARRied by retailer r. Dimension: pure number
                (binary).
             = 1.0, if brand b carried by retailer r.
             = 0.0, if brand b not carried by retailer r.
             = input from retailer sector.
                Equation 9.12, p. 278.

[65] See "The Consumer Decision to Shop," pp. 161–169.

EFPDPR(r)   EFfect of ProDuct PRominence in store type r. Dimension: pure number ratio).

$$= 1 - \text{ENXPF}\left[-\frac{\text{RPDPM(r)}}{C_{32}} \right].$$

RPDPM(r)   Retailer Product Display PRoMinence. Dimension: pure number (ratio).
                  = output from retailer sector model based on Prominence Scale. See Equation 9.14, p. 282.

C_{32} a constant determining the rate of change in effect with product prominence. Dimension: pure number.
                  = 2.0, as sample value.

A third factor influencing the probability of exposure to brand is the brand preference with which the consumer enters the store. Consumer attitude toward brand provides a measure of brand preference. A consumer who feels strongly about the value of a brand is more likely to notice it, to be accidentally exposed, than one who has neutral or negative attitudes. The function encompassing brand preference illustrated in Figure 8.19 is discontinuous at zero because only positive attitudes are relevant — the person who dislikes a brand will wish to ignore it.

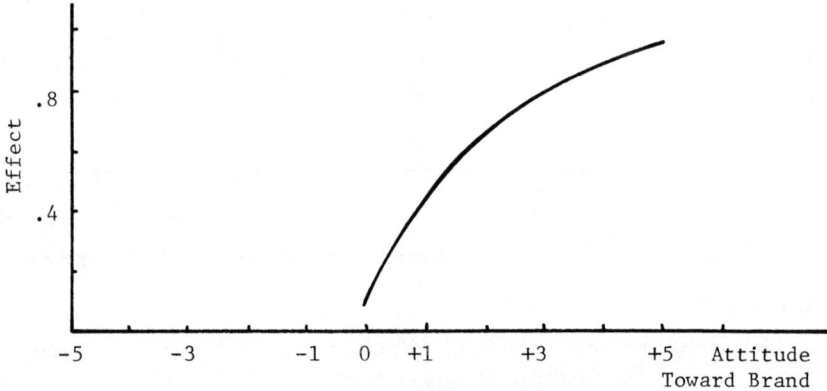

Figure 8.19. Effect of consumer brand preference on accidental exposure to product.

The probability of accidental exposure to brand b in retail outlet r as formulated above may be weighted by the consumer's brand preference to establish the probability of a particular consumer c being exposed to brand b in store r.

Equation 8.28

PRAXBR(c, r, b)	PRobability of consumer c being Accidentally eXposed to BRand b in store type r. Dimension: pure number. = EFBRPR(b, c) ∗ PREXBR(r, b).
EFBRPR(b, c)	EFfect of consumer c's BRand PReference for b.

$$= 1 - \text{ENXPF}\left[-\frac{C_{33} + \text{ATTBR}(b, c)}{C_{34}}\right],$$

if ATTBR(c) $\geq$ 0.
= 0.0, if ATTBR(c, b) < 0.

ATTBR(c, b)	ATTitude toward BRand b. Dimension: attitude scale units (range −5 to +5). = see Equation 8.42, p. 226.
C_{33}	a constant determining the threshold (zero attitude) level of the brand preference effect. Dimension: pure number. = .10 as sample value.
C_{34}	constant determining the rate of change of effect with attitude. Dimension: attitude scale units. = 2.0 as sample value.

Probability of Exposure to Point-of-Sale Promotion

For purposes of sequential structuring, exposure to a brand at point of purchase will be established as a prerequisite of exposure to point-of-sale material relating to that brand. Once brand exposure has been established, exposure to point-of-sale material is a function of placement. If the material has not been placed in the store, it is impossible for the consumer to encounter it.

Exposure to a particular point-of-sale display na in retail outlet r is thus determined by retailer r's placement of the display.

Equation 8.29

PREXPS(r, b, na)	PRobability of EXposure to Point-of-Sale promotion na in retail outlet r (given exposure to brand b). Dimension: pure number (binary). = RPLPSD(na, b, r) conditional on brand exposure.
RPLPSD(na, b, r)	Retailer PLacement of Point-of-Sale Display. = binary output from retailer model indicating placement of point-of-purchase piece na by retailer r. Based on Equation 9.16, p. 285. See Equation 9.3, p. 261.

The characteristics and content of point-of-sale promotion are defined in a manner analogous to that employed for media advertising in terms of the following variables developed in the manufacturer sector.[66]

PSDSIZ(na)	Point-of-Sale Display SIZe measured in terms of floor space required by display na. Dimension: square feet.
EVPSAW(n, na)	EValuation of Point-of-Sale Appeal Weighting (relative prominence) for appeal n in point-of-sale display na. Dimension: pure number (ratio).
EVPBPS(b, na)	EValuation of Prominence of Brand b in Point-of-Sale display na. Dimension: pure number.
EVPCWP(np, na)	EValuation of Product Characteristic np Weighting (relative prominence) for Point-of-sale display na. Dimension: pure number (ratio).

Assimilation of Point-of-Sale Promotion

Assimilation of point-of-sale promotion content is affected by the relative size of the display and consumer attitude toward appeals emphasized in it. Previous comments on the impact of attitude on assimilation of media advertising content are largely applicable to the effect of attitude on point-of-sale promotion assimilation.[67] When the advertising content specifiers are replaced with comparable descriptors for point-of-sale promotion, the previously developed probability of assimilation formulation becomes[68]

Equation 8.30

PRASPS(r, b, c) PRobability of consumer c ASsimilating Point-of-Sale promotion for brand b in retail outlet r. Dimension: pure number.

$$= \text{PREXPS}(r, b, na) * \frac{\text{PSDSIZ}(na) * \text{EFADAP}(c, na)}{\sum_{na=1}^{NA} \text{PSDSIZ}(na) * \text{EFADAP}(c, na)}.$$

PSDSIZ(na) Point-of-Sale Display SIZe measured in terms of floor space required by display na. Dimension: Square feet.
= input from manufacturer sector. See Equation 9.9, p. 274.

EFADAP(c, na) EFfect of ADvertising APpeals present in promotion na on probability of consumer c noting. Dimension: pure number.

$$= C_{21} + C_{22} * \frac{\sum_{ap=1}^{AP} |\text{ATITD}(ap, c)| * \text{EVPSAW}(ap, na)}{\sum_{ap=1}^{AP} \text{EVPSAW}(ap, na)}.$$

[66] See Equations 7.9 and 7.10.
[67] See "Probability of Assimilating an Advertisment," p. 190.
[68] See Equation 8.16, p. 192.

EVPSAW(ap, na)   EValuation of Point-of-Sale Appeal Weighting for appeal ap in promotion na. Dimension: pure number (ratio).

Response aspects of the assimilation process represented by memory update and awareness gain are formulated in a manner identical to that discussed for the media advertising case.[69] The process summarized in Equations 8.17 through 8.22 is duplicated, with appropriate point-of-sale variables replacing the previously used media promotion descriptors.

Equation 8.31

APPMEM(ap, b, c)   APPeals MEMory entry associating appeal ap with brand b in simulated mind of consumer c. Dimension: pure number.

$$= \text{APPMEM(ap, b, c)} + \text{EVPSAW(ap, na)}$$

$$* \frac{\text{EVPBPS(b, na)}}{4} * [C_{23} + C_{24} * |\text{ATITD(ap, c)}|].$$

PCHMEM(np, b, c)   Product CHaracteristic MEMory entry associating product characteristic np with brand b in simulated mind of consumer c. Dimension: pure number.

$$= \text{PCHMEM(np, b, c)} + \text{EVPCWP(np, na)}$$

$$* \frac{\text{EVPBPS(b, na)}}{4} * [C_{23} + C_{24} * |\text{ATITD(np, c)}|].$$

Equation 8.32

PRAGPS(na, b, c)   PRobability of brand b Awareness Gain by consumer c in response to Point-of-Sale display na. Dimension: pure number.

$$= \text{EFPCAG(na, c)} * \text{EFBPAG(na, b)}$$

$$* [1 + C_{27} * \text{AWARE(c, b)}].$$

EFPCAG(na, c)   EFfect of Perceived Content on Awareness Gain. Dimension: pure number.

$$= 1 - \text{ENXPF}[-\text{ELMXSA(na, c)}].$$

ELMXSA(na, c)   ELement of MaXimum SAliency in point-of-sale piece na as perceived by consumer c. Dimension: pure number.

= maximum of

$$\left\| \text{EVPCWP(np, na)} * \left| \frac{\text{ATITD(np, c)}}{C_{25}} \right| \right\|_{\text{np}=1 \text{ through NP}}$$

or

$$\left\| \text{EVPSAW(ap, na)} * \left| \frac{\text{ATITD(ap, c)}}{C_{25}} \right| \right\|_{\text{ap}=1 \text{ through AP}}.$$

[69] See "Formulation of the Selective Perception Process," p. 195.

EFBPAG(na, b)   EFfect of Brand Prominence on Awareness Gain.
                                 Dimension: pure number.

$$= \frac{EVPBPS(b, na)}{C_{26}}.$$

Complete definitions for standard variables and constants used in the preceding equation set are supplied in Equations 8.19 through 8.22.

Consumer-Salesman Interaction

While shopping in a retail outlet, the consumer may interact with a salesman. For purposes of this model, such contact will be assumed contingent on exposure to the product. A salesman will not talk to a customer about a totally unrelated product class — the consumer must indicate some interest in the product before the salesman will initiate comment.

Consumer exposure to information regarding a brand communicated via a retail salesman is influenced by the selling effort exerted in the retail outlet. In addition, factors contributing to brand exposure support selling effort by the salesman. The allocation of display area favoring exposure to a brand, for example, provides an environment conducive to the generation of selling effort on behalf of that brand. The probability of exposure to salesman selling effort in support of a brand may thus be expressed in terms of the level of such effort and the relative display prominence allotted the brand.

This probability of exposure to selling effort on behalf of brand b in retail outlet r may be expressed as

Equation 8.33

PREXSE(r, b)   PRobability of EXposure to Selling Effort on behalf of
                                 brand b in store r (contingent on product exposure).
                                 Dimension: pure number.

$$= C_{35} * \frac{RETSLE(r, b)}{\sum\limits_{b'=1}^{B(r)} RETSLE(r, b')} * \frac{RPDPRM(r, b)}{\sum\limits_{b'=1}^{B(r)} RPDPRM(r, b')}.$$

RETSLE(r, b)   RETail outlet r SeLling Effort on behalf of brand b.
                                 (Range 0 to 1.0). Dimension: units of selling effort
                                 (proportion of time).
                                 = input from retail sector. See Equation 9.15, p. 283.

RPDPRM(r, b)   Retailer outlet r Product Display PRoMinence for
                                 brand b. (Range 0 to 1.0). Dimension: pure number.
                                 = input from retail sector. See Equation 9.14A, p. 282.

B(r)   total number of Brands carried in product line by re-
                                  tailer r. Dimension: pure number.

$$= \sum_{b=1}^{B} CARRY(b, r), \text{ see Equation 9.12, p. 278.}$$

C_{35} scaling constant. Dimension: pure number.
                                  = .5, as sample value.

The major component of retail selling effort is salesman communication. Given exposure to selling effort the content of salesman communication and consumer response to same must both be established.

The salesman communication content is generated within the retail
sector model discussed in Chapter 9. Content specifiers are defined as

SCAPC(ap, b, r)   Salesman (retailer) Communication APpeal Content.
                     Dimension: pure number (ratio).

SCPCC(np, b, r)   Salesman (retailer) Communication Product Character-
                     istic Content. Dimension: pure number ratio.
                     = input from retail sector. See Equation 9.23, p. 292.

Brand prominence in salesman communication is assumed to be
maximum.

Assimilation of Salesman Communication

Formulation of the probability of assimilation of salesman communication follows the by now familiar appeals based representation.

Equation 8.34

PRASSC(r, b, c)   PRobability of consumer c ASsimilating Salesman
                     Communication regarding brand b generated in out-
                     let r. Dimension: pure numbers.
                     = PREXSE(r, b) * EFSEAP(r, c).

PREXSE(b, r)   PRobability of EXposure to Selling Effort for brand b
                     in outlet r (see Equation 8.32).

EFSEAP(r, c)   EFfect of SElling APpeals in communication of re-
                     tailer r salesman as perceived by consumer c. Dimen-
                     sion: pure number.

$$= C_{21} + C_{22} * \frac{\sum_{ap=1}^{AP} \left| ATITD(ap, c) \right| * SCAPC(ap, b, r)}{\sum_{ap=1}^{AP} SCAPC(ap, b, r)}.$$

SCAPC(ap, b, r)   Salesman Communication APpeal Content (see pre-
                     ceding section).

Following assimilation, the consumer's memory update and awareness gain processes operate against the content generated by the salesman in a manner directly analogous to that described for word-of-mouth response.[70]

Reaction to Product Use

Once a brand is purchased, the consumer has an opportunity to respond directly to the physical product as opposed to communication about the product.

Effect of Purchase on Brand Awareness

In the light of previously established definitions, a consumer's awareness of the brand purchased becomes 1.0 immediately following purchase. This is not to say that the consumer will continue to be aware of that brand as long as he owns it. However, awareness is achieved at time of purchase if it was not present prior to purchase.

Equation 8.35

AWARE(c, b) = 1, following purchase of brand b by consumer c.

Factors Influencing Response to Use

Positive reaction to product use may be supported by (1) high prepurchase attitude, (2) close correlation between perceived brand image prior to purchase and actual brand product characteristics, (3) high price effect in purchase — assumed "reasonable price."

Prepurchase Attitude. A high prepurchase attitude supports positive reaction to use because the consumer has a strong prepurchase commitment to the product. A strong positive bias makes it difficult for the consumer to find fault with the product because to react negatively he must admit that he has made a mistake in buying and that his strong prepurchase attitudes were unfounded.[71]

Perceived and Experienced Product Attributes. If the consumer gets what he wanted — if the correlation between perceived brand image and actual product characteristics is high — he will be satisfied. The product will be what he expected: it will perform in the way that he planned, and his purchase decision will have yielded the anticipated outcome.

---

[70] See "Response to Assimilated Word-of-Mouth Communication," p. 207, particularly Equations 8.25 and 8.26.

[71] The process of conflict resolution is discussed in detail in a later section.

Purchase Price.   If previously noted assumptions regarding the price-imputed quality interactions are correct, the more reasonable the price of the product appears in the eyes of the consumer, the less likely he will be to find fault with the product once he has purchased it. Because of the price-quality syndrome, he will expect less of a product that was purchased at what he considers to be a low or reasonable price than of one which he perceived as high priced.[72]

As an obvious corollary of the preceding observations, it follows that a negative reaction to product use will be supported by (1) a low or marginal prepurchase attitude, (2) major differences between perceived and experienced product characteristics, (3) low price effect in purchase (assumed high price image).

Use Opportunity.   Response to product usage is amplified by high use opportunity and dampened by low use opportunity. The more frequently a product is used, the more opportunity the consumer is given to react to the factors previously discussed, and the greater the emphasis placed on positive or negative attributes of the product use situation.

Probability of Positive Response to Product Use

In developing formulations for response to product use, only the probability of a positive (supporting) reaction will be explicitly considered. The probability of negative reaction will be derived from the positive equation set once it is complete.

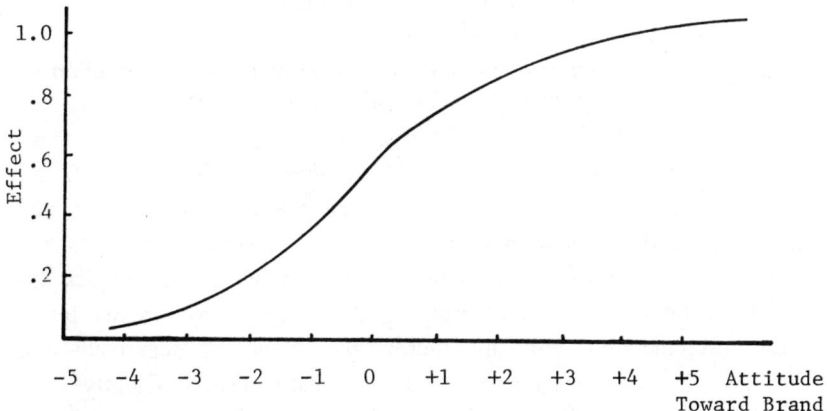

Figure 8.20. Effect of prepurchase attitude on positive response to product use.

[72] The impact of price on purchase is discussed under the heading, "Price Effects," pp. 173–175.

The Attitude Effect. The first condition to be considered is the contribution of prepurchase attitude to the probability of positive reaction to use after purchase. In keeping with previously discussed attitude saliency phenomena, an exponential weighting is applied to the magnitude of attitude toward the brand being used. This function is illustrated in Figure 8.20.

Equation 8.36

$EFATPR(c, b)$ EFfect of ATtitude on probability of Positive Reaction to use after purchase.

$$= C_{36} + \left[1 - ENXPF \left(-\frac{ATTBR(c, b)}{C_{37}} \right) \right] * C_{38},$$

if $ATTBR(c, b) \geq 0$,

$$= \left[ENXPF \left(+\frac{ATTBR(c, b)}{C_{37}} \right) \right] * C_{38},$$

if $ATTBR(c, b) < 0$,
≥ 0.0 by constraint.

$ATTBR(c, b)$ ATTitude toward BRand b held by consumer c. Dimension: attitude scale units.
      = see Equation 8.42.

C_{36} scaling constant establishing threshold (zero attitude) value for function. Dimension: pure number.
      = .5, as sample value.

C_{37} constant determining rate of change of function with attitude. Dimension: attitude scale units.
      = 2.0, as sample value.

C_{38} scaling constant establishing maximum contribution by attitude term. Dimension: pure number.
      = .5, as sample value.

Effect of Perceived versus Realized Attributes. The second factor to be considered is the difference between the consumer's perceived brand image, those characteristics which the consumer believes the brand purchased possesses, and the actual product characteristics exhibited by the product. In quantifying the assumptions already introduced in connection with this factor, the effects of negatively and positively viewed characteristics must be distinguished. Clearly it is desirable to find *less* than the expected number of *negative* attributes and/or *more* than the expected number of *positively* viewed product characteristics. This condition is represented by the following formulation illustrated in Figure 8.21.

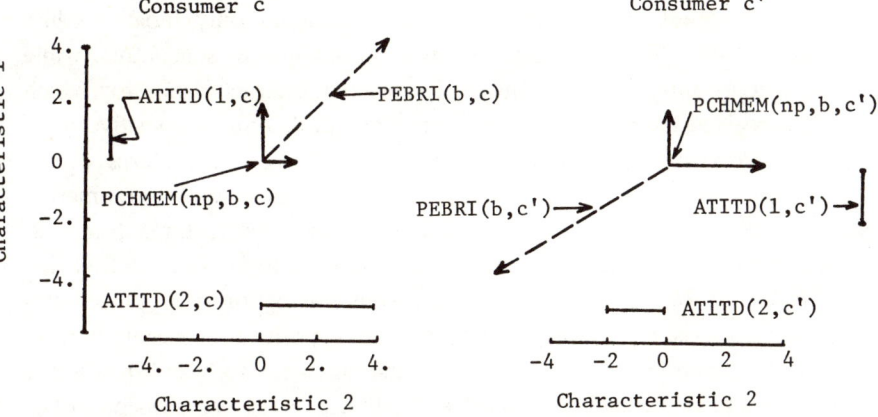

Figure 8.21. Illustration of perceived brand image formation for two-dimensional case.

Equation 8.37

EFIMPR(c, b)   EFfect of IMage on probability of Positive Reaction to use after purchase due to image effect.

$$= C_{39} + \left[\sum_{np=1}^{NP} [|PEBRI(np, b, c)|_{-only}\right.$$

$$- |PEBRI(np, b, c)|_{+only}] * (1 - PRDCHR(np, b))$$

$$\left. + \sum_{np=1}^{NP} PEBRI(np, b, c) * PRDCHR(np, b) \right]$$

$$* \frac{C_{40}}{\sum_{np=1}^{NP} |PEBRI(np, b, c)|}.$$

C_{39} a constant establishing the threshold (no difference) level for the function. Dimension: pure number.
= .5, as sample value.

C_{40} scaling constant determining rate of change of effect due to function. Dimension: units per attitude scale units.
= 1.0.

PEBRI(np, b, c)   PErceived BRand Image. Dimension: attitude scale units.
= derived function of noted communication (see Equation 8.41, p. 225).

PRDCHR(np, b)   PRoDuct CHaRacteristics actually present in brand b. Dimension: pure number (binary).
= input from the manufacturer sector. See Equation 7.1.

The first entry in the first summation includes only those product characteristics for which the perceived brand image is negative, while the second entry includes only those product characteristics for which the perceived brand image is positive. Thus probability of positive reaction is *increased* by the absence of expected negative features (entry 1, summation 1) or the presence of expected plus features (summation 2). It is *decreased* by the absence of expected plus features (entry 2, summation 1) or the presence of negative features (summation 2).

Effect of Use Opportunity. Increasing use opportunity places emphasis on existing factors tending toward a positive or negative reaction. In quantifying this concept, it is first necessary to establish whether other factors are leading toward a positive or negative decision. (The reference probability value is .5 because at this level both outcomes are equally likely.) If the net effect of other factors in the formulation is to produce a positive response probability greater than .5, the use opportunity coefficient effect will increase the existing positive bias. If, on the other hand, other factors produce a net value less than .5, the use opportunity effect will further reduce the probability of positive reaction.

Formulation of Positive Probability. Given the factors defined, in combination with the previously discussed effect of price on purchase function, the probability that consumer c will have a positive reaction to product use after purchase may be formulated as

Equation 8.38

PRPRAP(b, c)	PRobability of Positive Reaction After Purchase. Dimension: pure number.
	= EFATPR(c, b) * EFIMPR(c, b) * EFPPU(c, b) * EFUOPC(c).
EFATPR(c, b)	EFfect of ATtitude on probability of Positive Reaction to use after purchase.
	= see Equation 8.36.
EFIMPR(c, b)	EFfect of IMage on probability of Positive Reaction to use after purchase.
	= see Equation 8.37.
EFPPU(c, b)	EFfect of Price on PUrchase. Dimension: pure number.
	= see Equation 8.4.
EFUOPC(c)	EFfect of Use OPportunity Coefficient. Dimension: pure number.

$$= 1 + \frac{\text{USOPC(c)}}{C_{41}}, \text{ if remainder of PRPRAP(b, c)} \geq .5,$$

$$= 1 - \frac{\text{USOPC(c)}}{C_{41}}, \text{ if remainder of PRPRAP(b, c)} < .5.$$

USOPC(c)   USe OPportunity Coefficient. See Equation 8.1.

Formulation of Negative Probability.   Given the probability of positive reaction after purchase and forcing the consumer to react either
positively or negatively, the probability of negative reaction is simply
the probability of not having a positive response.

Equation 8.39

PRNRAP(c, b)   PRobability of Negative Reaction After Purchase.
$$= 1 - \text{PRPRAP(c, b)}.$$

Positive-Reinforcing Response

When a positive response occurs, the consumer's memory of product
characteristics and appeals is reinforced. The extent of reinforcement
has been hypothesized to be a function of the extent of response as
revealed in the reaction probability and the magnitude and bias of the
prevailing attitude toward the element. In equation form, this conditional reinforcement may be expressed as

Equation 8.40

APPMEM(ap, b, c)   APPeals ap MEMory associated with brand b of
consumer c. Dimension: pure number
$$= \text{APPMEM(ap, b, c)} * (1 + \text{PRPRAP(b, c)}$$
$$* \text{ATITD(ap, c)} * C_{42})$$
≥ 0.0, by constraint.

PRPRAP(b, c)   PRobability of Positive Reaction After Purchase.
$$= \text{see Equation 8.37.}$$

C_{42} scaling constant determining extent of memory update per probability step. Dimension: units per
attitude scale unit.
$$= 1.0, \text{ as sample value.}$$

PCHMEM(np, b, c)   Product CHaracteristic np MEMory associated with
brand b in simulated mind of consumer c. Dimen-
sion: pure number.
$$= \text{PCHMEM(np, b, c)} * (1 + \text{PRPRAP(b, c)}$$
$$* \text{ATITD(np, c)} * C_{42})$$
≥ 0.0, by constraint.

This process yields an increase in associations between the brand and positively valued attributes and a decrease in associations with negatively regarded characteristics following positive response to product use.

Negative-Weakening Response

When a negative response occurs, the consumer's memory of product characteristics and appeals is weakened by a proportionate amount according to the procedure established in Equation 8.38 as follows:

$$\text{APPMEM}(ap, b, c) = \text{APPMEM}(ap, b, c) * (1 - \text{PRNRAP}(b, c) * \text{ATITD}(ap, c) * C_{42})$$

$$\text{PCHMEM}(np, b, c) = \text{PCHMEM}(np, b, c,) * (1 - \text{PRNRAP}(b, c) * \text{ATITD}(np,c) * C_{42})$$

Thus in the negative reaction case, associations with positively regarded attributes are reduced while negatively based associations are incremented.

Brand Attitude Formation

As a result of response to product and communication experience over time, each consumer associates certain product characteristics and appeals with particular brands. The consumer's mental record of these associations is summarized in this model in the appeals and product characteristic memory entries (APPMEM(ap,b,c) and PCHMEM(np,b,c) respectively).

While the content of these memory cells is continually modified by experience, the consumer's attitude toward specific appeals and characteristics (ATITD(ap,c) and ATITD(np,c) respectively) remains constant over time.

Perceived Brand Image

The brand-specific information assimilated by a consumer and his attitude toward each content element provide the basis for his perceived image of the brand. Information perception in context of existing attitudes has already been introduced to explain the phenomenon of selective communication perception.[73] The consumer is expected to emphasize (be highly sensitive to) those elements of communication

[73] For a description of this formulation see "Assimilation of Point-of-Sale Promotion," p. 214.

content about which he feels strongly and to de-emphasize (be relatively indifferent to) those toward which he has little or no attitude.

Following arguments similar to those presented in support of selective perception, the consumer's subjective evaluation of a brand may
be described in terms of the interaction of a product attribute (appeal
or product characteristic) vectors based on consumer memory content
and subjective evaluation scalars based on consumer attitude. This
representation is illustrated graphically for the two-dimensional case
(NP = 2) in Figure 8.21.

The perceived brand image previously defined by the variable name
PEBRI(n,b,c) may be formulated as the dot product of the product
characteristic and appeal vectors.

Equation 8.41

PEBRI(n, b, c) — PErceived BRand Image of attribute n associated
with brand b in the simulated mind of consumer c.
Dimension: attitude scale units.

$$= \frac{APPMEM(ap, b, c) * ATITD(ap, c)}{\sum_{ap=1}^{AP} APPMEM(ap, b, c)}$$

$$= \frac{PCHMEM(np, b, c) * ATITD(np, c)}{\sum_{np=1}^{NP} PCHMEM(np, b, c)}.$$

APPMEM(ap, b, c) — APPeal MEMory entry associating appeal ap with
brand b in simulated mind of consumer c. Dimen-
sion: pure number.
= see Equation 8.17, for example.

PCHMEM(np, b, c) — Product CHaracteristic MEMory entry associating
product characteristic np with brand b in sim-
ulated mind of consumer c. Dimension: pure number.
= see Equation 8.18.

ATITD(n, c) — ATtITuDe toward characteristic n held by consumer c. Dimension: attitude scale units.
= consumer characteristic. See Table 8.1.

The concept of a perceived brand image has been frequently hinted
at in the literature. In a description of personality dimensions and response to automobile advertising, Pierre Martineau, for example, speaks
of "the current character of the brand in the minds of the general pub-

lic." [74] In the same article he comments on "the broad attitude that exists toward the car, comprising its product personality."

Attitude Toward a Brand

The preceding sections have been concerned with measurement of attitudes toward product characteristics and appeals. It is now appropriate to consider simulating the process through which these components are combined in a single "brand attitude." The conceptual role of a "brand attitude" (ATTBR(c,b)) was noted while developing representations of shopping and purchase behavior.

The consumer's attitude toward a brand should reflect the net effect of his perceived brand image. Brand attitude might therefore be formulated as the algebraic sum of all elements of the perceived brand image. Using this concept consumer c's attitude toward brand b may be expressed in terms of perceived brand image as

Equation 8.42

ATTBR(b, c)   ATTitude toward BRand b held by consumer c. Dimension: attitude units.

$$= \left[\sum_{ap=1}^{AP} PEBRI(ap, b, c) + \sum_{np=1}^{NP} PEBRI(np, b, c) \right]/2.$$

PEBRI(n, b, c)   PErceived BRand Image of attribute n of brand b as perceived by consumer c.
    = see Equation 8.41.

Inclusion of appeal as well as product characteristic elements in brand attitude provides a partial recognition of the symbolic status implications of consumption.[75] In this context, the brand name is viewed as a symbol to which product characteristics and appeals are linked by the consumer. In some instances, the brand name is more appropriately described as a product characteristic eliciting attitudinal response as a status symbol.[76] When an image component is added by the brand name or symbol, the Equation 8.41 formulation is modified to take account of this effect.

[74] P. Martineau, "A Case Study: What Automobiles Mean to Americans," in Ferber and Wales, *op. cit.,* Footnote 12, p. 48.

[75] See, for example, D. Riesman, "Food and Sex as Symbols," D. Riesman, R. Denney, and N. Glazer, *The Lonely Crowd* (New Haven: Yale University Press, 1961), pp. 141–148.

[76] W. Henry, "The Meaning of Gasoline Symbols" in Ferber and Wales, *op. cit.,* Footnote 12, pp. 206–231.

Attitude Toward a Retailer

The subtlety of consumer-retailer interactions is well illustrated by Ernest Dichter's comments regarding the shopper's relationship with sales personnel as a determinant of retailer choice.

Actually, proximity had very little to do with store selection. We found stores convenient to apartment houses and residential neighborhoods which were "isolated," which were shunned by the neighborhood, although they were clean and carried standard merchandise. They were avoided because the owners or sales personnel were considered intruders, they had failed to establish a sympathetic relationship with their neighbors.[77]

Other observers suggest that consumer-retailer interaction should be viewed in terms of rational problem solving.

The instrumental side of the American household involves rational foresight and skill in problem solving. The realization that buyers come into the market to solve problems is more reliable than the notion that selling is simply a matter of implanting habits or taking advantage of impulses in passive and muddle-headed consumers.[78]

Some studies suggest that the clientele of stores having very different images is more heterogenous than might be expected. This is particularly true in the case of large department stores that seem to attract a wide cross section of the population. On the basis of a study of customer records of Philadelphia department stores, one author concluded that the ". . . reputed appeal of certain stores for certain income groups has been greatly exaggerated. Regardless of reputation each seems to secure the same composition of patrons." [79]

Pierre Martineau, on the other hand, continues to place considerable reliance on the hypothesis that different socioeconomic groups are attracted to different types of stores.

The social class profiles of each store, even of the chain grocery supermarkets, that conceivably have universal appeal, indicate that the shopper senses instinctively whether this is a Lower Lower Class store or an Upper

[77] E. Dichter, "The Real Reason Why People Buy," *Advertising and Selling,* July 1948, p. 561.

[78] W. Alderson, *op. cit.,* Footnote 22, p. 184.

[79] Blankertz, "Shopping Habits and Income — A Philadelphia Department Store Study," *Journal of Marketing,* Vol. 14 (January 1950), p. 577.

Middle Class store. She isn't going to take a chance feeling out of place in a store where she considers she doesn't fit. . . . The shopper is intimidated by some stores, she feels that some are considerably beneath her. She is looking for the ones where she feels comfortable and where her goals are understood and respected. All of this has nothing to do with economics. The very shouting of bargains and sales . . . conveys to the High Status shopper that she doesn't belong in that kind of establishment. She avoids any milling mobs.[80]

It would appear that store image is a factor in the consumer's shopping-purchase process, although its importance varies significantly between individuals. This section is concerned with factors affecting the formation of consumer attitudes toward retailers. The impact of this attitude, once formed, is determined by other model segments.

Retailer Promotion Activities

The process through which a retailer generates advertising content and schedules promotion is modeled in Chapter 9. Working with local advertising media, the simulated retailer must choose between two broad courses of action. He may use mats, tapes, or film supplied by the manufacturer or create his own brand-oriented or institutional promotion. Brand-oriented advertisements may be described using previously developed content descriptors. Institutional advertising generated by the retailer in an attempt to enhance his consumer image requires additional consideration.

Within this system, retail institutional advertising appeals will be limited to (1) price, (2) quality, and (3) selection. Using this structure, retailer institutional advertising may be modeled in terms of appeal functions comparable to those employed in the brand-advertising case.

Institutional advertisement content generated by the retailer model is specified in terms of the proportion of promotion devoted to these three appeals. The variable transferring this institutional content from the retail sector to the consumer model is defined as follows:

Equation 8.43

> PRRADA(n, r) PRoportion of Retailer r Advertisement Devoted to Appeal n. Dimension: pure number.
>   = input from retail sector. See Equation 9.21, p. 291.

[80] P. Martineau, "The Pattern of Social Classes," in R. L. Clewett (ed.), *Marketing's Role in Scientific Management* (Chicago: American Marketing Association, 1957), pp. 241–242.

Probability of Exposure to Retail Advertising

Once retail advertising enters a media channel, it becomes part of the general media model structure developed earlier to describe the probability of consumer c being exposed to advertisement na. Because the retailer model developed in Chapter 9 is constrained to generate only one advertisement per retailer per time period, the previously encountered proliferation of up to NA distinct advertisements for a given brand is not possible in the retail promotion case.

Given this constraint the probability of exposure may be expressed as

Equation 8.44

> PREXRA(c, r, t) PRobability of consumer c EXposure to Retailer r's Advertisement at time t. Dimension: pure number.
> $$= AVMED(c, m(r)) * PRADEX(r, t).$$

> PRADEX(r, t) PRobability of ADvertising EXposure to advertisement r in media type m(r) at time t. Dimension: pure number.
> $$= see\ Equation\ 8.11A.$$

> AVMED(c, m(r)) AVailability of MEDia type m used by retailer r to consumer c. Dimension: pure number (binary).
> $$= see\ Equation\ 8.8.$$

Retail Advertising Assimilation

The assimilation of retailer advertisements involves processes already considered for manufacturer-generated promotion; the same factors determine whether or not the advertisement will be assimilated by the consumer. Formulation of the consumer probability of assimilating *brand-oriented* promotion originated by the retailer is identical to that for brand-specific media promotion summarized in Equation 8.16.[81] The probability of assimilation of *institutional* promotion content is developed in an analogous manner. However, due to the introduction of institutional content specifiers, the attitudinal effect formulation is slightly modified.

Equation 8.45

> PRNTRA(c, r, t) PRobability of consumer c assimilating Retailer r's (institutional) Advertisement at time t. Dimension: pure number.
>
> $$= PREXRA(c, r, t) * [EFADSZ(r) + EFADCL(r)]$$
> $$* EFADAP(c, r).$$

[81] See "Probability of Assimilating an Advertisement," p. 190.

EFADAP(c, r)　　EFfect of ADvertising APpeals in promotion by retailer r as perceived by consumer c.

$$= C_{21} + C_{22} * \frac{\sum_{n=1}^{3} |ATITD(n, c)| * PRRADA(n, r)}{\sum_{n=1}^{3} PRRADA(n, r)}.$$

ATITD(n, c)　　ATtITuDe of consumer c toward institutional appeal n. Dimension: attitude scale units.
= consumer characteristic (range -5 to $+5$).

PRRADA(n, r)　　PRoportion of Retailer r Advertisement Devoted to appeal n.
= see Equation 8.43.

C_{21} and C_{22}　　scaling constants.
= see Equation 8.14 for definition.

PREXRA(c, r, t)　　PRobability of consumer c EXposure to Retailer r Advertisement at time t. Dimension: pure number.
= see Equation 8.43.

EFADSZ(r)　　EFfect of ADvertisement SiZe in advertisement r.
= see Equation 8.13.

EFADCL(r)　　EFfect of ADvertisement CoLor in advertisement r.
= see Equation 8.14.

Consumer response to content of a retailer-generated advertisement is described by the generalized response model representing memory update and awareness gain described earlier in this chapter.[82]

The Perceived Retailer Image

Following reasoning analogous to that presented when developing the "perceived brand image," [83] the consumer's perception of a retail store may be summarized in a "Perceived Retailer Image" formulated in terms of memory content and attitudes.

Equation 8.46

PEREI(n, r, c)　　PErceived REtailer Image of appeal n associated with retailer r in mind of consumer c. Dimension: pure number.

$$= \frac{APPMEM(n, r, c) * ATTITD(n, c)}{\sum_{n=1}^{3} APPMEM(n, r, c)}.$$

[83] See "Representation of Response to Communication," p. 194.
[83] See "Perceived Brand Image," p. 224.

APPMEM(n, r, c)   APPeals MEMory entry associating appeal n with retailer r in mind of consumer c. Dimension: pure number.
= see Equation 8.17.

ATTITD(n, c)   ATtITuDe toward appeal n held by consumer c. Dimension: attitude scale units.
= consumer characteristic. See Table 8.1.

Attitude Toward a Retailer

Once the perceived retailer image has been established, the attitude toward a particular retailer may be defined as the algebraic sum of the elements of perceived retailer image. This formulation parallels that developed for the brand attitude in the preceding section.

Equation 8.47

ATTRET(r, c)   ATTitude of consumer c toward RETailer r. Dimension: attitude scale units.

$$= \sum_{n=1}^{3} PEREI(n, r, c).$$

PEREI(n, r, c)   PErceived REtailer Image of appeal n associated with retailer r in mind of consumer c.
= see Equation 8.46.

The Forgetting Process

The discussion thus far has been concerned with factors affecting information assimilation and attitude and awareness gain in the mind of the consumer. This section is concerned with the inverse of the learning process, forgetting.

Loss of Awareness

One form of awareness loss is a result of the specification that a consumer can be "aware" of only one brand at a time. The mutually exclusive nature of awareness imposes automatic forgetting of one brand as a prerequisite to attainment of awareness of a second brand.

A second form of forgetting is associated with awareness loss due to lack of exposure to product or information. In context of this system structure, the probability of losing awareness of brand b due to forgetting over time is dependent on three factors: (1) the time since communication regarding brand b was last assimilated, (2) the time since brand b was last seen or used, and (3) the level of existing attitude toward brand b.

The present model does not facilitate maintenance of an explicit record of lapsed time since consumer c last assimilated communication regarding brand b or was exposed to that brand. However, functions developed earlier in this chapter may be used to approximate the information that would be obtained by saving an actual time record of consumer experience. Previously developed assimilation formulations indicate the probable frequency of communication reinforcement and may be used to approximate the time lapse between successive communication responses. The probability of exposure to product provides an estimate of the time lapse between in-store product exposure, while the use opportunity function is indicative of use experience with a purchased brand.

The probability of awareness loss is inversely proportional to the probability of being exposed to the brand or communication regarding it. Product or a salesman may be encountered in any of R retailers carrying the brand. An advertisement may be noted in any of M media types, and word-of-mouth communication may be received from any of C-1 consumers. It is therefore necessary to sum probabilities over retailers, media types, and consumers to establish the probability of encountering a single source of memory reinforcement. Representation of cumulative response over time is achieved by a smoothing function.

Equation 8.48

SEFXFA(t, c, b)   Smoothed EFfect of eXposure on probability of Forgetting Awareness.

$$
= \text{SEFXFA}(t - 1, c, b) + C_{43} \left[1 - \sum_{na=1}^{NA(b)} \right.
$$

$$
\text{PRASAD}(c, na, t) - \sum_{c_t=1}^{CT(b)} \text{PRASWM}(c, c_t)
$$

$$
- \sum_{r=1}^{R} [[\text{PRAXBR}(c, r, b) + \text{PRSHP}(c)]
$$

$$
* [\text{PRASPS}(r, b, c) + \text{PRASSC}(c, r, b)]]
$$

$$
- \text{USOPC}(c) * \text{PROWN}(b, c)
$$

$$
\left. - \text{SEFXA}(t - 1, c, b) \right].
$$

PRASAD(c, na, t)   PRobability of consumer c ASsimilating ADvertisement na at time t.
                     = see Equation 8.16.

PRASWM(c, c$_t$)   PRobability of consumer c ASsimilating Word-of-Mouth communication generated by consumer c$_t$.
= see Equation 8.24.

PRAXBR(c, r, b)   PRobability of consumer c being Accidentally eXposed to BRand b in retail outlet r.
= see Equation 8.28.

PRSHP(c)   PRobability of consumer c SHoPping for product line (implied).
= see Equation 8.3A.

PRASPS(c, r, b)   PRobability of consumer c ASsimilating Point-of-Sale promotion for brand b in retail outlet r.
= see Equation 8.30.

PRASSC(c, r, b)   PRobability of consumer c ASsimilating Salesman Communication regarding brand b.
= see Equation 8.34.

USOPC(c)   USe OPportunity Coefficient.
= see Equation 8.1.

PROWN(b, c)   PRoduct OWNership indicator for brand b.
= see Table 8.1.

NA(b)   Number of Advertisements for which b(na) = b.

CT(b)   number of Consumer's generaTing word-of-mouth regarding brand b.

C$_{43}$ smoothing constant

Representation of the effect of existing brand attitude on the probability of awareness loss is based on the observation that high attitude toward a brand yields low probability of awareness loss. This relationship is illustrated in Figure 8.22.

Equation 8.49

EFATA(c, b)   EFfect of ATtitude on probability of consumer c forgetting Awareness of brand b.

$$= \text{ENXPF}\left[-\left|\frac{\text{ATTBR(b, c)}}{C_{44}}\right|\right].$$

C$_{44}$ scaling constant. Dimension: attitude scale units.
= 2.0 as sample value.

Because either existing attitude or exposure to communication and product may deter forgetting, the probability formulation is based on the smaller of the attitude effect or exposure — the factor (exposure or attitude) that constitutes the most effective deterrent to forgetting.

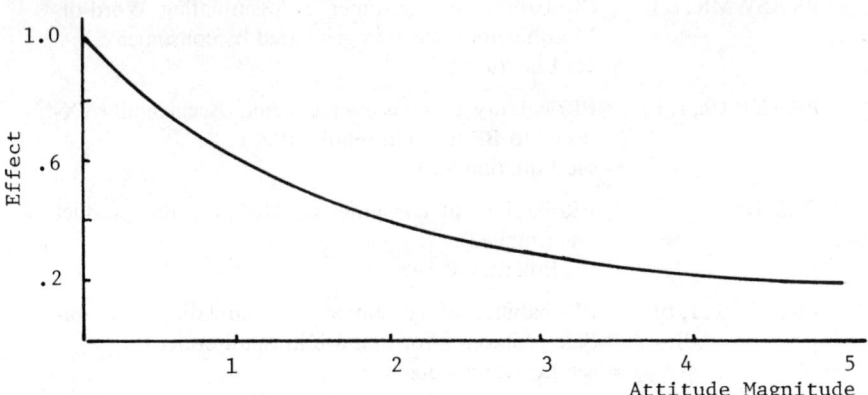

Figure 8.22. Effect of attitude on probability of forgetting awareness.

Equation 8.50

PRFGAW(c, b)   PRobability of consumer c ForGetting AWareness of
               brand b.
             = MINIMF(EFATA(c, b), SEFXFA(c, b)).

Memory Reduction Due to Forgetting

The major difference between memory reduction and awareness loss
rests on the distinction between general and specific information. Exposure to the product or any brand communication maintains awareness. Because awareness connotes a high level of cognizance, it is not
surprising to find the consumer less apt to forget specific attributes of
a brand of which he is aware rather than unaware. However, because
memory entries relate to specific product characteristics and appeals,
mere exposure is not sufficient to reinforce all existing memory. In the
case of memory, it is necessary to consider content noted rather than
simple existence or absence of exposure.

The effect of communication containing information supportive to
existing memory content on memory retention may be expressed in
terms of the smoothed probability of assimilating communication content relating to specific brand characteristics (product characteristics or
appeals).

Equation 8.51

SEFXML(t, n, c, b)   Smoothed EFfect of eXposure on consumer c Mem-
                      ory Loss associated with characteristic (product
                      characteristic or appeal) n in association with
                      brand b.

$$
= \text{SEFXML}(t - 1, n, c, b) + C_{43} * \left[\left[1 - \sum_{na=1}^{NA(b)} \right. \right.
$$

$$
\text{PRASAD}(c, na, t) * \left\{ \begin{array}{c} \text{EVAPWT}(n, na) \\ \text{or} \\ \text{EVPCWT}(n, na) \end{array} \right\}
$$

$$
- \sum_{c_t=1}^{CT(b)} \text{PRASWM}(c, c_t) * \text{CONWMC}(c_t, n, b)
$$

$$
- \sum_{r=1}^{R} \left[[\text{PRAXBR}(c,r,b) + \text{PRSHP}(c)] \right.
$$

$$
* \text{PRASPS}(r, b, c) * \left\{ \begin{array}{c} \text{EVPSAW}(n, na(r)) \\ \text{or} \\ \text{EVPCWP}(n, na(r)) \end{array} \right\}
$$

$$
+ \text{PRASSC}(c, r, b) * \left\{ \begin{array}{c} \text{SCAPC}(n, b, r) \\ \text{or} \\ \text{SCPCC}(n, b, r) \end{array} \right\} \left. \right] \right] * (1
$$

$$
\left. - \text{AWARE}(c, b) * C_{45}) - \text{SEFXML}(t - 1, n, c, b) \right].
$$

PRASAD(c, na, t)	PRobability that consumer c will ASsimilate ADvertisement na at time t.
	= see Equation 8.16.
EVPCWT(n, na)	EValuation of Product Characteristic WeighTing of characteristic n in advertisement na.
EVAPWT(n, na)	EValuation of APpeal n WeighTing in advertisement na.
PRASPS(c, b, r)	PRobability of consumer c ASsimilating Point-of-Sale promotion for brand b in retail outlet r.
	= see Equation 8.30.
EVPCWP(n, na(r))	EValuation of Product Characteristic Weighting of characteristic n in Point-of-sale piece na(r).
EVPSAW(n, na(r))	EValuation of Point-of-Sale Appeal n Weighting in promotion na(r).
PRASWM(c, c_t)	PRobability of consumer c ASsimilating Word-of-Mouth communication from consumer c_t.
	= see Equation 8.24.
CONWMC(c_t, n, b)	CONtents of Word-of-Mouth Communication regarding characteristic n of brand b generated by consumer c_t.
	= see Equation 8.7.
PRASSC(c, r, b)	PRobability of consumer c ASsimilating Salesman Communication regarding brand b in retail outlet r.
	= see Equation 8.34.

SCPCC(n, b, r)   Salesman Communication Product Characteristic n Content relating to brand b generated in retail outlet r.

SCAPC(n, b, r)   Salesman Communication APpeal Content relating to brand b generated in retail outlet r.

AWARE(c, b)   consumer c's AWAREness of product b.
= consumer descriptor, see Table 8.1.

The effect of existing memory content and magnitude of bias are also considered at the product characteristic and appeal level.

Equation 8.52

EPBIML(n, b, c)   Effect of Perceived Brand Image on Memory Loss associated with characteristic n of brand b in simulated mind of consumer c.

$$= \text{ENXPF} \left[-\left| \frac{\text{PEBRI}(n, b, c)}{C_{45}} \right| \right].$$

PEBRI(n, b, c)   PErceived BRand Image of characteristic n of brand b as perceived by consumer c. Dimension: attitude scale units.
= see Equation 8.41.

C_{45} scaling constant. Dimension: attitude scale units.
= 1.0, as sample value.

Forgetting Due to Conflict Resolution

Consumers seldom exhibit a microanalytical approach to choice situations. Reacting to a limited number of salient characteristics, they establish categorical likes and dislikes. This tendency to categorize as black or white produces pressure to resolve conflicting perceptions. The consumer is not apt to continue for long periods of time with directly conflicting attitudes about elements of a product; he is not apt to maintain a strong positive attitude toward one attribute and a strong negative attitude toward another recognized characteristic of a single product. Admitting that both characteristics are present in the same item creates conflict or dissonance that must be resolved. "The existence of dissonance gives rise to pressures to reduce the dissonance and avoid increases in dissonance." [84]

Festinger has referred to the process by which this conflict is resolved as cognitive dissonance resolution.[85] Because the response model may

[84] L. Festinger, *A Theory of Cognitive Dissonance* (Evanston, Ill.: Row, Paterson, and Company, 1957), p. 31.
[85] *Ibid.*, p. 80.

create directly conflicting attitudes in the simulated mind of the consumer, dissonance resolution may account for significant reductions in memory content. If the consumer associates several factors with a brand and his attitude toward one or more of these factors is in opposition (contrabiased) to the majority of his attitudes, the conflicting attitude(s) will be reduced in the direction of compliance with the majority attitude.

The process to be modeled in this context has been described in terms of the "congruity principle."

Whenever two signs are related by an assertion, the mediating reaction characteristic of each shifts toward congruence with that characteristic of the other, the magnitude of the shift being inversely proportional to the intensities of the interacting reactions.[86]

Two kinds of assertions are defined: (1) associative assertions (+), and (2) disassociative assertions (−). It is then predicted that

. . . Whenever two signs are related by an assertion, they are congruent to the extent that their mediating reactions are equally intense, either in the same (compatible) direction of excitation in the case of associate assertions or in opposite (reciprocally antagonistic) directions in the case of disassociative assertions.[87]

The congruity principle may be formulated in terms of perceived brand image as follows. If an element in the perceived brand image set is biased in opposition to the majority of the other elements in that set, the magnitude of the opposing element will be reduced.

This formulation has substantial empirical support. As an example, a study of student attitudes toward war and the effect of these attitudes on retention of information found that acceptable information was retained much longer than unacceptable data.[88]

The extent of positive or negative imbalance may be established by summing positive and negative brand image elements separately and examining the ratio of the two sums. This ratio indicates the extent to which bias favors the positive attitudes, while the inverse indicates

---

[86] C. E. Osgood, G. Suci, and P. Tannenbaum, *The Measurement of Meaning* (Urbana, Ill.: University of Illinois Press, 1957), pp. 200–201.

[87] *Ibid.,* p. 203.

[88] L. Postman and G. Murphy, "The Factor of Attitude in Associated Memory," *Journal of Experimental Psychology,* Vol. 33 (September 1943), pp. 228–238.

the extent to which prevailing attitudes favor the formation of a negative brand attitude.

Equation 8.53

EFCDML(n, c, b) EFfect of Cognitive Dissonance on Memory Loss regarding characteristic n associated with brand b in simulated mind of consumer c.

$$= \frac{ATITD(c, n)}{C_{46}} * \left[\frac{\sum\limits_{n=1}^{N} |PEBRI(n, b, c)|_{+only}}{\sum\limits_{n=1}^{N} |PEBRI(n, b, c)|_{-only}} \right],$$

if PEBRI(n, b, c) $\leq$ 0.0,

$$= \frac{ATITD(c, n)}{C_{46}} * \left[\frac{\sum\limits_{n=1}^{N} |PEBRI(n, b, c)|_{-only}}{\sum\limits_{n=1}^{N} |PEBRI(n, b, c)|_{+only}} \right],$$

if PEBRI(n, b, c) $>$ 0.0.

PEBRI(n, b, c) PErceived BRand Image of characteristic n associated with brand b in simulated mind of consumer c.
= see Equation 8.41.

ATITD(c, n) ATtITuDe of consumer c toward characteristic n. Dimension: attitude scale units.
= consumer characteristic. See Table 8.1.

C_{46} scaling constant. Dimension: attitude scale units.
= 5.0, as sample value.

This model implies that an individual's behavior will be consistent with his knowledge and beliefs and that the individual will attempt to maintain consistency between various attitudes that he holds. When placed in a situation in which inconsistency (dissonance) is created, he will act in a manner designed to reduce this dissonance (achieve consonance). Because dissonance is anxiety producing, the individual should attempt to avoid circumstances and communication that might produce dissonance.[89] This suggests that the selective perception formulations developed earlier might be modified to bias in favor of perception of congruent (positive attitude) content.

A study of the readership of automobile advertising by new and old car owners supports this assumption concerning selective exposure to information.

[89] Evidence in support of this theory in context of an attitude framework is provided by W. J. McGuire, "Cognitive Consistency and Attitude Change," *Journal of Abnormal and Social Psychology,* 60 (1960), pp. 345–353.

It was found that new car owners read advertisements of their own car more often than of cars they considered but did not buy and other cars not involved in the choice. These selected tendencies in readership were much less pronounced among old car owners. This finding supports the theoretical derivation that persons in general seek out consonant or supporting information after an important decision in an attempt to reduce dissonance resulting from it.[90]

This simulation is formulated on the assumption that the consumer will act to reduce dissonance, rather than accept and live with dissonance, through the use of one or more defense mechanisms (i.e., repression, displacement, or transference).[91]

For the individual who chooses to deal with conflicts without resolving them and who employs defense mechanisms, the theory of cognitive dissonance may fail in its most fundamental assumptions, "the pressure of dissonance gives rise to pressure to reduce that dissonance." However, evidence supporting the dissonance reduction model has been obtained in all markets investigated to date.

The probability of memory reduction based on interaction between the three factors just defined is summarized in Equation 8.54.

Equation 8.54

PRMRED(n, b, c)   PRobability of Memory REDuction of characteristic n associated with brand b in simulated mind of consumer c.
= MAXF[MINF(EFCDML(n, c, b), EPBIML(n, c, b)), SEFXML(t, n, c, b)].

This equation indicates that the probability of memory reduction is established by the greater of (1) the smoothed effect of exposure, and (2) the minimum of the effect of cognitive dissonance and the effect of perceived brand image. In the case of conflict between perceived brand image and cognitive dissonance, the factor supporting memory retention and therefore *least likely to lead to forgetting* will prevail, while in the interaction between the exposure and memory-based functions, the factor *most likely to lead to forgetting* will prevail.

[90] D. Ehrlich, *et al.*, "Postdecision Exposure to Relevant Information," *Journal of Abnormal and Social Psychology*, Vol. 54 (January 1957), pp. 101–102.

[91] For a discussion of this alternative approach see A. Freud, *Ego and the Mechanisms of Defense*, translated by C. Baines (New York: International Universities Press, 1964).

The Process of Memory Reduction

When memory reduction — forgetting — occurs, the content of the memory element is reduced to a percentage of its prereduction level. Use of a constant percentage rather than constant unit decrement reduces high exposure entries by more than low exposure entries but makes total forgetting — complete loss of memory — impossible. This formulation is consistent with accepted psychological theory.[92]

The forgetting process may be represented as

APPMEM(ap, b, c) APPeals MEMory entry associating appeal ap with brand b in simulated mind of consumer c. Dimension: pure number.
$$= \text{APPMEM(ap, b, c)} * (1 - C_{47}).$$

C_{47} constant determining proportion of memory content lost due to forgetting.
$$= .10 \text{ as sample value.}$$

PCHMEM(np, b, c) Product CHaracteristic MEMory entry associating product characteristic np with brand b in simulated mind of consumer c. Dimension: pure number.
$$= \text{PCHMEM(np, b, c)} * (1 - C_{47}).$$

Summary

This chapter has focused on the development of a quantitative model of consumer behavior limited in scope and detail by specifications developed in Chapter 3.

Review of Model Development

In beginning this chapter, four categories of consumer descriptors were defined. Demographic variables included geographic location — urban, suburban, or rural residency — and age. Socioeconomic factors were represented by income and education. Behavioral characteristics included product ownership and consumer media habits. Psychological attributes were summarized in attitude and awareness variables indicating consumer orientation toward product characteristics, appeals, brands, and retailers.

---

[92] See H. Ebbinghaus, *Memory* (translated by H. A. Ruger and C. E. Bussemius) (New York: Teacher's College, 1913). Evidence supporting this formulation was first presented by Ebbinghaus who found that retention curves were roughly logarithmic.

Representation of consumer behavior began with the three consumer actions established by the Chapter 3 specifications: shopping, purchase, and word-of-mouth generation. Consideration of the shopping decision led to the perceived need concept formulated in terms of consumer attitude, awareness, existing product ownership, and use opportunity. Perceived need in combination with income determined the consumer's shopping probability. Later in the chapter, the probability of accidental exposure to a brand in the course of normal shopping was formulated.

The consumer's probability of purchasing a specified brand in a particular retail outlet was formulated as a function of brand price, consumer income, consumer orientation toward the brand as reflected in attitude and awareness, and salesman selling effort at point of sale.

Consumer word-of-mouth generation — talking to another consumer about a brand — was related to consumer brand orientation. It was noted that a high probability of talking might exist immediately following purchase as a result of response to initial product use.

Representation of word-of-mouth communication content introduced the problem of describing information flow in terms of product characteristics and appeals contents.

Following representation of the three consumer actions, factors influencing consumer orientation were examined.

The consumer's probability of being exposed to media advertising, point-of-sale promotion, salesman presentations, and word-of-mouth comment were formulated. The concept of assimilation was introduced to describe consumer response to communication content. The previously introduced prominence scale was employed to measure the extent of brand identification in a communication.

The process of orientation change was formulated in terms of changes in consumer awareness and memory content as a result of assimilating communication. Response functions based on communication content and consumer preassimilation orientation established the probability of awareness gain and form of selective memory update.

Consumer reaction to product use was described as a function of consumer perceived brand image prior to purchase and actual characteristics of the brand determined through use. Product price as perceived by the consumer and consumer attitude toward the brand were also included in this formulation in which use opportunity served as a weighting factor.

The concept of Perceived Brand Image was quantified, using consumer memory content and attitudes toward product characteristics and appeals. Attitude toward a brand was derived as the net effect of elements of perceived brand image algebraically summed. Perceived Retailer Image and attitude toward the retailer were developed paralleling procedures followed for the brand case.

Exposure, assimilation, and response functions for retail promotion were considered separately from other communication effects with the basic communication model modified to account for specialized characteristics of retail institutional promotion.

The process of forgetting was considered in terms of memory reduction and awareness loss as a result of lack of exposure to information or product over time. Cognitive dissonance resolution was introduced as the basis for process models explaining the tendency for the consumer to develop internally consistent attitudes over time.

Graphic Summary of Interaction

Interaction characteristics of the model developed in this chapter are summarized in Figure 8.23, which is divided into three sectors representing the sources of information and product flow in the manufacturer and retailer sectors as well as major consumer sector action and response functions.

Figure 8.23 illustrates the generation of media advertising, point-of-sale promotion, product flow, and retail advertising support in the manufacturer sector. Media advertising generated by the manufacturer is transmitted directly to the consumer sector, while other elements of flow must pass through the retail sector before reaching the consumer. Media characteristics affecting the consumer's media advertising exposure are included in the manufacturer sector, although they might more appropriately be considered a function of a distinct communication channel.

The flow chart elements representing channel origination in the retail sector indicate the dependence of consumer sales on retailer stocking and order decisions. In a similar manner, retailer placement of point-of-sale promotion material is shown to be a necessary precondition of consumer exposure. Selling effort is represented as the product of a retailer decision to push a particular brand. The content of selling messages and generation of retailer advertising are similarly determined by the retailer model.

On the left of the consumer sector flow chart in Figure 8.23, the

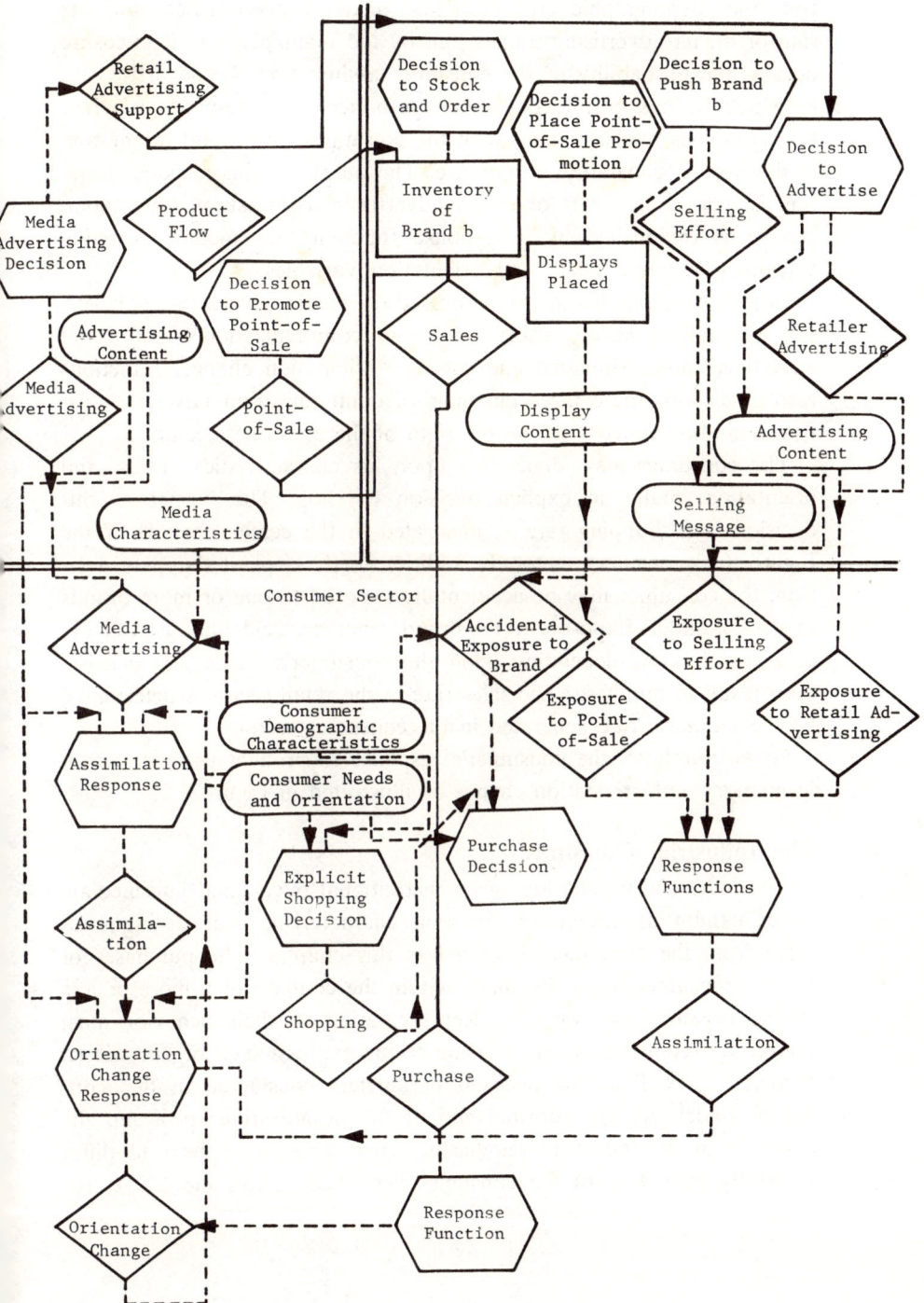

Figure 8.23. Macro flow chart of consumer-retailer-manufacturer interactions.

probability of media advertising exposure is shown to be a function of consumer demographic characteristics, media characteristics, and the rate of media advertising undertaken by the manufacturer. If exposure occurs, the probability of the consumer assimilating the advertisement to which he has been exposed is determined by a response function that combines media content with the consumer's need and orientation to develop a probability of response. The output of this response function is viewed as a rate of media advertising assimilation. Orientation change is established by a response function that modifies existing consumer memory, need, and orientation variables.

In a manner parallel to that discussed for media advertising, point-of-sale promotion, selling effort (salesman communication), and retail advertising are assimilated and produce orientation change. Functions associated with these three channels of communication flow are illustrated in abbreviated form on the right of the consumer sector.

The consumer may, depending upon his characteristics, needs, and orientation, make an explicit decision to shop. The output of this decision is a shopping rate as illustrated in the center channel of the Figure 8.23 consumer sector. In addition to the explicit shopping decision, the consumer may be accidentally exposed to one or more brands in a retail outlet. Exposure to the brand, whether accidental or explicitly determined, may, depending upon the consumer's needs and orientation, result in purchase. The sales rate in the retail sector is determined by the purchase rate generated in the consumer sector.

Given purchase, the consumer's response to product use may result in memory and orientation change as illustrated in Figure 8.23.

The Industrial Consumer

The industrial purchasing agent, institutional buyer, and intermediate buyer exhibit an important common characteristic that distinguishes them from the consumer simulated in this chapter. The purchases of the nonconsumer buyer are made within the confines of a more or less formal organization structure. Representation of their behavior must therefore encompass factors relevant to the expression of organizational influence as well as the decision parameters considered in this consumer model. At the informal end of the organization spectrum, the behavior of the industrial purchasing agent does not appear to differ markedly from that of the consumer described in this model. At the other extreme, organizational constraints may be controlling. Industrial purchasing behavior has been simulated using extensions of the basic action and response models developed for the consumer case in this chapter.

Chapter 9

A MODEL OF RETAILER BEHAVIOR

This chapter focuses on aspects of retailer behavior encompassed by the specifications developed in Chapter 3. The present objective is to develop a simulation of retailer behavior based on the macrostructure provided by these specifications. The resulting model, like its consumer counterpart, will be descriptive rather than normative. It will summarize an empirically verified description of the behavior of individuals filling the retailer's role in the marketing system.

The retailer model may represent the actions and responses of an institution or group of individuals as well as a single person. It is possible to look at the limiting case of an individual proprietorship in which all functions are performed by the same person. However, this model is oriented toward description of processes common to vast commercial complexes in which thousands of people perform highly functionalized jobs as well as the "Mom and Pop" store in which one or two people fill all functional capacities.

In developing this simulation, decision and response functions will be formulated as if each retailer were a single abstract individual. This approach need not conflict with the fact that larger retailers are enterprises in which many individuals serve in various capacities. The focus is on processes through which actions are taken and opinions formed. When applied to the proprietorship, the model should describe the actions and responses of the individual retailer. In the case of a large firm, it should encompass the actions of the enterprise — the consensus among different individuals who collectively respond to their environment and determine the policy and actions of the firm.

246

This model is to be used to examine interactions between the retailer and other elements of the marketing environment. It is not intended to encompass interpersonal interactions within the retail firm. As long as its limited specified functions are kept clearly in mind, the advantages realized from the abstract retailer-as-an-individual structure are substantial.

Description of a Retailer

Structural specifications for the retailer model parallel those of the Chapter 8 consumer model. Both models are cell simulations in which population elements of characteristic types are represented explicitly. Total population behavior is simulated through aggregation of the effects of actions taken by each cell unit with the impact of each unit weighted to reflect the relative importance of its characteristic type in the total population.

The first step in defining the cell model structure will be to specify characteristics that appear relevant as distinguishing attributes affecting retailer behavior. Once characteristics have been defined, retailer actions will be examined to establish relationships between retailer attributes and decision and response processes. Upon completion of this specification, action and response functions will be developed to provide a quantitative and testable model.

Demographic characteristics of the consumer population are also relevant as retailer descriptors. It is, for example, desirable to distinguish on the basis of geographic region so that retailers may be associated with consumer populations exhibiting regional product preferences. It is similarly useful to distinguish between rural, suburban, and metropolitan retailers.

Before delineating further characteristics of the retailer population it may be useful to review basic functions of the retailer specified in Chapter 3. Taking advantage of previous experience with the consumer model this review will be structed in terms of retailer actions having counterparts in the consumer model and those that are unique to retail business activities.

Consumerlike Activities of the Retailer

Those performing the retail function are members of the community in which they work and, as such, subject to influence by factors in the marketing environment previously noted as affecting the consumer, e.g., media promotion, word-of-mouth discussion, and product experiences. Although their objectives may differ from those of nonretailer consumer's, they are members of consumer society. It is therefore necessary to take account of the retailers' role as consumers and to recognize attributes affecting their consumerlike actions and responses. Consumer characteristics specified in Table 8.1 are relevant in this context.

The process through which retailers react to trade promotion is analogous to the previously discussed consumer media response. Similar considerations influence the probability of exposure to media and to specific advertisements. In both instances perception and evaluation of communication are influenced by pre-exposure attitude, awareness, and perceived brand image.

Product characteristics and appeals absent from the consumer realm may require the addition of new dimensions to the previously developed response structure. However, if the communication response model developed in Chapter 8 provides a meaningful description of the process through which a human recipient responds to communication content, it is applicable to both the retailer and consumer.

The Retailer as a Businessman

While the retailer's role as a member of the consumer community cannot be ignored, the major concern of this chapter is with his activities as a businessman.

The consumer and retailer are both concerned with (have attitude toward) a brand's quality, appearance, functional capabilities, and price. The retailer also has attitudes toward available margin, existing demand, manufacturer promotional support, extent of present retail coverage, level of price maintenance, degree of product differentiation, and product line composition.

The retailer in his role as a businessman forms expectations, makes plans for the future based on these expectations, and takes action to implement his plans. Two types of expectations may be noted. First, there are broad expectations relating to the business and economic climate. These influence the retailer's over-all optimism or pessimism and provide a bias affecting his planning. Second, there are brand specific expectations relating to expected unit sales, competitive pricing, margins, and promotional support. Both types of expectations are based on the retailer's perception and evaluation of present and historical conditions.

Specification of Retailer Characteristics

Model development does not begin with the definition of a final set of retailer characteristics in terms of descriptor variables. Characteristics specification and model development are interrelated processes. Development begins with a tentative list of characteristics and, as the model is synthesized, this list expands and contracts until, with the final statement of the model, the final set of descriptors required by the model is determined. Although this process may be more or less orderly, it inevitably involves a certain amount of cutting and trying. Ways of viewing a process which, on first formulation, appear wholly adequate, are found lacking as the model is developed or validation is attempted.

For purposes of presentation, this discussion of model formulation begins with the specification of retailer descriptors used in the final model. This organization provides a reasonably efficient means of communicating structure once a model has been developed. However, it is important to recognize that this sequence of presentation does not reflect the actual chronology of model development.

As indicated earlier, the retailer population will be divided into regional sections corresponding to specific geographic regions and urban, suburban, and rural locations.

Within each geographic area, retailers will be described in terms of demographic, economic, behavioral, and psychological characteristics. Within each of these categories, business-related characteristics will be added to previously noted attributes common to the retailer and consumer.

Demographic Characteristics

The simulated retailers are implicitly located in a geographic location and explicitly described as serving a substantially rural, suburban, or urban population. In addition, the type of retail outlet is indicated. In an appliance product model, for example, outlet classifications distinguish between hardware, furniture, appliance, and department stores.

Economic Characteristics

Business-related retailer attributes include average store-wide unit sales volume and average store-wide unit margin. The retailer's normative economic perspective is manifest in his expected percent markup.

Behavioral Attributes

Behavioral characteristics affect the retailer's relationship to various brands and product lines. A product mix descriptor indicates product lines stocked. Brands carried and inventories maintained are also specified. A media exposure index indicates which consumer and trade media are available to the retailer.

Two specialized behavioral attributes enter the model directly as parameters in ordering and point-of-sale functions. The first is an inventory requirement indicating the retailer's desired product backlog. The second reflects the retailer's size and establishes his perception of an optimal point-of-sale display size.

Psychological Attributes

Retailer orientation toward product is recorded, as in the consumer case, in terms of attitude toward each product characteristic. Attitude toward and awareness of each brand is derived and maintained for each retail cell.

It may be useful to think of the retailer attitude matrix as reflecting the *retailer's impressions of how consumers feel* about product characteristics and appeals. In reacting to consumer-oriented promotion, the retailer is therefore recording the response he believes a typical consumer would have to the promotion.

The retailer attitude set encompasses orientation toward five potential characteristics of selling and distribution programs in addition to the consumerlike product characteristics and appeals orientations. These unique retailer attitudes determine disposition toward price modification, price speculation, adding new brands, using advertising allowances, and allocating profits to advertising.

Retailer concern for competitor activity is reflected in an attitude toward other classes of retailers carrying the same or similar brands of product.[1] A matrix is maintained at the retailer level but is not recorded in each retailer cell because these attitudes appear to be consistent across retailer type; response to competitive activity is determined by retailer classification and size.

[1] An example of retailer competitive orientation is provided by W. Alderson and S. J. Shapiro, "Towards the Theory of Retail Competition," in Cox, Alderson, and Shapiro (eds.), *Theory in Marketing* (Homewood, Ill.: Richard D. Irwin, Inc., 1964), pp. 190–212.

Coding Characteristics

Table 9.1 summarizes the coding and organization of the four classes of retailer attributes described in the preceding paragraphs. Attributes are described under the heading *Characteristic*. The variable name associated with each attribute is indicated in the column headed *Variable*. The column headed *Gradations* specifies the degree of differentiation used in scaling and the column headed *Bits Required* indicates the number of binary bits of computer storage allocated to the characteristic in a single retailer cell.

TABLE 9.1. Variable Definition and Storage Allocation

Characteristic	Variable	Gradations	Bits Required
Geographic Location	*	*	*
Rural, Urban, Suburban Classification	RUSID(r)	3	2
Classification Type	RETTYP(r)	24	5
Product Mix (4 Levels in 7 Categories)	PROMIX(r)	4	21
Average Store-Wide Item Volume (Units)	AVSWVL(r)	15	4
Average Store-Wide Unit Margin ($)	AVSWUM(r)	15	4
Inventory Requirement	C_{15}	15	4
Optimal Point-of-Sale Size	OPTSIZ	15	4
Disposition Toward Price Modification	C_5-C_{10}	10	20
Disposition Toward Price Cutting	C_{35}	10	4
Disposition Toward Price Speculation	C_{16}	10	4
Expected Percent Markup Requirement	EXPCMU(r)	10	4
Disposition Toward Adding New Brands	C_{13}-C_{14}	10	4
Disposition Toward Use of Advertising Allowances	C_{21}, C_{23}	10	4
Disposition Toward Allocation of to Advertising	C_{22}, C_{24}	10	4
Brands of Product Carried	CARRY(b, r)	1	B
Media Availability (Consumer and Trade	MEDAV(m, r)	1	M
Attitude Toward PC Product Characteristics	ATITD(pc, r)	7	PC
Attitude Toward AP Appeals	ATITD(ap, r)	7	AP
Attitude Toward B Brands of Product	ATTBR(b, r)	7	B
Awareness of B Brands of Product	AWARE(b, r)	1	B

* Implicitly established as a function of model structure.

Representation of Behavior

In developing this model, the actions and responses of the retailer will be considered separately.

Retailer Actions

Consideration of actions will begin with the process through which the retailer evaluates past experience and determines the present state of the market. This evaluation focuses on dollar and percent markup and dollar and unit volume as basic measures employed by the retailer in describing his business experience. Following formulation of this procedure, the process of expectation formation will be examined. Considerations in this area emphasize sales and margins.

Decision functions will be formulated to yield action specifications. The pricing decision establishes the price for each brand and model. The drop decision deletes selected brands from the line, while the add decision produces an offer to carry other brands. The order decision determines the quantity and composition of orders sent to the distributor or manufacturer. The "push" decision determines the extent of selling effort exerted on behalf of each brand. The promotion decision controls local media promotion with content based on prepared mats or generated by the retailer. Placement of point-of-sale promotion is determined by the related decision function. An allocation decision establishes salesman utilization.

Retailer Responses

Retailer responses to the business environment relate to perceptions of the over-all business climate, local competitive conditions, trade advertising, interactions with manufacturer or distributor salesmen, and discussions with consumers. While the retailer may respond to objective measures of the business climate related to his sales and profits, his response to particular situations may be biased by subjective expectations.

Representation of response to competitive conditions is based on the matrix indicating attitude toward sales of competitive brands by other retailers in the same and adjacent regions. Response to trade advertising is described in terms of processes comparable to those considered when examining consumer response to media promotion.

In a similar manner retailer response to manufacturer or distributor salesmen parallels the consumer-retailer salesman interaction.

Retailer-consumer interactions are represented through a variation of the word-of-mouth communication model discussed in Chapter 8. If, as suggested earlier, the retailer's consumerlike attitude set is viewed as representing his conception of consumer beliefs, information from the consumer population serves to either verify or negate these assumptions regarding consumer attitudes toward brands, appeals, or product characteristics. In his role as a consumer (or modeler of consumers), the retailer responds to the content of consumer-directed media, subject to the same availability constraints that limit consumer media exposure.

The remainder of this chapter is devoted to the development of a microanalytic simulation of retailer behavior encompassing these actions and responses. This model is intended as a summary statement of a quantitative behavioral theory of retailer actions and responses. It is a generalized representation, encompassing attributes and processes common to retailers who sell a wide range of consumer products. In keeping with this objective, the structural framework of the model is designed to facilitate modification to encompass unique attributes associated with the marketing of particular goods.

Dimensional Analysis

The practice of dimensioning all variables in defining formulations followed in Chapter 8 will *not* be continued. Pure number units will not be dimensioned explicitly. Thus nondimensioned variables may be assumed to be pure numbers.

Retailer Actions

Experience Evaluation

Model exposition will begin with the retailer's evaluation of experience — his perception of the status quo in the market environment. At a macrolevel the retailer may evaluate business in general as reflected in his average store-wide gross margin. At a microlevel he may be concerned with the profitability of a single brand.

The Impact of an External Economy

The scope of this system has been limited by specification to selected actors and interactions; however, the retailer's evaluation of the business climate involves manifestations of a parameter falling outside specified boundaries. The factor in question is the economic climate — the level of business prosperity. This is not to imply that interactions producing aggregate economic conditions cannot be simulated. Major work is now being done to develop simulations of the total economy.[2] However, because description of such interactions is not one of the objectives of this study, over-all business activity will be summarized in an economic cycle presented exogenously to the model.

The retailer characteristic set includes average store-wide unit volume and gross margin figures that may be viewed as indications of that which will be realized in the outlet under normal economic and business conditions. If the economic situation is normal ($= 1.0$), the retailer will experience the average sales volume characteristic of his operation. Deviations from this norm will be a function of the economic cycle.

Equation 9.1

    RELAVS(r)   REaLized AVerage Sales in retail outlet r. Dimension: product units.
                = AVSWVL(r) $*$ ECYCLE(t).

    AVSWVL(r)   AVerage Store-Wide VoLume in outlet r. Dimension: product units.
                = Retailer characteristic, see Table 9.1.

    ECYCLE(t)   Economic CYCLE value at time t.
                = Exogenous input (expected range .5 through 1.5).

If realized average sales through the retail outlet are known and the average store-wide unit margin specified earlier as a retailer characteristic remains constant, the gross margin realized by the retailer is the product of average store-wide unit margin and realized average sales.

Equation 9.1A

    RELAGM(r)   REaLized Average Gross Margin of retailer r. Dimension: value units (dollars).
                = RELAVS(r) $*$ AVSWUM(r).

    AVSWUM(r)   AVerage Store-Wide Unit Margin of retailer r. Dimension: dollars per product unit.
                = Retailer characteristic, see Table 9.1.

[2] The work of G. Orcutt and others at the University of Wisconsin represents the most comprehensive approach to this problem. For a discussion of this project, see G. H. Orcutt, M. Greenberger, J. Korbel, and A. Rivlin, *Microanalysis of Socio-Economic Systems: A Simulation Study* (New York: Harper and Brothers, 1961).

The realized average sales and gross margin are of interest primarily as references against which product line performance may be evaluated. These measures of store-wide performance reflect experience across numerous product lines and, as such, provide a standard that may be applied when evaluating a particular product line as an element in the product mix.

Evaluation of Trends in Product Line Sales

The retailer may be concerned with the absolute number of units sold during a preceding period or the sales in that period relative to sales realized in earlier periods. The evaluation of relative performance over time may be viewed as a consideration of the sales trend. Most retailers are sensitive to seasonal demand characteristics, and it is reasonable to assume that evaluations of sales trends are corrected for known seasonal characteristics.

The retailer generally maintains records of or has a reasonable "feel" for brand sales during some past time period. For purposes of this model, the retailer will be assumed to possess an accurate summary of purchases in his outlet. Given this information, the trend perceived by the retailer is simply his differential sales experience during the two most recent time periods corrected for the average differential across brands experienced during comparable time periods in a previous year.

Equation 9.2

$TREND(t, b, r)$ TREND in sales of brand b in retail outlet r at time t.

$$= \frac{ACTUSL(t-1, b, r) - ACTUSL(t-2, b, r)}{ACTUSL(t-2, b, r)}$$

$$- SESLAJ(t-1, r)$$

$ACTUSL(t, b, r)$ ACTual Unit SaLes of brand b through retail outlet r at time t. Dimension: product units.

$$= \sum_{c=1}^{C_r} CPURCH(t, c, b, r).$$

$CPURCH(t, c, b, r)$ Consumer PURCHases of brand b in outlet r by consumer c at time t. Dimension: product units.

     = Summary statistic derived from output of consumer model based on probability of purchase PRPCH (c, b, r). See Equation 8.4.

C_r total number of Consumers who purchase in retail outlet r.

= Summary statistic derived from output of consumer model based on probability of purchase
PRPCH(c, b, r).

SESLAJ(t, r)   SEaSonaL AdJustment in sales of product line as
established by retailer r at time t.

$$= \left[\sum_{b=1}^{B(rt)} \frac{\text{ACTUSL}(t - 12, b, r) - \text{ACTUSL}(t - 13, b, r)}{\text{ACTUSL}(t - 13, b, r)} \right] * \frac{1}{B(rt)}.$$

B_{rt} total number of Brands in product line carried by
retailer r at time t.

In the preceding formulation, the trend and seasonal adjustments
have been expressed as percent rates of change to facilitate inclusion
as multipliers in later decision functions. A one-month time step is assumed.

Evaluation of Average (Prevailing) Price

In evaluating a particular product line, the retailer is concerned
with what might be described as the "prevailing price" for that line.
The average price charged for brands within a line does not accurately
reflect this concept. An unusually high- or low-priced, but relatively
obscure brand does not markedly affect retailer conception of the
generally prevailing price. However, prices charged for brands making
up the major portion of sales in a particular line strongly influence his
perception.

In developing a representation of the prevailing price concept, it is
necessary either to make assumptions regarding the scope and accuracy
of information available to a retailer or to simulate the interactions
through which he gains information about competitive pricing policies.
In this model, the retailer will be assumed to have perfect knowledge
of the prices being charged by his immediate competitors. This assumption is not unreasonable. As a result of direct investigation and indirect
feedback from consumers, retailers are generally aware of prices charged
for various brand-models in their area. The importance attached to the
pricing policy of another retailer is generally proportional to that competitor's sales volume in the brand in question. In order to develop a
weighting by sales volume, the retailer must have knowledge of the
sales level of his competitors. By way of salesmen and distributors,
most retailers seem to obtain a reasonably good estimate of "how" a
brand "is moving" in other outlets. The availability of such estimates
is assumed.

With the assumption of perfect price and sales information, the retailer's concept of prevailing price may be summarized as follows:[3]

Equation 9.2A

AVWPRC(b)   AVerage Weighted PRiCe being charged for brand b in region being considered. Dimension: value units (dollars) per product unit.

$$= \frac{\sum_{r=1}^{R} CARRY(b, r) * (PRICE(b, r) * ACTUSL(t - 1, b, r))}{\sum_{r=1}^{R} CARRY(b, r) * ACTUSL(t - 1, b, r)}.$$

CARRY(b, r)   brands being CARRied by retailer r.
= 1.0, if being carried,
= 0, if not being carried.
see Equation 9.12, p. 278.

PRICE(b, r)   PRICE being charged by retailer r for brand b. Dimension: value units (dollars) per product unit.
= see Equation 9.8, p. 270.

ACTUSL(t, b, r)   ACTual Unit SaLes of brand b in outlet r at time t. Dimension: product units.
= see Equation 9.2.

The use of the *CARRY* function in this formulation insures that only outlets carrying a brand will be included in deriving the prevailing price for that brand.

Given the assumption of perfect information, all retailers perceive the same weighted average brand price. Thus the prevailing price exists as a brand characteristic and is not retailer specific.

Evaluation of Average Brand Gross Margin

The contribution made by a particular product line is often evaluated in light of the average gross margin realized across all product lines carried by the store. Specific retailers may be concerned with percent margin, unit dollar margin, dollar flow, or gross dollar margin. In this model evaluation of performance will be described in terms of the gross dollar margin contributed by a given brand during a specified period of time. Formulations based on alternative measures of contribution could obviously be substituted for that used.

[3] A similar average price reference has been used by Kuehn in the development of market share models. See A. A. Kuehn, "How Advertising Performance Depends on Other Marketing Factors," *Journal of Advertising Research,* Vol. 2 (March 1962), pp. 2–10.

The average gross margin contributed by a brand is determined by the price charged by the retailer and the price at which the brand is available to him from the manufacturer or distributor.

Equation 9.2B

AVBRGM(r)   AVerage BRand Gross Margin in retail outlet r. Dimension: dollars.

$$= \frac{\sum_{b=1}^{B} HSTGMG(b, r) * CARRY(b, r)}{\sum_{b=1}^{B} CARRY(b, r)}.$$

HSTGMG(b, r)   HiSTorical Gross MarGin of brand b in outlet r. Dimension: dollars.
    $= [PRICE(b, r) - PRTRET(b, r)] * ACTUSL(t - 1, b, r).$

PRICE(b, r)   PRICE charged for brand b by retailer r. Dimension: dollars per product unit.
    = see Equation 9.8, p. 270.

PRTRET(b, r)   PRice To RETailer r charged by distributor or manufacturer of brand b — price at which b is available to r. Dimension: dollars per product unit.
    = input from distributor or manufacturer sector. See, for example, Equation 7.13.

Expectation Formation

The process of extrapolation through which the retailer attempts to develop expectations for the future must now be considered.

Sales Expectations

The retailer establishes expectations for the future under two types of circumstances. On the one hand he develops estimates of future sales for brands that he is carrying. On the other, he hypothesizes a level of sales that might be realized if he were to add certain brands to his line.

Sales Expectations for Brands Carried

In developing expected sales for brands already carried, past experience provides the basis for future expectations. This conclusion, based on discussions with retailers, has been validated by Cyert, March, and others at the Carnegie Institute of Technology. In developing "A Model of Retail Ordering and Pricing by a Department Store," they determined that the retailer's estimate of sales for a given period was based on sales experienced during a corresponding period in the previous year.[4]

Trend Extrapolation. In developing expectations for the future the retailer may note trends in demand that are not accounted for by seasonal variations. The trend formulation developed in Equation 9.2 provides a means of representing retailer extrapolation of the rate of change as well as the absolute level of sales experienced in preceding periods.

If competitive interactions are relatively stable and the retailer's position in the market well established, a model based on level and trend extrapolation provides a reasonable representation of expectation formation. If competition between brand manufacturers or retail outlets is substantial, additional factors require consideration.

The Effect of Perceived Distribution and Promotion. In examining sales estimation procedures followed by appliance, furniture, and food retailers, significant competition between brands or outlets has been found to sensitize the retailer to changes in promotion and distribution. When changes in promotional activity in support of a brand are observed, the retailer reasons that increased or decreased promotional emphasis will lead to a resulting increase or decrease in relative sales of that brand.[5] Increased competition through introduction of a brand in competitive retail outlets adversely affects the retailer's expected sales of that brand through his outlet. Conversely, a change in distribution favorable to an outlet produces favorable sales expectations for the coming quarter.

When estimating future sales, the retailer is concerned with the direction and rate of change of promotion and distribution rather than their absolute level.

Consideration of both promotion and distribution may constitute

---

[4] The specific rule for the product line considered was "the estimate for the next six months is equal to the total of corresponding six months of the previous year minus one-half of the sales achieved during the last month of the previous six month period." The indicated model is discussed in R. M. Cyert and J. G. March, "A Specific Price and Output Model," *A Behavioral Theory of the Firm* (Englewood Cliffs, N.J.: Prentice-Hall, Inc., 1963), p. 134.

[5] For example, a study of sales expectation formation by a furniture buyer showed that increased noting of trade promotion for a particular line-style and the expectation of increased consumer promotion led to increased sales expectations. See L. Yermack, "Toward Computer Models of the Selection of Merchandise, Allocation of Area, and the Total Contribution of Upholstered Furniture in a Department Store," Unpublished master's thesis, M.I.T., School of Industrial Management, 1962.

double counting on the part of the retailer who is already taking into account existing trends in the sales of a particular brand. The retailer, however, does not normally perceive this as a problem. Historical trends are seen as a function of conditions existing in the past. He considers historical trend extrapolation valid, so long as historical conditions prevail. As these conditions change, he anticipates corresponding sales change. The direction of change is predicted on the basis of his assessment of the new conditions as favorable or adverse to his brand or product line.

Quantification of Expectation Formation. Retailer perception of change in promotional support will be expressed in terms of the smoothed probability of exposure to promotion supporting a brand. This formulation is based on the communication exposure model developed in Chapter 8.

Retailer evaluation of competitive distribution is summarized in the matrix expressing the attitude of retailer r of type and size category t_r toward a retailer of type t_c carrying the same brand.

RETATM(t_r, t_c)   RETailer ATtitude Matrix element defining attitude of retailer of type t_r toward distribution of a brand he carries through a retailer of type t_c. Dimension: attitude scale units.
= retail population characteristic.

The extent of retailer concern is also a function of the volume of competitive business. A retailer may be unconcerned about isolated and incidental sales by a competitor but become increasingly alarmed as that competitor's volume in a brand increases. The importance of a competitive condition may be measured by weighting the attitude toward the competitive retailer by the sales of the brand under consideration through that competitor. The net effect of all attitudes thus weighted and combined represents the retailer's evaluation of the total competitive environment — an evaluation of the perceived desirability of the distribution pattern established for a brand.

These relationships, described as determinants of expected brand sales, may be summarized as follows:

Equation 9.3

EXPUSL(t, b, r)   EXPected Unit SaLes of brand b through outlet r at time t under conditions where brand b carried by retailer r at time t — CARRY(b, r) = 1.0.
= ACTUSL(t − 1, b, r) ∗ (1 + SESLAJ(t − 1, r)
+ PROMAJ(b, r) + DISTAJ(b, r) + TREND(b, r)).

ACTUSL(t, b, r)   ACTual Unit SaLes of brand b through outlet r at time t. Dimension: product units.
= see Equation 9.2.

SESLAJ(t, r)   SEaSonal AdJustment in sales of product line.
= see Equation 9.2.

PROMAJ(b, r)   PROMotional AdJustment.

$$= \left[\frac{\text{SPRADX}(t-1, b, r) - \text{SPRADX}(t-2, b, r)}{\text{SPRADX}(t-2, b, r)} \right] * C_1.$$

SPRADX(t, b, r)   Smoothed PRobability of ADvertising eXposure to promotion for brand b on part of retailer r.

$$= \text{SPRADX}(t-1, b, r) + \left[\left[\sum_{na=1}^{NA(b)} \text{PRADEX}(na, r) \right] \right.$$

$$\left. * \left[1 + \sum_{na=1}^{NA(b)} \text{RPLPSD}(na, r) * C_3 \right] \right.$$

$$\left. - \text{SPRADX}(t-1, b, r) \right] * C_2.$$

PRADEX(na, r)   PRobability of ADvertising EXposure to advertisement na by retailer r.
= see Equation 8.11.

NA(b)   Number of Advertisements promoting brand b.

C_1 Constant determining relative weighting attached to promotional component.
= 1.0 as sample value.

RPLPSD(na, r)   Retailer PLacement of Point-of-Sale Display na (relating to brand b).
= 1.0, if display placed,
= 0.0, if display not placed. See Equation 9.16, p. 285.

C_2 Smoothing constant specifying time period over which function formed.
= .5, as sample value.

C_3 Weighting constant indicating relative effect of point-of-sale placement and advertising exposure.
= 2.0, as sample value.

DISTAJ(b, r)   DISTribution AdJustment.

$$= C_4 * \frac{\text{ATTCMP}(t, b, r) - \text{ATTCMP}(t-1, b, r)}{\text{ATTCMP}(t-1, r)}.$$

C_4 Constant determining relative weighting attached to distribution component.
= 1.0, as sample value.

ATTCMP(b, r)   ATTitude toward CoMPetitive situation in relation to distribution of brand b (time reference is implicit). Dimension: attitude scale units.

$$= \frac{\sum_{t_e=1}^{TC(b)} RETATM(t_r, t_e) * ACTUSL(t-1, b, t_e)}{\sum_{t_e=1}^{TC(b)} ACTUSL(t-1, b, t_e)}.$$

t_r Type category of evaluating retailer.
                          $= RETTYP(r).$

t_e Type category of competive retailers.

TC(b)   Total number of Competitors carrying brand b.

RETATM(t_1, t_2)   RETailer ATtitude Matrix indicating attitude of retailer type t_1 toward retailer of type t_2 carrying same brand of product. Dimension: attitude scale units.

ACTUSL(t, b, r)   ACTual Unit SaLes of brand b through outlet r. Dimension: product units.
                          $=$ see Equation 9.2.

TREND(b, r)   TREND in sales of brand b through retail outlet r.
                          $=$ see Equation 9.2.

The seasonal, promotion, distribution, and trend adjustments enter the determination of expected unit sales as multipliers applied against the actual unit sales for the preceding period. If all of these factors are zero, the retailer's expectation for the present period will equal his experience in the preceding period.

Expected Unit Sales for Brands Not Carried

The formulation of expected unit sales for a brand not carried by the retailer will be developed using the previously discussed assumption of complete information availability.

Addition to Existing Line. Although not carrying the brand for which an expected sales estimate is desired, the retailer may have experience with other brands in the product line under consideration. In this instance, his sales expectation for the brand not carried is based on brands carried and available information regarding the total market brand share of the brand not carried. He assumes that brands with which he has no experience will, if added to his line, provide a brand share within his outlet comparable to that which they exhibit in the total market.

Addition of New Product Line. When asked to evaluate the potential sales that might be achieved by adding a brand in a new product line, the retailer has no experience on which to base an answer. Under these circumstances, he normally obtains through trade channels estimates (assumed to be accurate) of brand sales in a similar retail outlet in his area. This information may be modified to take account of differences in the volume of business that he and the noted outlet handle. With the exception of this correction, the brand performance experienced in the other outlet is accepted as an indication of probable performance in his store.

These two approaches to sales estimation when the brand for which the estimate is desired is not being carried, are summarized in Equation 9.3A. The first equation represents the condition where one or more brands is carried by the retailer $(B_r > 0)$. The second specifies the case when the retailer has no experience with the product line $(B_r = 0)$.

Equation 9.3A

EXPUSL(t, b, r)   EXPected Unit SaLes of brand b through outlet r.
= formulation for brand b not carried by retailer r at time t — CARRY(b, r) = 0.0.

$$= \frac{\sum_{b_r=1}^{B_r} \text{EXPUSL}(t, b_r, r)}{\sum_{b_r=1}^{B_r} \text{BRDSHR}(b_r)} * \text{BRDSHR}(b), \text{ if } B_r > 0,$$

$$= \text{ACTUSL}(t-1, b, r') * \frac{\text{AVSWVL}(r)}{\text{AVSWVL}(r')}, \text{ if } B_r = 0,$$

where: RETTYP(r) = RETTYP(r').

B_r total number of Brands carried in product line by retailer r at time t.

$$= \sum_{b=1}^{B} \text{CARRY}(b, r).$$

BRDSHR(b)   BRanD SHaRe of brand b — aggregate over region.

$$= \sum_{r=1}^{R} \frac{\text{ACTUSL}(t-1, b, r)}{\sum_{b=1}^{B} \text{ACTUSL}(t-1, b, r)}.$$

EXPUSL(t, b_r, r)   EXPected Unit SaLes of brand b_r carried by retailer r.
Dimension: product units.
= see Equation 9.3.

ACTUSL(b, r)   ACTual Unit SaLes of brand b through retail outlet r.
Dimension: product units.
= see Equation 9.2.

CARRY(b, r)   brands CARRied by retailer r.
                   = 1.0, if b is carried by r,
                   = 0.0, if b not carried by r,
                   = output of carry decision — see Equation 9.12, p. 278.

AVSWVL(r)   AVerage Store-Wide VoLume in retail outlet r. Dimen-
                   sion: product units.
                   = retailer characteristic. See Table 9.1.

Formation of Expected Gross Margins

Once the retailer has established an estimate of expected unit sales for a brand it is a simple matter for him to determine the gross margin that will be realized if the expected sales level is achieved. Given the price he must pay the distributor or manufacturer and the price he will charge consumers, the retailer knows the available dollar gross margin. Multiplying this gross margin by the expected unit sales he establishes the expected gross margin.

Equation 9.4

EXPGMG(b, r)   EXPected Gross MarGin on sale of brand b by re-
                   tailer r. Dimension: dollars.
                   $= [PRICE(b, r) - PRTRET(b, r)] * EXPUSL(t, b, r).$

PRICE(b, r)   PRICE charged for brand b by retailer r. Dimension:
                   dollars per unit.
                   = see Equation 9.8, p. 270.

PRTRET(b, r)   PRice To RETailer r charged by distributor or manu-
                   facturer of brand b — price at which b is available to r.
                   Dimension: dollars per unit.
                   = input from distributor or manufacturer model. See
                   Equation 7.13.

The Pricing Decision

The manufacturer normally establishes a suggested retail or "list" price for each brand-model. In some instances, this is a "fair-traded" price that the manufacturer seriously attempts to maintain. At other times, the list price constitutes little more than a uniform reference against which all retailers determine their "discounts" and actual selling price.

For purposes of formulation, the tautological conditions surrounding effectively policed fair-trade pricing will be disregarded. The process to be described is that through which the retailer arrives at a final retail price in the absence of manufacturer control. The concept of a "tentative price" will be used to follow the process through which the retailer considers the implications of charging a specific price *prior* to implementing that price.

Let us assume that the retailer initially considers charging the suggested list price communicated to him by the manufacturer. Certainly he is aware of this price. But how does he evaluate it? What alternative prices does he consider charging in lieu of the suggested list price?

The Effect of Available Margin on Pricing

The experienced percent markup established earlier as a retailer attribute often serves as the basis for an alternative to the suggested list price. The retailer, knowing his cost, applies his expected markup to determine the minimum price that will yield the normal margin.

At this point the retailer has two alternatives: (1) charge the list, and (2) charge the margin-based price. Retailer r has some probability of charging the margin-based rather than suggested list price for brand b and, assuming for the moment that this probability is known, his tentative price can be specified as

Equation 9.5

TENPRC(b, r)   TENtative PRiCe of brand b at retail outlet r based on outcome of margin-based versus suggested price consideration. Dimension: dollars per unit.
= SUGPRC(b), if outcome of random draw against PRMBP(b, r) is negative.
= MGBPRC(b, r), if outcome of random draw against PRMBP(b, r) is positive.

SUGPRC(b)   SUGgested retail PRiCe for brand b. Dimension: dollars per unit.
= input from manufacturer model. See Equation 7.13A.

MGBPRC(b, r)   MarGin Based PRiCe for brand b formulated by retailer r. Dimension: dollars per unit.
= PRTRET(b, r) * (1.0 + EXPCMU(r)).

PRTRET(b, r)   PRice To RETailer charged retailer r for brand b. Dimension: dollars per unit.
= input from distributor or manufacturer model. See Equation 7.13.

EXPCMU(r)   EXpected PerCent MarkUp on all products carried.
= retailer characteristic, see Table 9.1.

PRMBP(b, r)   PRobability of Margin-Based Price being charged for brand b.
= see Equation 9.6, p. 268.

Factors influencing the probability just referenced may be considered in terms of two conditions motivating the retailer to charge the margin-based price. The retailer may view the suggested list price as unrealistically low. In this situation, the retailer believes that the consumer is willing to pay a higher price than that suggested by the manufacturer because, in the course of his experience, he has found that consumers accept a higher markup than provided by the suggested list price. In this context the retailer exhibits symptoms of the price-quality syndrome noted in Chapter 8.

In some situations, the retailer may find that the suggested list price offers a margin substantially higher than is customarily received. Under this condition, he may reason approximately as follows:

The mark-up is unusually high. This unit is, competitively speaking, over-priced. With an usually high margin available competition will cut price. To put it another way, with the extra margin, I can promote a price advantage and still get my usual mark-up.[6]

The retailer frequently expresses the fear that his competitors may resort to price cutting when an unusually large margin or percentage markup is available. This suspicion of competitors, combined with a desire to take advantage of opportunities that permit him to promote lower-than-list prices to his consumers (to act as he "fears" his competitors will act), causes the retailer to reject unusually high margins or percentage markups.

The Impact of Percent Markup.   The observed effect of percentage markup on the probability of margin-based pricing is summarized in Figure 9.1. If the ratio of markup based on suggested price to the normally expected margin is less than 1.0, the probability of margin-based pricing decreases as the ratio increases. If the ratio is greater than 1.0, an increase in the ratio leads to an increased probability that the margin-based rather than a suggested list price will be charged. The impact of this ratio on the probability of margin-based pricing is determined by the retailer characteristic describing disposition toward price modification.

[6] Excerpts from interview with Metropolitan Boston appliance dealer regarding pricing of high margin line of television receivers. (M.I.T. Sloan Research Project 142, February 1960).

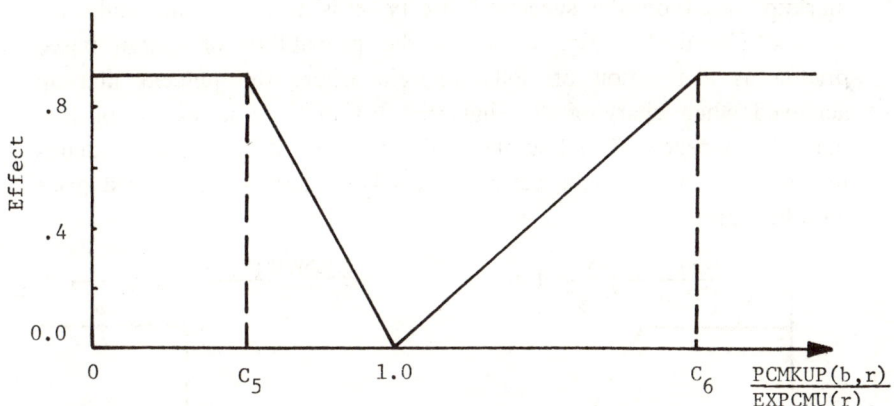

Figure 9.1. Effect of percent margin ratio on probability of margin-based pricing.

The Impact of Dollar Margin. Discussions with retailers reveal that when dealing with established products many outlets are as concerned with dollar margin as with percentage markup. The retailer's perception of available dollar margin at the suggested list price is based on the expected sales level,[7] the suggested retail price, and the price to the retailer.

The retailer's consideration of dollar margin is not independent of his analysis of percentage markup. When the percent markup is greater than expected, charging the list price may (depending on demand effects) yield a higher return than charging the margin-based price. Under these conditions, the decision to charge the suggested list price is dependent on expected volume yielding an acceptable dollar margin. As the margin available increases beyond the normally expected level, the probability that the margin-based price will be charged (that the price will be less than the suggested list price) increases. If the percentage markup is less than normally expected, the probability of the margin-based price being charged (of the price being increased above the suggested price) decreases as the margin increases.

These relationships are summarized in Figure 9.2. The solid line in this figure represents the effect of dollar margin on the probability that the margin-based price will be charged where the percentage

[7] Few retailers considered the possible existence of a price-sensitive consumer demand when discussing markups or gross margin. Their estimate of expected sales remained constant while the profit impact of alternative prices was discussed. (M.I.T. Sloan Research Project 142, February 1960).

markup based on the suggested list price is less than normally expected. The dashed line illustrates the probability of margin-based pricing as a function of dollar margin where the percent markup achieved when charging the suggested list price is in excess of that normally expected. Breakpoints in the Figure 9.2 function are determined by the retailer characteristic specifying disposition toward price modification.

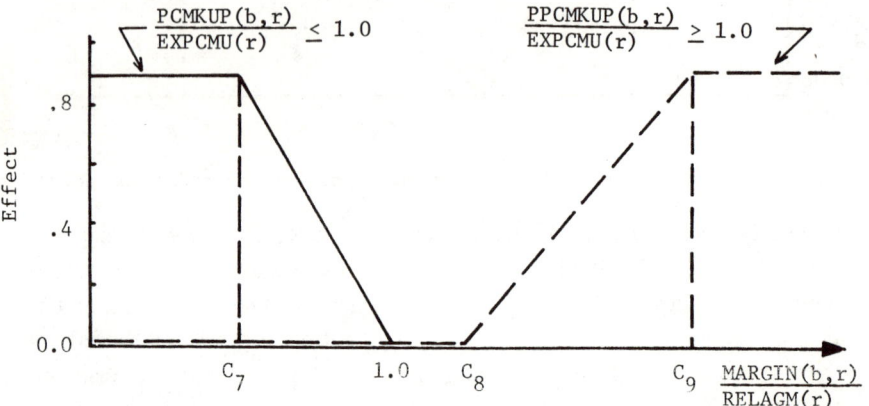

Figure 9.2. Effect of dollar gross margin on probability of margin-based pricing.

Using the "SRF3F" and "SRF2F" logistics introduced in Chapter 5 with the terms just defined, the probability of a margin-based price being charged for brand b by retailer r may be formulated as

Equation 9.6

PRMBP(b, r)   PRobability of Margin-Based Price being charged for brand b by retailer r.

$$= \text{SRF3F} \left(\frac{\text{PCMKUP(b, r)}}{\text{EXPCMU(r)}}, .9, 0, .9, C_6, 1.0, C_5 \right)$$

$$+ \text{SRF2F} \left(\frac{\text{MARGIN(b, r)}}{\text{RELAGM(r)}}, .9, 0, C_9, C_8 \right),$$

$$\text{if } \frac{\text{PCMKUP(b, r)}}{\text{EXPCMU(r)}} > 1.0,$$

$$= \text{SRF3F} \left(\frac{\text{PCMKUP(b, r)}}{\text{EXPCMU(r)}}, .9, 0, .9, C_6, 1.0, C_5 \right)$$

$$+ \text{SRF2F} \left(\frac{\text{MARGIN(b, r)}}{\text{RELAGM(r)}}, 0, .9, 1.0, C_7 \right),$$

$$\text{if } \frac{\text{PCMKUP(b, r)}}{\text{EXPCMU(r)}} \leq 1.0.$$

PCMKUP(b, r)   PerCent MarkUP available to retailer r charging suggested list price for brand b.

$$= \left[\frac{\text{SUGPRC(b)} - \text{PRTRET(b, r)}}{\text{PRTRET(b, r)}} \right].$$

EXPCMU(r)   EXpected PerCent MarkUp.
= retailer characteristic, see Table 9.1.

MARGIN(b, r)   MARGIN available to retailer r from brand b at expected sales level and suggested price. Dimension: dollar units.
$$= [\text{SUGPRC(b)} - \text{PRTRET(b, r)}] * \text{EXPUSL(b, r)}.$$

RELAGM(r)   REaLized Average Gross Margin of r — gross margin realized from average product carried. Dimension: dollar units.
= see Equation 9.1A.

C_5–C_9 Constants specifying the retailer's disposition toward margin pricing in terms of threshold and response. Values empirically derived for particular retailer.
= .5, 2.0, .5, 1.2, and 2.0, respectively, as sample values. See Table 9.1.

The Competitors' Effect on Pricing

Competitive pricing enters the pricing decision through the retailer's knowledge of the prevailing price charged in his area, as discussed while formulating Equation 9.2A.

The retailer is thus cognizant of the prevailing price and wishes to maintain a more or less competitive pricing policy, depending on his disposition toward pricing behavior specified in this model as a defining characteristic. For each retailer, there is some level of unfavorable price difference for which his probability of meeting the competitive price reaches a maximum. The precise level varies from retailer to retailer as a result of the previously noted disposition (sensitivity). Although data substantiating this function are weak, for purposes of formulation the probability will be assumed to increase linearly as illustrated in Figure 9.3.

The probability of retailer r meeting a competitive price on brand b may be summarized using the SRF2F logistic as follows:

Equation 9.7

PRMCP(b, r)   PRobability of Meeting Competitive Price on brand b.

$$= \text{SRF2F} \left(\frac{\text{TENPRC(b, r)}}{\text{AVWPRC(b)}}, .9, 0, C_{10}, 1.0 \right).$$

C_{10} constant establishing response limit as function of retailer disposition.
                                               = 1.20, as sample value.

TENPRC(b, r)   TENtative PRiCe of brand b at retail outlet r. Dimension: dollars per unit.
                                               = see Equation 9.5.

AVWPRC(b)   AVerage Weighted PRiCe being charged for b. Dimension: dollars per unit.
                                               = see Equation 9.2.

If the competitive price is not met, the retail price is the tentative price established on the basis of the choice between suggested list and

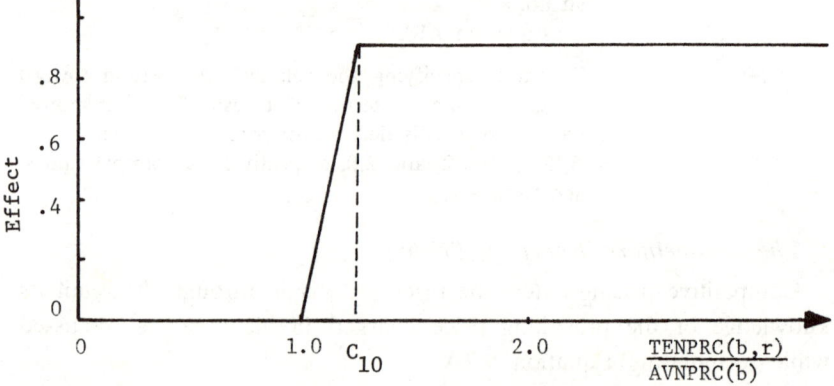

Figure 9.3. Effect of prevailing market price on probability of meeting competition.

margin-based prices. If competitive considerations are controlling, the retailer will charge what he perceives as the prevailing price in his area, the average weighted price developed in Equation 9.2A.[8]

Equation 9.8

PRICE(b, r)   PRICE charged for brand b by retailer r.
                                               = TENPRC(b,r), if PRMCP(b, r) yields negative outcome,
                                               = AVWPRC(b), if PRMCP(b, r) yields positive outcome.

Figure 9.4 illustrates the logic flow involved in the pricing decision as outlined in Equations 9.5 through 9.8. Following previously estab-

[8] Supplied with appropriate control parameters, this formulation is in basic agreement with that developed in the department store case by Cyert and March, in the article noted previously. Although the authors developed their model on a more ad hoc basis, the conclusions of this generalized formulation based on an independent exploration of retailer activities are in basic agreement with the Cyert-March model.

lished conventions, exogenous inputs are indicated by circles, factors developed endogenously within the model are represented within ovals, and decision points are indicated by hexagons. Decision outcomes are determined by comparing a number drawn randomly from a rectangular distribution of mean .5 and range 0 through 1.0 with the probability developed by the margin-based pricing and competitive pricing functions. If the random number drawn is less than the probability specified, an affirmative outcome is assumed.[9]

Product Line Composition

A product line consists of those brands which the retailer has previously carried and does not decide to drop, plus those brands which he decides to add to the line. Thus representation of factors determining product line composition involves modeling the retailer's decisions to add and drop brands in the product line.

The Decision to Drop a Brand

The retailer's decision to drop a brand previously carried appears to be influenced by two considerations. The first is the logical economic implications of experienced and expected gross margins associated with stocking the indicated brand. The second is the retailer's opinion of the brand, which may be adversely affected by consumer complaints, returns, changes in the product, advances made by competitive brands, or changes in brand policy.

Comments relating to retailer evaluation of gross margin made in discussing the pricing decision are equally applicable at this point.[10] The retailer's probability of dropping a brand decreases as the gross margin that he expects to receive from the sale of the brand increases.

The retailer recognizes a minimal margin level at which his probability of dropping the brand reaches a maximum value. This level is partially determined by his characteristics; however, it is also influenced by available references against which he compares the expected gross margin obtained from the brand in question. If the retailer is carrying other brands in the line, these are his reference. In the absence of reference brands, brand performance is compared with that of other product lines.

[9] This process is described in detail in Chapter 5. See "Stochastic Decision Processes," p. 107.

[10] For a review of this discussion see "The Effect of Available Margin on Pricing," p. 265.

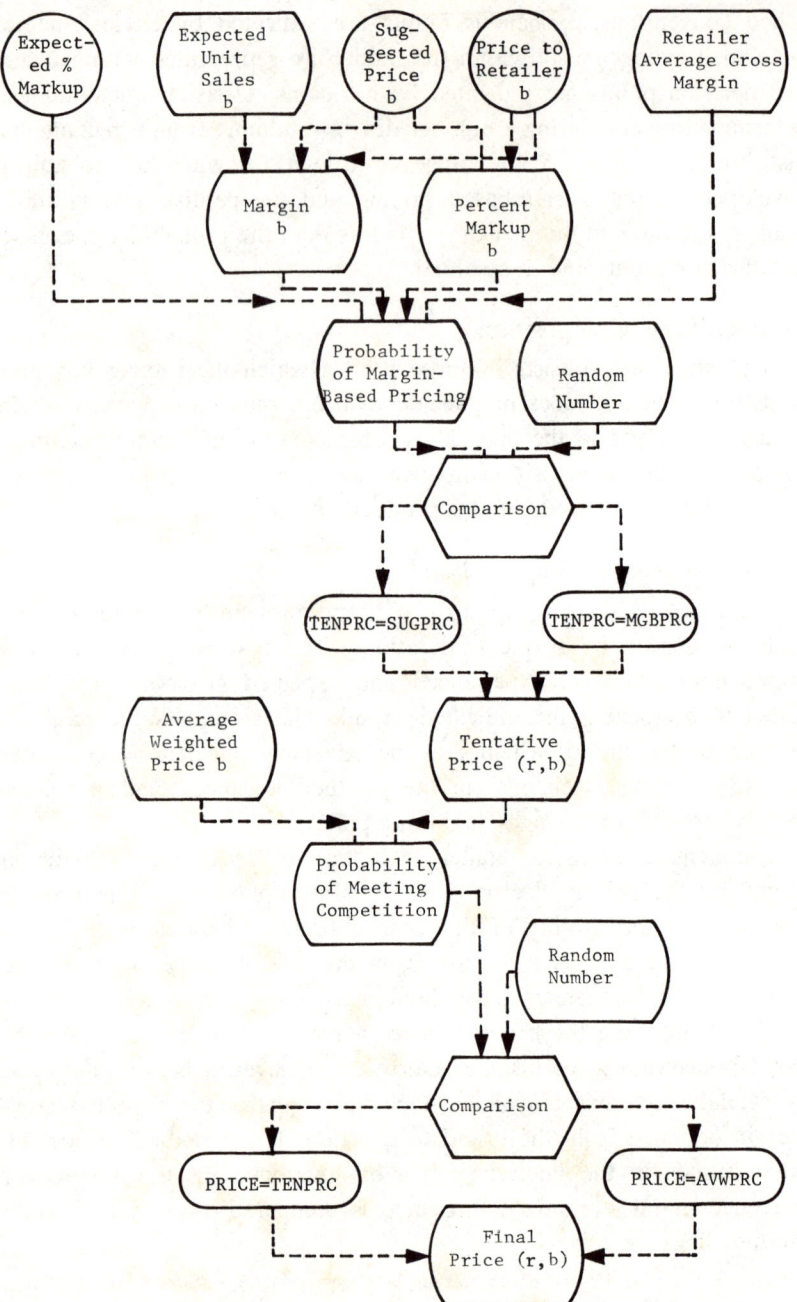

Figure 9.4. Pricing decision. Logical flow.

The retailer may continue to carry one or more brands despite an unfavorable economic evaluation. Cigarettes and certain convenience goods provide examples of product lines in which this behavior is consistently noted. In these situations, the retailer's margin-based probability of dropping a brand is reduced as a result of his subjective evaluation of the "advantages" of carrying the brand. In the cigarette example, brands are maintained to provide a selection. It is hoped that the customer coming into the store to pick up cigarettes will buy from other product lines offering an acceptable margin.

The retailer continues to stock brands for which he believes there is a selective demand even though he has concluded that this demand is not sufficient to provide desired gross margins. The retailer may stock a particular brand-model simply because of the status that he believes this brand gives his outlet (e.g., RCA Color Television in 1960). In each instance, the retailer modifies his margin-based probability as a result of a *positive* attitude toward some aspect of the brand in context of his outlet.

The attitude effect may be unilateral. A retailer will stock a brand because his attitude overrides his margin-based analysis. On the other hand, the author has yet to encounter a retailer who refuses to carry a brand that he believes will provide an expected *dollar* margin greater than his reference margins. Retailers have refused to carry a brand despite the existence of normal *percentage* markups. (E.g., one retailer interviewed refused to carry goods manufactured in certain countries toward which he believed his clientele had strong negative attitudes.) In this instance the retailer not only questioned the probability of the brand achieving the desired dollar margin but also believed that carrying the brand would result in a loss in store-wide gross margin due to customers refusing to purchase either the brand in question or any other product in the store. (This may, of course, be economic rationalization of an emotional response.) Thus the retailer's decision to drop a given brand appears to be based largely on his margin analysis, while his decision not to drop may be a function of nonmargin considerations.

The preceding discussion is summarized in Figure 9.5 illustrating the effect of gross margin and attitude on the probability of dropping a brand. The family of curves shown in Figure 9.5 indicates that the probability of a brand being dropped decreases as the ratio of expected margin to reference margin increases and that for each ratio value the probability of dropping decreases as attitude increases. The relationship between the attitude and margin variable is a function of weighting factors that, for purposes of the example plotted in Figure 9.5, have been assumed equal.

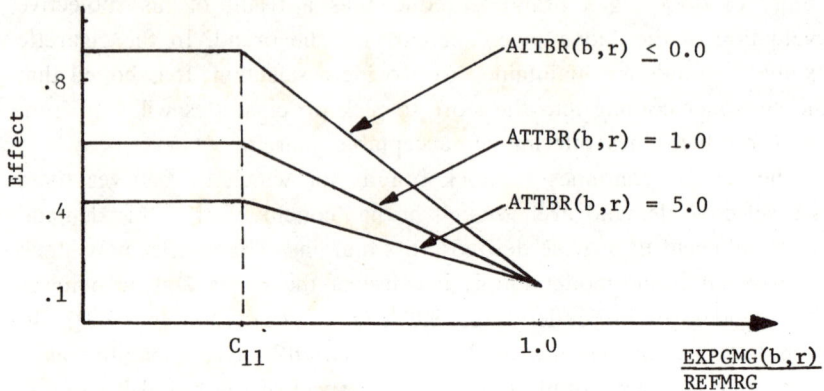

Figure 9.5. Effect of gross margin on probability of dropping brand.

Quantification of the concept just discussed requires explicit representation of the obvious condition that it is impossible to drop a brand that is not being carried — the probability that the retailer will drop a brand is 0 if that brand is not carried. To insure that this necessary condition will hold a variable that is 0 when the brand is not being carried and 1 when the brand is being carried is introduced as a multiplier. The remainder of the drop decision, formulated in terms of the probability that retailer r will drop brand b, can be expressed using an SRF2F logistic:

Equation 9.9

$\qquad$ PRDRBR(b, r) $\qquad$ PRobability that retailer r will DRop BRand b.

$$= \text{CARRY}(b, r) * \left[\text{SRF2F} \left(\frac{\text{EXPGMG}(b, r)}{\text{REFMRG}}, .1, .9, 1.0, C_{11} \right) \right.$$

$$\left. - C_{12} * [1 - \text{ENXPF}(-\text{ATTBR}(b, r))] \right],$$

if **ATTBR**(b, r) > 0.0.

$$= \text{CARRY}(b, r) * \text{SRF2F} \left(\frac{\text{EXPGMG}(b, r)}{\text{REFMRG}}, .1, .9, 1.0, C_{11} \right),$$

if **ATTBR**(b, r) $\leq$ 0.0.
Range: 0.0 to 1.0 by constraint.

EXPGMG(b, r)   EXPected Gross MarGin from sale of brand b through outlet r. Dimension: dollar units.
= see Equation 9.4.

REFMRG   REFerence MaRGin. Dimension: dollar units.

$$= \text{AVBRGM(r), if } \sum_{b=1}^{B} \text{CARRY(b, r)} \geq 2.0,$$

$$= \text{RELAGM(r), if } \sum_{b=1}^{B} \text{CARRY(b, r)} < 2.0.$$

AVBRGM(r)   AVerage BRand Gross Margin for retailer r.
= see Equation 9.2B.

RELAGM(r)   REaLized Average Gross Margin of retailer r.
= see Equation 9.1A.

C_{11} scaling constant.
= .4 as sample value.

C_{12} weighting constant applied to attitude effect.
= .5 as sample value.

ATTBR(b, r)   ATTitude toward BRand b held by retailer r. Dimension: attitude scale units.
= see Equation 8.42.

CARRY(b, r)   specification of brands CARRied by retailer r.
= 0.0, if brand b *not* carried,
= 1.0, if brand b carried.

Clearance Pricing Policies

If the retailer decides to drop a brand, considerations causing him to drop may motivate dumping of existing inventory. In this situation, he may adopt a clearance pricing policy with respect to the brand selling it at cost or some portion of normal markup. Clearance pricing appears to be associated with the existence of high inventory in the brand being dropped.[11] Comments by retailers interviewed in developing this model suggest that the probability of adopting a clearance pricing policy is a function of the ratio of existing and desired inventory, as illustrated in Figure 9.6. This relationship can be simply expressed as follows:

Equation 9.10

PRCLPR(b, r)   PRobability that retailer r will set CLearance PRice following dropping of brand.

$$= 1 - \text{ENXPF} \left[-\frac{\text{ACTINV(t, b, r)}}{\text{DESINV(t, b, r)}} * C_{35} \right].$$

[11] For a detailed discussion of this type of behavior, see Cyert and March, *op. cit.,* Footnote 4, pp. 140–144.

ACTINV(t, b, r)   ACTual INVentory of brand b in retail outlet r at
                   time t. Dimension: product units.
                   = see Equation 9.13.

DESINV(t, b, r)   DESired INVentory of brand b that retailer r would
                   like to have at time t. Dimension: product units.
                   = see Equation 9.13, p. 281.

C_{35} scaling constant reflecting disposition toward price cut-
                   ting (retailer characteristic, see Table 9.1).
                   = .5, as sample value.

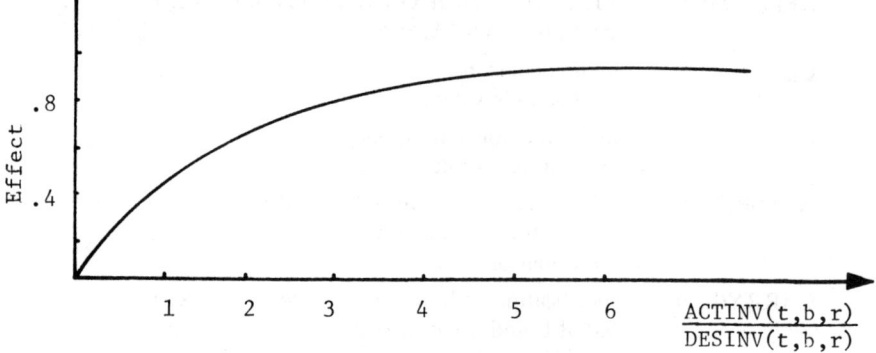

Figure 9.6. Effect of inventory level on probability of clearance pricing.

The Decision to Add a Brand

Comments made previously in context of the drop decision are in
several respects applicable to the decision to add a brand. Both margin-
based and attitudinal effects may be noted. The impact of margin is
comparable in the two situations; however, the attitude effect differs
from the relationship just discussed. The retailer exhibits a bias favoring maintenance of the status quo; he demands more of a brand that
is to be added than of a brand already carried. This bias is partially
manifest in the margin-based effect. A margin level that would be
sufficient to ensure a reasonable probability of maintaining a brand
within the line is not sufficient to motivate addition to the line.

The impact of attitude on the add decision is bilateral — negative
as well as positive attitudes are effective. Retailers may hesitate to add
a brand because of negative attitudes, while, as indicated, negative
attitudes do not provide a basis for dropping a brand that is performing
satisfactorily from the point of view of profit margin.

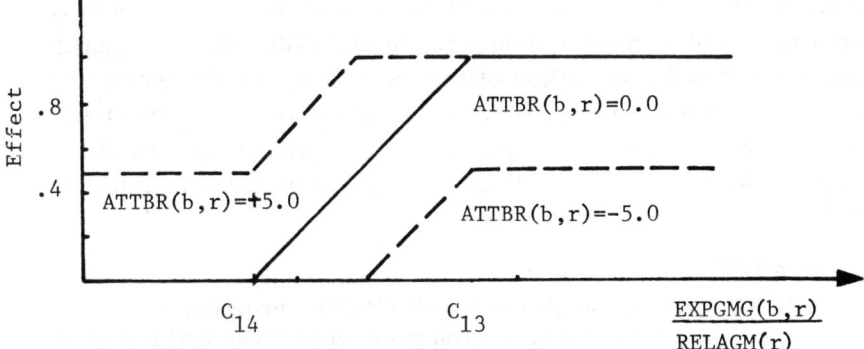

Figure 9.7. Effect of gross margin on probability of adding brand.

The extent of the attitude effect is not definitely established; however, the general function form observed to date is summarized in Figure 9.7 and presented in equation form.

Equation 9.11

PRADBR(b, r)   PRobability that retailer r will ADd BRand b.

$$= [1 - \text{CARRY}(b, r)] * \left[\text{SRF2F} \left(\frac{\text{EXPGMG}(b, r)}{\text{RELAGM}(r)},\right.\right.$$
$$1.0, 0, C_{13}, C_{14})$$
$$\left.\left.+ \text{SIGN} * C_{12} * [1 - \text{ENXPF} (-|\text{ATTBR}(b, r)|)] \right].\right.$$

Range: by constraint 0.0 to 1.0.
Where: SIGN = +1.0, if ATTBR(b, r) $\geq$ 0.0,
          = −1.0, if ATTBR(b, r) < 0.0.

C_{13} and C_{14} scaling constants specifying disposition toward adding a brand (retailer characteristics, see Table 9.1).
= 1.8 and .8, respectively, as sample values.

CARRY(b, r)   brands CARRied by retailer r.
= 1.0, if brand b carried by retailer r,
= 0.0, if brand b not carried by retailer r.

EXPGMG(b, r)   EXPected Gross MarGin on brand b anticipated by retailer r. Dimension: dollar units.
= see Equation 9.4.

RELAGM(r)   REaLized Average Gross Margin of retailer r. Dimension: dollar units.
= see Equation 9.1A.

ATTBR(b, r)   ATTitude of retailer r toward BRand b. Dimension: attitude scale units.
= see Equation 8.42.

Given the probability that retailer r will add or drop brand b, the outcome of the decision to modify the product line is simulated by drawing a random number from a rectangular distribution of mean .5 and range 0 to 1. Comparison of this variable against the appropriate probability provides the basis for determining whether a brand will be dropped or added. The previously referenced carry variable is modified by the outcome of these decisions as indicated in Equation 9.12.

Equation 9.12

CARRY(b, r)   specification of brands CARRied by retailer r.
            = 0.0, if drop decision based on PRDRBR(b, r) is positive,
            = 1.0, if add decision based on PRADBR(b, r) is positive.

For purposes of aggregate assessment, it is useful to establish the proportion of retailers of a given type carrying a brand. This retail sector descriptor can be easily derived from the carry variable.

Equation 9.12A

RPRCBR(b)   Retail PRoportion Carrying BRand b.

$$= \frac{\sum_{r=1}^{R} CARRY(r, b)}{R}.$$

The Order Decision

The ordering decision has probably received more attention than any other action taken by the businessman. Among the best known simulation-based work in this area is that previously cited by Cyert and March, Forrester, and Balderston and Hoggatt.[12] Forrester's work examining the impact of time delays, backlogs in pipelines between sectors, and the amplifying effect of decision rules is more relevant to later discussions of distributor activity than in the present retail situation. Research to date supports the previously noted Cyert and March contention that most retailers order at intervals substantially longer than the communication and shipping delays involved in the system and do not normally consider pipeline and communication backlogs or delays.

The retailer's decision to place an order for a specified number of

[12] For a discussion of this work see J. W. Forrester, *Industrial Dynamics* (Cambridge, Mass.: The M.I.T. Press and John Wiley & Sons, Inc., 1961), and F. E. Balderson and A. C. Hoggatt, "Simulation of Market Processes," IBER Special Publication No. 1, University of California, Berkeley, 1962.

brand units is based on his desire to (1) achieve an inventory sufficient to handle expected sales during the period covered by the order, and (2) to fill any back orders existing at the time when the order is placed.

The ordering process is not continuous. Orders are placed at intervals over time and, when an emergency arises, special orders are initiated. In situations where little or no retail inventory is maintained, orders may be placed on a daily basis to the distributor or manufacturer's warehouse from which normal delivery is achieved in a matter of hours. The sample formulation will assume a one-month order cycle in order to simplify time notation referencing the previously defined ex-

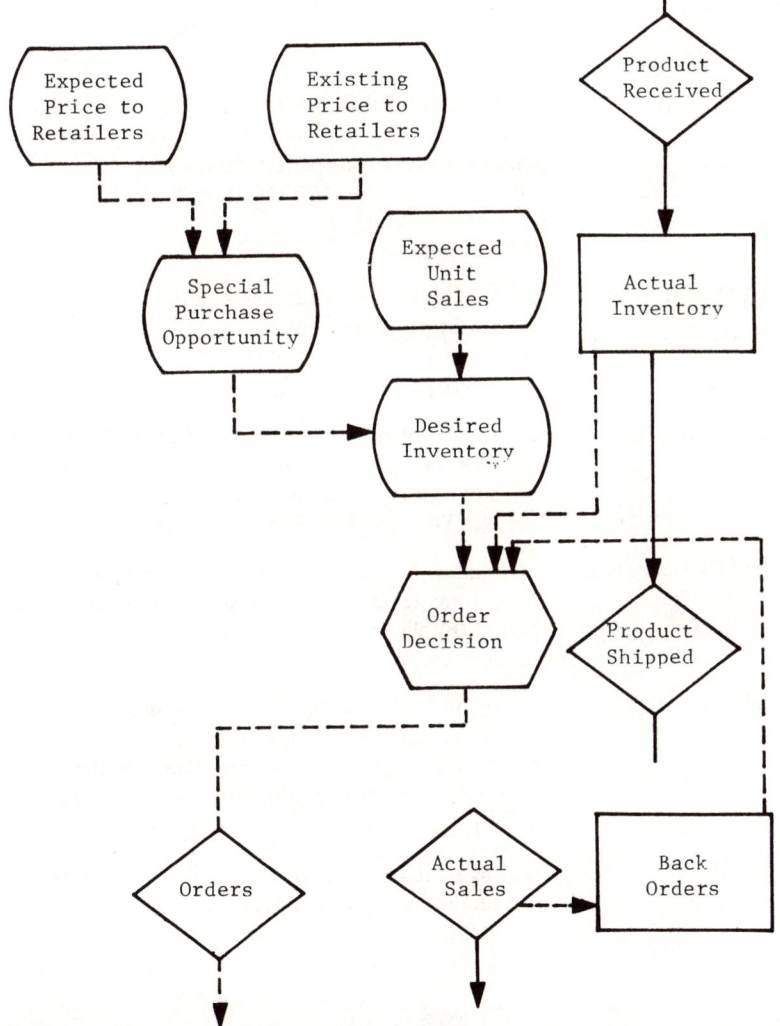

Figure 9.8. Flow chart of retailer order decision.

pected unit sales variable. Modification to take account of other ordering cycles involves explicit representation of the order period.

In addition to maintaining an inventory sufficient to cover expected sale, some retailers engage in what might be described as price speculation. These individuals are alert to opportunities to gain extra margin by obtaining product at a lower price as a result of quantity discounts or expected price increases. Their willingness to take on extra stock under such situations is determined by the extent of potential gain.

The basic retail order decision is summarized in Figure 9.8 and Equation 9.13.

Equation 9.13

ORDERS(t, b, d, r)   ORDERS to distributor from retailer r for brand b product at time t in units. Dimension: product or value units (per time period implicit).
= DESINV(t, b, r) − ACTINV(t, b, r) + BACORD(t, b, r),
≥ 0.0 by constraint.

ACTINV(t, b, r)   ACTual INVentory of brand b at outlet r at time t. Dimension: product units.
= ACTINV(t − 1, b, r) + RECPTS(t − 1, b, r) − ORDFLD(t − 1, b, r).

RECPTS(t, b, r)   RECeiPTS of brand b at retailer r from distributor at time t — goods received. Dimension: product units per time period (implicit).
= SHTRET(t − SHPDEL(d, r), b, r, d).

SHTRET(t, b, r, d)   SHipments of brand b To RETailer r by distributor d at time t. Dimension: product units per time period (implicit).
= input from distributor model.

SHPDEL(d, r)   SHiPping DELay in transport from distributor d to retailer r. Dimension: time units.
= function of system parameters — distributor characteristics (assumed significantly less than order interval).

ORDFLD(t, b, r)   ORDers FiLleD by retailer r at time t. Dimension: product units per time period (implicit).
= ACTUSL(t, b, r),
    if ACTUSL(t, b, r) ≤ ACTINV(t, b, r),

$$= \text{ACTINV}(t, b, r),$$
$$\text{if ACTUSL}(t, b, r) > \text{ACTINV}(t, b, r).$$

BACORD(t, b, r) BACk ORDers of brand b in retail outlet r at time t. Dimension: product units.
$$= 0.0, \text{ if ORDFLD}(t - 1, b, r) = \text{ACTUSL}(t - 1, b, r)$$
$$= \text{ACTUSL}(t - 1, b, r) - \text{ORDFLD}(t - 1, b, r),$$
$$\text{if ORDFLD}(t - 1, b, r) \neq \text{ACTUSL}(t - 1, b, r).$$

DESINV(t, b, r) DESired INVentory of brand b by retailer r at time t. Dimension: product units.
$$= C_{15}(r) * \text{EXPUSL}(t, b, r) * \text{SPPUOP}(b, r).$$

SPPUOP(b, r) SPecial PUrchase OPportunity in brand b as perceived by retailer r.

$$= C_{16}(r) * \frac{\text{EXPTRE}(b, r) - \text{PRTRET}(b, r)}{\text{EXPTRE}(b, r)}.$$

EXPTRE(b, r) EXpected Price To REtailers. Dimension: dollars per product unit.
$$= \text{PRTRET}(b, r), \text{ if FURPSP}(b) = 0,$$
$$= \text{FURPSP}(b, x), \text{ if FURPSP}(b) > 0.$$

FURPSP(b, x) FUture Retail Price SPecification by distributor or manufacturer x of product brand b. Dimension: dollars per product unit.
$$= \text{input from distributor or manufacturer sector. See Equation 7.13.}$$

PRTRET(b, r) PRice to RETailer r for brand b. Dimension: dollars per product unit.
$$= \text{input from distributor or manufacturer sector. See Equation 7.13.}$$

ACTUSL(t, b, r) ACTual Unit SaLes of brand b by retailer r at time t. Dimension: product units per time period (implicit).
$$= \text{see Equation 9.2.}$$

EXPUSL(t, b, r) EXPected Unit SaLes of brand b by retailer r at time t. Dimension: product units per time period (implicit).
$$= \text{see Equation 9.3.}$$

C_{15} Constant specifying desired inventory level.
$$= 5.0, \text{ as sample value. Retailer characteristic. See Table 9.1.}$$

$C_{16}(r)$ 1.0 as sample value. Constant specifying disposition toward price speculation.
$$= \text{retailer characteristic, see Table 9.1.}$$

The Product Placement Decision

To the extent that economic analysis prevails, the retailer will attempt to allocate available space on the basis of gross margin.[13] In a supermarket display, prominence may take the form of (1) relative facings — the area of product display exposed to the customer's view, or (2) location — on a well-traveled aisle or in a back corner, at eye level or in an unusually high or low position on the shelf. If an economically rational retailer is assumed, relative product line prominence can be expressed as the ratio of average gross margin realized on all brands in the product line to the average gross margin realized for all product lines carried by the store.

Equation 9.14

> RPDPM(r) Retailer r Product Display ProMinence for product class as whole.
>
> $$= \frac{AVBRGM(r)}{RELAGM(r)}.$$
>
> AVBRGM(r) AVerage BRand Gross Margin for product line in retail outlet r. Dimension: dollar units.
> = see Equation 9.2B.
>
> RELAGM(r) REaLized Average Gross Margin in retail outlet r. Dimension: dollar units.
> = see Equation 9.1A.

In a similar manner, relative brand display prominence is influenced by relative brand contribution.

Equation 9.14A

> RPDPRM(r, b) Retailer Product Display PRoMinence (relative) given brand b within class.
>
> $$= \frac{EXPGMG(b, r) * CARRY(b, r)}{\sum\limits_{b=1}^{B} EXPGMG(b, r) * CARRY(b, r)}.$$
>
> EXPGMG(b, r) EXPected Gross MarGin for brand b through outlet r. Dimension: dollar units.
> = see Equation 9.4.
>
> CARRY(b, r) brand b CARRied by outlet r.
> = see Equation 9.3A.

Differential advantage gained from space allocation may be counteracted by point-of-sale promotion or salesman action. Factors affecting

---

[13] A discussion of this procedure as followed by one retailer is provided in Yermack, *op. cit.*, Footnote 5.

placement of point-of-sale material are examined in a later section of this chapter. Generation of retail selling effort will be considered next.

The Decision to Exert Selling Effort

Three factors appear to influence the decision to "push" a particular brand. These are (1) the differential gain accruing to the salesman as a result of selling one brand as opposed to another, (2) the relative profitability to the store of selling one brand rather than another, and (3) the salesman's opinion regarding the relative merit of particular brands. If the retail salesman is the proprietor or receives a commission based on margin, the first and second consideration may be equivalent. On the other hand, if the salesman's interest and that of the enterprise are divergent, these two considerations will be in conflict.

The effect of relative profitability on retail "push" can be expressed in terms of the familiar ratio of expected brand gross margin to realized average gross margin. This factor reflects a retailer philosophy of fishing where the fish are biting, of pushing the product that is presently doing best. In following this procedure, the retailer may actually push a product that has a lower unit margin. When presented with this fact, the retailers on which this study was based rationalized their behavior by noting that "it's easier to sell the product which sells better." They believe that return measured in dollar-per-unit of energy expended is maximized by this behavior.

Cynical observers of the business world may question the existence of salesman evaluation of product characteristics as a consideration in the push decision. However, data gathered to date indicate that, particularly in situations in which the retailer and consumer have more than a passing relationship, the retailer-salesman pushes the brand that he believes to be the best, the brand toward which he has the highest attitude.

These observations are summarized in the following representation of retail selling effort generated on behalf of brand b in retail outlet r.

Equation 9.15

RETSLE(r, b)   RETail SeLling Effort on behalf of brand b in outlet r. Dimension: pure number — proportion of product selling time devoted to brand.

$$= C_{17} * (DSMCOM(b, r) + PRBINC(b, r)) + C_{18}$$

$$* ATTBr(b, r) + C_{19} * \frac{EXPGMG(b, r)}{RELAGM(r)}.$$

$$\leq 1.0, \text{ by constraint.}$$

DSMCOM(b, r)   Direct SalesMan COMpensation to salesmen in retail outlet r on sales of brand b. Dimension: dollars per product unit.

= input from manufacturer and/or distributor sectors. See Equation 7.41.

PRBINC(b, r)   PRoBabilistic INCentive to salesmen in retail outlet r on sales of brand b — includes contests and other probabilistic return situations. Dimension: dollars per product unit.

= input from manufacturer and/or distributor sectors. See Equation 7.41.

ATTBR(b, r)   ATTitude toward BRand b on part of retailer r. Dimension: attitude scale units.

= see Equation 8.42.

EXPGMG(b, r)   EXPected Gross MarGin on brand b in retail outlet r. Dimension: dollar units.

= see Equation 9.4.

RELAGM(r)   REaLized Average Gross Margin in outlet r. Dimension: dollar units.

= see Equation 9.1A.

C_{17} constant determining relative effect of compensation on selling effort. Dimension: units per dollar per product unit.

= .33, as sample value.

C_{18} constant determining relative effect of attitude on selling effort. Dimension: units per attitude scale unit.

= .33, as sample value.

C_{19} constant determining relative effect of margin ratio.

= .33, as sample value.

The Decision to Promote

Retailer promotion decisions determine the extent and content of promotion at point of sale, in formal media, and through salesman.

Point-of-Sale Display Placement

Two factors appear to influence the retailers placement of point-of-sale material. First is the ubiquitous margin consideration. The retailer naturally prefers to place point-of-sale material for (to emphasize) the brand that will provide the highest relative return. The second factor affecting placement of point-of-sale material is the physical size of the display involved. Because space is at a premium in most outlets, the retailer hesitates to devote space to the promotion of a particular brand rather than to several brands or a variety of products. The retailer's willingness to allocate space is a function of his size and volume in the brand to be displayed. Both factors are reflected in the retailer attribute specifying optimal point-of-sale display size. As the size of a display increases in relation to this optimal reference, the probability of its being placed decreases.

The observed interaction between expected gross margin and display size as determinants of the probability of point-of-sale display placement is summarized in Figure 9.9 for three values of the expected gross margin ratio. Because optimal size is in the numerator of the size ratio, *increasing values* on the horizontal axis *indicate decreasing* point-of-sale display *size*.

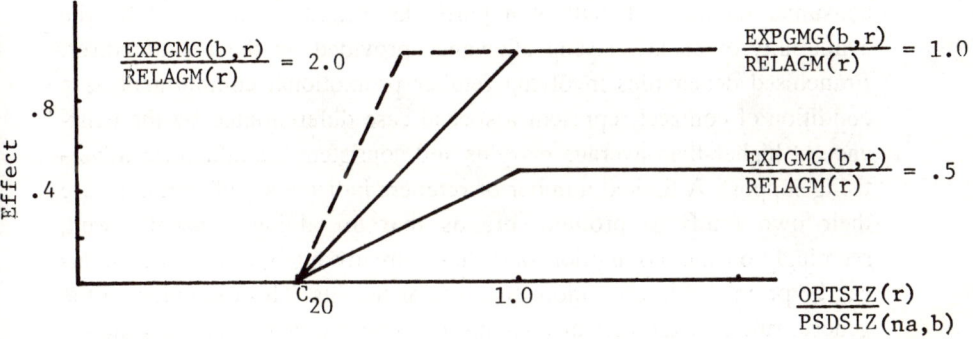

Figure 9.9. Effect of relative gross margin and display size on point-of-sale display placement.

The probability of a point-of-sale display na being placed by retailer r based on the reasoning just outlined is formulated using the "SRF2F" logistic as follows:

Equation 9.16

PRPSPL(na, b, r)   PRobability of Point-of-Sale display na for brand b being PLaced in retail outlet r.

$$= \text{SRF2F} \left(\frac{\text{EXPGMG(br)}}{\text{RELAGM(r)}} * \frac{\text{OPTSIZ(r)}}{\text{PSDSIZ(na, b)}}, \right.$$

$$\left. 1.0, 0, 1.0, C_{20} \right).$$

EXPGMG(b, r)   EXPected Gross MarGin on brand b in outlet r. Dimension: dollar units.
               = see Equation 9.4.

RELAGM(r)   REaLized Average Gross Margin in outlet r. Dimension: dollar units.
                    = see Equation 9.1A.

PSDSIZ(na, b)   Point-of-Sale Display SIZe — floor area required by display na. Dimension: square feet.
                    = input from manufacturer model. See Equation 7.9.

OPTSIZ(r)   OPTimal point-of-sale display SIZe for retailer r. Dimension: square feet.
                    = retailer characteristic, see Table 9.1.

C_{20} scaling constant determining threshold level.
                    = .5, as sample value.

Retailer Advertising in Consumer Media

The retailer's willingness to prepare and place advertising in local consumer media on behalf of a particular brand is influenced by the availability of an advertising allowance provided by the manufacturer. Franchised dealerships involving retailer promotional commitment as a condition of contract represent a special case differentiated by the existence of higher-than-average margins and consistent manufacturer advertising support. A limited number of retailers indicate a willingness to use their own funds to promote brands that are doing unusually well, seemingly on the assumption that these already high-performance items can be promoted to even more spectacular heights. This exception to the general rule that retailers are willing to spend the manufacturer's money but not their own, is most often encountered in large retail outlets where funds are made available under an umbrella advertising budget allocated to a department for the promotion of its products and allocated to specific brands on the basis of gross margin generation.

Because the probability of retailer placement of tie-in advertising is directly related to funds available, a simpler linear relationship represents observed conditions. Such a formulation is summarized below in the probability of media promotion generation by retailer r on behalf of brand b.

Equation 9.17

PRMDPG(b, r)   PRobability of MeDia Promotion Generation by retailer r on behalf of brand b.

$$= C_{21} * ADVALL(b) * EXPUSL(b, r) + C_{22}$$

$$* \left[\frac{EXPGMG(b, r)}{RELAGM(r)} - 1.0 \right].$$

ADVALL(b)   ADVertising ALLowance available on units of b. Dimension: dollars per product unit.
= input from manufacturer sector. See Equation 7.4.

EXPUSL(b, r)   EXPected Unit SaLes of brand b through outlet r. Dimension: product units.
= see Equation 9.3.

EXPGMG(b, r)   EXPected Gross MarGin on brand b through outlet r. Dimension: dollars.
= see Equation 9.4.

RELAGM(r)   REaLized Average Gross Margin received by retailer r. Dimension: dollars.
= see Equation 9.1A.

C_{21} constant reflecting retailer disposition toward use of advertising allowance. Dimension: units per dollar.
= .01, as sample value.

C_{22} constant reflecting retailer disposition toward use of own dollars in advertising.
= 2.0, as sample value.

If promotion is generated, the level — dollar expenditure — in local media is determined by the available advertising allowance, the brand margin, and the retailer's willingness to allocate funds from these sources to brand promotion.

Equation 9.18

LMDEX(b, r)   Local MeDia EXpenditure by retailer r in support of brand b.

$$= [C_{23} * \text{ADVALL}(b) + C_{24} * (\text{PRICE}(b, r) - \text{PRTRET}(b, r))] * \text{ACTUSL}(b, r).$$

ADVALL(b)   ADVertising ALLowance available on units of b. Dimension: dollars per product unit.
= input from manufacturer sector. See Equation 7.4.

PRTRET(b, r)   PRice charged To RETailer r for units of brand b. Dimension: dollars per product unit.
= input from distributor or manufacturer sector. See Equation 7.13.

PRICE(b, r)   PRICE charged for brand b by retailer r. Dimension: dollars per product unit.
= see Equation 9.8.

ACTUSL(b, r)   ACTual Unit SaLes of b by retailer r. Dimension: product units per time unit (implicit).
= see Equation 9.2.

C_{23} constant indicating retailer r's disposition toward use of
                     advertising allowances.
              = 1.0, as sample value.

C_{24} constant indicating retailer r's disposition toward use of
                     profit margin for advertising.
              = .10, as sample value.

Use of Prepared Advertising Mats

Use of manufacturer-prepared mats is related to retailer size. Large
outlets tend to develop their own promotional content, whereas smaller
outlets will use mats when available to avoid the expense of copy, layout,
and plate preparation. The probability of a retailer using a prepared
mat (assuming that he has decided to undertake local promotion) may
be expressed as a function of his size as reflected in realized average
sales (Figure 9.10).

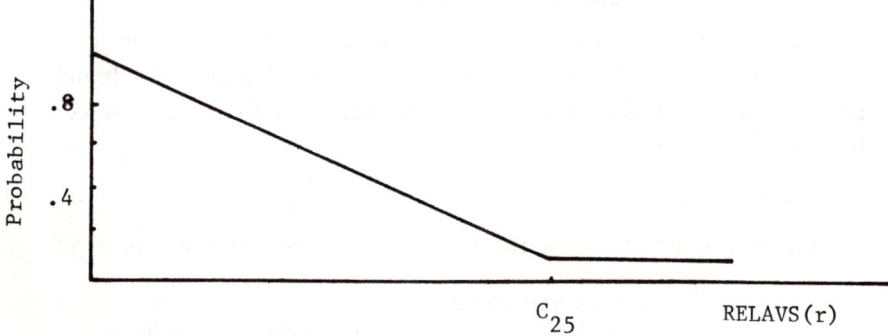

Figure 9.10. Probability of prepared promotion usage.

Equation 9.19

PRMATU(b, r)   PRobability of MAT Usage by retailer r running local
                  promotion for brand b — conditional on PRMDPG.
              = REMATA(b) $*$ SRF2F(RELAVS(r), .1, 1.0, C_{25}, 0).

REMATA(b)   REtail MAT Availability from brand b.
              = 1.0, if available,
              = 0.0, if not available.

RELAVS(r)   REaLized AVerage Sales — across all product lines
                  in retail outlet r.
              = see Equation 9.1.

C_{25} scaling constant determining upper limit of store size effect. Dimension: dollars.

= 150,000 as sample value.

Content of a Retail Promotion

If a prepared mat is used, the content of retail promotion is established by the manufacturer and communicated via the input-specifying mat content. The following comments relate only to content generated by the retailer who chooses *not* to use prepared promotion supplied by the manufacturer.

For purposes of this model, the retailer is limited to advertising content relating to three frequently encountered appeals. These are

1. A quality appeal: "We offer a carefully selected line of quality merchandise designed to meet the exacting standards of our discriminating clientele."
2. A price appeal: ". . . a wonderfully different kind of store and you pocket the difference."
3. A selection appeal: "choose from the widest selection of name brands available anywhere in New England. No need to waste time searching, the brand and model you want is on display at . . ."

Although the following rules are by no means exhaustive, they summarize preliminary conclusions regarding the relationship between operating characteristics of the retailer discussed earlier and the use of each of the appeals noted above.

As might be expected, the use of the quality appeal is correlated with higher-than-average percent markups across all products in the outlet. The use of a price appeal is somewhat less definitely associated with lower-than-average percent markups throughout the store. Analysis of this relationship is made difficult by price-leader promotions in which a particular item is promoted on the basis of price with the inference that a low price policy prevails throughout the outlet while, in fact, the promoted item is priced in marked contrast to the majority of products handled by the retailer. The use of the selection appeal is correlated with the presence of several brands within a given product line. In no instance was this appeal found in use by a retailer stocking only one brand in the promoted product line.

In the case of both the quality and price appeal the SRF2F logistic may be used to represent noted interactions. The relationship between number of brands carried and the use of the selection appeal is more appropriately represented by an exponentially weighted function. (See Figure 9.11.)

Equation 9.20

WGTAP(1, r) WeiGhT given quality APpeal 1 in advertisement generated by retailer r.

= SRF2F (EXPCMU(r), 1.0, .10, C_{26}, C_{27}).

EXPCMU(r) EXpected PerCent MarkUp for retailer r.
= Retailer characteristic, see Table 9.1.

C_{26} and C_{27} scaling constants determining upper and lower response limits.
= 1.00 and .30, respectively, as sample values.

WGTAP(2, r) WeiGhTing given price APpeal 2 in advertisement generated by retailer r.
= SRF2 (EXPCMU(r), 0, 1.0, C_{28}, C_{29}).

C_{28} and C_{29} scaling constants determining upper and lower response limits.
= .80 and .10, respectively, as sample values.

WGTAP(3, r) WeiGhTing given selection APpeal in advertisement generated by retailer r.

$$= 1 - \text{ENXPF}\left[-C_{29} * \frac{\sum_{b=1}^{B} \text{CARRY}(b, r)}{B}\right].$$

CARRY(b, r) brands CARRied by retailer r.
= see Equation 9.12.

B total number of Brands available in region.

C_{29} scaling constant.
= 3.0, sample value.

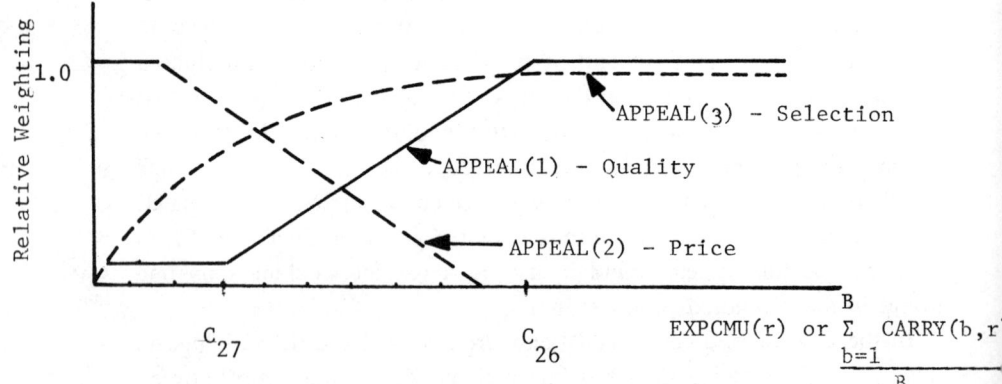

Figure 9.11. Appeal weightings in retailer-generated promotion.

Because a retailer may make some use of all three appeals it is necessary to consider the relative weighting given each appeal in a particular advertisement. Given Equation 9.20, the proportion of an advertisement devoted to each appeal may be calculated.

Equation 9.21

PRRADA(n, r)   PRoportion of Retailer r Advertisement Devoted to Appeal n.

$$= \frac{WGTAP(n, r)}{\sum\limits_{n=1}^{3} WGTAP(n, r)} .$$

Name Identification and Retailer-Prepared Advertisements

While manufacturer prepared mats present a wide range of retailer name prominences, advertisements generated by the retailer generally demonstrate a high level of name prominence achieved through the use of a distinctive logo and layout procedure or the more obvious mechanism of devoting large space to the retailer name.

The retailer name prominence is supplied as input in the case of a manufacturer-generated mat. In a retailer-generated advertisement, the maximum prominence scale value 4.0 will be assumed.

Equation 9.22

RNAMPR(na)   Retailer NAMe PRominence in content of advertisement na.
    = RTNMPR(na, b), if mat from b is used.
    = 4.0, if retailer generated advertisement.

RTNMPR(na, b)   ReTailer NaMe PRominence in mat na for brand b.
    = input describing brand b mat na.

Retailer-Salesman Communication at Point of Sale

The probability of retailer-salesman communication at point of sale was previously established as the probability of retailer selling effort on behalf of brand b expressed in Equation 9.15.

Given that selling effort exists, the content of communication between the retailer and consumer must be defined. Observation of retailer behavior suggests that the communication content is frequently determined by point-of-sale material available to the salesman at the time when communication is generated.[15]

---

[15] With the single exception of a salesman employed by a manufacturer and operating on location in the retail outlet, prepared salesman communication dif-

In addition, when more than one piece of point-of-sale information is available, content is biased toward the larger display. It has been observed, for example, that where both a placard and brochure were present, the salesman consistently "played back" the content of the placard before presenting information contained in the brochure.

In the absence of point-of-sale promotional material, it is unlikely that the retailer-salesman will generate point-of-sale communication. Factors supporting retail selling efforts are conducive to the placement of point-of-sale material. (See Equations 9.15 and 9.16.) Salesman communication generated in the absence of point-of-sale material is analogous to consumer word-of-mouth communication. Under these circumstances, the formulation for communication content summarized in Equation 8.7 is applicable.

Characteristics of retailer-generated communication content are summarized in the following formulations for appeals and product characteristic content.

Equation 9.23

$SCAPC(n, b, r)*$ Salesman (retailer) r Communication APpeal Content regarding appeal n in association with brand b.

$$= \sum_{na=1}^{NA(b)} EVPSAW(n, na) * RPLPSD(na, r),$$

$$\text{if } \sum_{na=1}^{NA(b)} RPLPSD(na, r) > 0.0,$$

$$= PEBRI(r, n, b), \text{ if } \sum_{na=1}^{NA(b)} RPLPSD(na, r) \leq 0.0.$$

$EVPSAW(n, na)$ EValuation of Point-of-Sale Appeals Weighting.
                   = input describing content of point-of-sale piece. See Equation 7.10.

$RPLPSD(na, r)$ Retailer r PLacement of Point-of-Sale Display na.
                   = 1, if display is placed,
                   = 0, if display is not placed.

$NA(b)$ total number of promotions relating to brand b.

$PEBRI(r, n, b)$ PErceived BRand Image of appeal n as associated with brand b in simulated mind of retailer r.
                   = see Equation 8.41.

---

fering in context from coincident point-of-sale promotion was not encountered in a study of 16 appliance retailers. (M.I.T. Sloan Research Project 142, March 1960.)

Equation 9.24

    SCPCC(n, b, r)*   Salesman (retailer) r Communication Product Characteristic Content regarding product characteristic n in association with brand b.

$$= \sum_{na=1}^{NA(b)} EVPCWP(np, na) * RPLPSD(na, r),$$

$$\text{if } \sum_{na=1}^{NA(b)} RPLPSD(na, r) > 0.0,$$

$$= PEBRI(r, np, b), \text{ if no point-of-sale display present.}$$

    EVPCWP(np, na)   EValuation of Product Characteristic np Weighting in Point-of-sale promotion na.
                     = input from manufacturer sector. See Equation 7.10.

This concludes the discussion of retailer decisions. In the following section of this chapter retailer responses to inputs received from other sectors in the marketing environment will be considered.

Retailer Responses

As indicated earlier in this chapter, retailer responses may be conveniently categorized in terms of the retailer's businessman and consumer orientations. As a businessman, the retailer responds to the prevailing business climate, competitive conditions in his area of operation, trade advertising, manufacturer and distributor salesmen, and consumers. As a consumer, he encounters and may respond to the complete range of consumer media. In addition, his exposure to point-of-purchase displays placed in his own outlet is assured. Because retailer-consumer interactions provide for extensive word-of-mouth communication, the retailer's nonbusiness word-of-mouth interchanges may be ignored.

Response to the Business Climate

Retailer attitude toward the existing business climate is largely determined by sales trends observed during the preceding period. This perception may be summarized in a rate of expectation change described in terms of the attitude construct as illustrated in Figure 9.12 and summarized in equation form.

---

* SCPCC and SCAPC by the *retailer* (n, b, r) should not be confused with the similarly identified *salesman* (n, b, s) variables.

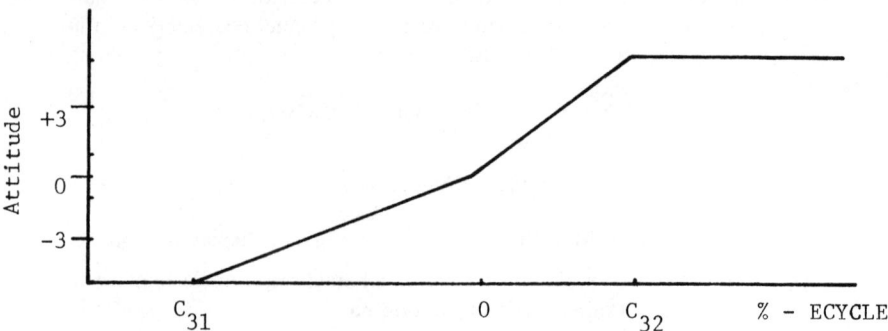

Figure 9.12. Effect of change in economic cycle on attitude toward business climate.

Equation 9.25

ATTBCL(r)   ATTitude toward Business CLimate.
                   $= -5 + \text{SRF3F (GRORAT(r), } 10.0, 5.0, 0.0, C_{32}, 0, C_{31}).$

GRORAT(r)   GROwth RATe as perceived by retailer r.

$$= \sum_{b=1}^{B(r)} \left[\frac{\text{EXPUSL}(t, b, r) - \text{ACTUSL}(t - 1, b, r)}{\text{ACTUSL}(t - 1, b, r)} \right].$$

EXPUSL(t, b, r)   EXPected Unit SaLes of brand b through outlet r at
                   time t.
                   = see Equation 9.3.

ACTUSL(t, b, r)   ACTual Unit Sales of brand b through outlet r at
                   time t.
                   = see Equation 9.2.

B(r)   total Brands carried in product line by retailer r.

C_{32} and C_{31} constants specifying response limits.
                   $= +.30$ and $-.20$ as sample values.

Response to Competitive Conditions

As noted earlier, an attitude matrix indicating retailer orientation toward other outlets carrying brands that he is stocking is supplied exogenously to the model. The retailer's aggregate attitude toward competitive conditions for a product line may be summarized in the net value of his attitude toward the condition existing with respect to each of the brands making up that product line.

Equation 9.26

ATTREC(r)   ATTitude of retailer r toward REtail Competition. Dimension: attitude scale units.

$$= \frac{\sum\limits_{tc=1}^{TC} \left[RETATM(t_r, t_c) * \sum\limits_{b=1}^{B} ACTUSL(b, t_c) \right]}{\sum\limits_{tc=1}^{TC} \sum\limits_{b=1}^{B} ACTUSL(b, t_c)}.$$

RETATM(t₁, t₂)   RETailer ATtitude Matrix indicating attitude of retailer of type t_1 toward retailer of type t_2 carrying brands stocked by him. Dimension: attitude scale units.
        = exogenously supplied input.

ACTUSL(b, t_c)   ACTual Unit SaLes of brand b through retailers of type t_c. Dimension: product units.

$$= \sum_{r=1}^{R_{tc}} ACTUSL(b, r).$$

R_{tc} total number of Retailers of type tc.

Response to Trade Advertising

The media response model introduced in Chapter 8 may be applied to the retailer's response to trade advertising by expansion to encompass trade media and appeals and product characteristics relevant to the retailer (i.e., high margins, warranty backup, liberal credit policies, etc.). In view of the detailed discussion of this structure undertaken in Chapter 8, further elaboration of this representation would be redundant.[16]

The probabilities of exposure, assimilation, and response (awareness gain and memory update) as well as forgetting and dissonance resolution developed in Chapter 8 may be used without modification in the present context to describe retailer responses.

Response to the Manufacturer or Distributor Salesman

The retailer's probability of being exposed to a salesman representing a manufacturer or distributor is a function of that salesman's call schedule. The scheduled call rate corrected for average rate of call completion, reduced to take account of abortive calls, provides a measure of this exposure probability.

---

[16] The reader interested in reviewing the assumptions underlying the use of this model is referred to the discussion "Consumer Exposure and Responses to Media Communication" in Chapter 8.

Equation 9.27

$PREXSM(r, d_b)$ PRobability that retailer r will be EXposed to Sales-
Man representing distributor d handling brand b.
$= RCCMPL(S_{d_b}, rt_r)$.

$RCCMPL(S_{d_b}, rt_r)$ Rate of Call CoMPLetion by salesman S_{d_b} in employ
of distributor d_b, carrying brand b calling on retailers
of type rt_r in region of location.
= input from salesman model, proportion of retailers
of type rt successfully contacted during call period.

Given this exposure probability, previously developed formulations
for the probability of assimilation and response (awareness gain and
memory update) as developed in Chapter 8 (Equation 8.34) are applicable.

Retailer-Customer Interactions

Studies of retailer-consumer interactions suggest that the customer
expects the merchant to emphasize the customer's status through exaggerated deference, yielding in minor arguments, expressions of interest
in the customer's personal affairs, and the performance of various small
personal services.[17]

One series of motivation studies concluded that the housewife needed
". . . to feel important, to feel that she was in control of the sales visit,
and to feel that she was an efficient shopper. . . ." [18]

Pierre Martineau indicates that expectations with regard to the retailer
are a function of the customer's socioeconomic position. "The lower-
status shopper expects the clerk to be 'just people.' The Upper Middle
Class woman expects them to be high-salaried servants." [19]

Otto Pollak has suggested that the consumer-retailer interaction may
be seriously affected by the tendency for the shopper to use the purchase
situation as a vehicle.

. . . for the expression of hostility in what may appear, not only to others
but even to herself, as acceptable forms. . . . Irrationality can influence
. . . the relationship established between the buyer and the salesman. The

[17] T. Caplow, *The Sociology of Work* (Minneapolis: University of Minnesota
Press, 1954), p. 119.

[18] J. H. Newman, "New Insights, New Progress, for Marketing," *Harvard Business Review,* Vol. 35 (November–December 1957), p. 101.

[19] P. Martineau, "The Pattern of Social Classes," R. L. Clewett (ed.), *Marketing's Role in Scientific Management* (Chicago: American Marketing Association,
1957), p. 242.

phenomena of "displacement" may operate in that relationship. A woman who cannot afford to express antagonism toward her husband or her children may find the salesman a convenient target. In a buyer's market, the salesman is notoriously vulnerable, and vulnerability always attracts the displacement of aggression.[20]

Within the structure of this simulation, these intricacies of the consumer-retailer interaction are subsumed under formulations developed in Chapter 8.

Exposure to Customer Comment

The simulated consumer's presence in a simulated retail outlet is a prerequisite of retailer-consumer interaction at point of purchase. In formulating this interaction from the consumer's point of view, it was assumed that brand-oriented discussion with the retailer would be preceded by exposure to the brand in question.

Assuming independence, the probability that a consumer who has entered the store will be exposed to a brand *and* generate word-of-mouth communication regarding that brand may be expressed as

Equation 9.28

$\text{PREXWM}(r, c_r)$ PRobability of retailer r being EXposed to Word-of-Mouth communication by consumer c_r who has entered outlet r.

$= \text{PREXBR}(r, b) * \text{PRWMG}(c_r, b)$.

$\text{PREXBR}(r, b)$ PRobability of EXposure to BRand b in retail outlet r.
$=$ see Equation 8.27.

$\text{PRWMG}(c_r, b)$ PRobability of Word-of-Mouth Generation by consumer c_r regarding brand b.
$=$ see Equation 8.5.

Given interaction, the content of word-of-mouth communication is determined by the model developed in Chapter 8 and summarized in Equation 8.7.

Assimilation of Customer Comments

The impact of consumer word-of-mouth comment is largely determined by the retailer's evaluation of the extent to which the consumer is representative of his clientele. Reactions communicated to a retailer by a nonrepresentative customer may be totally disregarded.

[20] O. Pollak, "Symptomatic Factors in Consumer Behavior," in Cox, Alderson, and Shapiro, *op. cit.,* Footnote 1, p. 285–286.

The assimilation process may be formulated in terms of the Chapter 8 Equation 8.27 representation, with the following modification.

Equation 9.29

PRAWM(r, c) PRobability that retailer r will Assimilate Word-of-Mouth communication generated by consumer c.

$$= \text{PREXWM}(r, c_r) * [1 - \text{INCDFR}(c_{rt}, c_r) - \text{AGEDFR}(c_{rt}, c_r) - \text{EDUDFR}(c_{rt}, c_r)].$$

PREXWM(r, c_r) PRobability of retailer r being EXposed to Word-of-Mouth communication generated by consumer c_r.

= see Equation 9.28.

INCDFR(c_{rt}, c_r) INCome DiFfeRential between consumer c_r and the total clientele of regainer, r, c_{rt}.

$$= C_{29} * \frac{\sum\limits_{c_{rt}=1}^{\text{CRT}(r)} \text{INCOM}(c_{rt})}{\text{CRT}(r)} - \text{INCOM}(c_r),$$

$$\text{if } \sum \frac{\text{INCOM}(c_{rt})}{\text{CRT}(r)} > \text{INCOM}(c_r),$$

$$= 0.0, \text{ if } \sum \frac{\text{INCOM}(c_{rt})}{\text{CRT}(r)} \leq \text{INCOM}(c_r).$$

AGEDFR(c_{rt}, c_r) AGE DiFfeRential between consumer c_r and the total clientele of retailer r, c_{rt}.

$$= C_{30} * \left| \frac{\sum\limits_{c_{rt}=1}^{\text{CRT}(r)} \text{AGEID}(c_{rt})}{\text{CRT}(r)} - \text{AGEID}(c_r) \right|.$$

EDUDFR(c_{rt}, c_r) EDUcation DiFfeRential between consumer c_r and the total clientele of retailer r, c_{rt}.

$$= C_{31} * \frac{\sum\limits_{c_{rt}=1}^{\text{CRT}(r)} \text{EDUCA}(c_{rt})}{\text{CRT}(r)} - \text{EDUCA}(c_r),$$

$$\text{if } \sum \frac{\text{EDUCA}(c_{rt})}{\text{CRT}(r)} > \text{EDUCA}(c_r),$$

$$= 0.0, \text{ if } \sum \frac{\text{EDUCA}(c_{rt})}{\text{CRT}(r)} \leq \text{EDUCA}(c_r).$$

INCOM(c) INCOMe of consumer c.
= attribute of consumer cell, see Chapter 8.

AGEID(c) AGE of consumer c.
= attribute of consumer cell, see Chapter 8.

EDUCA(c) EDUCAtion of consumer c.
= attribute of consumer cell, see Chapter 8.

CRT(r) total number of Consumers who shop in ReTail outlet r.

Once consumer communication is assimilated, probable retailer response may be determined using the communication response model summarized in Equations 8.25 and 8.26. These formulations indicate the probability of awareness gain and extent of memory update that will occur as a result of word-of-mouth communication assimilation.

Consumer response to retailer comments is handled in the consumer model through formulation of the consumer's response to retail selling activity. (See Equations 8.33 and 8.34.)

Consumerlike Retailer Responses

The response model developed in Chapter 8 is directly applicable to the representation of retailer responses in two contexts in which the retailer and consumer are indistinguishable. These are (1) consumer media exposure and response, and (2) response to point-of-sale displays.

Responses to Consumer Media

Although the retailer's orientation based on past experience may be different from that of any consumer, the process through which he is exposed to, assimilates, and responds to promotion transmitted via consumer media is indistinguishable from that of the consumer. The concept and formulations summarized in Equations 8.8 through 8.22 are incorporated into the retailer model by substituting the retailer identification code r in lieu of the consumer identification code c.[21]

Response to Point-of-Purchase Display

Retailer exposure and response to point-of-purchase display material for brands that the retailer is *not* carrying may be described by the previously developed consumer point-of-sale display response model (Equations 8.29 and 8.30). Exposure to material for brands carried may be assumed while assimilation continues to be determined by the response model.[22]

Equation 9.30

PREXPS(r, b)   PRobability that retailer r will be EXposed to Point-of-Sale material for brand b.
= 1.0, if CARRY(b, r) = 1.0.

[21] For a review of the media exposure and response model, see "Consumer Exposure and Response to Media Communication," Chapter 8, p. 185.

[22] Consumer response to point-of-sale promotion is discussed in "Experience at Point of Sale," Chapter 8, p. 209.

CARRY(b, r)   brands CARRied by retailer r.
              = 1.0, if brand b carried,
              = 0.0, if brand b not carried.

Summary

This chapter has focused on the development of a simulation of retailer behavior designed to function in conjunction with the Chapter 8 consumer model and representations of behavior associated with other market sectors formulated in later chapters.

Decision and response processes within the retail sector have been formulated as if each outlet were operated by an abstract individual retailer. Business-related descriptors in addition to previously established consumer characteristics identified each retail cell.

Model development began with an examination of processes through which retailers evaluate existing market conditions ranging from the general state of the economy to trends in product line sales and relative brand performance. Factors influencing the retailer's expectations for the future were then considered and sales and margin estimating procedures were derived.

Representations of decision processes establishing price, product line composition, orders, product placement, selling effort, and promotion under various competitive and market conditions were then developed. Determinants of retailer promotional communication were assessed in the course of formulating media and salesman communication content generation functions.

Retailer response to business and trade conditions was described in terms of attitudes toward other retailers carrying specified brand combinations. Response to media, point-of-sale, and salesman promotion was represented using the consumer response structure developed in Chapter 8. The impact of consumer-retailer interactions was manifest in retailer response to word-of-mouth communication interpreted in light of characteristics of his clientele.

Chapter 10

A MODEL OF DISTRIBUTOR BEHAVIOR

The objective of this chapter is to develop a simulation encompassing major distributor actions and responses. Specifications developed in Chapter 3 provide the framework for this discussion. Taking advantage of similarities in the roles of retailer and distributor, this development will be based on the retailer model formulated in the preceding chapter. Familiarity with the retailer simulation will be assumed.

Description of a Distributor

For reasons comparable to those discussed in the retail context, distributor decision and response functions will be formulated as if each distributor were a single abstract individual. The distributor model will be a cell simulation in which members of an artificial distributor population described in terms of selected attributes are explicitly represented. As in the retailer and consumer models, total population behavior will be established through accumulation of individual cell behavior.

Management Control of Distribution Channels

It is sometimes suggested that the manufacturer controls the distribution channels through which his goods are distributed and is able to select and direct the activities of each link in the chain joining him to the ultimate consumers of his product.[1]

If this were true, management's concern with distributor behavior

[1] See, for example, C. F. Phillips and D. J. Duncan, *Marketing Principles and Methods* (3rd ed.; Homewood, Ill.: Richard D. Irwin, Inc., 1956), p. 562.

would be negligible. Examination of actual business relationships suggests, however, that the concept of direct manufacturer control of distribution channels is inaccurate and misleading.[2] Middlemen are relatively free agents who exercise a substantial degree of autonomy in responding to information and product flow through the system while making decisions as businessmen and purchasing agents for their customers. In the words of Wroe Alderson, distributors and retailers ". . . constitute a loose coalition engaged in exploiting joint opportunity in the market." [3]

Activities of a Distributor

When defining attributes for the retail population, the retailer's consumerlike activities were separated from his behavior as a businessman and decision maker. It may be useful to maintain this categorization in order to determine similarities and differences between retailer and distributor.

Consumerlike Distributor Behavior

In the previously developed simulation, the retailer was viewed as a member of consumer society — as an individual influencing and influenced by consumer opinion. Representations of retailer response processes were modeled on those of consumers.

Although the distributor may be characterized as an intermediate consumer, he is substantially removed from the consumer market. His decisions are more often based on business information — trends in sales, market share, promotional expenditures and the like — than on subjective evaluations of probable responses to a brand by a particular clientele. The distributor may be affected by salesman and trade promotion containing policy communiqués. However, his reaction to such communication is more appropriately represented by direct memory update than by the selective perception and response process associated with consumer and retailer reaction to information presentation. Direct consumer contact on the part of the distributor is rare and, for purposes

[2] For a discussion of this problem see P. McVey, "Are Channels of Distribution What the Textbooks Say?", *Journal of Marketing,* Vol. 24 (January 1960), pp. 61–65.

[3] W. Alderson, "The Development of Marketing Channels," in R. M. Clewett (ed.), *Marketing Channels for Manufactured Products* (Homewood, Ill.: Richard D. Irwin, Inc., 1954), p. 30.

of this model, the potential impact of consumer word-of-mouth inter-action will be ignored.

While the distributor is recognized to be a member of the consumer population, his consumerlike behavior and responses are relegated to a position of secondary importance.

The Distributor as a Businessman

It is in his role as a businessman that the distributor most closely parallels behavior of the retailer. Both distributor and retailer form expectations, make plans for the future, and take actions based on these plans. Previously developed formulations of retailer business decisions provide a useful starting point for analysis of distributor decision making.

When formulating expectations relating to the future business and economic climate or the future sales performance of a brand or product line, the retailer and distributor are sensitive to similar factors. Their future expectations are often congruent — faced with comparable evidence, they arrive at comparable conclusions. Expected unit sales, gross margin, average sales, average gross margins, and trends, or rates of change in these variables over time are viewed as a relevant descriptor of the business environment by the distributor as well as the retailer.

Both distributor and retailer maintain normative references against which conditions existing in the market are evaluated. Desired margin, sales volume, promotional support, profit potential, and associated concepts found to be important to the retailer are also referenced by the distributor.

The Distributor as Decision Maker

Five of the seven retailer decision areas identified in Chapter 9 have direct equivalents in the distributor sector:

1. The decision to carry (stock) a product line and/or brand.
2. The decision to order specific quantities of a brand-model for delivery at a given time.
3. The decision to exert selling effort in an attempt to "push" a particular product line or brand-model.
4. The pricing decision.
5. The decision to drop — liquidate existing stocks of — a product line and/or brand-model.

Two decision areas of importance to the retailer are totally irrelevant insofar as the distributor is concerned. While the retailer may make independent decisions relating to local media promotion and the placement of point-of-sale promotion, the distributor normally serves as a transfer agent handling manufacturer-generated material. He is not apt to generate promotional material independently. Similarly, while both distributor and retailer are concerned with pricing policy, the retailer is more apt to be involved in competitive pricing activities than is the distributor. In the pricing context, the distributor, particularly in a franchised situation, is more apt to function as agent of the manufacturer than as an independent decision maker.

In structuring the retailer model, the roles of store manager and salesman or clerk were combined in a single abstract entity. In the distributor case, administrative and selling functions will be isolated. Two distinct entities, the distributor and distributor salesman, will be simulated within separate sector models. As a result of this structure, it will be necessary to examine the distributor's interactions with his salesmen as manifest in hiring, firing, scheduling, and compensation decisions.

Distributor Attributes

Defining characteristics of the distributor will be categorized in terms of the four previously used classifications: demographic, economic, behavioral, and psychological. Continuing the comparison between retailer and distributor, characteristics of the distributor will be referenced to comparable retailer attributes defined in Chapter 9. Table 10.1 provides an appropriately cross-referenced summary of distributor characteristics.

The Table 10.1 column headed *Distributor Characteristic* identifies each attribute. The *Variable* column specifies the variable name used in the distributor model to reference this characteristic. The column headed *Gradation* specifies the number of unique values used in measuring the variable, while the *Bits Required* column indicates the number of binary bits of computer storage allocated to the characteristic. The column headed *Retail Variable* references the variable names of comparable retailer model characteristics.

A single demographic characteristic is noted in Table 10.1 in contrast to the retailer case in which retailer-type and rural-urban-suburban classifications were used.

Three economic variables comparable to measures employed in the

TABLE 10.1.   Distributor-Retailer Characteristics Comparison

Distributor Characteristic	Variable	Gradation	Bits Required	Retail Equivalent Variable
Demographic				
Geographic Location	Implicit	—	—	Implicit
Economic				
Average Total Dollar Volume	AVTOTV	1	8	AVSWVL
Standard Markup	MARKUP	10	4	EXPCMU
Average Gross Profit	AVGRPR	10	4	RELAGM
Average Product Line Gross Profit	AVPLGP	10	28	—
Salary Paid Salesmen	SALARY	20	5	—
Commission Paid Salesmen	COMMIS	20	5	—
Behavioral				
Brands Carried	CARRY	1	10	CARRY
Product Mix — 7 Categories	PRDMIX	4	21	PROMIX
Number Calls/ Salesman/Period	NCPSPP	1	8	—
Number on Sales Force	NSALFC	1	8	—
Normal Call Period in Days	NCALPD	1	8	—
Maximum Number on Sales Force	MXSDES	20	5	—
Psychological				
Disposition to "Weed" Product	C_5	10	4	C_{11}
Disposition to Add Product Line	C_1, C_2	10	4	C_{13}, C_{14}
Disposition to Change Brands Carried	C_3, C_4	10	4	C_{11} -C_{14}
Desired Number of Days Inventory	C_9	15	4	C_{15}
Disposition Toward Price Speculation	C_{10}	10	4	C_{16}

retailer case are used as descriptors of the distributor population. Two additional variables relating to distributor sales force compensation are also included.

Under the "Behavioral" heading, two variables comparable to previously discussed retailer brand and product line characteristics are defined in addition to three variables relating to distributor behavior vis-à-vis the sales force. The media availability variable set that was of importance in both consumer and retailer models is absent from the distributor specifications.

Four previously discussed psychological variables are included in the distributor model. These relate to the distributor's disposition toward adding product line, changing brands, and engaging in price speculation, and his concept of a desired inventory. Because media response is not being considered in describing distributor behavior, the attitude variables that appeared as psychological descriptors of the retailer are not specified for the distributor.

Distributor Behavior

Model development will begin with the processes through which past experience and the present state of the market are evaluated. This will be followed by an examination of expectation formation establishing expected unit sales for each brand being distributed or considered for distribution. As in the retail case, expected unit sales figures in combination with the outcome of pricing decisions yield brand specific gross profits.

Formulation of distributor decision functions will focus on several decisions previously considered from the retailer's point of view. These are the pricing decision, decisions to carry and drop brands from the product line, and the order decision. Sales force management adds new decision areas to the distributor's action set. He must develop call schedules determining the allocation of salesman time among various retailers, hire salesmen to fill vacancies, and remove nonproductive salesmen.

Formulation of the distributor's sales management decisions will specify one side of an interaction simulation that will be completed by the Chapter 11 representation of salesman behavior.

The distributor's responses to the business climate will be described in terms of reactions to margins, competitive conditions, and brand performance as reflected in retail purchases. His responses to trade promotion will be represented as direct assimilation of policy information rather than subjective response to appeals and product characteristics. This formulation ignoring the effects of consumer interaction, consumer media promotion, and trade promotion may be expected to produce simulated behavior that will appear more "rational" — less subjective — than that generated by the retailer model.

Similar decision inputs at the distributor and manufacturer levels (both distributor and manufacturer focus on distributor sales as an indication of the state of the market) yield similar expectations within the manufacturer and distributor sectors. Manufacturers consequently report that they are better able to "understand" and anticipate distributor responses based on "business factors" than consumer and retailer actions determined in part by "whims and fancy." [4] This finding might be anticipated because the communication channels linking distributor and manufacturer are often direct — the decision makers communicate without intermediaries — while communication between manufacturer and retailer or consumer involves intermediaries who may filter and distort the flow of information.

A Model of Distributor Behavior

The remainder of this chapter is devoted to the development of a model of distributor behavior based on specifications established in Chapter 3 and characteristics outlined in Table 10.1. The model focuses on behavior applicable to a broad range of products. Unique attributes of distributors of specific product lines may be treated as exceptions to or expansions of this generalized model.

The procedure for specification of variable dimensions adopted in Chapter 9 will be maintained in this chapter. Pure number variables and functions will not be explicitly dimensioned.

Evaluation of Existing Sales

Because the distributor's basic function is to supply goods — to satisfy existing demand — he is sensitive to the orders that he receives from retailers whom he services. Ignoring for the moment time delays inherent in communication from retailer to distributor, the sales experienced by the distributor may be represented as the cumulative orders generated during a time period by all retailers whom he supplies with product.

Equation 10.1

ACTUSL(t, b, d)   ACTual Unit SaLes of brand b through distributor d at time t. Dimension: product units per time period.

$$= \sum_{r=1}^{R_d} ORDERS(t, b, d, r).$$

[4] Remarks taken from interviews conducted in a study of distributor-manufacturer relations in the appliance industry. (M.I.T. Sloan Research Project 142, 1959.)

ORDERS(t, b, d, r)   ORDERS for units of b generated by retailer r at time t and directed to distributor d. Dimension: product units per time period.
= see Equation 9.13.

R_d total number of Retailers serviced by d.
= system constant.

The distributor, like the retailer, is sensitive to that which he perceives as seasonal demand and "significant sales trends." The distributor does not generally appear to be more sophisticated in his evaluation of trends or seasonality than the retailer. However, the data with which the distributor works may be broader based and, as such, more representative than that available to the retailer.

Evaluation of Seasonal Cycle

The distributor's evaluation of seasonality for a product line made up of B brands may be formulated in terms of a seasonal adjustment factor comparable to that developed in the retail model. A one-month decision time step is assumed.

Equation 10.2

SESLAJ(t, d)   AdJustment required to take account of SEaSonaLity of demand for product line as perceived by distributor d.

$$= \sum_{b=1}^{B(d)} \left[\frac{ACTUSL(t - 12, b, d) - ACTUSL(t - 13, b, d)}{ACTUSL(t - 13, b, d)} \right] / B(d).$$

ACTUSL(t, b, d)   ACTual Unit SaLes of brand b through distributor d at time t. Dimension: product units per time period.
= see Equation 10.1.

B(d)   total Brands in distributor d product line.

$$= \sum_{b=1}^{BTOT} CARRY(b, d).$$

CARRY(b, d)   specifications of brands CARRied by distributor d.
= 0.0, if brand not carried,
= 1.0, if brand carried.

BTOT   the TOTal number of Brands that might potentially be carried as part of the product line being considered in the simulation.
= system parameter.

Evaluation of Sales Trends

Once the distributor decides what portion of the fluctuation in demand over time he will attribute to "seasonality," his estimate of sales trend is effectively established. The distributor does not normally attempt to correlate specific market developments with changes in sales. He is more apt to assume that all changes not attributable to seasonal fluctuations are an indication of trend. The distributor is not concerned with causality. He simply notes that "there seems to be a trend."

That which the distributor perceives as a short-term (one-month) trend is easily expressed (assuming a one-month decision time step) in a form analogous to that employed earlier in the retailer model.

Equation 10.3

> TREND(t, b, d)   TREND in sales of brand b as perceived by distributor d at time t.
>
> $$= \frac{ACTUSL(t-1, b, d) - ACTUSL(t-2, b, d)}{ACTUSL(t-2, b, d)}$$
>
> $$- SESLAJ(t, d).$$

> ACTUSL(t, b, d)   ACTual Unit SaLes of brand b through distributor d at time t.
>   = see Equation 10.1.

> SESLAJ(t, d)   AdJustment required to take account of SEaSonaLity of demand for product line as perceived by distributor d at time t.
>   = see Equation 10.2.

Distributor Knowledge of Brand Shares

As a result of discussions with other distributors and feedback from the manufacturer, most distributors seem to possess relatively accurate estimates of brand market shares. The assumption that the distributor has perfect information regarding brand sales in the market in which he is operating will be introduced as an approximation to the actual condition of relatively accurate, but not perfect, information.

Equation 10.4

> BRDSHR(b)   BRanD SHaRe of brand b in region as a whole.
>
> $$= \frac{\sum_{d=1}^{DTOT} ACTUSL(t-1, b, d)}{\sum_{d=1}^{DTOT} \sum_{b=1}^{BTOT} ACTUSL(t-1, b, d)}.$$

> DTOT   TOTal number of Distributors operating in the region being simulated.
>   = system parameter.

A "noise" factor may be introduced as a multiplier in this equation to represent deviations of distributor perceived brand shares from absolute truth. Given information regarding the extent of such deviations, random variation of an appropriate magnitude may add substantially to the realism of simulated behavior.

Lacking data on which to base such a formulation, there is no reason to believe that random fluctuation is more appropriate than a consistently biased estimate oriented, for example, toward overestimation of market shares for brands carried. In this situation, model economy favors use of the simplest estimate based on the assumption of perfect information.

Using his knowledge of sales and prices, the distributor develops the basic measures of profitability discussed earlier in context of retailer brand performance evaluation. He is also aware of dollar and percent markups, and gross margins achieved through various brands and product lines.

Expectation Formation

While the distributor bases many decisions on expectations for the future, his estimates of what will happen tomorrow are based largely on his experiences today and yesterday.

The distributor is most concerned with the brands that he is presently distributing. His best historical data relate to these brands because he regularly places orders for them, and the most rudimentary ordering procedure requires maintenance of some information.

The distributor's concept of "trends" may be somewhat more sophisticated than the retailer's and, as noted earlier, he has a broader base from which to view developments over time. However, the approach to estimation encountered at the two levels is not very different. If anything, distributors appear to be slightly more conservative and to tie their estimates more closely to historically realized performance than do retailers.

Salesmen may succeed in convincing a retailer that a forthcoming promotional campaign will have a substantial effect on the sales of a particular brand and, as such, induce the retailer to stock more product than would be justified on the basis of a strict analysis of historical brand performance. At the distributor level, the importance of this kind of prestocking is greatly reduced. Increased stocking may be noted at the distributor level at the same time as the retail level; however, *the reasons* for placing orders are different. While the retailer may be ordering on the basis of expectations with little basis in experience, the distributor is stocking to replenish inventory depleted by the retailer's orders. From the distributor's point of view, orders are real and, being unaware of the motivations of the retailer, he is acting on what appears to him to be established historical fact — the orders were received — rather than future expectations.

Sales Expectations for Brands Carried

Sales expectations for a brand that the distributor is carrying and has carried for sufficient time to have historical performance experience can be simply described in terms of past sales. The most important factor in the distributor's mind is normally recent performance reflected in sales during the preceding month. Recognizing the existence of seasonal and trend factors, he may, however, correct this experienced sales level to reflect what he perceives as *"established growth characteristics"* for the brand.

Equation 10.5

EXPUSL(t, b, d)   EXPected Unit SaLes of brand b through distributor d at time t. Dimension: product units per time unit. Where: CARRY(b, d) = 1.0.
$$= \text{ACTUSL}(t-1, b) * (1 + \text{SESLAJ}(t) + \text{TREND}(t, b)).$$

ACTUSL(t, b)   ACTual Unit SaLes of brand b through distributor d at time t. Dimension: product units per time period.
$$= \text{see Equation 10.1.}$$

SESLAJ(t, d)   AdJustment required to take account of SEaSonaLity of demand for product line as perceived by distributor d.
$$= \text{see Equation 10.2.}$$

TREND(t, b, d)   TREND in sales of brand b as perceived by distributor d at time t.
$$= \text{see Equation 10.3.}$$

Sales Expectations for Brands Not Carried

The distributor attempting to develop sales expectations for a brand that he has not previously carried faces one of two circumstances. (1) He has had experience with other brands in the product line and is considering adding the brand under investigation to expand his line or replace a brand that will be dropped. (2) He has not previously handled the product line and has no directly applicable experience on which to base his consideration of this brand. The circumstances existing in a particular case can be established by examining the CARRY(b,d) array specifying brands carried by each distributor.

The Existing Product Line Case. Identifying the brand under consideration as b_1 the situation in which the distributor is considering adding b_1 to an existing product lne is expressed as follows:

Equation 10.6

$$CARRY(b_1, d) = 0.0.$$

$\quad$ B(d) $\qquad\qquad$ > 0.0.

$\quad$ B(d) $\qquad\qquad$ total Brands in product line carried by distributor.
$\qquad\qquad\qquad$ = see Equation 10.2.

In this situation, the distributor relies on experience gained in handling other brands in the product line in arriving at his estimate of expected sales for b_1. Making use of experience-based expectations summarized in Equation 10.5, the distributor relates his sales in brands carried to market wide sales (brand shares) to obtain a sales estimate for the new brand whose market-wide brand share is also known.

Equation 10.7

$\quad$ **EXPUSL(t, b_1, d)** $\quad$ EXPected Unit SaLes of brand b_1 through distributor d under conditions as summarized in Equation 6. Dimension: product units per time period.

$$= \left[\frac{\sum_{b=1}^{B(d)} ACTUSL(t - 1, b, d)}{\sum_{b=1}^{B(d)} BRDSHR(b)} \right] * BRDSHR(b_1).$$

$\quad$ **ACTUSL(t, b, d)** $\quad$ ACTual Unit SaLes of brand b through distributor d at time t. Product units per time period.
$\qquad\qquad\qquad$ = see Equation 10.1.

$\quad$ **BRDSHR(b)** $\qquad$ BRanD SHaRe of brand b in region as a whole.
$\qquad\qquad\qquad$ = see Equation 10.4.

$\quad$ b_1 $\qquad\qquad\qquad$ variable specifying brand for which expected unit sales are being calculated.

$\quad$ **B(d)** $\qquad\qquad\qquad$ total Brands in product line carried by distributor d.
$\qquad\qquad\qquad$ = see Equation 10.2.

The New Product Line Case. As indicated, the distributor may consider adding a brand in a new product line — a line in which he has not previously carried any other brands. This situation can be described as follows:

Equation 10.8

CARRY(b_1, d)   specification of brand b_1 CARRied by distributor d.
= 0.0.

B(d)   total Brands in product line carried by d.
= 0.0.

In this situation, the distributor is faced with the problem of estimating the unit sales that will be realized by adding the new product line represented by brand b_1. Having no experience with the relevant product line, he is supplied by the manufacturer (or obtains through trade sources) an estimate of brand performance through similar channels in another area. Under the assumption of perfect information availability, the distributor has access to actual sales data as indicated in Equation 10.4. Subject to the limitations inherent in the omniscience assumption, the distributor's behavior under these circumstances may be described as follows:

Equation 10.9

EXPUSL(t, b_1, d)   EXPected Unit SaLes of brand b_1 through distributor d under conditions specified in Equation 10.8.

$$= \frac{ACTUSL(t - 1, b_1, d') * AVTOTV(d)}{AVTOTV(d')}.$$

ACTUSL(t, b_1, d)   ACTual Unit SaLes of brand b through distributor d'.
= see Equation 10.1.

AVTOTV(d')   AVerage TOTal dollar Volume through distributor d'.
= distributor characteristic. See Table 10.1.

The Pricing Decision

Formulation of the retailer pricing decision as outlined in Chapter 9 involved consideration of competitive interaction within the market. The distributor is by comparison relatively passive once a pricing policy has been agreed upon with the manufacturer. The markup defined as a characteristic attribute of each member of the distributor population constrains that member to maintain a price to his retailer customers that is related to the price charged him by the manufacturer by a constant factor — his characteristic markup.

The extent of behavioral variation encountered is indicated by a study of hardware, dry goods, and drug outlets in the southern United States. Use of the manufacturer suggested resale price was reported in 20% of the dry goods cases, 33% of the hardware cases, and 59% of the drug trade pricing examples. The extent of adherence to the suggested resale price was correlated with manufacturer emphasis on adherence to the "suggested" resale price. When buyers pricing at suggested resale levels were asked to indicate their reasons for doing so, the presence of adequate markup at the suggested price was most frequently mentioned while manufacturer insistence on price maintenance received the second largest number of mentions.[5]

In practice this markup may not be constant although consistent markup policies will be followed. There is, however, no substantive gain to be realized in the context of this system by introducing a range of markups.

Given the indicated markup structure the pricing decision reduces to a tautology based on the manufacturer's price to the distributor and the distributor's standard markup.

Equation 10.10

PRTRET(b, r)   PRice To RETailer r for brand b. Dimension: dollars per product unit.

$$= \text{MANFPR(b)} * (1 + \text{MARKUP(d)}).$$

MANFPR(b)   MANuFacturers PRice for b. Dimension: dollars per product unit.

= input from manufacturer sector. See Equation 8.12.

MARKUP(d)   distributor d's MARKUP over MANFPR(b).

= distributor characteristic. See Table 10.1.

Expected Gross Profit Determination

Once the distributor has established expected unit sales for a brand, his expected gross profit — the total profit that would be realized from the sales of this brand at the expected level — can be specified as a function of the manufacturer's price, the expected unit sales, and the characteristic markup.

Equation 10.11

EXGRPR(b, t)   EXpected GRoss PRofit on sales of b at time t. Dimension: dollars.

$$= \text{MANFPR(b)} * \text{MARKUP(d)} * \text{EXPUSL(t, b, d)}.$$

EXPUSL(t, b, d)   EXPected Unit SaLes of brand b through distributor d during period t. Dimension: producer units per time period.

= see Equations 10.5, 10.7, and 10.9.

[5] A. J. Alton, "The Influence of Manufacturer's Price Policies Upon Price Determination by Wholesalers," *Miami Business Review,* October 1957, pp. 1–4.

Because this simulation relates to a single product line, profit experience with other product lines must be specified exogenously as a distributor characteristic. The average gross profit realized across all product classes carried by the distributor (previously defined as a distributor characteristic) serves this reference function.

Equation 10.12

> AVGPR(d)   AVerage GRoss PRofit for all product classes. Dimension: dollars.
> = distributor characteristic. See Table 10.1.

The Decision to Offer to Carry

Two conditions comparable to those used to classify procedures for establishing expected unit sales may influence the decision to offer to carry.

The New Product Line Case

The distributor considering the addition of a brand as a means of adding a new product line $(B(d) = 0)$ is concerned with expected brand performance in contrast to the performance experienced in other lines within his store. For reasons comparable to those discussed in Chapter 9, the appropriate measure of brand performance at the distributor level

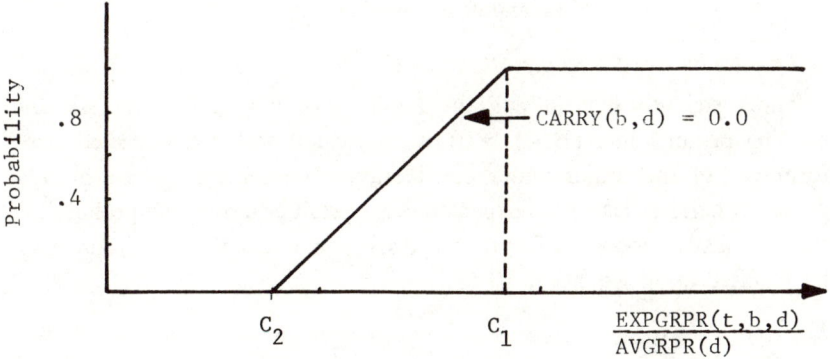

Figure 10.1. Effect of gross profit on probability of offer to carry.

appears to be the expected or realized gross profit associated with carrying a particular brand.[6] In the absence of experience with another

---

[6] The interaction between percentage and dollar margins as measures of profitability is discussed in "The Effect of Available Margin on Pricing," Chapter 9, pp. 265.

brand in the same product line, the distributor's reference is the average gross profit realized on other products carried. The impact of relative gross profit on the probability that the distributor will offer to carry a new brand in a new product line is comparable to that previously noted for the retailer.[7] This relationship based on the SRF2F logistic is summarized in Figure 10.1.

Equation 10.13

PROFTC(b, d)   PRobability that distributor d will OFfer To Carry brand b.

$$= [1 - \text{CARRY}(b, d)]$$

$$* \text{SRF2F}\left[\frac{\text{EXGRPR}(t, b, d)}{\text{AVGRPR}(d)}, 1.0, 0, C_1, C_2\right].$$

CARRY(b, d)   specification of brands CARRied by distributor d.
= see Equation 10.2.

EXGRPR(t, b, d)   EXpected GRoss PRofit to distributor d from sales of brand b at time t. Dimension: dollars.
= see Equation 10.11.

AVGRPR(d)   AVerage GRoss PRofit of distributor d. Dimension: dollars.
= distributor characteristic, see Table 10.1.

C_1 and C_2 constant specifying distributor's disposition toward adding new brands, see Table 10.1.
= 1.8 and .8, as sample values.

The Established Product Line Case

The distributor considering the addition of a brand in an already existing product line $(B(d) > 0)$ is concerned with the expected performance of the brand under consideration referenced against brands presently carried. Using the expected gross profit criterion, the probability that the distributor will offer to carry a brand under this condition may be restated as in Equation 10.13.

Equation 10.13A

PRDOTC(b, d)   PRobability that Distributor d will Offer To Carry brand b.

$$= [1 - \text{CARRY}(b, d)]$$

$$* \text{SRF2F}\left[\frac{\text{EXGRPR}(t, b, d)}{\text{AVGPBC}}, 1.0, 0, C_3, C_4\right].$$

[7] The impact of gross margin on the retailer's probability of adding a brand is summarized in Equation 9.11.

CARRY(b, d)   specification of brands CARRied by distributor d.
                   = see Equation 10.2.

C_3 and C_4 disposition toward changing brands carried, see Table
                   10.1.
                   = 1.5 and .9 as sample values.

EXGRPR(t, b, d)   EXpected GRoss PRofit of distributor d from sales
                   of brand b at time t. Dimension: dollars.
                   = see Equation 10.11.

AVGPBC(d)   AVerage Gross Profit on Brands Carried. Dimension:
                   dollars.

$$= \frac{\sum_{b=1}^{\text{BTOT}} \text{CARRY}(b, d) * \text{EXGRPR}(t, b, d)}{B(d)}.$$

BTOT   TOTal Brands produced.
                   = system parameter.

B(d)   number of Brands carried in product line.
                   = see Equation 10.2.

Implications of Exclusive Distribution Agreements

In developing the retail model it was assumed that shipments would be received in response to orders subject only to limitations imposed by available inventory at the manufacturer or distributor level and time delays inherent in the channels of distribution. This formulation ignored the effect of franchised retailer contracts and other forms of exclusive distribution agreements.

In developing the distributor model it is important that the potential for exclusive distribution be noted. The distributor relationship desired by a firm is specified as an output from the manufacturer sector. The variable EXCLSV indicates the manufacturer's willingness to distribute through a single franchised distributor in a particular region.

Equation 10.14

EXCLSV(b)   EXCLuSiVe distribution indicator for brand b.
             = 0, if brand b is not distributed under an exclusive arrangement.
             = 1, if brand b is distributed under an exclusive arrangement.
             = see Equation 7.3.

If an offer to carry made to a company specifying exclusive distribution is accepted, the distributor must drop all other brands after a specified period of time. Normally, the new brand may be added without delay. If the manufacturer to whom an offer is made does not specify an exclusive relationship, the distributor may continue to carry other brands. Addition of the new brand does not modify his relationship with other brand manufacturers except insofar as experience with the new brand provides a new performance reference that was not previously available.

In situations where exclusive distribution agreements are adopted by all or a majority of leading brand manufacturers, the distributor cannot carry more than one brand, and the average profit calculated in Equation 10.13A is the average gross profit on competitive brands. Under this condition, $(B(b) = 1)$, the appropriate comparison is made between the single brand carried and the single brand proposed for addition.

If the distributor is faced with a market in which a limited number of brands distribute exclusively, between-brand comparisons involve the expected gross profit from all brands carried (b') and from a single exclusive brand (b) considered for addition.

Equation 10.13B

PRDOTC(b, d) PRobability that Distributor d will Offer To Carry brand b.

$$= [1 - \text{CARRY}(b, d)]$$

$$* \text{SFR2} \left[\frac{\text{EXGRPR}(t, b, d)}{\sum\limits_{b'=1}^{B(d)} \text{EXGRPR}(t, b', d)}, 1.0, 0, C_3, C_4 \right].$$

Given: $B(d) > 1$ and $\text{EXCLSV}(b) = 1.0$.
              = see Equation 10.13A for variable definitions.

The Decision to Drop a Brand

In examining distributor decisions to drop a brand from the line carried, two types of behavior are observed. The first is associated with addition of an exclusively distributed brand as just discussed. The distributor who elects to add a brand distributed under exclusive contract must have concluded that it is profitable to drop brands previously carried. Under the second condition, the distributor may drop a poorly performing brand without replacing it with a new item.

The distributor's decision to drop a brand because of poor performance is comparable in structure to the retailer decision summarized in Equation 9.9 of Chapter 9. If retailer and distributor use comparable criteria (dollar flow, gross margin, net margin, or percent return) when evaluating the relative merits of brands, their manifest behavior will not be noticeably different. In each instance, the decision maker has established performance limits within which he is willing to continue to carry the brand. If these limits are exceeded, the brand will be dropped.

Formulation of this decision based on the expected gross margin concept discussed is summarized below.

Equation 10.15

PRDRBR(b, d)   PRobability of distributor d DRopping BRand b.

$$= \text{CARRY}(b, d) * \text{SRF2}\left[\frac{\text{EXGRPR}(t, b, d)}{\text{AVGRPR}(d)}, .1, .9, 1.0, C_5\right].$$

= see Equation 10.13 for further variable definition.

C_5 constant indicating distributor disposition toward dropping brands (see discussion that follows).
= .4, as sample value.

Variables appearing in Equation 10.15 should be familiar as a result of preceding development. The constant C_5 indicates the distributor's willingness to "weed out" nonproductive brands. Some distributors are slow to change their product line composition even when substantial evidence of nonproductivity is present. Others constantly review the performance of each brand with an eye toward removal of brands that do not maintain activity above a minimal or average level.

The Order Decision

The objective that the distributor attempts to achieve through the order decision is analogous to previously discussed retailer goals. In both instances, the order decision is directed toward maintaining an inventory level considered appropriate by the ordering agent in light of expected sales.

Ordering procedures encountered by the author during the development of this model may be categorized in terms of two classes of behavior.

The first classification relates to distributors serviced by a local warehouse or factory sufficiently close so that time delays involved in order processing and shipment are small in comparison to the ordering decision period. The second classification encompasses order decisions made under circumstances in which delays are sufficiently large to require consideration of orders and shipments backlogged in transit between the distributor and manufacturer.

Ordering under the Fast-Service Condition

The conditions under which order and shipment backlogs can be ignored might be described as the "fast-service" case. Order handling by both food product and appliance retailers located in and around the Boston area was found to comply with this model.[8] The distributor maintains relatively small inventories while depending on the factory or regional warehouse to maintain back-up inventory or accepting the fact that out-of-stock situations will occur. The desired inventory is established as a multiple of the expected unit sales over the time period and the amount ordered is the discrepancy between desired and existing inventory. Back orders are accumulated, however, shipments to cover back orders are often received prior to the next ordering time. This relatively simple order procedure may be expressed as follows:

Equation 10.16

ORDERS(t, b)	ORDERS for brand b to manufacturer or central warehouse at time t. Dimension: product units per time period (implicit).
	$= \text{DESINV}(t, b) - \text{ACTINV}(t, b) + \text{BACORD}(t, b)$.
DESINV(t, b)	DESired INVentory of brand b at time t. Dimension: product units.
	$= C_9 * \text{EXPUSL}(t, b)$.
ACTINV(t, b)	ACTual INVentory of brand b at time t. Dimension: product units.
	$= \text{ACTINV}(t - 1, b) + \text{RECPTS}(t - 1, b) - \text{ORDFLD}(t - 1, b)$.
RECPTS(t, b)	RECeiPTS from manufacturer of brand b during time period t. Dimension: product units per time period (implicit).
	$= \text{SHTDST}(t - 1, b, d)$.
SHTDST(t, b, d)	SHipments of b To Distributor d by manufacturer. Dimension: product units per time period (implicit).
	$=$ output of manufacturer sector. See Equation 9.2.
ORDFLD(t, b)	ORDers for brand b FiLLeD at time t. Dimension: product units per time period (implicit).
	$= \text{ACTUSL}(t, b, d),$
	if $\text{ACTUSL}(t, b, d) \leq \text{ACTINV}(t, b, d).$

[8] Research on which this formulation is based was conducted under the sponsorship of the M.I.T. Sloan Research Fund. See A. E. Amstutz and B. C. Hood, "Interim Report on Marketing Systems Research," Cambridge, M.I.T., July 1960.

$= \text{ACTINV}(t, b, d),$

if $\text{ACTUSL}(t, b, d) > \text{ACTINV}(t, b, d).$

BACORD(t, b)   BACk ORDers for brand b at time t. Dimension: product units.

$= \text{BACORD}(t - 1, b) - \text{BACSHP}(t - 1, b),$

if $\text{ORDFLD}(t - 1, b) \geq \text{ACTUSL}(t - 1, b, d),$

$= \text{BACORD}(t - 1, b) + \text{ACTUSL}(t - 1, b, d)$

$- \text{ORDFLD}(t - 1, b, d),$

if $\text{ORDFLD}(t - 1, b) < \text{ACTUSL}(t - 1, b, d).$

BACSHP(t, b)   BACk SHiPments of brand b at time t. Dimension: product units per time period (implicit).

$= \text{ACTINV}(t, b) - \text{ACTUSL}(t, b, d),$

if $\text{ACTINV}(t, b) - \text{ACTUSL}(t, b, d)$

$< \text{BACORD}(t, b),$

$= \text{BACORD}(t, b),$

if $\text{ACTINV}(t, b) - \text{ACTUSL}(t, b, d)$

$\geq \text{BACORD}(t, b).$

$= 0.0,$ if $\text{ACTINV}(t, b) < \text{ACTUSL}(t, b, d).$

C_9 constant determining desired inventory level. Distribution characteristic, see Table 10.1. Dimension: time units.

$= 2.0,$ as sample value.

In developing these equations, a one-day order period and time step were assumed (a time step multiplier of 1.0 is thus implicit in all rate to backlog conversions). Under this assumption, the weighting constant C_9 is expressed in days of desired inventory, the time reference t refers to a particular day, and the reference $t - 1$ refers to the preceding business day. For time steps of other than one day, it would be necessary to change these equations to take explicit account of the time step multiplier.

Ordering under the Slow-Service Condition

In the slow-service situation, the distributor takes account of noted delays in the system by ordering in advance. Because his procedure normally involves ordering at fixed intervals, his view of the distribution process is discrete rather than continuous. He recognizes that decisions made today determine the quantity of goods received at some time in the future — the existence of delays in the system necessitates forecasting of expected unit sales over a period of time.[9] Inaccurate

[9] Forrester has given substantial consideration to the effect of pipeline and clerical processing delays in the generation of inventory cycles under various order

forecasts are viewed as producing lost sales or excess inventory. Back orders are explicitly recognized, with the distributor distinguishing between back orders covered by orders to the manufacturer and those requiring action.

If existing inventory levels are greater than desired, the distributor will reduce his orders, taking into account the excess of inventory that may be carried forward into future time periods. He will not normally take explicit account of early inventory depletion in establishing estimates for the next period. His estimated inventory requirements are based on expected unit sales. In his mind, the impact of existing inventory drain is accounted for by sales estimation procedures.

This process may be summarized as follows:

Equation 10.17

> ORDERS(t, b)   ORDERS for brand b to manufacturer or warehouse at time t.
> $$= \text{DESINV}(t, b) - \text{CARFWD}(t, b).$$
>
> CARFWD(t, b)   CARry ForWarD of brand b at time t. Dimension: product units per time period.
> $$= \text{DESINV}(t - 1, b) - \text{ACTINV}(t - 1, b),$$
> if $\text{DESINV}(t - 1, b) > \text{ACTINV}(t - 1, b)$,
> $$= 0.0, \text{ if } \text{DESINV}(t - 1, b) \leq \text{ACTINV}(t - 1, b).$$
>
> DESINV(t, b)   DESired INVentory of brand b. Dimension: product units.
> $$= C_9 * \text{EXPUSL}(t + \text{DELAY}, b).$$

This carry-forward takes account of any excess of actual over desired inventory at decision time.

Back order considerations are totally ignored in this formulation because under the pure slow-service case the distributor is *unable* to obtain shipment of goods without substantial delays. In this situation he does not back order — he does not promise delivery and then place an order to obtain the materials to make his promise. Excess of demand over supply is, of course, reflected in the estimate of demand for future periods embodied in the expected unit sales formulation.

The Conglomerate Case

In the pure fast-service case, the distributor simply ignores the all but irrelevant delays in the distribution system. In the pure slow-

---

procedures. See, for example, J. W. Forrester, "Industrial Dynamics: A Major Breakthrough for Decision Makers," *Harvard Business Review*, Vol. 36 (July–August 1958), pp. 37–66.

service case, he accepts substantial delays as a fact of business life and addresses himself to the problem of estimating sales at some point in the future and living with the results of his estimate. In certain product situations (for example, automobiles) the distributor may exhibit characteristics of both the slow- and fast-service condition. Through sharing and pooling arrangements with distributors in adjacent regions he is able to modify the pure slow-service procedure when excess inventory of a desired model exists in another region. In many instances, however, an item in great demand in one region will be in short supply in all regions so that the over-all impact of this type of activity is of marginal importance.

Special Purchase Opportunities

The distributor, like the retailer, may take advantage of special purchase opportunities as they arise. The distributor's behavior and response to an opportunity to obtain goods at a price or other market advantage may be represented through modification of the desired inventory formulations in Equations 10.16 and 10.17 to reflect the probability of the distributor taking advantage of a particular purchase opportunity. As an example, distributor response to an expected price change may be summarized in a manner analogous to that discussed earlier for the retailer.[10]

Equation 10.18

DESINV(t, b)	DESired INVentory of brand b at time t.
	$= C_9 * \text{EXPUSL}(t, b) * (1 + \text{SPPUOP}(b, d))$.
SPPUOP(b, d)	SPecial PUrchase OPportunity.
	$= C_{10} * \dfrac{\text{EXMFPR}(b) - \text{MANFPR}(b, t)}{\text{MANFPR}(b, t)}$.
EXMFPR(b)	EXpected ManuFacturer PRice for brand b. Dimension: dollars per product unit.
	$= \text{MANFPR}(b, t)$, if $\text{FUDPSP}(b) = 0$.
	$= \text{FUDPSP}(b)$, if $\text{FUDPSP}(b) > 0$.
FUDPSP(b)	FUture Distributors Price SPecification for brand b. Dimension: dollars per product unit.
	= input from manufacturer sector. See Equation 7.12.
MANFPR(b, t)	MANuFacturer's PRice for brand b at time t. Dimension: dollars per product unit.
	= input from manufacturer sector. See Equation 7.12.

[10] The retailer's response to special purchase opportunity is included in Equation 9.13.

C_9 constant determining desired inventory as number of
                           days expected sales. Dimension: time units. Distributor
                           characteristics, see Table 10.1.
                           = 3.0, as sample value.

C_{10} constant determining distributor's disposition toward
                           price speculation. Distributor characteristic, see Table
                           10.1.
                           = 5.0, as sample value.

Shipments to Retailers

For purposes of this model the scheduling of shipments to individual
retailers and allocation of existing goods in the event of shortages will
be ignored. Formulation of detailed product handling functions would
not contribute to the conceptual development of this chapter. Need-
less to say, appropriate formulation can easily be developed given the
allocation or scheduling algorithm to be employed.

In the interest of completeness, it should be noted that shipments
to retailers must be scheduled. At an aggregate level total shipments
will be a function of orders previously received. Assuming FIFO
processing of orders and appropriate bookkeeping to identify individual orders, the shipment variable can be specified in terms of the orders
filled expression developed in Equation 10.16.

Equation 10.19

SHTRET(t, b)   SHipments To RETailers of brand b at time t. Dimen-
                    sion: product units per time period.
                    = ORDFLD(t − WRHSDL, b).

ORDFLD(t, b)   ORDers for brand b FiLleD at time t.
                    = see Equation 10.16.

WRHSDL   WaReHouSe DeLay.
                    = system parameter. Dimension: units of time.

The Salesmen Allocation Decision

Representation of the distributor's relationship with salesmen requires preliminary definition of two characteristics that influence the
outcome of distributor-salesman interactions. These are the salesman's
productivity and his willingness to change employers. Other differentiating salesman attributes are defined in Chapter 11.

The salesman's historical generation of orders over time provides a
common measure of productivity. For purposes of this model the aver-

age monthly sales produced over a one-year period will be used as a representative performance index.

Equation 10.20

> AVGSAL(s)   the AVeraGe monthly SALes generated by salesman s during the preceding year. Dimension: dollars per month.
> = Salesman descriptor statistic maintained by the salesman model, see Chapter 11.

In the salesman model, orientation toward present employer is developed as a function of experience and conditions of employment. A salesman's interest in alternative employment is communicated through a binary availability variable.

Equation 10.21

> AVAILA(s)   AVAILAbility indicator for salesman s.
> = 1, salesman is considering alternative employment,
> = 0, salesman is fully committed to present employer.

Value of a Retail Outlet

Discussions of call scheduling procedures with distributors suggest that two factors may be controlling in the distributor's conception of salesman call allocation among retail outlets.

First, the distributor is concerned with compatibility between the line carried by a retailer and the line which he offers. There is no point in a salesman spending time with a retailer carrying only a limited number of products offered by the distributor if he has the alternative of spending that time with a retailer who might potentially buy a large number of the products in the distributor's line.

The second factor noted by distributors is retailer size. Obviously there is an advantage to be gained from allocating maximum time to retailers generating substantial sales volume in appropriate product lines.

In developing call schedules the distributor must evaluate the relative worth of each retail outlet that might potentially be visited by a salesman in his employ. The same outlet may be of very different value to distributors carrying different product lines. The retailer's product mix was specified as a defining characteristic of retailer population members by the model structure developed in Chapter 9.[11] In a similar manner the distributor's product mix is defined in Table 10.1.

---

[11] See Table 9.1, for a summary of retailer attributes.

The distributor is also concerned with the relative profitability of products within his lines. Given the choice, he would prefer to sell his highest profit item. The average gross profit realized on a sale in product line n will be used as a measure of product line profitability.

Given these descriptors the value of retail outlet r to distributor d may be expressed as follows:

Equation 10.22

VALROL(r, d)   VALue of Retail OutLet r to distributor d. (Relative Index). Dimension: dollars.

$$= \sum_{n=1}^{7} \text{PROMIX}(n, r) * \text{PRDMIX}(n, d) * \text{AVPLGP}(n, d)$$

$* \text{AVSWVL}.$

PROMIX(n, r)   importance of PROduct line n in MIX of retail outlet r.
= prominence scale value — retail descriptor. See Table 9.1.

PRDMIX(n, d)   importance of PRoDuct line n in MIX of distributor d.
= prominence scale value — distributor characteristic, see Table 10.1.

AVSWVL(r)   AVerage Store Wide VoLume through retail outlet r. Dimension: units.
= retailer characteristic, see Table 9.1.

AVPLGP(n, d)   AVerage Product Line Gross Profit on unit in product line n sold by distributor d. Dimension: dollars.
= distributor descriptor, see Table 10.1.

Developing a Call Schedule

Given an evaluation of the relative worth of each retailer as specified in Equation 10.22, the distributor may order all retailers according to their potential value to the firm. Differential call costs may be introduced to establish net values. The retailers are then allocated to salesmen with higher priority retailers usually allocated to more productive salesmen.

Allocation based on this procedure involves ranking the salesmen by historical performance (AVGSAL(s)) and then giving the highest priority retailers to the first salesman subject to limitations imposed by the number of calls that the salesman can make during a specified call period, NCALPP(s). Although distributors seem to prefer this type of allocation, operating under the assumption that higher profits are most easily attained by "using your best bait where the most fish are biting," practical implementation is obviously limited by economies realized from regional allocation when the geographic area to be covered is large.[12]

The procedure outlined in this section is indicative of thinking underlying distributor use of salesmen. It represents the distributor's best intentions. Implementation is, as already noted, limited by "practical" problems. In addition to difficulties of scheduling, geographic coverage, and salesman turnover, the distributor does not normally establish an explicit rating. Priority setting tends to be less systematic, more ad hoc.

Variables associated with the scheduling process are summarized in Equation 10.23.

Equation 10.23

VALROL(r, d) VALue of Retail OutLet r to distributor d. Dimension: dollars.
= see Equation 10.22.

NSALFC(d) Number of men on SALes ForCe for distributor d. Dimension: calls.
= count based on hiring and drops by distributor d as outlined in following sections.

NCPSPP(d) Number of Calls Per Salesman Per Period.
= distributor descriptor, see Table 10.1.

NCALPD(d) Normal CALl PerioD for salesmen employed by distributor d. Dimension: units of time.
= distributor descriptor, see Table 10.1.

SMCSCH(r, d) SalesMan Call SCHedule for retailer r established for salesman of distributor d.
= 1.0, if call scheduled,
= 0.0, if no call scheduled.

Sales Force Maintenance Decision

For purposes of his model distributor sales force maintenance can be summarized in two basic decisions: (1) the decision to hire a new salesman to fill a vacancy, and (2) the decision to remove a nonproductive salesman.

[12] An applicable case study in the allocation of salesman through the use of an operations research analysis is presented by A. A. Brown, F. T. Hulswit, and John D. Kettelle, "A Study of Sales Operations," *Operations Research,* Vol. 4 (June 1956), pp. 296–308.

Hiring Salesmen to Fill Vacancies

This simulation abstracts from the complex interactions between employer and potential employee by assuming that the distributor has access to information regarding salesman availability. As noted earlier, salesman disposition toward changing jobs is revealed by an indicator (AVAILA(s)) that is equal to 1 if the salesman is disposed to consider offers from a distributor.

Distributors appear to be most concerned with the past productivity of a salesman, and attempt to evaluate on this basis. In the model, available salesmen are ranked by the distributor in terms of past productivity as revealed in average sales generated over a specified time period (2 years in the case of the Chapter 11 salesman model). The distributor then makes offers to the salesmen in order of productivity. The distributor's offer consists of a salary and commission that are evaluated by the salesman using criteria discussed in Chapter 11. If a salesman accepts the distributor's offer, he is hired and added to the sales force.

The distributor will normally consider all available applicants at the initial salary and commission rate before taking the more drastic step of raising either salary or commissions. This behavior appears to result from the usual requirement that salary and commission scales be applied across all sales employees. Bringing on a new man at a higher rate thus affects the rate structure (or morale) of the entire sales force.[13]

The compensation schedule established by the distributor is maintained as a descriptive characteristic applicable to all salesmen in his employ.

Equation 10.24

SALARY(d)   SALARY paid sales force members. Dimension: dollars per time period.
= distributor characteristic, see Table 10.1.

COMMIS(d)   COMMISsions paid sales force members. Dimension: pure number (percent).
= distributor characteristic, see Table 10.1.

The number of salesmen considered appropriate for handling a given market varies markedly from distributor to distributor. Three com-

---

[13] A thorough discussion of the compensation problem is provided by H. Tosdal, "How to Design a Salesman's Compensation Plan," *Harvard Business Review,* Vol. 31 (September–October 1953), pp. 61–70.

peting electronic distributors in the New York area were, for example, equally confident that two, seven, and eighteen salesmen were appropriate for serving what was essentially the same geographic and product market. The maximum number of salesmen desired by a particular distributor is therefore viewed as a distributor characteristic and included in Table 10.1.

Equation 10.25

 MXSDES(d) MaXimum number of Salesmen DESired by distributor d.
     = distributor characteristic, see Table 10.1.

If the desired number of salesmen cannot be obtained at the salary and commission rate originally offered, one or both of these will be increased. Most distributors with whom this condition was discussed seemed more willing to adjust salary offers than to change the commission structure.

Removal of Nonproductive Salesmen

The distributor's evaluation of salesman performance focuses on sales generation. However, as might be expected, the length of association between salesman and distributor affects the stability of the relationship. Although these factors will be treated as independent, there is some evidence that because the salesman with a longer association is more familiar with the business and has had more opportunity to develop profitable accounts, there may be substantial interdependence.

The ratio of the individual salesman's average sales generation to that

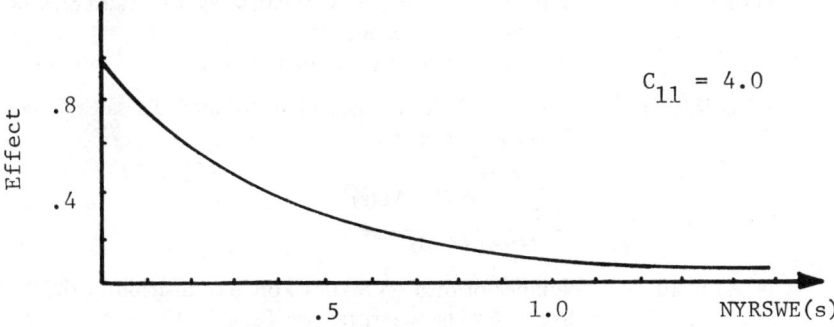

Figure 10.2. Effect of years with employer on probability of drop.

of the sales force as a whole is representative of distributor measures of relative performance. The number of years the salesman has been with his present employer provides a simple measure of extent of association.

The effect of these factors may be summarized in terms of the probability that the distributor will drop salesman *s* as illustrated in Figures 10.2 and 10.3.

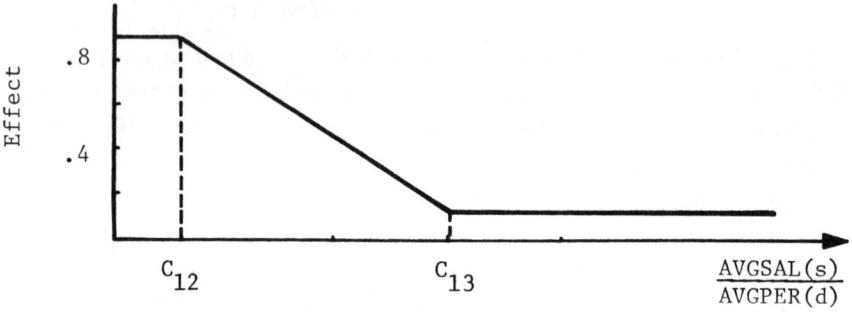

Figure 10.3. Effect of relative performance on probability of drop.

Equation 10.26

PRDRSM(s, d)   PRobability that distributor d will DRop SalesMan s.

$$= \text{ENXPF} \left(-\frac{\text{NYRSWE(d, s)}}{C_{11}} \right)$$

$$* \text{SRF2} \left(\frac{\text{AVGSAL(s)}}{\text{AVGPER(d)}}, .9, .1, C_{12}, C_{13} \right).$$

NYRSWE(s)   Number of YeaRs that salesman s has been With present Employer. Dimension: time units.
                 = count maintained by salesman model.

AVGPER(d)   AVeraGe PERformance of distributor d's sales force. Dimension: dollars.

$$= \frac{\sum_{s=1}^{\text{NSALFC(d)}} \text{AVGSAL(s)}}{\text{NSALFC(d)}}.$$

NSALFC(d)   Number of men on SALes ForCe of distributor d.
                 = distributor characteristic, see Table 10.1.

C_{11} constant determining impact of time with employer on probability of being dropped.
                 = 4.0, as sample value.

C₁₂ scaling constant determining performance ratio value
for which maximum probability is achieved.
= .3, as sample value.

C₁₃ scaling constant determining performance ratio value
for which minimum probability is achieved.
= 1.5, as sample value.

AVGSAL(s) AVeraGe month SALes generated by salesman s.
= see Equation 10.20.

Distributor Exposure and Response to Business Communication

Distributor exposure and response to communication is not explicitly simulated within this model. As noted earlier, trade media advertising of the type considered in the retailer sector did not appear relevant to distributors studied while formulating this model. Despite lack of specific promotion inputs, the distributor possesses information regarding brand shares, competitive sales conditions, prevailing prices, and salesman performance. Most of this information is obtained either from manufacturers and their salesmen or from other distributors. Information assimilated by the distributor is equivalent to that achieved through a high level of media communication assimilation. In this circumstance, media promotion is redundant. It has no impact because it provides no new information content.

In the consumer and retailer case, automatic assimilation of promotional communication content could not be assumed. It was therefore necessary to describe the process of perception through which selected content is assimilated. The distributor, on the other hand, has a need for business data. There is no question of its relevance to him. Available data are assimilated.

These conclusions regarding media and promotions are most applicable to major metropolitan areas in which distributors are in relatively close contact with manufacturers' salesmen and each other. Conditions in geographically isolated locations can be quite different. In the absence of close personal contacts, promotion to the trade assumes increased importance.

Summary

This chapter has focused on the role of the distributor. Similarities and contrasts between the distributor and retailer have been noted, and characteristic attributes differentiating members of the distributor population have been defined.

Representation of distributor behavior started with the processes through which existing market conditions are evaluated and future expectations formed. This was followed by the development of decision functions representing behavior associated with pricing, product line composition, and order generation.

Distributor decisions relating to the maintenance and allocation of a sales force were discussed and procedures for establishing call schedules noted. Factors that influence the hiring and firing of salesmen were reviewed in the context of probabilities of adding or dropping salesmen who exhibit specified characteristics.

The chapter concluded with a brief discussion of information assimilation by the distributor.

Chapter 11

A MODEL OF SALESMAN BEHAVIOR

This chapter is concerned with characteristics, actions, and responses of salesmen employed by manufacturers or distributors. Specifications developed in Chapter 3 provide the framework for a simulation of behavior consistent with model structures developed in preceding chapters. The orientation continues to be descriptive rather than normative, with the model providing a quantitative statement of relationships affecting salesman action and response.

Description of a Salesman

The salesman is an intermediary through whom information and orders are transferred from one sector of the marketing system to another. It is, however, inaccurate to think of the salesman as a passive communication channel. As a human actor on the market stage, the salesman is differentiated from passive communication channels by the distinctive attributes of an active element.

Within this system structure, the salesman may serve as an intermediary between the manufacturer and distributor, the manufacturer and retailer, or the distributor and retailer. He will not, by definition, serve as intermediary between retailer and consumer because the functions of retail salesmen are subsumed in the retailer model.

Because descriptions of the manufacturer, retailer, and distributor have now been completed, the role of the salesman may be described in terms of interactions with each of these active elements.

Salesman-Manufacturer Interactions

This system's focus on the consumer market precludes representation of an industrial salesman calling on a manufacturer. The relationship between salesman and manufacturer is therefore limited to that of employer-employee. In this context, three classes of interactions are relevant. The first relates to compensation, the second involves bilateral communication between manufacturer and salesman, and the third concerns the flow of orders generated by the salesman and transmitted to the manufacturer.

Compensation-Related Interactions

The manufacturer's salary and commission schedule may affect the salesman in two ways. First, it may influence his willingness to change employers — the salesman who considers his pay scale satisfactory is less willing to switch jobs than one who is dissatisfied with his compensation. Second, it may influence his willingness to devote extra effort to his job — his motivation.

While salesman morale appears to be related in part to compensation, it is difficult to define the effect precisely. Salesmen with opportunity for substantial economic gains are highly motivated. However, there is evidence that the marginal value of additional compensation may decrease to the point where the salesman prefers to coast along on compensation generated earlier in the year rather than exert additional effort to obtain returns of questionable marginal value.[1]

Communication-Related Interactions

Three types of salesman-manufacturer communication are relevant in context of this system. The first class relates to the transfer of information regarding brand-model characteristics and/or appeals from manufacturer to salesman. It is through this mechanism that the salesman's promotional message content is established.

A second class of communication relates to the salesman's transfer of information from the retailer and distributor to the manufacturer. This type of information flow will be considered part of the research

[1] This problem is discussed in H. Tosdal, "How to Design the Salesman's Compensation Plan," *Harvard Business Review,* Vol. 31 (September–October 1953), pp. 61–70.

function and separated from the normal operating activities of the manufacturer.[2]

A third class of communication relating to the manufacturer's desired sales force allocation is the suggested call schedule. This communication may affect morale if the salesman's desired allocation of effort and that suggested by the manufacturer are in conflict.

Order Flow Interactions

The manufacturer's final assessment of salesman performance is based on orders generated by the salesman or attributed to his efforts on a regional or store basis. Although the salesman may at times modify the order flow (moving orders from one point in time to another or generating large unit orders with unspecified delivery dates), interactions relating to this flow may be viewed primarily in terms of manufacturer monitoring of sales performance. Commission-based compensation plans involve order flows because commissions payable are determined by the magnitude of order flow (or shipments based on earlier orders).

Salesman-Distributor Interactions

If the salesman interacting with the distributor is an employee, previous comments regarding the salesman-manufacturer interaction are applicable. Interactions between the salesman employed by a manufacturer and a distributor customer involve a different set of relationships.

The Distributor as Employer

The salesman employed by the distributor engages in the three types of activity just discussed. His actions may be complicated by the existence of a broader range of products and/or brand-models than are normally present in the manufacturer case; however, the same interactions occur, and, for purposes of this model, comparable employer-employee considerations will be assumed.

Communication and compensation-related interactions at the distributor level may be complicated by inputs from the manufacturer level. The manufacturer may establish incentive compensation schemes directly affecting the distributor salesman and generate communication

[2] The research function is discussed in Chapter 12.

regarding special purchase incentives as well as product and promotional data for use by the salesman.

The Distributor as Customer

Within the structure of the Chapter 10 Distributor Simulation, the salesman has no influence on the distributor sector. Communication response models of the type employed in the retailer model are required to simulate the salesman's influence on distributor order timing and expectation formation.[3]

Salesman-Retailer Interactions

Two types of retailer-salesman interaction are noted. The first is associated with missionary selling activities and the second with the regular order-taking call.

The Missionary Salesman

Interactions between retailer and missionary salesmen serve one function. The salesman provides the retailer with information regarding characteristics or appeals associated with a particular brand-model. He may also present his view of competitive conditions in the retailer's market and comparative brand performance data from other markets.

The Order Taker

The order-taking salesman's major role is to restock or remind the retailer to reorder. Although he may provide limited communication of brand characteristics and appeals, this function is normally secondary to stock maintenance.

The Manufacturer-Supported Retail Salesman

In some retail outlets (particularly the large appliance discount house) one finds salesmen on the payroll of manufacturers selling a particular brand of product (e.g., Hoover Vacuum Cleaners) to the retailer's customers. The abstraction made in developing the Chapter 9 retailer model precludes explicit representation of this type of salesman activity. Representation of the retailer as a single individual precludes identification of independent salesmen in a retail outlet. The model structure could be expanded to permit inclusion of this class of behav-

---

[3] See "Distributor Exposure and Response to Business Communication," Chapter 10, p. 331.

ior; however, the advantages to be gained from such modification are not obvious.

Specification of Salesman Characteristics

Following the procedure established in earlier chapters, demographic, behavioral, economic, and psychological characteristics by which salesman cells will be differentiated within the model structure must be defined. Each class of attribute will be considered separately.

Demographic Attributes

Two salesman characteristics, his geographic location and present employer, can be reasonably classified as demographic. These variables locate the salesman in a particular geographic area and associate him with a specific distributor or manufacturer. Geographic location is identified implicitly within the system structure, while the variable EMPLOY(s) identifies the salesman's present employer.

Behavioral Attributes

Three characteristics of the salesman's behavior are important determinants of action within this model:

1. The salesman's productivity, manifest in the average rate of sales generated over a predetermined time period.
2. The extent of his association with his present employer as reflected in the number of years he has been in that employ.
3. His present customer set, established by a matrix indicating the customers on whom he is scheduled to call.

These attributes are referenced by the variables NYRSWE(s), AVGSAL(s), and SMCSCH(s), respectively.

Economic Attributes

The salesman's economic characteristics relate to his compensation schedule. The salesman's most recent level of compensation is indicated by the variables SALARY(s) and COMMIS(s) representing his salary and commission rate, respectively.

If the salesman is employed by a manufacturer or distributor handling several brands or products, a separate commission rate is specified for each brand-model within the product line.

Psychological Attributes

This model encompasses two psychological characteristics. The first relates to the salesman's disposition toward his present and alternative employers. The second factor might be described as a personality component of selling effort or "level of involvement in the selling role."

The salesman's disposition toward new employment opportunities will be indicated by the availability variable AVAILA(s). His relative level of involvement or willingness to expend energy in the selling role will be specified by the variable EFFORT(s). This performance variable represents a crude attempt to take account of the observed fact that some salesmen are dynamic in their approach to selling while others are indifferent and blasé. For purposes of model development, historical performance and selling effort will be used to represent more complex personality characteristics related to the salesman's effectiveness in the selling role.

In discussing the "mystique" of supersalesmanship, R. M. McMurry suggests that

> . . . the possessor of an *effective* sales personality is a *habitual "wooer,"* *an individual who has a compulsive need to win and hold the affection of* *others.* Along with the winning instinct, several less glamorous, more pedestrian qualifications are important: (1) *a high level of energy . . .* (2) *abounding self-confidence . . .* (3) *a chronic hunger for money . . .* (4) *a well-established habit of industry . . .* [and] (5) *a state of mind which* *regards each objection, resistance, or obstacle as a challenge.*[4]

Sociopsychological characteristics of salesmen have been summarized in terms of the correlation between several attributes and "salesman performance." [5]

There is no significant relationship between intelligent test scores . . . Independent measures of personality traits . . . Age . . . Measurable character traits . . . Level of education . . . (or) . . . level of sales activity and sales success among individual salesmen.
Salesmen differ from nonsalesmen in four important ways:
A. Salesmen are persuasive rather than critical.

[4] R. N. McMurry, "The Mystique of Super Salesmanship," *Harvard Business Review,* Vol. 39 (March–April 1961), pp. 117–118.
[5] S. N. Stevens, "The Application of Social Science Findings to Selling and the Salesman," in *Aspects of Modern Marketing,* AMA Management Report No. 15 (New York: American Management Association, Inc., 1958), pp. 87–89.

B. Salesmen are intuitive rather than analytical.
C. Salesmen have higher average energy level (expressed in activity).
D. Salesmen are more strongly motivated by the desire for prestige, power, and material gains than by a service ideal or the need for security.

While failing to define either factor in measurable terms, Mayer and Greenberg maintain that

. . . a good salesman must have at least two basic qualities: empathy and ego drive. *Empathy,* the important central ability to *feel* as the other fellow does in order to be able to sell him a product or service, must be possessed in large measure. Having empathy does not necessarily mean being sympathetic. One can know what the other fellow feels without agreeing with that feeling. But a salesman simply cannot sell well without the invaluable and irreplaceable ability to get a powerful feedback from his client through empathy.

The second of the basic qualities absolutely needed by a good salesman is a particular kind of *ego drive* which makes him want and need to make the sale in a personal or ego way, not merely for the money to be gained. His feeling must be that he *has* to make the sale; the customer is there to help him fulfill his personal need. In effect, to the top salesman, the sale — the conquest — provides a powerful means of enhancing his ego. His self-picture improves dramatically by virtue of conquest, and diminishes with failure.[6]

The salesman's relative level of involvement or willingness to expend energy may be considered representative of the ego drive concept introduced by Mayer and Greenberg. The second dimension of their personality description is not explicitly represented.

Past performance is adopted as an indication of potential future success in the sales role to compensate for the lack of effective means of quantifying personality characteristics. This emphasis on past performance as a basis for evaluation is consistent with much of current practice. However, the need for a relevant personality classification structure is clearly indicated in the present context where a basis for quantitative assessment of salesman potential would be of great value.

Summary of Attributes

Salesman characteristics and related reference variables are summarized in Table 11.1.

[6] D. Mayer and H. Greenberg, "What Makes a Good Salesman," *Harvard Business Review,* Vol. 42 (July–August 1964), pp. 119–125.

TABLE 11.1.   Variable Definitions and Storage Allocation

Characteristics	Variable	Gradations	Bits Required
Geographic Location	—	—	—
Present Employer (d or b)	EMPLOY	1	20
Number of Years with Employer	NYRSWE	10	4
Salesman Call Schedule	SMCSCH	1	24
Availability for Employment	AVAILA	1	1
Average One-Year Sales Rate	AVGSAL	250	8
Relative Involvement	EFFORT	10	4
Salesman Salary	SALARY	10	4
Salesman Commission Rate	COMMIS	10	4

Representation of Salesman Behavior

The attributes noted in the preceding section will be used to distinguish between simulated salesmen. Relevant behavior must therefore be described in terms of these attributes and inputs received from other sectors.

Salesman Actions

Models representing salesman actions must encompass processes through which the salesman generates communication, tenders a resignation or accepts an employment offer, and devotes effort to selling activity. While these actions are all observable, direct measurement of selling activity is difficult. The level of selling effort must be inferred from the salesman-customer interaction time devoted to various brands. Behavior may nevertheless be validated by direct observation.

Salesman Responses

Four response mechanisms must be described by a model of salesman behavior. These relate to salesman response to (1) promotional communication, (2) observed brand-model product characteristics, (3) his present job, and (4) offers received from potential employers.

Representation of response to promotion and brand characteristics may range from assumptions of full knowledge as used in the distributor model to detailed response formulations of the type developed for the consumer in Chapter 8. The salesman's response to his present job and alternative employment opportunities is similar in some respects to the retailer's business climate evaluation or the distributor's decision to add or delete brand or product lines. In both instances, the decision maker is influenced by economic considerations, habit, attitudes, and beliefs as he attempts to arrive at a "rational" decision in the presence of uncertainty.

Model Formulation

Formulation of the salesman simulation will be divided into five major sections devoted to the representation of selling effort, sales generation, communication, the decision to seek employment, and the decision to accept employment.

Salesman Selling Effort

In considering factors affecting the salesman's willingness to devote effort to a particular brand, it is useful to differentiate between the salesman employed by the distributor and the manufacturer's employee.

The Distributor Salesman

The salesman employed by a distributor may be expected to allocate his energies among various brands on the basis of potential return. He will devote more effort to a brand paying high commission than to one for which he receives low payment. Manufacturers employing sales forces to distribute their own and other companies' products take explicit account of this behavioral expectation by paying higher commissions on products of their own manufacture.[7]

Personality differences between salesmen result in differential selling effort generation in comparable situations. Some salesmen simply work harder — they put more effort into selling than others. Within this system, individual differences will be expressed solely in terms of relative involvement (ego drive), EFFORT(s) as defined in Table 11.1.

Notwithstanding individual differences, salesmen seem willing to work harder when they feel they are getting "a good deal" as opposed to an average or below-average level of compensation. The salesman's motivation to devote effort on behalf of a particular brand is therefore formulated as a function of commissions received on sales of that brand.

[7] As an example, a leading manufacturer and distributor of laboratory equipment pays a commission of 6% on items of their own manufacture and a commission of 2% on products manufactured by other companies but carried by their sales force.

The effectiveness of commissions received as a result of direct sales-man compensation plans originated by a manufacturer is determined by the availability of comparable compensation from manufacturers of other brands.

The motivating effect of commissions paid by distributors is deter-mined by the level of commission paid relative to the prevailing com-mission structure in the industry.

In the absence of special incentives, salesmen emphasize faster-mov-ing brands within the line. Salesmen also tend to push products that are moving well. It seems easier for them to talk about a product that is already generating substantial sales — "to move with the trend" — than to discuss a relatively unestablished brand.

These relationships may be summarized in equation form:

Equation 11.1

SALSLE(b, s, d)   SALesman SeLling Effort in support of brand b by salesman employed by distributor d. Dimension: pure number units (proportion of time).

$$= \text{EFFORT(s)} * \left[\frac{\text{DSMCOM(b, d)}}{\text{AVMNCM(d)}} \right.$$

$$\left. + \frac{\text{ACTUSL(t} - 1, \text{b, d)}}{\text{AVBRSL(t} - 1, \text{d)}} * \frac{\text{COMMIS(s)}}{\text{INAVCM}} \right].$$

≤ 1.0, by constraint.

EFFORT(s)   Extent of involvement (ego drive) — measure of rela-tive EFFORT expended by salesman s. Dimension: pure number units (proportion of time).
= salesman descriptor (range 0 to 1.0), see Table 11.1.

DSMCOM(b, d)   Direct SalesMan COMpensation provided distributor d by manufacturer of brand b. Dimension: dollars per product unit.
= input from manufacturer model, see Equation 8.4.

AVMNCM(d)   AVerage MaNufacturer CoMpensation available to salesmen employed by distributor d. Dimension: dol-lars per product unit.

$$= \frac{\sum_{b=1}^{B(d)} \text{DSMCOM(b, d)}}{B(d)}.$$

B(d)   total Brands carried by distributor d.
= function of distributor model (integer), see Equation 10.2.

ACTUSL(t, b, d)   ACTual Unit SaLes of brand b through distributor d at time t. Dimension: product units per time period.
= function of distributor model, see Equation 10.1.

AVBRSL(t, d)   AVerage BRand SaLes through distributor d at time t. Dimension: product units per time period.

$$= \frac{\sum_{b=1}^{B(d)} ACTUSL(t, b, d)}{B(d)}.$$

COMMIS(s)   COMMISsion rate earned by salesman s. Dimension: dollars per product unit.
= COMMIS(d).

COMMIS(d)   COMMISsion paid by distributor d. Dimension: dollar units per product unit.
= function of distributor model, see Equation 10.24.

INAVCM   INdustry AVerage CoMmission. Dimension: dollar units per product unit.

$$= \frac{\sum_{d=1}^{D(IREG)} COMMIS(d)}{D(IREG)}$$

D(IREG)   total number of Distributors in region IREG.
= system parameter (integer) — simulation control.

In situations where a differential commission rate is paid on different brands by the distributor, the commission variable COMMIS(d) must be expanded to specify the commission paid on each brand COMMIS(b, d). The salesman's commission schedule variable may be similarly expanded to COMMIS(b, s).

The Manufacturer Salesman

In the case of a salesman employed by a manufacturer rather than a distributor, selling effort in support of one or more brands produced by that manufacturer can be represented in a manner analogous to Equation 11.1 with the following exceptions. First, relative sales levels are not relevant to allocation of effort because the manufacturer salesman is generally concerned with a limited product line. Second, compensation comparisons reference other manufacturers rather than distributors.

The previous formulation may be modified to account for these exceptions as follows:

Equation 11.2

SALSLE(b, s)   SALesman SeLling Effort in support of brand b by salesman in employ of manufacturer of brand b. Dimension: pure number (proportion of time).

$$= EFFORT(s) * \frac{DSMCOM(b) + COMMIS(b)}{AVCOM}.$$

EFFORT(s)   extent of involvement (ego drive) — measure of relative EFFORT.
$= $ see Equation 11.1.

DSMCOM(b)   Direct SalesMan COMpensation provided by manufacturer of brand b. Dimension: dollars per product unit.
$= $ input from manufacturer model, see Equation 7.4.

COMMIS(b)   COMMISsion paid by manufacturer of brand b. Dimension: dollars per product unit.
$= $ input from manufacturer model, see Equation 7.14.

AVCOM   AVerage COMpensation paid by brand manufacturers to salesmen in their employ. Dimension: dollars per product unit.

$$= \frac{\sum_{b=1}^{BHSF(IREG)} DSMCOM(b) + COMMIS(b)}{BHSF(IREG)}.$$

BHSF(IREG)   total number of Brand manufacturers Hiring Salesmen in region IREG.
$= $ system parameter (integer) — simulation control.

Attributed Sales Generation

In earlier chapters, the average sales rates attributed to a salesman has been noted as a basis of performance evaluation. Because this descriptor is required by other sectors, it must be generated as output from the salesman model.

As indicated in Table 11.1, each salesman's call schedule is specified in an array (SMCSCH(x, s)) indicating the retailers or distributors x on whom salesman s will call during an average call period. Sales attributed to salesman s may be simply specified as the product of the call schedule variable and shipments to the appropriate outlet. This formulation is expressed for the distributor case in the following equation.

Equation 11.3

SALES(t, d, s)   SALES attributed to salesman s employed by distributor d at time t. Dimension: dollars.

$$= \sum_{r=1}^{R(IREG)} \left[\sum_{b=1}^{B(d)} SMCSCH(r, s) * PRTRET(d, r, b) \right.$$

$$\left. * ORDFLD(t, r, b) \right].$$

SMCSCH(r, s)   SalesMan Call SCHedule indicating assignment of retail outlet r to salesman s.
= 1, if outlet assigned,
= 0, if outlet not assigned.
= see Equation 10.23.

PRTRET(d, r, b)   PRice To RETailer r for product of brand b charged by distributor d. Dimension: dollars per product unit.
= see Equation 10.10.

ORDFLD(t, r, b)   ORDers for brand b from retailer r FiLleD at time t. Dimension: product units per time period.
= see Equation 10.16.

R(IREG)   total number of retailers in Region IREG.
= system parameter (integer) — simulation control.

B(d)   total Brands carried by distributor d.
= function of distributor model (integer), see Equation 10.2.

Equation 11.3 can be easily modified to represent the attributed sales generation for a manufacturer employed salesman by the substitution of appropriate order, pricing, and scheduling variables from the manufacturer sector in lieu of comparable variables from the distributor model. In developing Equation 11.3, the aggregate order filled and shipment variables from the Chapter 10 distributor model have been expanded to take account of allocation to individual retailers.

Given the sales attributed to a particular salesman, the average sales characteristic can be derived. In the case of the one-year-average monthly sales rate specified in Table 11.1., this attribute may be defined as follows. (A one-day time step with 260 business days per year is assumed.)

Equation 11.4

AVGSAL(s)   AVeraGe SALes (over 1 year period) attributed to salesman s.

$$= \frac{\sum_{t=T}^{T-259} SALES(t, s)}{12}.$$

Determinants of Communication Content

The content of salesman communication is determined by available information sources. In the simplest case, the salesman follows an approach outlined by the manufacturer. In the absence of manufacturer content specification, selling aids prepared for use by the retailer or distributor on whom the salesman is calling may be influential. Salesman communication content frequently parallels the characteristics and appeals emphasis of the brochure or point-of-sale display that he is distributing.

In the absence of a suggested sales message or selling aids, the salesman is left wholly to his own devices. In this situation, he is not unlike the consumer whose communication generating behavior was discussed in detail in Chapter 8. Except for a higher probability of exposure to promotion relating to the product line that he is selling, the salesman's response mechanisms are comparable to those of the consumer, and, in the absence of other sources of communication content, his communication does not vary substantially from that of an equally informed consumer generating word-of-mouth communication.

Manufacturer-Determined Communication Content

The majority of manufacturer-employed salesmen and a substantial number of those employed by distributors have access to suggested selling approaches prepared by the brand manufacturer. Within this system, proposed content received from the manufacturing sector defines suggested selling communication in terms of the proportion of communication devoted to each of np product characteristics and n product associated appeals, EVSPCW(np, b) and EVSAPW(n, b), respectively.

Communication Content Based on Selling Aids

In the absence of a suggested selling approach, the salesman relies on the content of brochures, broadsides, and other point-of-sale material in developing his own selling message. The communication content of point-of-sale piece na has been defined in terms of the variables EVPCWP(np, b) and EVPSAW(n, b), indicating the proportion of the material devoted to specific product characteristics and appeals respectively. Because point-of-sale material is prepared by the brand manufacturer, these communication descriptors are also generated within the manufacturer sector and appear as inputs to the salesman sector.

Salesman-Determined Communication Content

The preceding comments imply that available content will be assimilated and retransmitted as part of the salesman's selling message. This disregards the salesman's subjective response to communication content through which certain characteristics or appeals may be emphasized while others are totally ignored. Predispositions may affect response to communication, produce selective recognition, and result in inaccurate transfer of content.

A representation of the subjective perception and response process was developed in Chapter 8 as part of the simulation of consumer behavior. It may be reasonable to assume that the salesman does not have relevant predispositions — that his own attitudes, if any, do not affect his selling message. If this assumption is unacceptable, the subjective perception and response model may be applied to the salesman.

In the absence of other sources of communication content, the salesman's selling message can be based only on his conception of brands gained from experience over time. This subjective conception of a brand has been previously defined as the "perceived brand image." [8]

Formulation of Communication Content

The content of salesman communication under the three conditions discussed can be summarized using the previously noted variables. The product characteristic content of this communication is defined as follows.

Equation 11.5

SCPCC(np, b, s)   Salesman s Communication Product Characteristic Content associating characteristic np with brand b. (Proportion of communication devoted to characteristic np.)

$$= \text{EVSPCW(np, b), if} \sum_{np=1}^{NP(b)} \text{EVSPCW(np, b)} > 0.0,$$

$$= \text{EVPCWP(np, na, b), if} \sum_{np=1}^{NP(b)} \text{EVSPCW(np, b)} = 0$$

$$\text{and} \sum_{np=1}^{NP(b)} \text{EVPCWP(np, na, b)} > 0.0,$$

[8] See "Brand Attitude Formation," Chapter 8, particularly Equation 8.41.

$$= \text{PEBRI}(np, b, s), \text{ if } \sum_{np=1}^{NP(b)} \left[\text{EVSPCW}(np, b) \right.$$

$$\left. + \sum_{na=1}^{NA(b)} \text{EVPCWP}(np, na, b) \right] = 0.0.$$

EVSPCW(np, b)   EValuation of Salesman Product Characteristic np Weighting in brand b's proposed detail.
= input from manufacturer sector, see Equation 7.16.

EVPCWP(np, na, b)   EValuation of Product Characteristic np Weighting in Point-of-sale promotion piece na (being distributed by salesman s).
= input from manufacturer sector, see Equation 7.10.

PEBRI(np, b, s)   PErceived BRand Image of attribute np associated with brand b in simulated mind of salesman s.
= response model parameter, see Equation 8.41.

In a similar manner, brand-associated appeals communicated by the salesman may be expressed in terms of comparable content descriptors as follows.

Equation 11.6

SCAPC(n, b, s)   Salesman s Communication APpeals Content associating appeal n with brand b. (Proportion of communication devoted to appeal n.)

$$= \text{EVSAPW}(n, b), \text{ if } \sum_{n=1}^{N(b)} \text{EVSAPW}(n, b) > 0.0,$$

$$= \text{EVPSAW}(n, na, b), \text{ if } \sum_{n=1}^{N(b)} \text{EVSAPW}(n, b) = 0.0$$

$$\text{and } \sum_{n=1}^{N(b)} \text{EVPSAW}(n, na, b) > 0.0,$$

$$= \text{PEBRI}(n, b, s), \text{ if } \sum_{n=1}^{N(b)} \left[\text{EVSAPW}(n, b) \right.$$

$$\left. + \sum_{na=1}^{NA(b)} \text{EVPSAW}(n, na, b) \right] = 0.0.$$

EVSAPW(n, b)   EValuation of Salesman APpeal n Weighting in brand b's proposed detail.
= input from manufacturer sector, see Equation 7.16.

EVPSAW(n, na, b)   EValuation of Point-of-Sale Appeal n Weighting in display na for brand b.
= input from manufacturer sector, see Equation 7.10.

The summations over n in Equations 11.5 and 11.6 provide a check for the existence of any nonzero element in the set of product characteristics or appeals weightings. Content is absent only if all elements of the set are zero.

References to promotional piece na assume that the promotion thus designated is being distributed through the salesman to the appropriate retailers or distributors. Explicit formulation of this condition is a simple matter of subscript specification.

Probability of Communication Generation

Because the salesman's major selling activity is communication — communication generation is the sole measurable manifestation of selling effort — the probability of communication generation is proportional to the salesman's selling effort $(SALSLE(b, s))$ as formulated in Equation 11.1.

The Decision to Seek Employment

The salesman's satisfaction with his present employment and interest in considering alternative employment is influenced by three factors in his environment. The first relates to the extent of his association with his present employer, the second to his present level of compensation and what he might expect to receive in another situation, and the third to his perception of the market for the product that he is now selling.

Effect of Extent of Employer-Employee Association

The salesman's interest in new employment opportunities decreases as his length of association with a single employer increases. The salesman's level of satisfaction, feeling of job security, familiarity with product, markets, and customers, as well as access to more profitable accounts all increase as he spends time with an employer. As time passes, the salesman's investment in a particular situation and the corresponding gains that he can realize from that situation increase.

If only this dimension of the decision to seek employment is considered, it is evident that the salesman's probability of considering alternative positions is greatest during the early part of his association with a particular employer. It is generally accepted, however, that a salesman should not leave a new employer until he has worked with him for a "reasonable" period of time. (Salesmen employed by appliance distributors seem to consider a period of approximately six months to be "reasonable.") Although this concept of fair play undoubtedly has its limits in the case where an unusually advantageous offer is made, under normal circumstances the probability of the salesman initiating an action to change jobs during the first few months of new employment is low.

As the extent of association increases beyond this period, the probability of his being interested in an alternative situation decreases as the result of his investment in the present situation. For purposes of this model, the extent of association with present employer will be measured by the variable NYRSWE(s, t) reflecting the number of years during which salesman s has been associated with his present employer as of time t.

Effect of Relative Compensation

The salesman's interest in alternative employment is influenced by the relative merits of the compensation program offered by alternative employers. The previously referenced average commission rate does not appear to be as relevant as the maximum rate being paid in the salesman's region. Although the average may more accurately reflect actual conditions in the market, the highest paying compensation program available to comparable salesmen is more often used as a reference by salesmen in discussing alternative opportunities — someone in the region is getting this "better deal," and the existence of this reference reduces the relative attractiveness of the salesman's own compensation program.

Effect of Market Conditions

The salesman is naturally sensitive to developments in the market in which he is selling. He is more apt to be interested in leaving a company operating in a contracting market than one facing an expanding demand. It is difficult to establish the time perspective taken by the salesman in evaluating market trends. The evaluation is a personal one based on individual experience in that segment of the market with which the salesman has contact. For purposes of this model, the salesman's market experience will be approximated by the average sales measure, AVGSAL(s), established by Equation 11.4.

Formulation of Decision to Seek Employment

As has been suggested by the preceding discussion, the salesman's evaluation of alternative employment opportunities is a continuing process. Under precisely the right conditions, practically any salesman is willing to consider changing jobs. Each of the factors noted influences the probability that a particular salesman will be interested in considering an alternative employment opportunity at a specified time. This decision process can most easily be represented in terms of a probability of salesman action as summarized in Figure 11.1 and the following equations.

Equation 11.7

PRSCAE(s)
: PRobability of Salesman s Considering Alternative Employment opportunities.

$$= \text{EFHICP(s)} + \text{EFASOC} + C_4 * \frac{\text{SALES}(t, s)}{\text{SALES}(t - 1, s)}.$$

EFHICP(s)
: EFfect of HIgh ComPensation on probability of salesman s considering alternative employment.

$$= C_1 * [\text{HICOM(s)} - \text{SALARY(s)} - \frac{\sum\limits_{b=1}^{B(d)} \frac{\text{COMMIS}(s, b)}{\text{PRTRET}(b, d, t)}}{B(d)}$$

$$* \text{AVGSAL(s)}]/\text{HICOM(s)}$$

EFASOC(s)
: EFfect of length of ASsOCiation on probability of salesman s considering alternative employment.

$$= C_2 * \text{ENXPF}(-\frac{\text{NYRSWE}(s, t)}{2.0}), \text{ if NYRSWE}(s, t) \geq C_4$$

$$= 0.0, \text{ if NYRSWE}(s, t) < C_3.$$

HICOM(s)
: HIghest available COMpensation available to salesman s. Dimension: dollars.

$$= \text{Maximum of}$$

$$\left| \text{SALARY}(s') + \frac{\sum\limits_{b=1}^{B(d')} \frac{\text{COMMIS}(s', b)}{\text{PRTRET}(b, d', t)}}{B(d')} * \text{AVGSAL}(s') \right|$$

$d' = 1$ through D.
$s' = 1$ through S.

SALARY(s)
: SALARY (dollars) paid to salesman s. Dimension: dollars.
: = input from distributor or manufacturer sector, see Equation 7.14, and Equation 10.24.

COMMIS(s, b)
: COMMISsion paid salesman s on brand b. Dimension: dollars per product unit.
: = input from distributor or manufacturer sector, see Equation 7.14, and Equation 10.24.

PRTRET(b, x, t)   PRice To RETailer charged for brand b by distributor or manufacturer x at time t. Dimension: dollars per product unit.
                     = input from distributor or manufacturer sector, see Equation 7.13, or Equation 10.10.

AVGSAL(s)   AVeraGe SALes generated by salesman s. Dimension: dollars.
                     = see Equation 11.4.

NYRSWE(s, t)   Number of YeaRs Salesman s With present Employer as of time t. Dimension: time units.
                     = NYRSWE(s, t − 1) + TIMINC,
                       if EMPLOY(s) at time t = EMPLOY(s) at time t − 1.
                     = 0.0, if EMPLOY(s) at time t ≠ EMPLOY(s) at time t − 1.

EMPLOY(s)   EMPLOYer identification indicating distributor or manufacturer by whom salesman s employed.
                     = salesman characteristic, see Table 11.1.

TIMINC   TIMe INCrement (DT) expressed in fraction of year.
                     = system parameter.

SALES(t, s)   SALES generated by salesman s at time t. Dimension: dollars.
                     = see Equation 11.3.

C_1 through C_3 scaling Constants indicating relative weightings applied to each effect as determinant of probability.
                     = .33, as sample values.

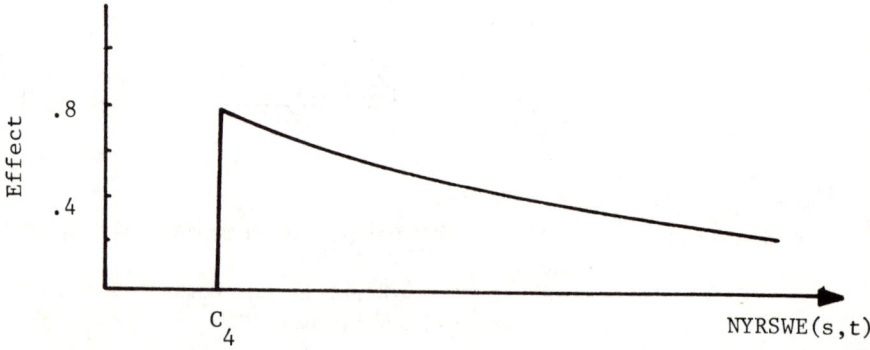

Figure 11.1. Effect of length of association on salesman considering other employment.

Salesman Availability

Given the probability that salesman s will consider alternative employment, his interaction with prospective employers can be formulated in two alternative ways. One approach is to interrogate the salesman whenever a brand manufacturer or distributor is seeking additional personnel to determine whether or not he would be interested in considering an offer. The salesman's response to this interrogation is then established stochastically on the basis of the salesman's probability of considering the alternative.

An alternative formulation treats Equation 11.7 as the probability of the salesman considering *any offer* rather than a particular offer. Taking this view, the salesman will either consider all opportunities or none and a single test based on the probability establishes a binary outcome that governs the salesman's consideration of offers until a different outcome is established by a later test.

The second (binary outcome) formulation will be used in this model. Representation of the salesman's availability — his willingness to consider alternative employment offers by any distributor or brand manufacturer — is summarized in Equation 11.8.[9]

Equation 11.8

> AVAILA(s)   AVAILAbility of salesman s.
> = 1.0, if outcome of PRSCAE(s) $\geq$ RANNOF,
> = 0.0, if outcome of PRSCAE(s) $<$ RANNOF.

The Decision to Accept Employment

If the salesman considers an offer by a distributor or manufacturer, it is necessary to determine whether or not that offer will be accepted. In the real life situation, the salesman's probability of accepting a particular offer is related to the net gain that, in his opinion, would be achieved by changing employment.

The salesman is, of course, concerned with the relative compensation that he would receive in the proposed and present situation. The relative compensation is, however, not the whole story. The salesman may turn down an offer consisting of substantially improved compensation if, in his opinion, he will have to work harder or under less de-

---

[9] The use of the RANNO routine to establish a binary outcome based on a probability is discussed in Chapter 5.

sirable conditions in the new job. It is in this sense that the term "net gain" is used here. The salesman appears to consider the relative gain in compensation in light of the relative increase or decrease in the amount or nature of work that he will be expected to perform in order to receive the compensation.

The decision to accept employment can thus be represented in terms of the salesman's evaluation of the alternatives available along two dimensions — compensation and workload or employment conditions.

Effect of Relative Compensation

Within this model, compensation consists of commissions and salary. Comparative evaluation of salary involves a trivial direct comparison; however, evaluation of commission-based profit requires an assumption regarding the sales against which the new employer's commissions would be applied. In most situations examined in this study, the salesman made the assumption that if he accepted the new employment he would be selling at approximately the same dollar level that he generated in his existing employment situation.

The salesman's evaluation along the compensation dimensions is thus represented in terms of the difference between his present and the offered salary plus the difference between his present and the offered commission rate applied against his present average dollar sales level.

Effect of Working Conditions

Within the context of this system only one aspect of working conditions has been specified. The number of calls per salesman per period and the normal call period for a manufacturer or distributor, provide a measure of the average workload of their salesmen.

Measurement of Net Gain

In evaluating alternatives in terms of workload and compensation, the salesman is concerned with the expected change along each dimension as a result of moving from his present situation to the proposed employment alternative. This is an apples and oranges comparison through which the salesman attempts to equate workload and compensation. Relative change along each dimension may be expressed as a percentage to solve dimensional problems; however, the attendant assumption that the effect of a specified percentage increase in compensation may be neutralized by a comparable percentage increase in the requisite workload requires validation.

Probability of Accepting Employment Offer

The net gain approach establishes a formulation based on the difference between compensation and work-load based ratios. Small differences favoring the offering employer would not be expected to cause a salesman to change positions. However, as the favorable differential approaches 20 or 30 percent it is almost certain that the salesman who has already decided to consider alternative employment will make a change.[10] These conditions are appropriately described by an exponential relationship of the type illustrated in Equation 11.9 and Figure 11.2.

Equation 11.9

PRSMAE(s) PRobability of SalesMan Accepting Employment.

$$= C_5 * \text{ENXPF}\left(C_6 * \right.$$

$$\left[\frac{[\text{COMMIS(o)} - \text{COMMIS(s)}] * \text{AVGSAL(s)} + \text{SALARY(o)} - \text{SALARY(s)}}{\text{COMMIS(s)} * \text{AVGSAL(s)} + \text{SALARY(s)}} \right.$$

$$\left. - \frac{\dfrac{\text{NCPSPP(o)}}{\text{NCALPD(o)}} - \dfrac{\text{NCPSPP(s)}}{\text{NCALPD(s)}}}{\dfrac{\text{NCPSPP(s)}}{\text{NCALPP(s)}}} \left. \vphantom{\frac{a}{b}} \right] \right).$$

COMMIS(s)   COMMISsion presently received by salesman s. Dimension: dollars per product unit.
= COMMIS(b), if s employed by b,
= COMMIS(d), if s employed by d,
= .0001, if s unemployed.

COMMIS(o)   COMMISsion being offered. Dimension: dollars per product unit.
= COMMIS(b'), if offer made by manufacturer of brand b',
= COMMIS(d'), if offer made by distributor d'.

SALARY(s)   SALARY presently received by salesman s. Dimension: dollars per time period.
= SALARY(b'), if s employed by b',
= SALARY(d'), if s employed by d',
= .0001, if s unemployed.

[10] Evidence in support of the measurement technique implied by this formulation is weak. While salesmen did change employers consistently when alternative differences of this magnitude were encountered, the fact that they had already decided to "look around" raises questions regarding the impact of differential magnitude on their decision outcome.

SALARY(o)   SALARY being offered. Dimension: dollars per time
             period.
             = SALARY(b'), if b' making offer,
             = SALARY(d'), if d' making offer.

NCPSPP(s)   Number of Calls Per Salesman Per Period in present
             employment.
             = NCPSPP(d) or NCPSPP(b), depending on employer.

NCPSPP(o)   Number of Calls Per Salesman Per Period in situation
             offered.
             = NCPSPP(d) or NCPSPP(b) as function of offerer.

NCALPD(s)   Normal CALl PerioD of present employer.
             = NCALPD(d) or NCALPD(b) as function of employer.

NCALPD(o)   Normal CALl PerioD of offerer.
             = NCALD(d') or NCALPD(b') as function of offerer.

$C_5 - C_6$ Scaling constants.
             = .01 and 20 as sample values.

Call schedule parameters appearing in Equation 11.9 are established
for the manufacturer sector in Equation 7.15, and for the distributor in
Equation 10.23.

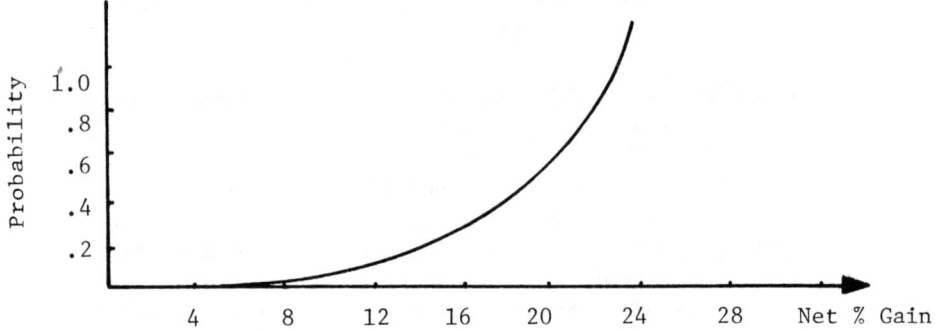

Figure 11.2. Probability of offer acceptance.

Summary

This chapter has focused on the development of a generalized model
of salesman behavior. Beginning with a description of the salesman's
role in the marketing system, basic characteristics of salesman interactions with manufacturer, distributor, and retailer were established.

Attributes differentiating between types of salesmen were defined to serve as specifications for an artificial salesman population and salesman actions and responses were reviewed.

Model formulations developed in this chapter may be summarized in terms of

1. The level of selling effort devoted to a brand.
2. The level of sales generated.
3. The content and extent of communication generated.
4. The decision to seek employment.
5. The decision to accept an employment offer.

While measures of salesman performance and motivation (effort) were established in this model as partial manifestations of the "ego drive," these descriptors leave much to be desired. The elusive quality of these attributes of the successful salesman is aptly revealed by Robert McMurry's description of a salesman who brings ". . . romance and excitement into lives which are otherwise drab, errant, and sterile." The qualities to be defined are those exhibited in

. . . the close used with great success by one specialty salesman of silverware. With his sample he carries two tall candlesticks. As he approaches his close he places his gleaming silver place setting on black velvet display pads on the dining room table, lights his candles, and turns off the lights. In the romantic atmosphere which he has thus created, he makes his final pitch. He tells the prospective housewife:

"Madam, there are three apocalyptic moments in every woman's life: when the man she loves tells her he loves her and wants to marry her; when she holds her first born in her arms; and finally, when she looks down on her first sterling table service. Sign here, Madam. Please use this pencil and press hard; there are four carbons." [11]

[11] McMurry, Footnote 4, *loc. cit.*

Chapter 12

REPRESENTATION OF REMAINING MARKET SECTORS

Descriptions of behavior and inputs associated with the marketing decision maker, consumer, retailer, distributor, and salesman have now been completed. Two sectors defined in Chapter 3 remain to be described. These are the research agent and the government.

Representation of Research and Government

Description of behavior associated with the research agent and government involves special problems that distinguish these sectors from those modeled in previous chapters.

The role of research agent is particularly difficult to define within the context of this system because the system itself is designed to serve as a tool of research. Thus representation of simulation-based research requires modeling of the simulation process (a procedure creating problems not unlike those facing the painter whose objective is to create a picture of himself painting a picture of himself painting a picture of himself painting a picture of . . .).

In a more traditional context, the research function may be described in terms of the research agent's effect on the content and rate of information flow from various market sectors to the manufacturer. This approach followed in Chapter 3 will be continued throughout the descriptive portions of this discussion.

Because relevant governmental actions are highly product specific, generalized description of behavior within the government sector is not particularly useful. While relevant government actions and responses have been represented in specific market simulations, they require a level of model development that is substantially beyond the scope of this exposition. For purposes of this discussion, the impact of government will be assessed in terms of constraints imposed on behavior within various sectors of the market environment.

The Research Agent

Two types of research simulation may be incorporated in a system. The first is behavioral simulation of research agent actions and responses. The second uses the simulation as an artificial environment in which individuals perform (simulate) the research function. This chapter is concerned with the first type of simulation. The second is discussed in Chapter 14.

The characteristics of a simulated research agent may be conveniently described with reference to the functions performed by his real-world counterpart.

Research Functions

Nine functions of the research agent will be considered in this chapter. While certain of these activities are directly amenable to simulation using procedures comparable to those developed in earlier chapters, others are, for reasons to be considered later, inappropriate for representation using this technique. The nine functional areas of research agent behavior may be defined as (1) problem definition, (2) hypothesis formation, (3) variable definition, (4) source determination, (5) methodology, (6) data acquisition, (7) data organization, (8) data analysis (interpretation), and (9) reporting.

Behavior associated with each of these functions will be described and its amenability to simulation noted. Examples based on previously developed sector models will be referenced where appropriate.

Problem Definition

The first step in an orderly research process is problem definition. The research agent alone or in combination with the manufacturer must determine what is to be learned from the research activity. If the problem is not stated in terms of decision alternatives, the information generated through later research steps may be inapplicable to a decision function and, as such, useless.

Problem definition should serve to focus the attention of the manager and the research agent on a specific aspect of the environment. Factors considered must be actionable in that management has the ability to take some action with respect to them and relevant in that their states influence the outcome of behavior within the market. The problem is one of defining relevant goals — of avoiding the previously noted "confusion between effectiveness and efficiency that stands between doing the right things and doing things right." [1]

In developing various sector models the need for information from outside the sector has become apparent. In certain cases requisite data have been explicitly generated within other sectors and transferred from one sector to another. In other instances transfer has not been specified; however, the decision maker has been assumed to have access to the specified data.

Within the simulated environment problem definition begins with the model builder's recognition of the need within a sector for information from another sector. Previously established retailer, distributor, and salesman requirements for information regarding relative brand performance illustrate this aspect of problem definition.

Hypothesis Formation

Once the problem area (information requirement) has been defined, the relationships to be researched must be specified as a testable assumption. Hypothesis formation may involve the statement of a formal null hypothesis or specific model to be tested. Under any circumstances, the research designer should be able to say something about the findings that he expects to encounter and the effect that these or alternative findings will have on specific decisions.

The distributor's interest in alternative brand performance provides an example of hypothesis formation within the simulated environment. The distributor assumes a relationship between brand performance in the market as a whole and potential performance within his outlet. Data regarding brand performance are of value as an input to his decision to carry. The distributor who is predisposed to add a brand to

[1] P. F. Drucker, "Managing for Business Effectiveness," *Harvard Business Review,* Vol. 41 (May–June 1963), p. 54.

his product line may initially assume above-average brand performance in the market. This assumption becomes a hypothesis to be tested through research. Research findings affect his decision outcomes because determination of below-average performance results in rejection, while the brand is added if above-average performance is established.

Variable Definition

The final statement of hypotheses to be tested is in terms of a variable for which values are to be obtained. The question "What is to be measured?" must be answered.

The variable defined must be valid — it must measure what is required in order to test the stated hypothesis. Within the simulation, as an example, the appropriate variables for testing the previously noted market share hypothesis are the actual unit sales of the brands within appropriate market segments.[2] Once a simulation has been developed, the relation between variable and process in the simulated environment is unequivocally established. However, in the real world environment lack of variable validity is the source of many research failures.[3] Simulations of research agent behavior may therefore encompass mechanisms for establishing probabilistic reliance on a particular variable as a "valid" measure of a process.

Source Determination

The research agent must determine who or what will be researched in order to obtain the desired data. The appropriate data source is normally defined in terms of attributes specifying the target area or group.[4]

The research target must be valid in view of the measurement to be taken. The proposed source must "know enough" to provide the requisite information. The validity of responses obtained through research are directly dependent upon those with whom the researcher

[2] Brand share data enters decision processes in Equations 9.3A, 9.4, and 9.11.

[3] For a discussion of this point, see "Validity and Reliability of Surveys," in E. J. McCarthy, *Basic Marketing: A Managerial Approach* (Homewood, Ill.: Richard D. Irwin, Inc., 1960), pp. 196–197.

[4] An excellent discussion of the processes through which target market definition is accomplished is provided by "Coordinating Research Approaches: The Complete Marketing Audit," Ferber and Verdoorn, *Research Methods in Economics and Business* (New York: The Macmillan Company, 1962), pp. 486–542.

communicates having relevant experience on which to base their responses.[5] In the simulated environment it is not sufficient to define the target group in terms of desired demographics. It is also necessary to ensure that the simulated respondent is capable of responding to relevant conditions — requisite response mechanisms must have been included in the model structure.

Once response capabilities have been established, an appropriate research target is defined in terms of attributes of the simulated population that differentiate cells appropriate for inclusion in the research sample from those that should be excluded. As an example, in simulated consumer research within the sector specified by the Chapter 8 model, research targets may be defined in terms of consumer age, income, education, brand ownership, or attitudes toward product characteristics, appeals, brands, or retailers.[6]

Methodology

Sample Selection. Given specification of a research target, the research agent must establish a sampling design determining the proportion of the target group to be contacted. If all eligible population members are not to be included in simulated research designs, models must establish the procedures to be followed in selecting a limited sample from the total population.

In some simulated research it is desirable to encompass the entire universe. This is the case, for example, when evaluating the extent and content of competitive advertising and promotion. In this instance, the simulated research process incorporates the entire universe — all promotion in all media generated by all competitors during the selected time period.

In other situations, a representative sample from the population is adequate to provide required data. Simulated research focusing on the behavior of particular consumer subgroups has been structured to obtain "responses" from a sample within the simulated consumer population exhibiting desired attributes, e.g., specified income and age characteristics.

Simulation of the sample selection process is a relatively straight-

---

[5] For a discussion of this problem see A. Politz, "Finding Out What Consumers Will Buy," *Steel,* Vol. 143 (July 14, 1958), pp. 106.

[6] Available consumer attributes are summarized in Table 8.1.

forward modeling activity once mechanisms facilitating sample acquisition have been established.

The simulated environment may be used to test procedures designed to evaluate sample reliability and bias. Simulated populations have effectively demonstrated the limitations of blind random sampling and the benefits realized by obtaining equal or proportionate representation of all relevant population subsections within the sample.[7]

In a sample drawn from the simulated Chapter 8 consumer population it is a simple matter to establish, for example, that greater assurance of a representative sample is achieved by an orderly selection process, rather than through a random selection of cells, ensuring that consumers having appropriate characteristics are included in the correct proportion.

Interview Procedures. Simulations of research agent behavior have been designed to duplicate three interview approaches normally described as observation, interview, and experimentation.

Following the observation procedure the simulated research agent monitors and reports on specified behavior within a sector. He may, for example, monitor variables specifying the extent of salesman customer interaction, traffic (brand exposure) within a store, or retailer inventory maintenance.

When implied as opposed to observable actions are to be monitored, the simulated research agent is programmed to apply interview or survey approaches in an attempt to gain attitude, exposure, or experience-based information from simulated respondents. Telephone, mail, and personal interview procedures have been simulated.

Data Acquisition

When the observation approach is followed, simulated data acquisition may involve nothing more than monitoring the flow of physical items or people. When an interview procedure is adopted, interaction between the research agent and respondent as well as respondent reactions to the topic, specific questions, or the interviewer must be modeled. If, under conditions prevailing, it is reasonable to assume that the interviewee will be able and willing to provide direct answers in

[7] An easily simulated example of the random sample fallacy is provided in R. Ferber, *Statistical Techniques in Market Research* (New York: McGraw-Hill Book Company, 1949), pp. 221–222.

response to interviewer questions, a direct "memory dump" of respondent orientation variables may be appropriate.

In other situations the simulated research agent may seek information which cannot be obtained through direct questioning.

There are many things that we need to know about a consumer's reaction to a product that he can't tell us because they are to some extent socially unacceptable. For instance, the snob appeal of a product vitally influences its sales, but it is a thing that the consumer will not like to discuss
explicitly. It is important information for us, but its socially unacceptable
character makes it hard or impossible for the respondent to tell us.

In other cases, the consumer is influenced by motives of which he is
perhaps vaguely aware but which he finds difficult to put into words. The
interviewer-respondent relationship puts a good deal of pressure on him
to reply and to make sense in his reply. Consequently he gives us stereo-
typical responses that use clichés which are commonly acceptable but do
not necessarily represent the true motives.[8]

In this situation, it is unreasonable to permit the simulated researcher
to have direct access to the mind of the simulated respondent. The
model builder must represent the process of projective testing through
which the human researcher presents ambiguous stimuli and evaluates
the structure imposed by the respondent as he reacts to these stimuli.

Assessment of the implications of alternative data acquisition procedures is beyond the scope of this chapter.[9] For present purposes it
is sufficient to note that objective interview techniques can be easily
simulated, and, because individual orientations are known (the content
of simulated minds may be accessed), information that would be
obtained through the successful application of projective techniques is
available.

Two sources of bias that may affect the accuracy of data acquired
using the previously discussed techniques have been modeled. The
first is interviewer bias and the second, question bias.

Interviewer bias may be simulated through selective response models
of the type discussed in Chapter 8. Such models have been used to
cause the simulated interviewer to interpret responses by the simulated

---

[8] M. Haire, "Projective Techniques in Market Research," *Journal of Marketing,*
Vol. 14 (1950), pp. 649–656.
[9] For a discussion of the strengths and weaknesses of both objective and projective techniques see R. Ferber and H. G. Wales (eds.), *Motivation and Market
Behavior* (Homewood, Ill.: Richard D. Irwin, Inc., 1958).

interviewee on a selective basis. If each simulated interviewer perceives the situation subjectively, different interviewers from the artificial population reporting the same situation will provide conflicting data.

Question bias refers to the effect of question wording on the respondent. Leading questions — questions that suggest an appropriate answer — are an example of this type of bias. Within a simulation system, representation of question bias requires external evaluation of the effective content communicated by a particular questioning procedure.

Data Organization

Once data have been gathered, the research agent must organize the resulting information for purposes of analyses. Models developed for this purpose are normally designed to aggregate or categorize responses. The organization process may modify information content and bases of microdifferentiation are lost through aggregation. Categorization of data to facilitate certain types of comparisons emphasizes certain relationships while excluding others. In short, realistic problems are created by the simulated research agent.

Data Analysis

Analysis involves the application of various models to data in an attempt to gain meaning that is not evident from direct observation of the data. Simulations of analysis generally involve the application of historical correlations or statistical extrapolation models. The simulated research agent may be equipped to correlate factors in the historical environment with conditions existing at the present time or to extrapolate current trends as predictions of conditions at a future time.

Historical Explanation. The real-world researcher's analysis of past conditions is more often than not a post mortem. Management is more frequently concerned with the reason for failure than the cause of success. In the presence of failure, they feel a compulsion to "find out what went wrong." When faced with success, there is little motivation to determine why the situation is developing favorably. It is a normal human failing to assume that success is related to what one does ("we were at the right place at the right time with the right product and the right approach"),[10] while poor performance leads

---

[10] Comment by a product manager describing the "reason" for the success of a newly introduced food product. (Cambridge, Mass.: M.I.T., Sloan Research Project 142, February 1960).

naturally to a desire to explain ". . . the one missing link in the otherwise solid chain. . . . We did everything right, except. . . ." [11]

The rationalizing function of this form of "research" has not been
simulated. However models of adaptive behavior in which historical
review changes sensitivity — modifies decision or response model parameters — have been incorporated in simulation structures.

Future Prediction. Research agent predictions have been summarized in 9 "important" areas of action: [12]

1. Analysis of territorial potentials.
2. Competitive position of company products.
3. Analysis of market size.
4. Customer acceptance of new product.
5. Variations in territorial yield.
6. New products demand estimates.
7. Economic research.
8. Comparative studies of competitive products.
9. Determining market characteristics.

This list includes characteristics of the economy which are beyond
the scope of systems discussed in this book. It also references product
market attributes which are completely compatible with previously
formulated model structures.

The process of future prediction was simulated to a limited extent
in the "expectation formation" functions developed for the distributor
and retailer in previous chapters.

Reporting

Two classes of reporting procedures available to the research agent
providing information to management may be simulated. The first
involves communicating complete data at a specified level of aggregation. Under these circumstances manager response formulations must
account for content loss through aggregation and, if data are presented
in detail, reduced utilization due to sheer bulk of output.

The alternative reporting procedure provides detailed output on a

---

[11] Comment from an interview with an appliance manufacturer describing problems encountered in launching a new model. (Cambridge, Mass.: M.I.T., Sloan
Research Project 142, February 1960).

[12] R. D. Crisp, *Marketing Research* (New York: McGraw-Hill Book Company,
Inc., 1957), p. 65.

selective basis specified by management developed criteria. Simulation of this procedure requires specification of the detail in which information is to be maintained and representation of the process through which it is monitored and referred to management when conditions meeting predetermined criteria arise.

Research Agent Simulation — A Summary

Macrocharacteristics of research agent simulations noted in the preceding discussion are illustrated in Figure 12.1. The upper portion of that figure uses the flow of product into inventory as an example of one class of data acquisition. In this example, the input rate at which goods are received is summed over time and across type. Given a specified time base, the first summation may be used to develop an average rate of flow over time. The rate of change in this average may also be formulated as indicated by the delta sign in the flow chart.

The summation across type may involve store types, product classes or brands and may be presented at a point in time as an average rate or over time as a rate of change in the average rate. Information relating to backlogs may be handled in a manner analogous to that just discussed for rates of flow. Successive levels of a backlog may be accumulated over time or across types in order to establish an average level, and the rate of change may be developed as a measure of trend.

Although Figure 12.1 emphasizes physical product as the element of flow, similar remarks could be made with regard to the flow of orders, promotional material, or cash. Sampling and aggregation functions are easily performed by the research agent whenever the quantity to be measured is explicitly observable and direct measurement of the channel content is possible. "Orders" and "product" may be defined in terms of attributes of the type discussed in earlier specifications, sampled, and measured directly.

A second type of research information collection illustrated in the lower half of Figure 12.1 involves assessment of response-based conditions that cannot be specified and measured directly. The flow chart representation indicates a filtering function affected by the respondent's reaction to promotion, perceived and cumulative perceived exposures, and response to the research agent.

Despite the existence of filtering, the research agent obtains from the respondent a reported rate of exposure — a number that can be manipulated to develop averages or classification statistics through

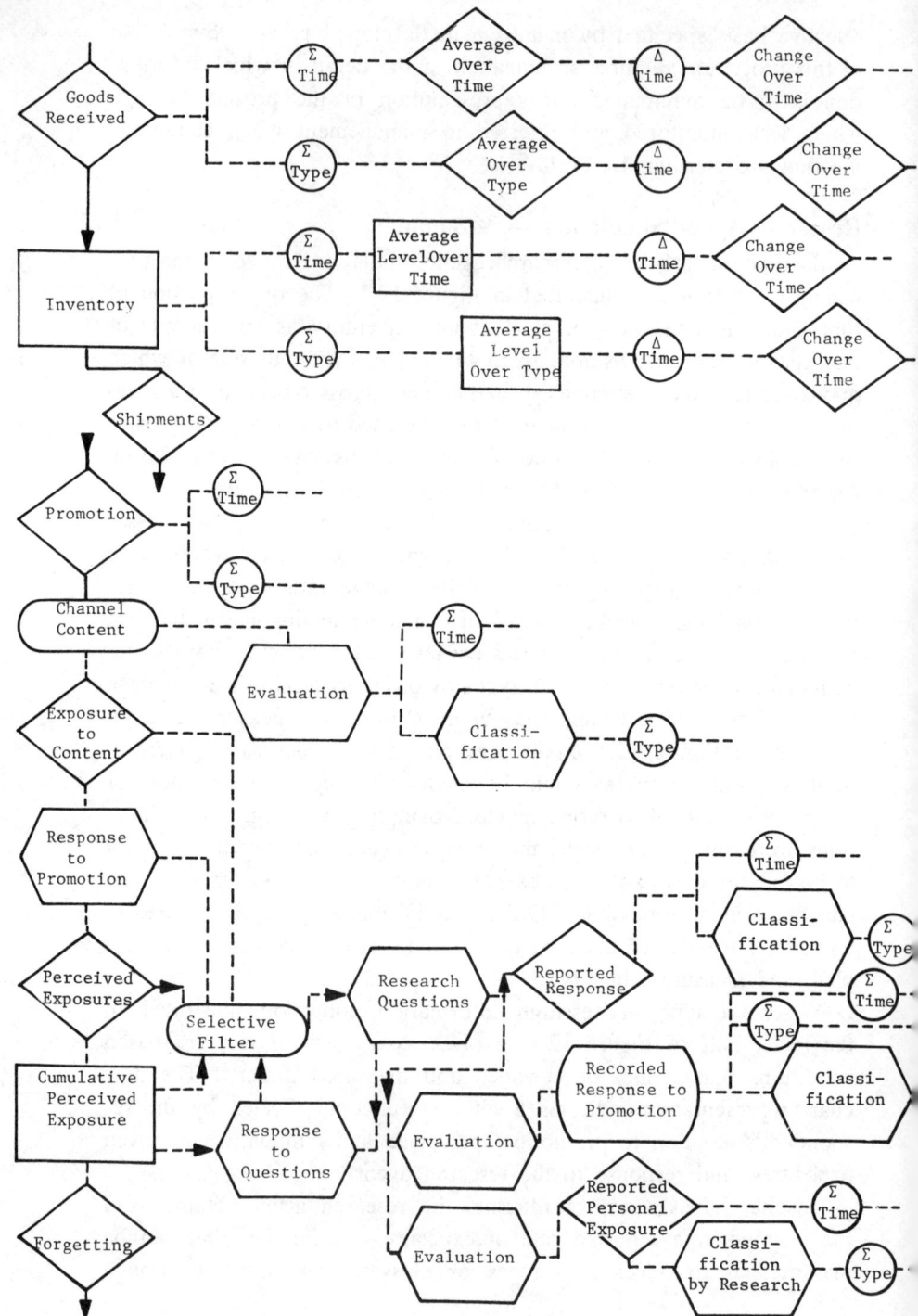

Figure 12.1. Representation of selected research functions.

procedures previously discussed. If the research agent attempts to move beyond exposure rates to determination of response to promotional content, additional complexities are introduced. Yes-no answers of the type obtained in researching exposure are no longer adequate. The respondent must express his feelings and emotions in words that the research agent must interpret, record, and combine with the answers of other respondents. Here the decision functions of the research agent are of particular importance. He must decide whether or not Mrs. Jones' comment that an advertisement was "about how clean product X gets your clothes" is equivalent to and should be classified with Mrs. Smith's remarks that "the ad talked about how product X has more washing power."

As illustrated in the flow chart, these evaluations and classifications produce data from which averages and rates of change over time may be developed to represent consumer response to a particular promotion or campaign. These numbers can be manipulated with the same ease as those reporting the quantity of physical product in inventory; however, the differential impact of research agent perceptions in the two cases should be evident.

The Government

The objective in this section is to consider factors encompassed by simulations of government actions and responses influencing behavior within the marketing environment. The impact of government agencies on decision areas including intercompany relations, competitive practices, promotion, packaging, and pricing will be discussed with reference to the Clayton Act, the Federal Trade Commission Act, and the Robinson-Patman Act.

Government Functions

Within the structure of this simulation the role of government has been previously defined in terms of passive and active behavior. Passive behavior involves monitoring channels of communication and product flow within the marketing system. Associated processes of selective information assimilation are not unlike those attributed to the research agent. The government's active role is manifested in constraints limiting alternatives available to decision makers within the manufacturer, distributor, and retailer sectors and increased uncertainty regarding some decision processes.

The Effect of Government on Competitive Interaction

Simulations of government impact on competitive interactions are based primarily on considerations associated with the Clayton Act of 1914 and the attendant Sherman Antitrust Act of 1890. Because both acts are founded on the concept that competition is good for the economy, simulated response functions are designed to be sensitive to actions that may be interpreted as tending to create monopolies or restrain trade. Such response functions are generally oriented toward measures of competitive market shares on the assumption that large market share and "monopoly control" are equated by the government. Government sector simulations are also designed to monitor intercompany communication with response functions sensitized to covariance that might be construed as manifestations of collusion or conspiracy in restraint of trade.

Response functions based on Clayton Act prohibitions against price discrimination, tie-in contracts, and exclusive arrangements, the effect of which might be ". . . to substantially lessen competition or tend to create a monopoly in any line of commerce" have also been programmed. The vagaries of the Clayton Act, attributable in large part to the inability of Congress or the courts to define consistently actions that will "substantially lessen competition," make it difficult to establish threshold values for these functions. This modeling problem reflects general management uncertainty rather than structural inadequacy. Managers are simply not able to establish clear standards for operating in a competitive market in compliance with the Clayton Act.[13]

Among the most specific comments regarding the position of the Antitrust division of the Department of Justice with regard to Sections 1 and 2 of the Sherman Act and Section 7 of the Clayton Act which this author has encountered are those contained in an address by Victor R. Hansen, former Assistant Attorney General in charge of the Antitrust division, presented to the American Economic Society of

---

[13] A relatively specific description of the Act and its potential implications for the business community is provided by R. W. Harbeson, "The Clayton Act: Sleeping Giant of Antitrust?" *The American Economic Review,* Vol. 48 (March 1958), pp. 92–104.

New York City in 1958.[14] To the extent that comments of the type made by Mr. Hansen can be obtained and accepted as valid, the problems of both operating manager and simulation designer are greatly simplified.

The Federal Trade Commission Act

While the agency established by the Federal Trade Commission Act in 1914 has been charged to take actions in situations involving "unfair methods of competition," neither the statute establishing the Commission nor its actions have clearly defined the meaning of these five simple words.

Behavioral representation of the constraints imposed by this agency is dependent on careful definition of the language in documents such as the Federal Trade Commission's *Guide Against Deceptive Pricing* for evaluating pricing representations in advertising.[15] Corporate legal counsel is normally called upon to make assumptions clarifying ambiguities and to indicate the extent to which consistent policies based on this guide may be assumed before probable courses of action by this agency in reviewing questions of corporate promotional activity are simulated.

In the language of this guide, the determination of ". . . whether or not pricing practices are violative of the laws administered by the commission . . ." is to be made

". . . in view of the requirements of the Federal Trade Commission Act, as amended, and principles enunciated by the courts in the ajudication of cases. The foremost of these principles are

1. Advertisements must be considered in their entirety as they would be read by those to whom they appeal.
2. Advertisements as a whole may be completely misleading although every sentence separately considered is literally true. This may be because things are omitted which should be said, or because advertisements are composed or purposefully printed in such a way as to mislead.
3. Advertisements are not intended to be carefully dissected with a dic-

---

[14] V. R. Hansen, Address Before the Metropolitan Economic Association, New York City, October 31, 1958, reprinted in S. Walters, M. Snider, and Morris Sweet, *Readings in Marketing* (Cincinnati, Ohio: Southwestern Publishing Company, 1962), pp. 759–772.

[15] *Guide Against Deceptive Pricing*, Federal Trade Commission, adopted October 2, 1958 (Washington, D. C.: U. S. Government Printing Office).

tionary at hand, but rather to produce an impression upon prospective purchasers.

. . .

7. Pricing representations, however made, which are ambiguous will be read favorably to the accomplishment of the purpose of the Federal Trade Commission Act, as amended, which is to prevent the making of claims which have the tendency and capacity to mislead.

The guide further details specific types of actions which are considered prima facie violations of the Act. These are exemplified by the following comments relating to price advertising.

No statement which represents or implies a reduction or saving from an established retail price or from the advertiser's usual and customary retail price should be used if, (a) an artificial mark-up has been produced to provide the basis for the claim, (b) the claim is based on infrequent or isolated sales, or (c) the claim is based on a past price (i.e., one not immediately preceding the price used in the recent, regular course of business) unless this fact is clearly and adequately disclosed.[16]

Given this type of specification prepared by the Commission and/or counsel familiar with the findings of the Commission and courts, it is possible to specify response parameters for models describing probable actions by this government agency in response to specific conditions arising in the market.

The Robinson-Patman Act

Certain proscriptions established by the Robinson-Patman Act of 1936 provide a reasonably clear basis for the imposition of constraints. Among these is ". . . any price discrimination between different purchasers of similar qualities, which may tend to injure competition." Simulations have been based on the assumption that any selective action might be construed as "tending to injure competition" and that only the manufacturer who does not differentiate between customers is reasonably safe from FTC action in this sphere.[17] There are, of course, associated problems of maintaining customers, but these do not concern the Commission.

---

[16] *Ibid.*

[17] A useful discussion of other alternatives available to marketing management is provided by W. David Robbins, "A Marketing Appraisal of the Robinson-Patman Act," *Journal of Marketing*, Vol. 24 (July 1959), pp. 15–21.

The development of Robinson-Patman based response models has generally introduced frustrating definitional problems. It is agreed, for example, that the manufacturer may change price in the face of competition providing he can prove that he was "meeting competition" and acting in "good faith." [18] Model development also raises an important question of management objectives. Does the decision maker wish to avoid government intervention completely? Several courses of action are open to the manufacturer who in the words of one author chooses to ". . . lawfully discriminate." He must, however, be prepared to carry to the courts his contention that his brand of discrimination is "legal." Defenses based on product differentiation, market separation, noninjurious discrimination, costs, and meeting competition have been proposed for ". . . the intelligent marketer . . . (who wishes to) . . . steer a careful course between the Scylla of ultra lawful apathy and the Charybdis of complete abandon." [19]

Simulation of Government Activity

Macrocharacteristics of a simulation of one form of government action within the marketing environment — monitoring and response to promotion content — is outlined in Figure 12.2. The response function is influenced by both the extent of promotion as reflected in the rate of promotion existing at a particular point in time and the content of that promotion. Output from the response function may lead to formulation and initiation of action that, after a process delay (assumed to be a function of the response), results in the issuance of a directive. Assuming that the manufacturer generating the promotion challenges the directive, a further delay associated with litigation is encountered before issuance is achieved or stopped.

This simplified representation leaves numerous questions unanswered. Which attributes of promotional content or rate of promotion cause the government to respond? What factors influence the extent of government response and the outcome of litigation? These highly relevant questions must be answered before an operating model can be achieved.

Simulation of behavior within the government sector is frustrated by the catchall phrases that appear in much documentation prepared by

[18] One of the more understandable discussions of this area is provided in McCarthy, *op. cit.*, Footnote 3, pp. 655–658.

[19] F. D. Buggie, "Lawful Discrimination in Marketing," *Journal of Marketing*, Vol. 26 (April 1962), pp. 1–8.

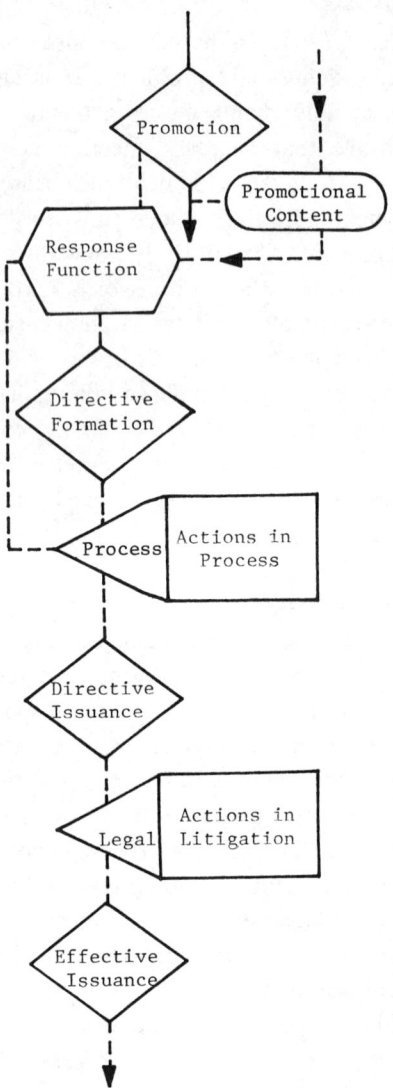

Figure 12.2. Representation of a typical government action.

government agencies. As an example, a booklet prepared by the Small Business Administration as a "small marketer's aid," which provides a reasonably precise specification of "practices regulated" such as "inducing discriminatory allowances," and "selling used items as new" concludes with a general statement against "employing any other false or misleading representation which deceives or has the capacity to deceive." [20] In the absence of definitions of that which may be considered to have "the capacity to deceive," logical representations developed on the basis of the specific proscriptions are, at best, incomplete.

Government Simulation — A Summary

While simulation of all aspects of government-corporation interaction may not be a realistic goal, models establishing the probability of government action under specified conditions have been developed and validated based on guidelines of the type discussed in the preceding sections.

Factors external to the government sector also influence the probability of government intervention. The applicability of government constraints in a system is, for example, a function of the products to which it relates. In some markets in which one or two large companies have been the focus of Federal Trade Commission and Justice Department action the government sector may be of great importance and substantial design sophistication is required. In working with other product markets the government sector may be all but ignored. For example, in markets in which regional manufacturers are an important element or major producers are medium-sized companies, reasonable freedom and even disregard of clear prohibitions are encountered.[21]

Applications of the generalized models discussed in Chapters 8 through 11 in specific product markets have included constraints representing the influence of major legislation as limiting conditions on competitive response. Such formulations normally provide a starting point from which more complete simulations are developed.

Consideration of the objectives a simulation system is designed to achieve leads to the question of whether actual government behavior or the action which manufacturers assume the government may take is more relevant. To the extent that manufacturer expectations or confusion result in the adoption of specific competitive policies, represen-

---

[20] D. R. Reel, "Small Business and Federal Trade Commission," *Small Marketers Aids Annual No. 2* (Washington, D. C.: Small Business Administration, 1960), pp. 8–9.

[21] For example, in one instant food market despite specific FTC positions on deceptive pricing, national manufacturers use two standard package sizes, the 5 cent off and the 10 cent off.

tation of actual as opposed to assumed government actions can be irrelevant.[22]

Summary

This chapter has examined the potential impact of research agent and government sectors on formulations developed in previous chapters. Salient attributes of behavior within each sector have been examined and macrocharacteristics of reaction and response models have been noted. Behavior within the research sector was found amenable to quantification although the applicability of specific model structures differs markedly among applications. Quantitative representation of actions taken by government agencies was found to be particularly difficult. Available guidelines at times support limiting constraint models, and in working with certain product lines it is possible to employ simplifying assumptions or ignore the effects of government action.

[22] For an example of manufacturer responses to the Robinson-Patman Act and other price-oriented legislation, see McCarthy, *op. cit.,* Footnote 3, pp. 660–664.

Chapter 13

TESTING AND VALIDATION OF SYSTEM PERFORMANCE

Testing and validation of simulation systems incorporating input and model structures of the type described in Chapters 7 through 12 have been in process since 1959. Various types of testing will be illustrated in this chapter using examples drawn from work based on these models. Data requirements and evaluation criteria will also be considered.

The Purposes of Testing

Tests of model-based systems are generally designed to evaluate either reliability or validity. Although this chapter is concerned primarily with validation, it is important to recognize the objectives associated with each type of testing.

Reliability Testing

Tests of reliability focus on reproducibility of results. In testing reliability one determines whether successive replications of a given system will reproduce within acceptable limits results obtained at one point in time. Various objective statistical tests may be used to establish confidence intervals with respect to the reliability question, which might be phrased, "Are the results obtained on sequential runs sufficiently alike to justify the assumption that they are two samples drawn from the same population of data?"

377

Validity Testing

Tests of validity are concerned with "truth." While reliability may be assessed using normal statistical techniques, there are no objective measures of truth.

The "truth" of a mathematical theorem has nothing at all to do with whether or not it actually describes any physical objects or events. As Wilson puts it, mathematics ". . . is based on 'axioms' which do not necessarily apply to any part of nature." [1] As an example, the field of plane geometry is built on certain basic definitions and assumptions; a triangle is defined in a certain way, and so is a right angle. Given these axioms, it is possible to deduce the familiar theorem that the length of the side opposite the right angle (the "hypotenuse") is equal to the square root of the sum of the squares of the other two sides. This result is "true" regardless of whether there really is any such thing as a "triangle" or a "right angle." . . . Thus, the use of a mathematical model to represent objects and events in marketing rests squarely on the very broad and general assumption that the axioms of one or more branches of mathematics are legitimate statements when applied to some aspect of the marketing process. [2]

In the absence of objective measures, the researcher must turn to a subjective evaluation of the consistency of the model's performance with theory and prior knowledge.

Models and Reality

Models are used by men to structure environments in which they must make decisions. Although models are designed to represent aspects of reality, they must always abstract from the real situation. While embodying certain attributes of that situation, they cannot duplicate all characteristics of reality.

Precision and Validity

When models are vague and general, their connection with reality is not apt to be questioned. An economic growth model is accepted for

[1] E. Bright Wilson, Jr., *An Introduction to Scientific Research* (New York: McGraw-Hill Book Company, Inc., 1952), p. 31.

[2] R. D. Buzzell, *Mathematical Models and Marketing Management* (Cambridge, Mass.: Harvard University Press, 1964), p. 14.

what it is — a simplified representation of certain attributes of a complex situation. In contrast, when one encounters highly precise mathematical or logical models describing a situation in terms of the carefully structured conventions of a formal language, the problem of assessing the validity of the model becomes more acute. Rigorous analysis and precise mathematical representation convey an aura of validity. It is sometimes difficult to remember that precise modeling may lead to a thoroughly documented but totally wrong conclusion. Assumptions embodied in authoritative equations and conclusions summarized in computer-prepared graphs often go unchallenged on the premise that "the scientific method" is predestined to reveal profound truths.

Assumptions and Realism

In final analysis, the validity of a model can be established only by examining the realism of the assumptions on which it is based. But what does it mean to assert that an assumption is "unrealistic"? In many instances this statement simply reveals that the individual making the assumption and the one evaluating it have different perceptions of the world.

In simplest terms, the model is "realistic" if it corresponds to — represents the salient attributes of — that which it is designed to model. A model is "realistic" if it duplicates the relevant characteristics of the "real" situation.

Turing has suggested that if a person knowledgeable in the area to be modeled, a person having experience with relevant reality, cannot distinguish the model from the real situation when provided with responses from both the model and the real situation, the model is realistic.[3]

The information provided to the observer using the Turing test is clearly determined by the context in which the reality of the model is to be evaluated. The attributes considered relevant will be determined by the proposed use of the model. Similarly, in developing models for use by marketing management, it is difficult to discuss the realism of a model without considering the functions which the model is to perform — the objectives that the manager wishes to achieve by using the model.

The validity of behavioral models of the type developed in earlier

[3] A. M. Turing, "Computing Machinery and Intelligence," *MIND*, Vol. 59 (October 1950), pp. 433–460.

chapters is often compared unfavorably with that of models employed by the physical scientist. Tracing the development of scientific models of the type developed by Euclid and Galileo, Churchman reaches the conclusion that

. . . the so-called "facts" of science exist only because the scientist has been bold enough to make assumptions. We can't measure angles without assuming a lot about the physical world. We can't measure velocities without assuming a lot about the mechanisms of clocks.

The more we want to know about a particular thing, the more we have to assume about the whole world. If a man is satisfied to experience Nature in a gross way, he can be modest about his beliefs. *The more he wants to learn about Nature in a precise manner, the more he must be willing to extend his power to believe.*

Hence, we have arrived at a conclusion about the manner in which the models of science are tested and, therefore, become realistic. As the tests become more precise, the need to assume about reality becomes greater. The more realistic a certain aspect of a model becomes, the greater the need to make assumptions that have not been tested.[4]

Tests of Validity

Tests of validity may be applied with varying degrees of rigor. When testing systems of the type considered in this chapter, five levels of validation may be distinguished. These include tests focusing on (1) viability, (2) stability, (3) consistency, (4) duplication of historical conditions, and (5) prediction of future states.

Tests of Viability

The term "viability" is used by Balderston and Hoggatt in discussing market simulation testing.

. . . our first concern in scheduling runs of the model was to establish its *viability:* that is, its ability, under plausible initial conditions and parameter settings, to generate behavior over time. . . .

It may appear transparently simple to demand that a model of this type merely exhibit persistent behavior, but this is a first requirement that may in fact fail to be met. We may then ask what accounts for the viability of the model. Do the initial conditions and parameter settings of the model

[4] C. W. Churchman, "Reliability of Models in the Social Sciences" in P. Langhoff (ed.), *Models, Measurement, and Marketing* (Englewood Cliffs, N. J.: Prentice-Hall, Inc., 1965), pp. 23–38, pp. 32–33.

guarantee viability, thus removing strength from the assertion that the model's capability in this regard is a significant test of its usefulness, *or* can we claim that the model's viability is evidence that it illuminates important features of the real-world system which serves as its background? . . .

Viability, in the sense in which we have used the term, is a quite weak condition on our dynamic system. It does not require that *equilibrium* be achieved, but only that behavior should persist over a significant time interval.[5]

Tests of Stability

A second level of model validation demands stability within the simulation structure for variables or processes that are known to be stable in the real-world environment. In testing the previously referenced model Balderston and Hoggatt hypothesize that average prices, physical commodity flow, number of suppliers, wholesalers, and retailers, and average profits ". . . will attain a narrow band of fluctuation after the completion of an interval of transition." [6] Their purpose in making these assumptions is

. . . to enforce some advance focus on the question of whether the model attains a steady state. For each variable taken by itself, of course, the discovery that it does or does not stabilize may serve as a basis for further investigation and analysis. It may be asked what limits of variation through time are specified so that a variable whose values fall inside these limits may be said to be reasonably stable, and one whose values fall outside may be said to call for rejection of the stability hypothesis. This is an old issue in the descriptive statistics of time series analysis.[7]

Tests of Consistency

A third type of model validation is concerned with consistency between model behavior and behavior observed in the real world. In its most fundamental form this is a test of "face validity."

Partly because of the intuitive suspicion of "purely statistical" relationships, most executives (and most researchers as well) apply another kind of test — that of "face validity." This means two things: (1) the extent to which the assumptions of a model agree with known facts, and (2) the internal consistency or "deductive veracity" of the model. At least in the

[5] F. E. Balderston and A. C. Hoggatt, *Simulation of Marketing Processes, Institute of Business and Economic Research,* University of California, Berkeley, 1962, pp. 32–33.

[6] *Ibid.,* p. 62.

[7] *Ibid.,* pp. 60–61.

early stages this is usually the key test of a model; if it does not "make sense," development of a model is not likely to be pursued for long.[8]

"Sensitivity testing" may be considered as one form of consistency evaluation. When conducting sensitivity tests, inputs to the model (or parameter values within the model structure) are varied between expected limits and the response of the model is examined to determine whether the sensitivity of the system is comparable to the observed sensitivity of the real-world environment.

Duplication of Historical Conditions

One of the more stringent tests of model validity focuses on the ability of the system to duplicate behavior observed in the real world at a particular point in time. Tests of the system's ability to duplicate historical behavior require that the model be initialized with parameter values and population distributions equivalent to those existing in the actual environment at a particular time. Inputs duplicating those supplied to the real-world environment during the test period (e.g., advertising, pricing, and product actions taken by competitors) are also supplied to the simulation. The response of the simulation manifest in the time paths of relevant variables and the terminal state of relevant population distributions is then compared with data describing the response of the actual environment. The validity of the model is evaluated in terms of the correspondence between simulated and actual conditions.

Prediction of Future Conditions

From the standpoint of system evaluation the difference between historical simulation and future prediction is largely a matter of showmanship. From the management planner's point of view, the distinction is more substantive. A properly conducted simulation test duplicates all conditions of a future prediction in that the system beginning from point of initialization moves through time into the simulated future without having access to information regarding the actual state of the real world at a comparable point in time. In the case of historical simulation, the model is being asked to answer the question, "What happened *when* these conditions existed?" In predicting future response, the system is being asked, "What would happen *if* these conditions were to exist?"

[8] Buzzell, *op. cit.,* Footnote 2, p. 52.

An extreme position on the question of how models should be tested holds that the *only* test is that of *prediction*. One operations researcher says flatly that "a good model is one that makes correct predictions."

The test of prediction implies that one cannot judge a model until it has been used over a period of time sufficient to make comparison of actual results with predictions. This leaves open the question of how the model can be evaluated without waiting for such a period of time. One approach is to use the model to make "pseudo prediction" of *past* results. For obvious reasons this approach can be used only if past data are separated into two (or more) groups, since it would be meaningless to "predict" the same data on which the model itself was based.

A basic difficulty with the criterion of prediction is that no model can be expected to predict *exactly*. . . . If exact prediction is highly unlikely, then, "how good" must the prediction be to constitute a "good" model? [9]

Data Requirements

The preceding discussion has tacitly assumed that requisite data describing conditions in the real world in appropriate detail are available. In fact, the generation and evaluation of data appropriate for testing often requires major expenditures of time and money as well as substantial imagination.

Use of Aggregate Statistical Data

Much of the aggregate statistical data generated through traditional market research is inadequate to provide references for the validation of a simulation model. Guy Orcutt, whose extensive work with microanalytic simulation has been noted previously, comments as follows.

Highly aggregative time series simply do not begin to contain enough degrees of freedom to permit extensive testing and estimation. This would be true even if the observations in such series resulted from well planned experiments. In fact, the available aggregative series are highly auto-correlated, highly multi-collinear, are frequently poor measures of what we want to measure and frequently do not measure short run developments, and are imbedded in an operating system involving many relatively rapid feedbacks. All this only compounds the already apparent drawbacks of estimation and testing based only on highly aggregative time series. [10]

[9] *Ibid.,* pp. 51–52.

[10] G. H. Orcutt, "Views on Simulation and Models of Social Systems," Hoggatt and Balderston (eds.), *Symposium on Simulation Models: Methodology and Applications to the Behavioral Sciences* (Cincinnati, Ohio: Southwestern Publishing Company, 1963), p. 223.

The validation of detailed functions within a microanalytic simulation requires the generation of data at a sufficient level of detail (disaggregation) to permit examination of relationships describing behavior at a microlevel.

Estimation and testing problems abound even when conducted using observations on micro-units, but at least one can have an enormous body of unplanned experiments to work with. These unplanned experiments may be observed in great detail at very frequent intervals and they do involve wide ranges of variation in the variables. At the micro level, there are frequently cases in which variables we would have liked to vary do in fact vary and in which other variables we would have liked to hold constant do remain constant.[11]

Data for Function Validation

Consideration of the data required for validation of the various functions developed in preceding chapters should make clear the unique data requirements of a microanalytic simulation. It is, for example, necessary to develop data on the purchase behavior of consumers categorized in terms of the attributes defined in Chapter 8. In addition to the requirement for microdata, the use of the attitude and awareness variables necessitates generation of information which is not produced in the course of normal market research.[12]

Parameter Values

When generalized model structures are adapted for description of behavior associated with a particular product, market scaling constants used to achieve model sensitivity must be set to values corresponding with observed behavior in that market.

Parameter estimation for a process model involves many problems other than simple data collection.

The problems of parameter estimation have, of course, been much discussed in statistical and economic literature. A major advance has been the proof that unbiased and efficient estimates can be obtained only by acknowledging the simultaneity of the equations of a model. If this result carries over to

---

[11] *Ibid.,* p. 223.
[12] Measurement procedures followed in developing attitude and awareness data are summarized in Chapter 5.

computer process models, obtaining maximum likelihood estimates of all parameters in such models will be a forbidding task.[13]

Manufacturer Sector Inputs

If a simulation model is to be used to describe either conditions that existed under specified historical circumstances or conditions that might exist at times in the future, historical or assumed future actions and responses of competitive manufacturers operating in the marketing environment must be specified. Values for variables specified in Chapter 7 must either be provided as input or established through decision rules representing assumed competitive behavior.

Requisite inputs can be generated. Historical data covering relevant parameters for substantial periods of time have been generated in specific industries. The generation of such data does, however, require substantial expenditures of time and money and the development of specialized measuring techniques designed to obtain the specific inputs required by the simulation model.

Data Describing Individual Behavior

Data representing the behavior of individual consumers, retailers, distributors, or salesmen require that reasonably large sample panels be interviewed using specialized techniques at frequent intervals. Data generated by established commercial panels of the type maintained by the Market Research Corporation of America and the *Chicago Tribune* can provide useful guidelines; however, in most instances, it is necessary to supplement such sources with specially designed panels established for the purpose of generating information required to validate and initialize functions within the simulation.

Model Testing and Validation

The remainder of this chapter is devoted to testing and validation procedures used in conjunction with simulation systems based on models of the type described in previous chapters. Seven aspects of testing will be discussed. These are (1) establishing functional forms, (2) setting parameter values, (3) decision and response function testing, (4) testing

---

[13] R. M. Cyert and James G. March, *A Behavioral Theory of the Firm* (Englewood Cliffs, N. J.: Prentice-Hall, 1963).

simulated sector behavior at the individual level, (5) testing simulated sector behavior at the population level, (6) testing subsystem interactions (interactions between one or more sectors), and (7) total system performance.

Establishing Functional Forms

Models of the type being discussed are initially developed on the basis of theory and observation. The model builder theorizes that certain behavior may be expected by individuals exhibiting specified attributes. Although it may be a relatively simple matter to determine the direction of an effect — whether the attribute will increase or decrease the probability of the action — validation of the relationship between the observed attribute and behavior requires the generation and analysis of data.

In this section, the validation of three functional forms developed as part of models presented in earlier chapters is discussed. Functions considered are (1) the effect of attitude on purchase, (2) the effect of attitude toward appeals on noting a promotion, and (3) the effect of display size on point-of-sale display placement.

Effect of Attitude on Purchase

The discussion summarized in Equation 8.4 concludes that consumer attitude toward a brand influences probability of purchase. Attitude is assumed to be positively correlated with purchase — a positive attitude is considered more likely to yield purchase than a negative attitude. Beyond this point, the form of the proposed relationship is based on analysis of the proportion of consumer panel members indicating each of the eleven brand attitudes who, on their most recent purchase, bought that brand. The interview procedure employed was that discussed in Chapter 5.[14] Data presented in this example are based on 900 interviews in the Metropolitan Boston area during August 1959.

Table 13.1 summarizes data obtained for two frequently purchased items, a dairy product, and a frozen food. This table indicates the number of respondents in each brand attitude category and the number and percent of respondents having each brand attitude who, on their purchase, bought that brand. The fifth column of Table 13.1 indicates the predicted level of purchase for each attitude category based on the Equation 8.4 formulation, with sample values used for scaling constants. These data are also plotted in Figure 13.1.

[14] See interview procedure p. 97.

TABLE 13.1. *Proportion Having Attitude Who Purchase*

Attitude Scale	Dairy Product			Frozen Food			Function Effect
	Pur-chasers	Number	Percent	Pur-chasers	Number	Percent	
+5	327	392	83	115	262	44	1.0
4	31	51	60	21	54	39	.67
3	50	111	45	25	98	26	.45
2	17	51	33	6	51	12	.30
+1	15	59	25	9	72	12	.20
—	12	109	11	42	283	15	.13
−1	2	25	08	—	18	—	.10
2	2	19	10	—	15	—	.08
3	2	15	13	1	11	09	.05
4	1	17	05	—	10	—	.03
−5	1	39	07	—	14	—	—
Total		888			888		

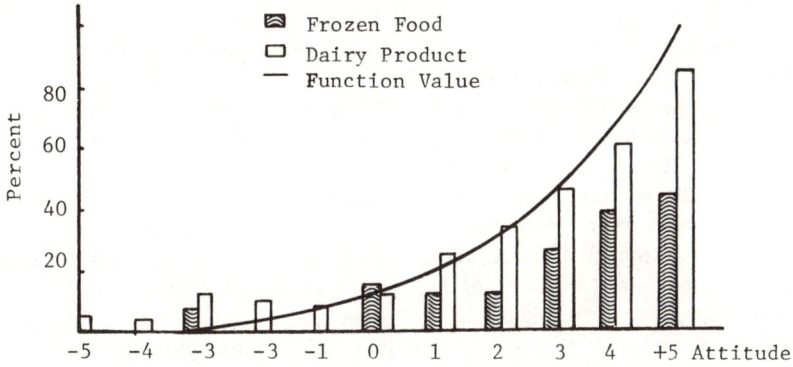

Figure 13.1. Proportion of population attitude groups who purchase.

Effect of Advertising Appeals on Assimilation

The probability of a consumer assimilating (gaining cognizance sufficient to support unaided recall) a communication has been expressed as a function of consumer attitude toward appeals used in the communication as summarized in Equation 8.15.

Data on which this formulation was based were developed during pretest interviews studying consumer response to two alternative promotional campaigns. Neither campaign had been used previously in the area in which the interviews were conducted, and it is reasonable to assume that the consumers had not been exposed to the promotion prior to the interview.

The research concerned the use of two appeals in promotion for a food product. The first appeal emphasizing the qualities that made this product particularly desirable as a diet food will be described as the "diet" appeal. The second appeal relating to the introduction of a "bright, new package," judged to add substantially to the product's visual appeal, will be referred to as the "package" appeal.

Data were obtained from a sample of 500 women in the Metropolitan Boston area using the following interview procedure.

The interview was divided into two sections. At the beginning of the first section the woman was informed that the interviewer was "interested in finding out about factors that women consider important when purchasing various products." Using the attitude scale measure discussed in Chapter 5,[15] each respondent was shown the attitude scale, given the explanation of its use discussed earlier, and asked to indicate, "how you feel about these factors as characteristics of bread, bacon, butter, milk, etc." The woman's response to each question was noted by the interviewer.

In the second section of the interview the respondent was told "we would like to get your opinion of some of today's advertising. This book contains some sample advertisements of the type used by many companies. Would you please look at it. Take as long as you like. After you have finished I would like to get some opinions from you."

After the woman completed examination of the book, she was asked, "do you remember seeing an ad for . . . bread . . . ?" If she responded affirmatively the interviewer would then ask, "do you recall what it said?" The information (playback of content) was recorded by the interviewer. The interviewer then asked "do you think this was a good ad?" The woman's comments were noted by the interviewer although these data were not used.

The third question was added in order to justify the contention of interest in the woman's opinion and to de-emphasize the playback question. In the absence of the third question, the playback inquiry appeared to be a test of the woman's memory. With the addition of the third question, the playback request was interpreted as a means for the interviewer to ensure that she and the woman were talking about the

[15] B. S. Greene, "Attitude Measurement," in Lindzey (ed.), *Handbook of Social Psychology,* Vol. I (Cambridge, Mass.: Addison-Wesley Publishing Company, Inc., 1954), pp. 335–369.

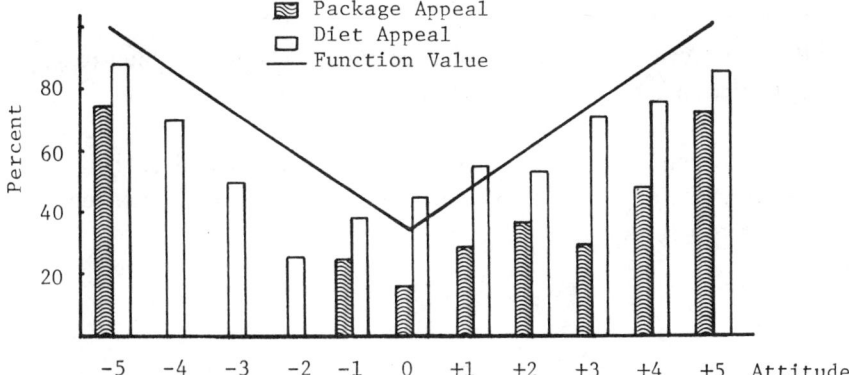

Figure 13.2. Effect of attitude on communication playback.

same advertisement. There were different advertisements for the same product present in the portfolio.

The results of this interview series are summarized in Table 13.2 and Figure 13.2. Table 13.2 indicates the proportion of those interviewed having specific attitudes toward each appeal who gave substantial playback for either the diet advertisement or the package advertisement. Predicted relative playback based on the Equation 8.15 formulation is also noted in Table 13.2. Data are illustrated in Figure 13.2.

TABLE 13.2. *Effect of Attitude on Communication Playback*

Attitude Scores	Diet Appeal			Package Appeal			Function Effect*
	Play-backs	Number	Percent	Play-backs	Number	Percent	
+5	62	74	84	32	45	71	1.0
4	32	43	75	14	24	58	.87
3	21	30	70	2	7	29	.74
2	29	56	52	7	19	37	.60
+1	22	41	54	45	161	28	.46
—	57	133	43	33	205	16	.33
−1	12	31	39	2	8	25	.46
2	2	8	25	—	—	—	.60
3	7	14	50	—	—	—	.74
4	12	17	70	—	—	—	.87
−5	23	26	89	3	4	75	1.0
Total		473			473		

* Normalized to 1.0

Effect of Point-of-Sale Display Size on Placement

Previous formulations of retailer decisions relating to point-of-sale display placement were based on the contention that available space influences the retailer's probability of placing a point-of-sale display. The relationship summarized in Equation 9.16 was based on data obtained from 20 appliance retailers carrying a similar brand complement in the Greater Boston area.

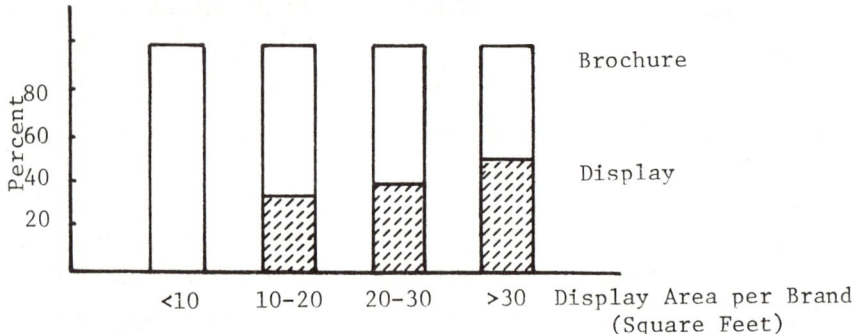

Figure 13.3. Proportion of stores placing point-of-sale material.

Data were obtained when the manufacturer of a brand carried by all 20 outlets simultaneously made available through distributors a full-color foldout brochure illustrating the product line and a 2-foot by 3-foot base stand-up display approximately 6 feet in height. The salesman calling on the retailers offered both types of point-of-sale material at no cost to the retailer. Table 13.3 and Figure 13.3 indicate the level of

TABLE 13.3. Effect of Display Space on Point-of-Sale Placement

Display Space*	Brochure Placement			Display Placement		
	Place-ment	Number	Percent	Place-ment	Number	Percent
<10	2	2	100	—	2	—
10–20	9	9	100	3	9	33
20–30	5	5	100	2	5	40
>30	4	4	100	2	4	50

* Area (square feet) per brand carried.

acceptance of each type of material as a function of available display area divided by number of brands carried.

Setting Parameter Values

Once functional forms have been established, population parameters must be initialized to reflect the actual distribution of specified attributes among population members. Data of the type discussed in the preceding section may be used for this purpose.

Initialization of Brand Attitude Variables

Initial brand attitude distributions may be established using data obtained while evaluating the effect of attitude on purchase. The proportion of the population having particular brand attitudes is a natural end product of this interview procedure. Table 13.4 and Figure 13.4 contain

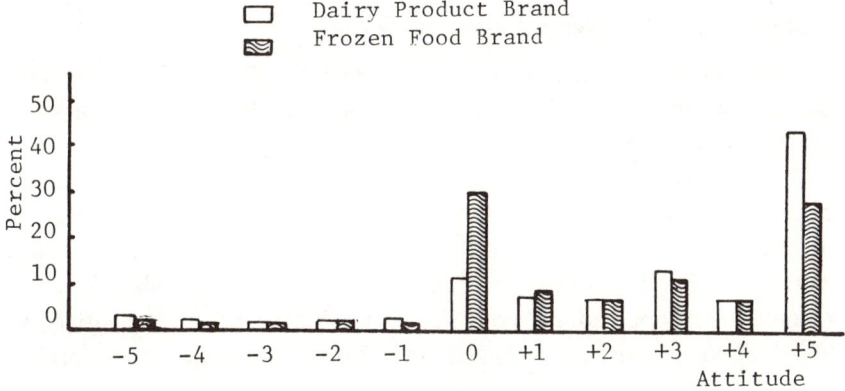

Figure 13.4. Population distribution of attitude toward two brands.

population figures for the dairy product and frozen food analyzed previously in Table 13.1.

Initialization of Appeals Orientation

In a similar fashion the predisposition of the population toward appeals may be established from data obtained when evaluating the effect of advertising appeals on assimilation. The distribution of attitudes toward diet and package appeals associated with the food product discussed previously are summarized in Table 13.5 and Figure 13.5.

TABLE 13.4. *Population Distribution of Attitudes toward Two Brands*

Attitude Score	Dairy Product		Frozen Food	
	Number	Percent	Number	Percent
+5	392	44	262	29
4	51	06	54	06
3	111	13	98	11
2	51	06	51	06
+1	59	07	72	08
—	109	12	283	32
−1	25	03	18	02
2	19	02	15	02
3	15	01	11	01
4	17	02	10	01
−5	39	04	14	02
Total	888	100%	888	100%

Decision and Response Function Testing

The previously noted research examining the effect of attitude on purchase is indicative of the testing required to determine the impact of one factor entering a decision function.

Because the orientation variables, attitude and awareness, are used extensively in these models, substantial time has been devoted to exploring the relationships between these variables and various aspects of consumer behavior. Research of the type described in Table 13.1 is focused at the population level. The relationship between these variables and individual purchase behavior has also been studied. "The prob-

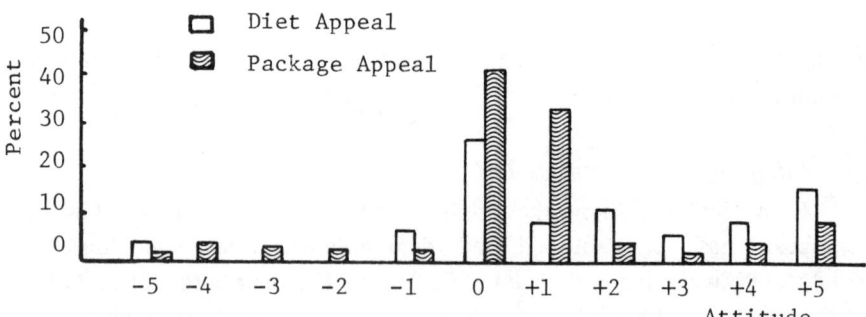

Figure 13.5. Population distribution of attitude toward two appeals.

TABLE 13.5. *Population Distribution of Attitude toward Two Appeals*

Attitude Score	Diet Appeal		Package Appeal	
	Number	Percent	Number	Percent
+5	74	16	45	10
4	43	09	24	05
3	30	06	7	01
2	56	12	19	04
+1	41	09	161	34
—	133	27	205	43
−1	31	07	8	02
2	8	02	—	—
3	14	03	—	—
4	17	04	—	—
−5	26	05	4	01
Total	473	100%	473	100%

ability that an individual consumer will purchase one or more units of a particular brand of a particular product within an arbitrary time period" was investigated by C. R. Sprague in 1961.[16] He found a function based on the product of the individual attitude and awareness scores positively correlated with last brand purchased at the 99 percent confidence level. Sprague further concluded that, in the steady state, the attitude and awareness variables can be used to predict probability of purchase and noted that there was evidence that the degree of correlation between the orientation variables and last brand purchased was dependent on product availability.

An example of response function testing is provided by the previously discussed data linking attitude toward advertising appeals content with assimilation. The test described was one of a series conducted in developing the selective perception functions presented in Chapter 8.[17]

Simulated Individual Behavior

The next level of testing to be considered examines operating characteristics of a sector model to determine whether the behavior exhibited by a single simulated member of the sector population is consistent with

[16] See C. R. Sprague, "A Method of Estimating Consumer Probability of Purchase," Unpublished Bachelor's Thesis, Sloan School of Management (Cambridge, Mass.: Massachusetts Institute of Technology, 1961).

[17] See "Consumer Exposure and Response to Media Communication," Chapter 8, p. 185.

expectations based on data from the real world. An example of this type of testing is provided by Exhibit 13.1, which contains output generated by the Chapter 8 consumer model operating in an appliance market simulation.

```
          SIMULATION APP-03 TEST RUN APRIL 4, 1965  1400 HOURS


-- CONSUMER 0109 NOW BEGINNING WEEK 117  --    FEBRUARY 19, 1962

    - REPORT MONITOR SPECIFIED.  TO CANCEL PUSH INTERRUPT.

    - CHARAC - REGION NE SU, AGE 25-35, INCOME 8-10K, EDUCATION COLLEG

    - BRANDS OWN 3, 6 YEARS OLD.  RETAILER PREFERENCE 05, 11, 03

    - MEDIA AVAILABLE 1 0 0 1 0 0 0 0 1 1 1 1 0 0 0 0 0 0 0 0 0 0 0 0

    - ATTITUDES .  1    2    3    4    5    6    7    8    9   10   11   12

        ............................................................

        PROD CHAR .  0   +1   +1    0   -3   -1    0   +5    0   +3    0    0
        APPEALS    . -3    0   +1   +5    0   -3   +3    0    0    0   +5    0
        BRANDS     . +2   +1   +3   +2
        RETAILERS  . +1   -5   +3   +1   +5   -5   -5   +1   -1   -3   +5   +1
                   . -3   +1   -1   +3   +1   +1
        AWARENESS  .  1    0    0    0

    - MEMORY DUMP FOLLOWS.  BRANDS LISTED IN DESCENDING ORDER 1 TO 4

    PRODUCT CHARACTERISTIC MEMORY              APPEALS MEMORY


  .  .  .  .  .  .  .  .  .  .  .  .  .  .  .  .  .  .  .  .  .  .  .  .  .
  1  2  3  4  5  6  7  8  9 10 11 12 . 1  2  3  4  5  6  7  8  9 10 11 12
  .  .  .  .  .  .  .  .  .  .  .  .  .  .  .  .  .  .  .  .  .  .  .  .  .

  2  3 15  0  5  5  4 14  8  7  1  3 . 8  9  7  3  1 11  7  4  4  3  9  3
  8  0  6  4  9  5  4 13  0  3  6  7 . 6  8  0  7  0  9  2  4  3 10  3  1
  0  6 15  7  0  3 11  3  5  2  5  7 . 0  4  8 10  9  2 14  3  9  7  9  5
  7  9  3  7  3  2  7  2  6 12 14  2 . 0  9  7  8 13  9 11  6  0  2  5  9


        - MEDIA EXPOSURE INITIATED

              - MEDIUM 003 APPEARS IN WEEK 117 -- NO EXPOSURES
              - MEDIUM 004 APPEARS IN WEEK 117
                  - EXPOSURE TO AD 013, BRAND 3 -- NO NOTING
                  - EXPOSURE TO AD 019, BRAND 4
                      - AD 109, BRAND 4 NOTED.  CONTENT FOLLOWS
                      - PROD. C 11 P = 4,   4 P = 2,
                      - APPEALS  5 P = 2,   7 P = 2, 12 P = 2,
              - MEDIUM 007 APPEARS IN WEEK 117 -- NO EXPOSURES
              - MEDIUM 012 APPEARS IN WEEK 117
                  - EXPOSURE TO AD 007, BRAND 2
                      - AD 007, BRAND 2 NOTED.  CONTENT FOLLOWS
                      - PROD. C  8 P = 3, 12 P = 1,
                      - APPEALS  2 P = 1,   4 P = 1,   6 P = 1,   10 P = 1,
                  - EXPOSURE TO AD 013, BRAND 3 -- NO NOTING
                  - EXPOSURE TO AD 004, BRAND 1 -- NO NOTING
              - MEDIUM 016 APPEARS IN WEEK 117 -- NO EXPOSURES
              - MEDIUM 023 APPEARS IN WEEK 117 -- NO EXPOSURES
```

Exhibit 13.1. Simulated individual consumer behavior. Part I.

```
        - WORD OF MOUTH EXPOSURE INITIATED

                - EXPOSURE TO CONSUMER 0093 -- NO NOTING
                - EXPOSURE TO CONSUMER 0104 -- NO NOTING
                - EXPOSURE TO CONSUMER 0117 -- NO NOTING

        - NO PRODUCT USE IN WEEK 117

        - DECISION TO SHOP POSITIVE -- BRAND 3 HIGH PERCEIVED NEED
                                    -- RETAILER 05 CHOSEN

        - SHOPPING INITIATED

                - CONSUMER DECISION EXPLICIT FOR BRAND 3 -- NO SEARCH
                - PRODUCT EXPOSURE FOR BRAND 3
                        - EXPOSURE TO POINT OF SALE 008 FOR BRAND 3
                            - POS 008, BRAND 3 NOTED.  CONTENT FOLLOWS
                            - PROD. C  3 P = 4,  6 P = 4,
                            - APPEALS  5 P = 2,  7 P = 2,  10 P = 2,  11 P = 2,
                - NO SELLING EFFORT EXPOSURE IN RETAILER 05

        - DECISION TO PURCHASE POSITIVE -- BRAND 3, $ 38.50

                - DELIVERY IMEDAT
                - OWNERSHIP = 3, AWARENESS WAS 2, NOW 3

        - WORD OF MOUTH GENERATION INITIATED

                - CONTENT GENERATED, BRAND 3
                        - PROD. C  3 P = +15,  8 P = +15,
                        - APPEALS  4 P = +50,  11 P = +45

        - FORGETTING INITIATED -- NO FORGETTING

    -- CONSUMER 0109 NOW CONCLUDING WEEK 117   --   FEBRUARY 25, 1962

    -- CONSUMER 0110 NOW BEGINNING WEEK 117    --   FEBRUARY 19, 1962


    QUIT,
    R 11.633+4.750
```

Exhibit 13.1. Simulated individual consumer behavior. Part II.

The Exhibit 13.1 output is a detailed, step-by-step report of the activities of an artificial consumer cell during one simulated week. The week chosen for illustration includes both shopping and purchase; however, in the case of an appliance market simulation this is infrequent behavior exhibited once every five years for the average consumer. Thus some simulated consumers in this environment do not make a purchase or even shop during a five-year simulation cycle.

With reference to Exhibit 13.1, the behavior of simulated consumer No. 109 may be described as follows.

Initiation of a Simulated Week

The first line of output following the standard report title indicates that consumer 109 is beginning simulated week No. 117 based on data

applicable to the week beginning Monday, February 19, 1962. The
second line of output refers to the fact that a detailed report of this
consumer's activity has been requested and gives the option to cancel
the detailed output.[18]

Consumer Characteristic Specifications

The information provided beginning with the third line of output
identifies characteristic attributes of consumer 109. The output specifies
that he is a suburban (SU) resident of New England (NE) and between
25 and 35 years of age. His income is between $8,000 and $10,000 per
year, and he has a college education. At present he owns a product of
brand 3 manufacture purchased 6 years previously.

Consumer 109's retailer preferences favor retailers 5, 11, and 3 in that
order. He subscribes to or otherwise has available media of types 1, 4,
9, 10, 11, and 12. Media of types 2, 3, 5, 6, 7, 8, and 13 through 24 are
not available to him.

Consumer 109's attitudes are summarized in a matrix indicating his
orientation toward 12 product characteristics, 12 appeals, 4 brands, and
18 retailers. This matrix indicates, for example, that his highest product-
characteristic-oriented attitude is toward characteristic 8, which he
regards very highly (+5), while his highest appeals attitudes are toward
appeals 11 and 4. From the retailer attitude set, his preference for
retailers 11 and 5 (both +5 attitudes) and 3 or 16 (both +3 attitudes)
may be established.[19] The final entry in the orientation matrix indicates
that consumer 109 is aware of brand 1.

Consumer Memory Content

The line stating MEMORY DUMP FOLLOWS. BRANDS LISTED
IN DESCENDING ORDER 1 THROUGH 4 introduces the printout
of consumer 109's present simulated memory content. This memory
dump is a record of noted communications retained by the consumer,
relating specific product characteristics and appeals to each of the four
brands. From this report it can be established, for example, that con-

---

[18] The Figure 13.6 output was generated on a 1050 remote access console communicating with the M.I.T. Compatible Time Sharing System computer. This
simulation is programmed to permit modification of previous instructions via an
"interrupt" procedure.

[19] The system has been programmed to handle equal attitudes by giving preference to the numerically lowest index value. Thus retailer 5 is given preference
over retailer 11, while retailer 3 is given preference over retailer 16.

sumer 109 has retained 14 communication exposures associating product characteristic 8 with brand 1, 13 exposures relating product characteristic 8 with brand 2, and 14 exposures associating appeal 7 with brand 3.

Media Exposure and Response

The entry in the report following the memory dump indicates that the simulation segment representing media exposure processes has become operational. Six media appear (are published or broadcast) during week 117. Consumer 109 is not exposed to medium 3 because that medium is not available to him (see media availability indicator in the characteristic output). Media 4 also appears in week 117 and because this medium is available to consumer 109 he may be exposed to relevant advertisements appearing in it. The output indicates that he was exposed to an advertisement for brand 3 but did not assimilate (note) that communication. On the other hand, an advertisement for brand 4, also present in medium 4 during week 117, was assimilated as indicated by the line reading ADVERTISEMENT 19, BRAND 4 NOTED. CONTENT FOLLOWS. The output message then indicates that advertisement 19 contained a reference to product characteristic 11 with a prominence of 4 and a reference to characteristic 4 having a prominence of 2. Advertisement 19 also contains references to appeals 5, 7, and 12 with 2.0 prominences.

Consumer 109 did not see medium 7, although it appeared in week 117; however, he was exposed to three advertisements in medium 12, which also appeared during that week. The advertisement for brand 2 was assimilated while the advertisements for brands 3 and 1 were not. The brand 2 advertisement discussed characteristics 8 and 12, with prominence of 3 and 1, respectively, and referenced appeals 2, 4, 6, and 10, all with a minimal prominence of 1.

Media 16 and 23 also appeared in week 117 but were not seen by consumer 109.

Word-of-Mouth Exposure

The next entry in the report following the media exposure section indicates that consumer 109 was exposed to word-of-mouth comment generated by consumers 93, 104, and 117, but failed to note communication from any of these individuals. Had noting occurred, a message content report comparable to that generated for advertising would have been printed specifying the information content noted.

Product Experience

The next entry in the report specifies that consumer 109 did not have product experience during week 117. Had he made use of the product, a report of his response to product use indicating product characteristics or appeals, if any, emphasized by the use experience, would have been printed.

Decision to Shop

The next entry in the Exhibit 13.1 output indicates that consumer 109 has made an explicit decision to shop, that his highest perceived need is for brand 3, and that his first choice retailer is 5. The next line indicates that simulation representing in-store experience has been initiated and the consumer is shopping.

In-Store Experience

The first entry within the SHOPPING INITIATED section notes that the consumer is exhibiting behavior associated with the explicit decision-to-shop option and is seeking brand 3 (there is therefore NO SEARCH activity — no opportunity for accidental exposure). Retailer 5 must have been carrying brand 3 because the next entry in the report indicates that consumer 109 has been exposed to brand 3 in retail outlet 5.

Retailer 5 has also placed point-of-sale display material for brand 3 as indicated by the output specifying that the consumer has been exposed to a specific point-of-sale piece and noted its content. In this case, the point-of-sale promotion emphasizes appeals 3 and 6 and product characteristics 5, 7, 10, and 11 as attributes of brand 3. Either retailer 5's salesmen are not actively engaged in pushing brand 3, or they are busy with other customers. In any event, consumer 109 is not exposed to selling effort while shopping in retailer outlet 5.

Decision to Purchase

The line of output stating DECISION TO PURCHASE POSITIVE — BRAND 03, $38.50, specifies that consumer 109 has made a decision to purchase brand 3 at a price of $38.50. The line following the decision to purchase statement indicates that retailer 5 can make immediate delivery of brand 3. In the event that he was out of stock or unable to supply, appropriately differentiated messages would have appeared in this location.

Response to Purchase

Because consumer 109 has now purchased brand 3 his awareness, which was favoring brand 2, is changed to favor brand 3.[20]

Word-of-Mouth Generation

As a proud owner of brand 3 product, consumer 109 initiates word-of-mouth comment regarding his new acquisition. The content of his communication regarding brand 3 emphasizes product characteristics 3 and 8 and appeals 4 and 11. These are the appeals and product characteristics toward which he has the highest perceived brand image as indicated in the previous memory dump.[21]

Forgetting

The FORGETTING line indicates that consumer 109 did not lose any of his existing memory content during week 117.

The final output line indicates that consumer 109 has concluded week 117. The remaining output is a result of the run being terminated at that point in the simulation process.

Simulated Population Behavior

The behavior of the population groups within each simulation sector is described in terms of variables derived from simulated individual behavior. Population output is normally presented as the proportion of purchases allocated to each brand of product (brand shares), changes in population attitude distributions toward brands, and changes in the perceived brand image for each brand held by a significant population segment. Sample outputs are provided in conjunction with the discussion of total system performance.

---

[20] Because the original orientation matrix output for consumer 109 showed awareness of brand 1 and his awareness at time of purchase had changed to brand 2, the advertisement that he noted for brand 2 must have resulted in an awareness shift favoring that brand.

[21] The specific situation illustrated may be somewhat confusing to those studying this output carefully. Prior to entering the store, consumer 109 had 15 noted and retained exposures toward product characteristic 3. The packing structure used to retain memory representation is limited to 4 binary bits with the result that no consumer can remember more than 15 exposures to a given appeal or product characteristic. As a result of this constraint, the point-of-sale promotion that consumer 109 noted and that related to characteristic 3 did not increase his memory associated with that attribute.

Subsystem Testing

Prior to total system testing, it is often desirable to examine particular aspects of the interactions between sector models. This form of testing in which one or more sectors of the model are treated as a subsystem is not conceptually different from the total system tests discussed below. The fundamental distinction between subsystem testing and total system testing is a matter of complexity, with the subsystem test involving a subset of the elements involved in total system operations.[22]

Total System Performance

Tests of total system performance are designed to examine characteristics of the simulation under conditions determined by test inputs. As an example, the performance of a food product market simulation based on models discussed in preceding chapters will be examined.

Test Conditions

The example to be considered involves validity testing based on the viability, stability, consistency, and duplication criteria discussed earlier in this chapter. The problem context is the introduction of a new product in a regional market in which a large national competitor has the predominant share, while four smaller companies are, at the time of introduction, splitting the remaining market among themselves.

The market test encompassed a period of 14 weeks during the spring and early summer and was conducted in a major metropolitan area in New England. At the conclusion of the 14-week test, promotion and distribution efforts for the new product were terminated.

Throughout the test market period, data required from the manufacturer sector were obtained for the company introducing the new product and its major competitor. The four small competitors were not considered in this simulation. Sixteen weeks following completion of the test, a final set of data was obtained to provide an indication of steady state conditions following consumer forgetting.

[22] For examples of subsystem testing see A. E. Amstutz and B. C. Hood, "Interim Report, Marketing Systems Research" (Sloan Research Fund Project 142) (M.I.T. Working Paper, July 1960), Sloan Research Project 142 Memorandum I–27 (Dated 7/29/59 as modified 8/14/59) and Sloan Research Project 142 Memorandum I–29 (Dated 8/14/59).

Initial Conditions

Initial conditions established for the consumer population model reflected attitude and product use conditions existing at the beginning of the test. Table 13.6 and Figure 13.6 summarize initial attitude distributions for the test market population. Both indicate the attitude scores for the new product and its major competitor as reported by 789 individuals interviewed prior to the introductory campaign.

TABLE 13.6.   Initialized Product Introduction Attitude Distribution

Attitude Score	Promoted Product		Competitive Brand	
	Number	Percent	Number	Percent
+5	27	3	445	57
4	—	—	39	5
3	—	—	83	11
2	—	—	47	6
+1	16	2	49	6
—	711	91	31	4
−1	13	2	25	3
2	—	—	8	1
3	—	—	17	2
4	—	—	19	2
−5	22	3	26	3
Total	789		789	

The company introducing the new product had well-established distribution in the test market area and was successfully marketing a broad line of associated products through outlets used for the test. Because stocking had begun during the week when initial condition interviews were conducted, some consumers had already encountered the product and others had already associated the new product name with its manufacturer. This limited product experience, association of product with manufacturer brand name, and unwillingness to admit lack of opinion about anything are responsible for the existence of positive and negative attitudes among a small portion of the population during the first interviews.

Comparative attitude distributions for the new product and its major competitor are illustrated in Figure 13.6.

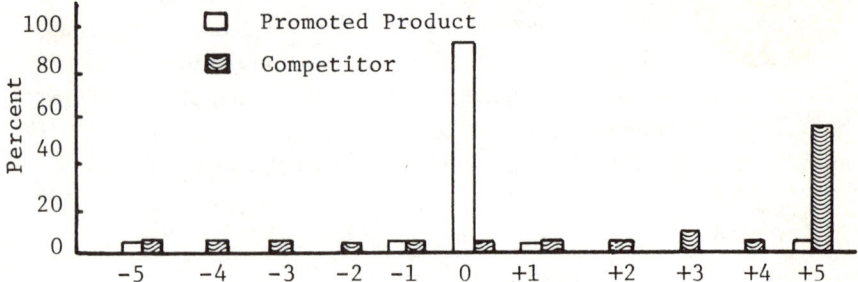

Figure 13.6. Initialized new product introduction. Attitude distribution.

Time Path Data

Table 13.7 indicates the brand share, attitude, and awareness values existing in the test market at 2-week intervals throughout the test and

TABLE 13.7.   New Product Introduction Time Paths — Actual

Time in Weeks	New Product			Competitive Brand		
	Brand Share	Attitude	Aware-ness	Brand Share	Attitude	Aware-ness
t_0	6%	—	5%	65%	+3.3	51.6%
$t_0 + 2$	9	—	—	64	—	—
$t_0 + 4$	16	+ .2	15	57	+3.6	53.2
$t_0 + 6$	27	+ .5	13	55	+3.1	52.9
$t_0 + 8$	33	+ .7	21	40	+2.8	55.7
$t_0 + 10$	28	+1.0	24	41	+2.6	53.0
$t_0 + 12$	23	+1.1	26	47	+2.8	56.0
$t_0 + 14$	30	+1.0	27	42	+2.9	54.0
$t_0 + 30$	12	+ .3	8	62	+3.4	51.0

16 weeks following completion of the test. Brand share measures are based on a 16-store retail audit, while the attitude and awareness variables are calculated following procedure specified in Chapter 5.

Table 13.8 contains the values for brand share, attitude, and awareness variables as generated by the market simulation operating with inputs describing conditions that existed in the test market during the specified period. Comparing Tables 13.7 and 13.8, it will be noted that while the actual brand share at time of initialization in the test market was 6 per-

TABLE 13.8.   New Product Introduction Time Paths — Simulated

	New Product			Competitive Brand		
Time in Weeks	Brand Share	Attitude	Aware-ness	Brand Share	Attitude	Aware-ness
t_0	0%	+0.0	0%	65%	+3.3	50. %
$t_0 + 2$	5	+ .2	2	65	+3.3	53.
$t_0 + 4$	15	+ .6	9	64	+3.5	58.
$t_0 + 6$	33	+1.1	20	61	+3.7	62.
$t_0 + 8$	38	+1.5	29	52	+3.7	57.
$t_0 + 10$	38	+1.7	35	47	+3.8	53.
$t_0 + 12$	36	+1.6	37	50	+3.8	53.
$t_0 + 14$	34	+1.5	37	57	+3.8	54.
$t_0 + 30$	17	+ .5	18	69	+3.7	58.

cent, due to the prestocking activity noted earlier, the simulation was initialized with a brand share of 0 for the new product while the major competitor was given the existing brand share. Percentages indicated for the simulation are based on a consumer sector model containing 1000 artificial consumers.

Model-Data Comparisons

Figures 13.7 through 13.10, Exhibit 13.2, and Table 13.9 provide comparisons between activity in the actual market and that developed by the simulation system.

Figure 13.7 illustrates the time paths of population attitude scores for

TABLE 13.9.   New Product Attitude Distribution at Period $t_0 + 14$

	New Product Distribution	
Attitude Score	Actual	Simulated
+5	13%	17%
4	4	11
3	6	8
2	3	5
1	3	3
—	67	51
−1	1	2
2	1	1
3	0	0
4	1	1
5	1	1

the new product and its major competitor. The solid line indicates actual data obtained from the market test, while the dotted line illustrates values generated by the simulated population. As will be evident from the examination of Figure 13.8, the simulation produced somewhat higher

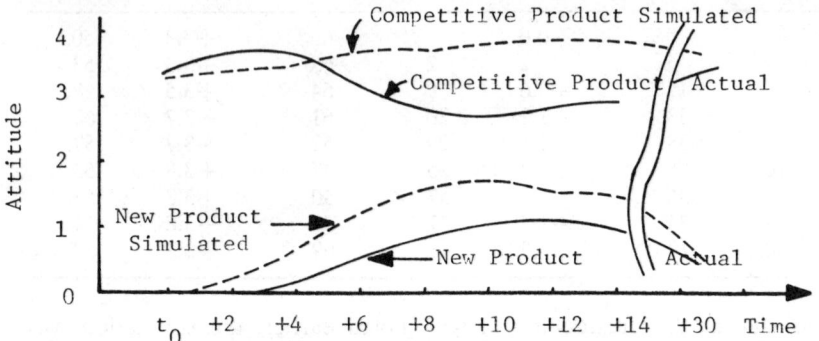

Figure 13.7. Time paths for new product introduction: attitudes.

population attitude scores than were realized in the actual market. In addition, the phenomenon of decreasing attitude toward the major competitor was not accounted for by the simulation. Consideration of conditions existing in the market during this test have led to the conclusion that the loss in attitude experienced by the competitor was a result of factors not encompassed by the model described in Chapter 8.

Figure 13.8 illustrates the time paths of simulated and actual popula-

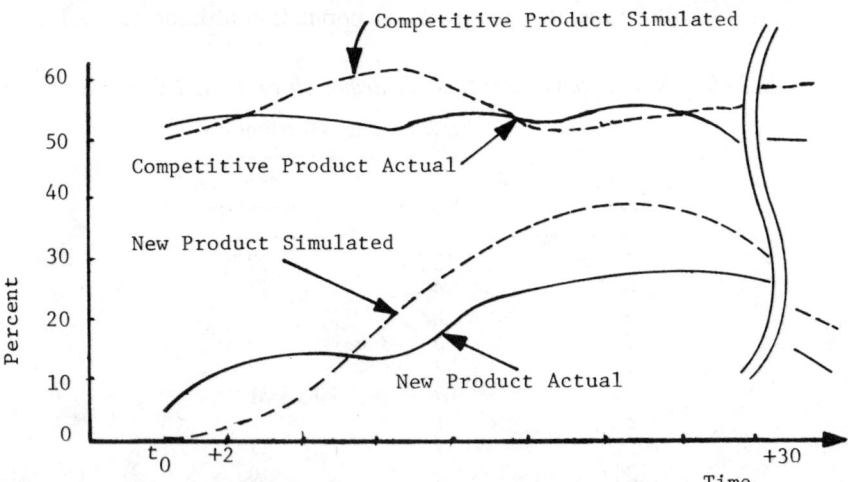

Figure 13.8. Time paths for new product introduction: awareness.

tion awareness during the same period. Awareness for the simulated population was initially at zero rather than the 5 percent value established in the interviews. As in Figure 13.8, solid lines indicate data from the actual market, while dotted lines reference output from the simulation. As in the attitude case, awareness variables predicted by the simulation are somewhat higher than those encountered in the actual environment.

Figure 13.9 illustrates the brand share time path for the new product and its major competitor as simulated and measured in the actual market. As illustrated, the actual competitive impact of the new product on the major brand was greater than that simulated, while higher brand shares were realized for both the new and old product in the simulation than

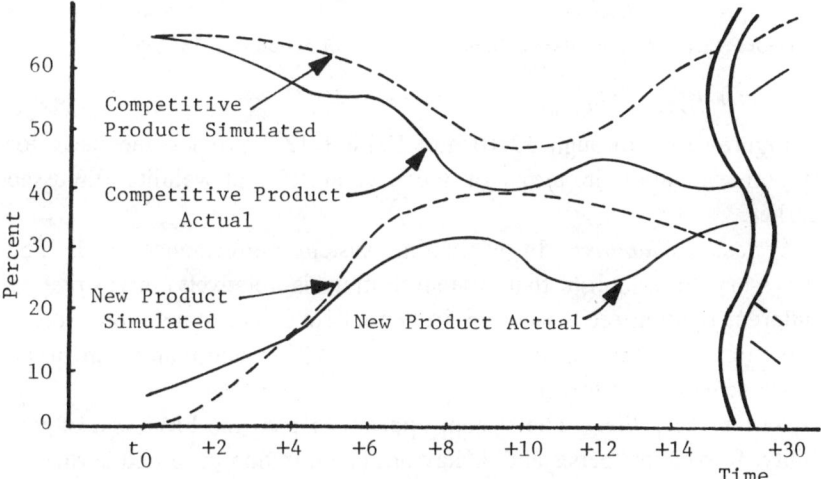

Figure 13.9. Time paths for new product introduction: brand share.

in actuality. It is natural to hypothesize relationships between the previously noted attitude discrepancies and the brand share conditions noted in this table.

Table 13.9 and Figure 13.10 illustrate the relative attitude distributions for the new product at the conclusion of period $t_0 + 14$. A comparison of this distribution with the initialized new brand attitude distribution illustrated in Figure 13.6 indicates the extent of consumer orientation change created by the test market as simulated and actually experienced. Figure 13.10 provides more detailed information on the previously noted discrepancy between realized and simulated population attitude scores as plotted in Figure 13.8. More consumers within the simulated population are found in each of the positive attitude categories than is the case within the actual test market population.

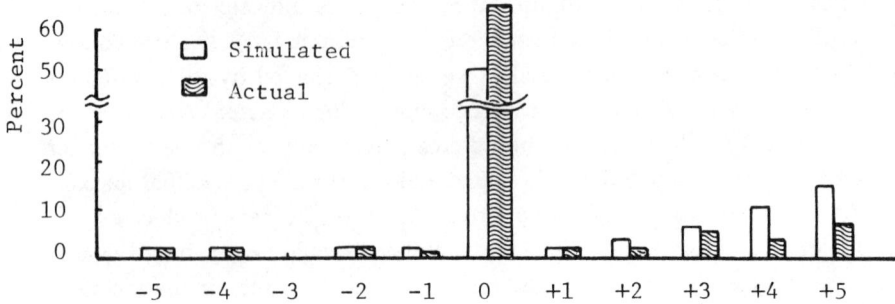

Figure 13.10. New product attitude distribution at period $t_0 + 14$.

Model Evaluation

Figures 13.6 through 13.10 and Exhibit 13.2 provide the basis for system evaluation in terms of the several tests of validity discussed earlier.

System Reliability. In evaluating system performance, it is first necessary to establish that system output is relatively insensitive to different random seeds used on sequential runs. The simulation used to generate the output illustrated in Figure 13.9 produced interrun brand share deviations of less than 1.5 percent.

System Viability. The system appears to pass the basic test of viability. It exhibits "persistent" behavior. The question proposed earlier by Balderston and Hoggatt must be answered by the reader. Do the initial conditions, parameter settings, and inputs required by the Chapter 8 model guarantee viability and thus remove the strength of "the assertion that the model's capability in this regard is a significant test of its usefulness, or can we claim that the model's viability is evidence that it illuminates important features of the real world system which serves as its background?" [23]

System Stability. The question of system stability is a relative one that must be assessed in light of the limits that the observer wishes to impose. In a sense, the stability test is not appropriately applied at this point because inputs to the system were fluctuating and stability testing is normally conducted with constant inputs.

[23] Balderston and Hoggatt, *op. cit.,* Footnote 5.

System Consistency. The basic question of system consistency raised by Buzzell in the previously noted comments[24] must be answered with reference to the Chapter 8 formulations before the output of the simulation run can be considered. In response to questions of sensitivity, the simulation is, as noted previously, more sensitive in terms of attitudes and awareness response than the actual test market population.

System Duplication of Historical Conditions. Does this simulation duplicate salient attributes of the actual test market? There is no absolute answer. Certainly the time paths have certain similarities to those recognized in the actual data; however, discrepancies are evident. While many comments could be made pro and con the assertion that the system does or does not duplicate historical conditions, the argument would be difficult to resolve. The fundamental problem remaining has been well summarized by Cohen and Cyert.

The likelihood that a process model will incorrectly describe the world is high, because it makes some small assertions about the nature of the world. There are various degrees by which any model can fail to describe the world, however, so it is meaningful to say that some models are more adequate descriptions of reality than others. Some criteria must be devised to indicate when the time paths generated by a process model agree sufficiently with the observed time paths so that the agreement cannot be attributed to mere coincidence. Tests must be devised for the "goodness of fit" of process models with the real world. The problem of validation becomes even more difficult if available data about the "actual" behavior of the world are themselves subject to error.[25]

In final analysis, simulation performance must be evaluated in terms of management requirements and intended system applications. Initial tests frequently focus on the qualitative evaluation of the reasonableness of population segment behavior over time. As an example, Exhibit 13.2 illustrates the cumulative prescription market shares generated by two general practitioners operating in a simulated drug product environment. These 2 doctors prescribed only one relevant drug during the first 2 weeks of simulated activity. However, as the year progressed, they tried 6 other drugs. Their cumulative brand shares for the 10 brands are shown at week 52.

[24] Buzzell, *op. cit.,* Footnote 2.
[25] K. J. Cohen and R. M. Cyert, "Computer Models in Dynamic Economics," in Cyert and March, *op. cit.,* Footnote 13, p. 319.

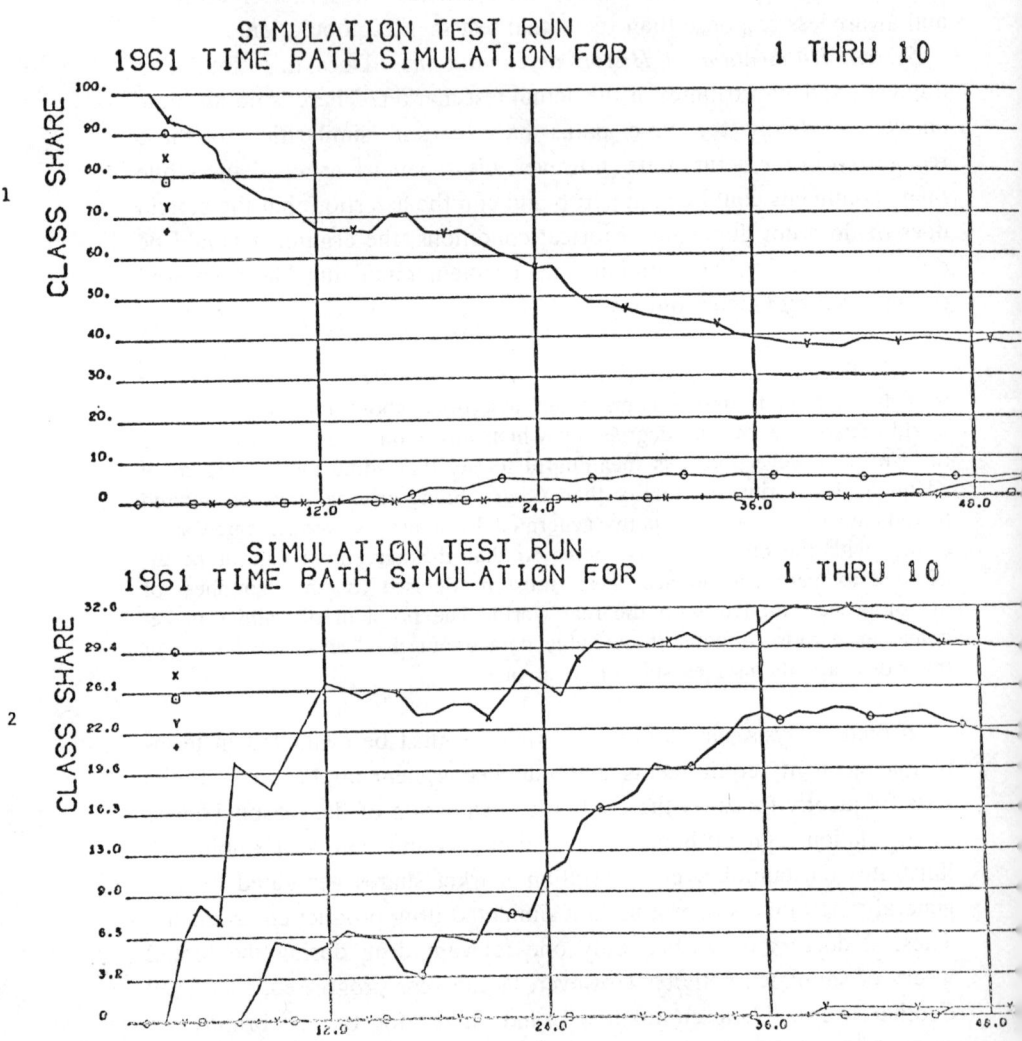

Exhibit 13.2. Sample output: Two doctors.

While management evaluation may begin with the type of over time Turing test, illustrated in Exhibit 13.2, this output is useful primarily as a basis for assessing system stability. Two simulated doctors are no more representative than two real-world practitioners. Meaningful tests of system response require examination of the behavior exhibited by major population segments.

Management evaluation of total system performance is normally based on measures requiring aggregation of simulated cell behavior. In the doctor case, for example, population behavior was validated by analyzing the proportion of prescriptions allocated to each (brand shares), and changes in knowledge, attitudes, and perceived brand images of important population segments.

Exhibit 13.3 illustrates the brand shares of 10 frequently used drugs resulting from 100 simulated doctors' treatment of several thousand patients. Inputs for this simulation run specified the content and related media allocation for all journal, direct mail, salesman detail, and convention promotion generated by competitors operating in the relevant market area during 1961.

Analytic procedures applied in later stages of management system evaluation may be summarized with reference to data plotted in Exhibit 13.3. The first test performed following this simulation established that the rank order of brand shares at the end of 1961 in the real and simulated worlds were equivalent. Actual versus simulated data comparisons are presented in Table 13.10.

The absolute value of brand shares generated by the simulation and

TABLE 13.10. Rank Order Brand Share Comparisons

| | | Year End Rank | |
| | | --- | --- |
Identification	Rank as Initialized	Simulated	Actual
1 — Y	4	2	2
1 — 0	5	6	6
1 — X	6	5	5
1 — +	8	8	8
1 — □	10	10	10
2 — □	1	1	1
2 — 0	2	3	3
2 — X	3	4	4
2 — +	7	7	7
2 — Y	9	9	9

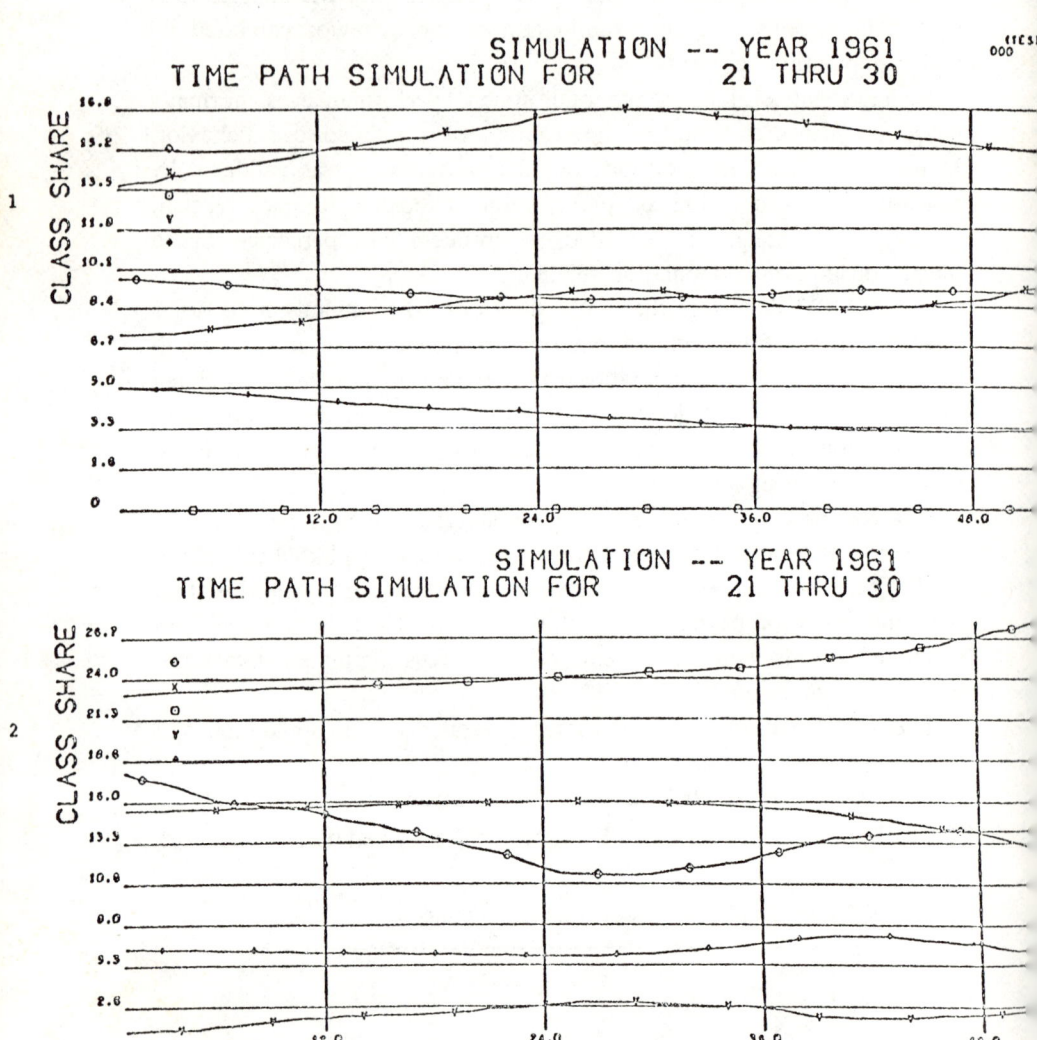

Exhibit 13.3. Sample output: 100 doctors.

TABLE 13.11.   Absolute Brand Share Comparison

| | | Year End Value | | |
Identification	Initialization Value	Simulated	Actual	Difference (Magnitude)
1 — Y	13.7%	15.0%	16.1%	−1.1%
1 — 0	9.7	9.1	8.7	+ .4
1 — X	7.3	9.3	9.0	+ .3
1 — +	5.0	3.2	2.8	+ .4
1 — □	0	0	0	—
2 — □	23.2	27.6	28.8	−1.2
2 — 0	18.1	13.0	12.7	+ .3
2 — X	15.6	13.9	14.4	− .5
2 — +	6.2	5.9	5.5	+ .4
2 — Y	1.0	2.5	2.0	+ .5
Σ	99.8%	99.5%	100.0%	5.1%

real-world population were then examined. As indicated in Table 13.11, the total error between actual and simulated brand shares at the end of 1961 was 5.1 percent.

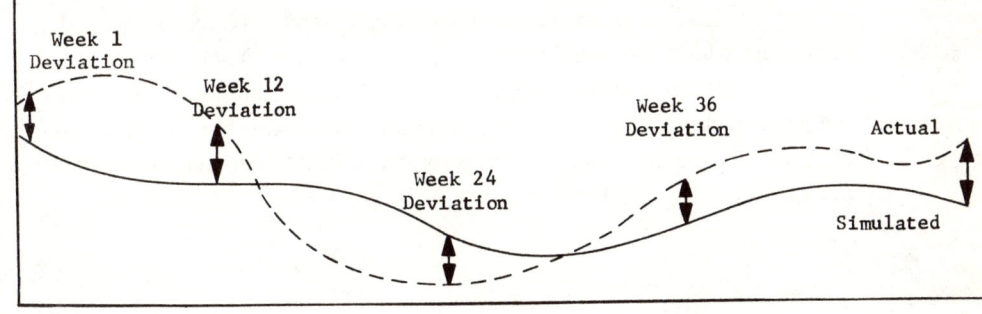

$$\text{Total Deviation for Brand } b = \sum_{t=1}^{52} \text{Actual}(b,t) - \text{Simulated}(b,t)$$

$$\text{Average Error for Ten Brands} = \frac{\sum_{b=1}^{10} \text{Total Deviation}}{520}$$

Figure 13.11. Over time brand share deviation: calculation procedure.

A final class of performance test focuses on the extent of correspondence between actual and predicted brand shares throughout the entire time period covered by the simulation. Figure 13.11 illustrates the procedure used to obtain this measure for the 1961 simulation test data. The maximum error in simulation based prediction for any brand was 5.2 percent, while the average error over this time period was .7 percent.

Summary

This chapter has focused on the testing and validation of simulation systems encompassing microanalytic behavioral models. Relationships between models and reality have been examined and five tests of validity proposed. These are (1) viability, (2) stability, (3) consistency, (4) duplication of historical conditions, and (5) prediction of future conditions.

Specialized data requirements associated with the evaluation of simulation system performance have been discussed and types of data required for various tests noted.

The simulation of individual behavior was discussed with reference to output obtained from a test run of the Chapter 8 consumer model operating within an appliance market simulation. Total system performance evaluation was considered with reference to population outputs obtained from a total market simulation based on test market data obtained during a 14-week food product introduction and a one-year prescription drug market test.

Chapter 14

EDUCATIONAL APPLICATIONS OF BEHAVIORAL SIMULATION

The system of behavioral models described in this book was developed in part to serve as a realistic artificial environment in which students of management would encounter representative business problems. This chapter focuses on the use of the previously discussed market structure and models in a total market environment simulation at the M.I.T. Sloan School of Management.[1]

Since 1959, the author and his associates at the Sloan School of Management have been experimenting with management games based on microanalytic computer simulation.[2] The structure of these games has increased in scope and complexity as educational objectives have been refined.[3] Systems now in use make possible a unique approach to management education based on the use of microanalytic simulation.

---

[1] Material presented in this chapter was discussed earlier in A. E. Amstutz and H. J. Claycamp, "The Total Market Environment Simulation — An Approach to Management Education," *Industrial Management Review*, Vol. 5 (Spring 1964), pp. 47–60.

[2] For a discussion of earlier development work see "The Complex Marketing Game — Accomplishments and Opportunity," in W. Alderson and S. Shapiro (eds.), *Marketing and the Computer* (Englewood Cliffs, N. J.: Prentice-Hall, Inc., 1963), pp. 424–443.

[3] Early versions of the game are described in A. E. Amstutz, *The M.I.T. Marketing Game — 650 Version,* School of Industrial Management Working Paper (Cambridge, Mass.: M.I.T., 1960) and A. E. Amstutz, *The M.I.T. Marketing Game — 709 Version,* School of Industrial Management Working Paper (Cambridge, Mass.: M.I.T., 1962).

Differentiating Characteristics of Business Games

Many types of management games succeed in stimulating student interest and involvement by providing a common reference — a dynamic case — that serves as a basis for class discussion of business problems.[4]

The effectiveness of many business games is limited by (1) structures that permit only limited input and constrain the player-manager to manipulation of a small number of gross quantitative descriptors (e.g., aggregate dollar expenditures in advertising, research, and product development), (2) highly aggregate output that provides little or no basis for meaningful research (e.g., one or two regional sales revenue figures and financial reports based on these numbers and the expenditure input, (3) operating procedures that frustrate orderly, analytical thinking (e.g., decision period turnaround times of from fifteen to twenty minutes).

This chapter is not intended as a detailed analysis of the strengths and weaknesses of alternative business games.[5] The present objective is to describe the use of the system structure and models described in earlier chapters as an artificial business environment in which students of management may gain realistic experience.

Objectives for a Business Game

Objectives motivating the development of the M.I.T. management games based on total market environment simulations might be summarized as follows:

1. To present relevant management problems in a realistic context.
2. To provide an opportunity for game managers to make business-oriented decisions of realistic complexity.
3. To create an environment capable of supporting realistic experimentation in the use of analytical and research techniques appropriate to problem formulation, decision making, and evaluation of results in the real world.

[4] See, for example, "Sales Management Plays 'The Game,'" *Sales Management,* Vol. 88 (January 19, 1962), pp. 43–47.

[5] For a discussion of this question see A. E. Amstutz, "Management Games — A Potential Perverted," *Industrial Management Review,* Vol. 5 (Fall 1963), pp. 29–36.

Characteristics of Relevant Management Problems

Beginning with the first objective, to present relevant management problems in a realistic context, it is necessary to ask "What makes a problem realistic?" In answering this question, five characteristics of business problems requiring management action may be noted.

1. Realistic business problems involve qualitative as well as quantitative factors.
2. Management problems are complex — they cannot be described by models involving one or two variables and linear relationships.
3. Relevant decision elements are interrelated — it is difficult or impossible to isolate one variable and consider it alone and without regard for its interaction with other variables.
4. Alternative approaches are available to the manager — there is seldom a single right answer standing in marked contrast to obviously wrong answers.
5. Business problems move in crowds — the manager is seldom able to devote his entire attention to a single problem. He is continually faced with many interrelated problems, all of which must be considered and solved.

Characteristics of a Realistic Artificial Environment

The preceding description of relevant management problems suggests two major attributes of an artificial environment in which such problems can be generated, analyzed, and solved. First, the environment must be complex. The models representing behavior within it cannot be simple first-order approximations to reality. They must be sufficiently complex to encompass the major characteristics of behavior within each sector of the relevant environment. Second, the artificial environment must be consistent. Although elements within the environment may be stochastic, the structure must be stable, and interactions within the simulation must have continuity comparable to that experienced within a real-world market environment.

If the environment is to provide an opportunity for game managers to make realistically complex decisions, flexible input/output capability is of primary importance. A flexible input structure permits the game decision maker to make use of the variables (qualitative and quantitative) available to his real-world counterpart. It enables him to control the priority ranking of decision elements and to focus on certain variables while ignoring all others. He is thus able to structure the decision situation in terms of factors that appear relevant to him. The problem of the game designer is to achieve an input system that will accept a range of specifications compatible with the range of factors that managers with different perspectives consider important as they view a particular management problem. The input system may suggest variables for consideration but should not demand that actions be taken with respect to any variable. The simplified, wholly numeric input forms used in most business games are entirely unsatisfactory.[6] Input forms should permit communication of vast amounts of information or no information. The level of detail must be determined by the player-manager, not by the input form.

In a similar manner, the outputs obtained from the game environment must be flexible and determined by the game participant. There will, of course, be standard operating reports containing basic financial and market information generated by most corporations. In addition, output corresponding to information available in the real world at the local library should be provided in the game world to those having the insight to request it. Game models and output structure must also be capable of providing data generated in response to specific research programs planned by the player-manager. This requires implementation of certain aspects of the research sector discussed in Chapter 12 and an output system incorporating report generators designed to present information content specified by the players.

The use of behavioral cell models of the type formulated in earlier chapters in combination with synthetic population structures facilitates the desired input/output flexibility and simplifies implementation of a broad research capability.

Characteristics of the Desired Decision Process

The third objective stated earlier referred to "problem formulation, decision making, and evaluation of results." It is difficult to discuss the implications of this objective without first defining more explicitly this decision-making process that the game environment is to support. The process is continuous; however, it may be conceptually divided into eight discrete steps: (1) problem statement, (2) analysis, (3) explica-

---

[6] Typical input forms are discussed in *ibid.*, pp. 30 and 31.

tion, (4) evaluation, (5) decision, (6) implementation, (7) monitoring, and (8) review.

The Problem Statement

In developing a statement of the problem, the player-manager must answer a series of questions that will help to define and limit the focus of his attention. The time perspective of the problem must be established in terms of time remaining before action is required. The time perspective, in combination with an assessment of the importance of alternative outcomes, establishes the priority to be allocated this problem in relation to other problems requiring consideration at the same time. Available information determines the perceived structure of the problem. Evaluation of information availability serves to structure the problem by defining the terms in which it will be expressed.

Analysis

The second step in the decision-making process, analysis, can be conveniently considered in terms of the focus of the investigation on factors within or outside the corporation. Within the corporation, the focus is on the goal structure of the enterprise as interpreted by the decision maker and the resources available to him. Factors external to the corporation are examined in context of the corporation's objectives. Because information about conditions in the external world is more sparse than that relating to internal company operations, areas of analysis in the external environment may be categorized in terms of data at hand (present knowledge) and data to be obtained (information desired).

Explication

In the third phase of the desired decision process, the decision maker organizes that which he knows and/or assumes in explicit and testable models. This aspect of decision making is often ignored; however, it is crucial to the realization of testable hypotheses and measurable objectives.

Evaluation

In evaluating the circumstances surrounding the problem, the player-manager restates his desired objective in terms of the explicit measurable outcomes that he wishes to achieve. Implicit in this statement is the formulation of criteria of evaluation — statements of factors to be considered in choosing between alternative courses of action. Once this has been done, alternative means of achieving desired outcomes can be examined.

Decision

If the preceding steps of the process have been performed, actual choice of a given strategy from the range of available alternatives is a relatively simple task. If rational behavior on the part of the player-manager is assumed, the decision outcome would be expected to optimize in terms of established criteria subject to the constraints of limited information, inability to consider all possible outcomes, and uncertainty.

Implementation

Once a course of action has been chosen, the decision must be implemented. Responsibilities must be assigned and tactics related to each element of strategy must be scheduled. Appropriate monitoring and evaluation procedures must also be scheduled.

Monitoring

In the seventh step of the process, the player-manager monitors activity within the simulated market to determine his degree of success in achieving stated objectives. Events in the market place or competitive actions may motivate reconsideration of previously established criteria of evaluation. Changes in underlying structure or the appearance of unexpected conditions may necessitate reanalysis or implementation of alternative strategies.

Review

In the final step of the desired decision process, the player-manager reviews his perception of the problem situation, which at this point may be quite different from his first conception, and enumerates problems remaining to be considered. If the original conception of the problem was accurate (if his original model of the environment was correct), criteria appear to have been appropriate, and objectives have been successfully achieved, the process may terminate. If, as is more likely, problems remain, step eight provides the input for step one and the entire sequence is repeated.

The sequence of steps in the desired decision process is summarized in Figure 14.1.

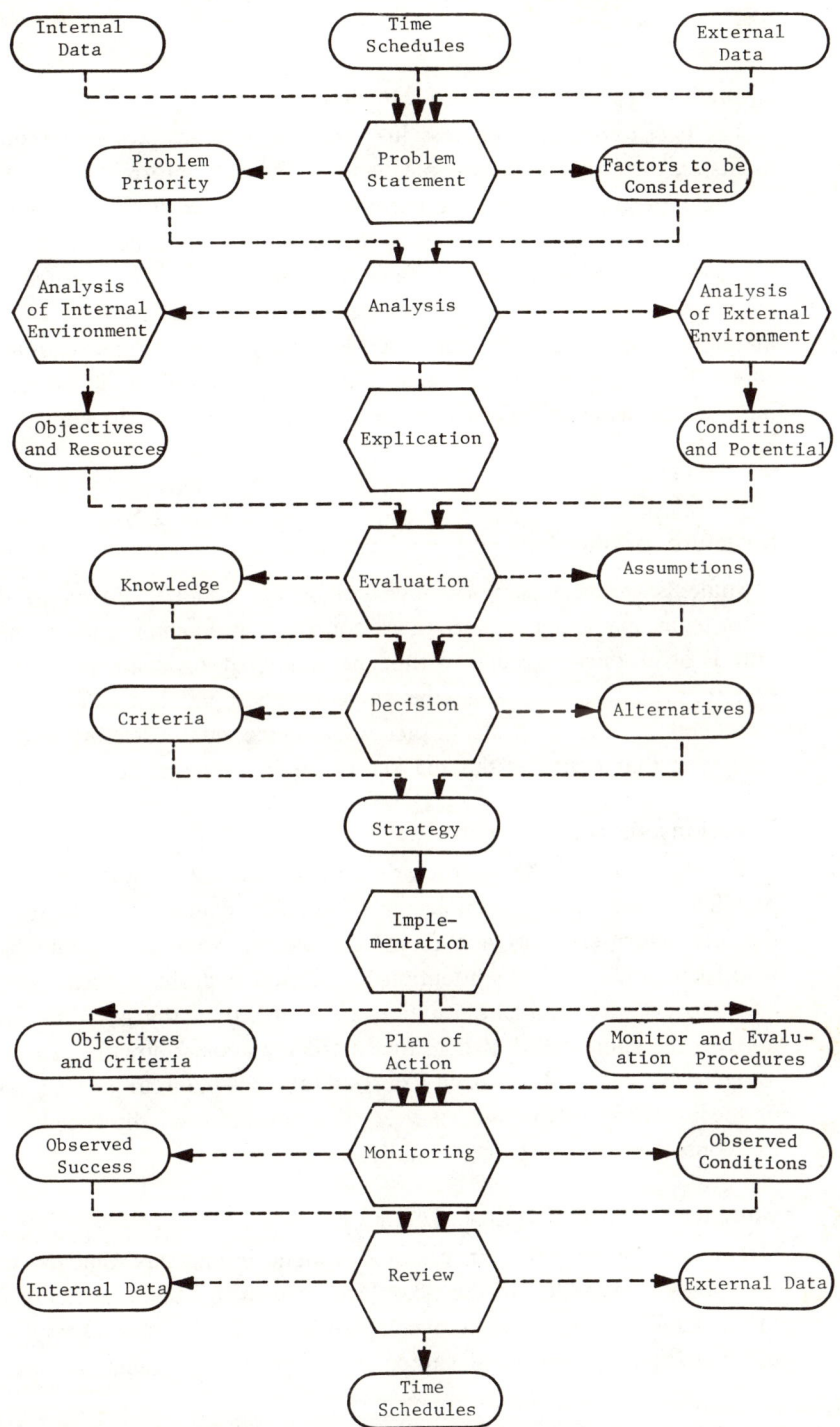

Figure 14.1. Graphic summary of desired decision process.

Implications of the Desired Decision Process

The decision-making process just outlined imposes stringent requirements on the structure of a game. It must generate information required by the indicated process and permit techniques learned in operations research, statistics, and marketing research courses to be applied with consistent and relevant results. As noted in Chapter 12, a simulation-based research approach emphasizes techniques designed to aid the manager in modeling relevant functions and identifying and estimating values for important parameters. Thus the development of models of the type discussed in earlier chapters becomes a part of the educational process.

Structure of the External Environment

Students within a game-oriented course are divided into teams with each team managing a particular company producing one or more brands of product marketed within the simulated environment. In addition to the company teams, the game involves the instructor, a control team described in detail below, a game administrator, and the computer that contains the marketing environment simulation.

Functions of the Instructor

To some extent, the instructor's role in the game situation closely parallels that in the normal lecture-discussion course. That is to say, the instructor serves as a combination lecturer and discussion leader who focuses the student's attention on particular problem areas or specific aspects of a problem situation encountered in the game or readings. In the game-based course, the instructor's role is greatly expanded — he also acts in the capacity of general consultant to one or more of the company teams and as over-all coordinator of the activities of the control team and game administrator.

Functions of the Control Team

The control team is a necessary element in the environment of a game based on models of the type developed in this book. It is through the control team that qualitative information relating, for example, to the content of promotional campaigns is evaluated (using the prominence scale discussed in Chapter 7) and scaled for communication to the computer. The control team evaluates communication content of creative work prepared by the company teams for transfer to retailers, distributors, salesmen, and consumers within the simulated environment.

Functions of the Game Administrator

The role of the game administrator is self-explanatory. He is responsible for the administration of all activities concerned with the game environment including preparation of inputs, processing of computer runs, checking of outputs, and dissemination of reports. In addition to transferring information from the quantitative input forms prepared by the students and control team to punched cards, the game administrator must also translate special report requests and research plans into a form appropriate for processing by the computer.

Functions of the Computer System

Inputs prepared by the game administrator are communicated to the computer that runs the simulation providing inputs to the sector models and generating reports for each company, the control team, the game administrator, and the instructor. Information supplied to the companies is of three types: (1) quarterly profit-and-loss and balance sheet statements, sales analyses, inventory and production reports, other standard outputs describing the operations of the company in the various regions of the simulated country in which it is active, and end-of-year reports similar to those that would normally be published by competitive companies; (2) environmental data generated in response to requests by a particular company team for information that is freely available in the real world but not included in the regular reports; (3) the results of specific research activities scheduled by a particular company team.

Operation reports made available to the control team, game administrator, and instructor provide detailed information on sector model performance. This information, comparable to that which would be obtained from a highly accurate survey of business conditions, encompasses variables defined in earlier chapters including distributor and retailer performance and expectations, salesman effort and availability, consumer purchase, communication response, perceived brand image, and attitudes toward product characteristics and appeals.

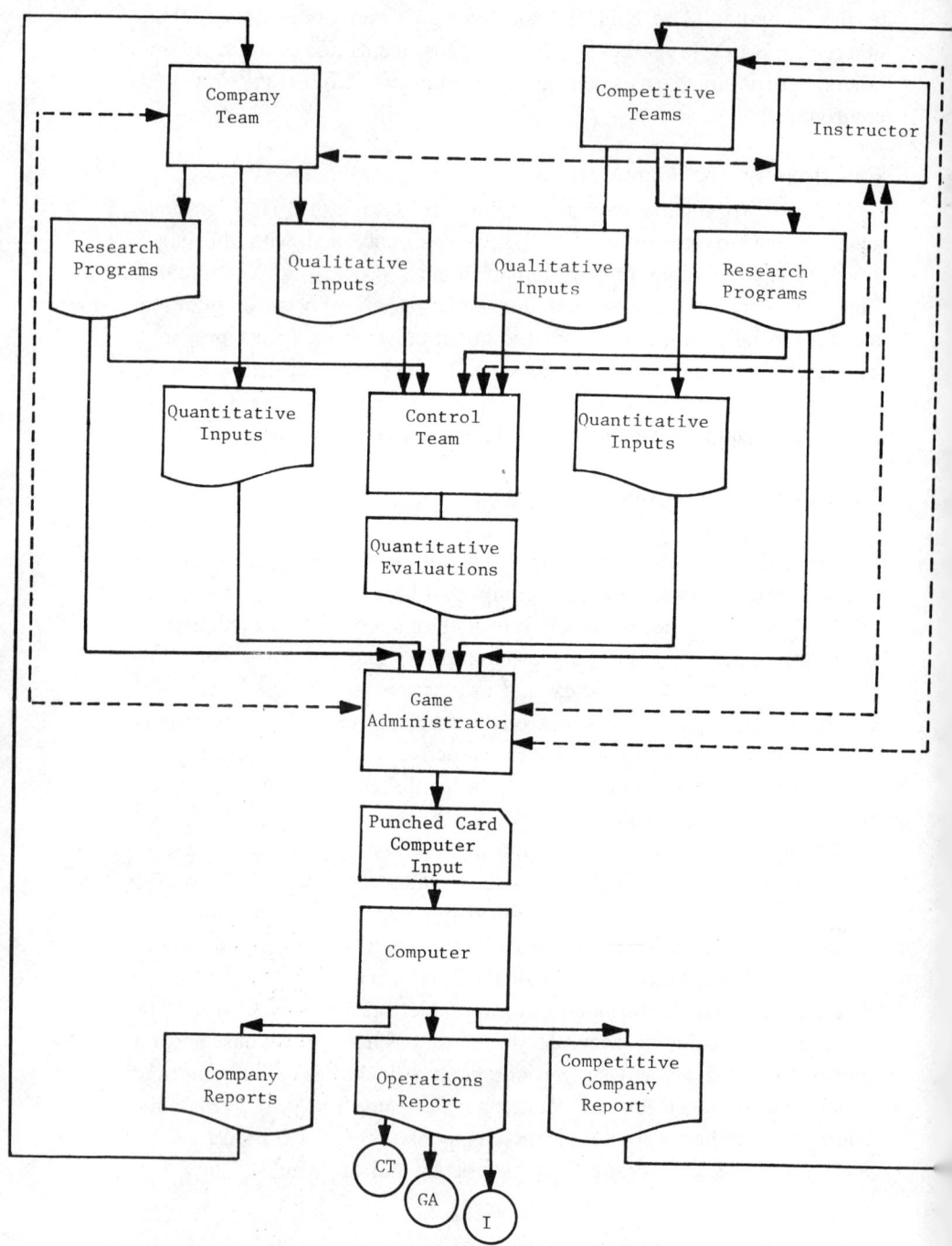

Figure 14.2. Flow of information within the external environment.

Information Flow Within the External Environment

The flow of information within the external game environment is summarized in Figure 14.2. The major actors in the external environment — the player-managers, the control team, the instructor, the game administrator, and the computer — are shown as rectangles. *Formal* communication between elements is indicated by *solid lines* with an arrow indicating the direction of such communication. The medium of communication is indicated as either printed reports or punched cards. *Informal* channels of communication are indicated by *dashed lines*.

As illustrated in Figure 14.2, informal communication flows among the company teams, the instructor, and the game administrator. Communication among company teams is limited. All communication between the company teams and the control team is formalized through the medium of qualitative input forms or research programs. The teams communicate quantitative inputs directly to the computer with the game administrator serving as a translator. The computer communicates directly with the company teams and with the control team, game administrator, and instructor through reports prepared for each of these elements. As indicated earlier, the qualitative inputs received by the control team are evaluated and transferred to the game administrator as scaled and quantitative inputs. All inputs communicated to the computer on punched cards are, of course, quantitative.

Structure of the Simulation

The simulation used in the M.I.T. Marketing Game is based on modifications of the sector models described in Chapters 7 through 12 with parameter values established to represent conditions existing in up to 30 geographic regions of the continental United States. Population distributions correspond to 1960 Census figures. Twenty-one of the geographic regions correspond to the 21 largest Standard Metropolitan Statistical Areas in terms of total population, age distribution, income distribution, degree of urbanization, etc. The remaining 9 regions represent the balance of the 9 standard census areas and have the same correspondence between represented and actual parameter distributions. Although it is based on the year 1960, the reproduced economy is not static. The economic cycle variable discussed in previous chapters is subject to fluctuations representing changes in the over-all economy.

Geographic regions exhibit differential rates of growth as in the real economy.

The simulation encompasses the five sector models described previously. These are (1) the manufacturer sector (Chapter 7), (2) distributors (Chapter 10), (3) selling agents — salesmen (Chapter 11), (4) retailers (Chapter 9), and (5) consumers (Chapter 8). The simulated manufacturers are controlled by the company teams who supply inputs comparable to those defined in Chapter 7. The functions of research agent and government discussed in Chapter 12 are performed by the game administrator and control team, respectively.

The Manufacturer Sector

Because operating decisions are made by the management teams, the manufacturer sector consists primarily of functions required to implement the decisions of the operating management and to handle the bookkeeping activities for the firm. Functions performed by the manufacturer sector simulation within the artificial environment include (1) ordering and making payment for raw materials in response to production schedules set by the operating management in the external environment (subject to capacity constraints), (2) implementing production and shipment allocation policies introduced by the management in the external environment, (3) processing orders and back orders from distributors and/or retailers, (4) implementing the promotional schedule developed by the company team in the external environment, (5) transmitting to the distribution system policy communiqués relating to pricing, distribution policy, sales force allocation and compensation, ordering policies, etc.

The Distributor Sector

The simulated distributor population is capable of several of the actions and responses described in Chapter 10. Their simulated decision capabilities include processing retailer orders; inventory maintenance; generation of orders to the simulated manufacturing operation; pricing; and sales force composition, allocation, and compensation.

The distributor model used in the game differs from that described in Chapter 10 in that it contains a selective response model that facilitates response to product characteristic and appeals content of advertising and promotion media and salesman promotion as well as communication from the producer regarding pricing, distribution, and ordering policies. In addition, the distributor is given the ability to respond to information generated by the retailer whose communication content relates to sales, orders, pricing, selling effort, or inventory problems.

The Salesman Sector

The salesman model employed in the game simulation is a somewhat simplified version of that described in Chapter 11.

The Retailer Sector

Behavior of the simulated retailer duplicates that discussed in Chapter 9 with certain simplifying modifications. The retailer responds to the content of both trade and consumer advertising along a limited set of dimensions and is assumed to be cognizant of prevailing pricing and ordering policies. Word-of-mouth interactions between retailer and consumer are not modeled in the game system.

The Consumer Sector

A simulated population of 1000 consumers resides in each of the 30 separate geographic regions. Descriptive attributes are initialized to correspond to appropriate regional demographic distributions. Exposure to advertising media, selling presentations, and word-of-mouth communication are formulated in the manner discussed in Chapter 8. Responses to communication and product, perceived need recognition, knowledge acquisition, perceived brand image formation, purchase decisions, and word-of-mouth generation are also based on formulations discussed earlier.

The Government Sector

The control team performs the regulatory function normally associated with governmental agencies. Thus the simulated government may intercede with cease and desist orders if the content of promotional communications differs markedly from the facts of the marketing situation or if pricing practices, certain forms of direct compensation, and intercompany actions represent violations of the Sherman Antitrust, Clayton, or Robinson-Patman Acts as discussed in Chapter 12.

Use of the Simulated Environment

The Course Structure

Courses based on the total market environment simulation can be characterized as a synthesis of the more traditional lecture and discussion approach to functional management decision making, the case study approach, and an experimental laboratory. The game serves as the integrative element. It is a dynamic and continuing problem environment — an experimental laboratory — in which the student learns by participating in the process of management decision making.

The game provides a common reference point for instructor and students — a dynamic case study based on situations that arise in the simulated environment. Developments within this environment are affected by decisions previously made by the player-managers. Thus the operating performance of the simulated companies constitutes feedback that must be analyzed by the student in an attempt to determine the results of his decisions.

Role of the Student Manager

The student is the decision maker. He must continue to operate in, and live with, the environment that he has helped to create. Mistakes cannot be ignored — they must be lived with and overcome. The student is competing against his peers and is responsible for the results of his decisions. This situation may be contrasted to the normal case study approach in which the student uses information gratuitously supplied to second-guess professional managers at a single point in time. In the game situation, the student must obtain the information necessary to evaluate the effectiveness of his own program from the environment he has helped to create.

The game is the integrative element of the course rather than an adjunct exercise inserted in an otherwise structured course. With this focus on the game, the major responsibility of the student is to manage his company. Readings, lectures, and discussions are all oriented toward the same objective — helping the student become a better manager. Thus the student and instructor have a common frame of reference and a unified purpose — to apply knowledge and techniques, regardless of where they are taught in the curriculum, to the task at hand.

The major criterion of relevancy becomes, "Does it offer a promise of improving management ability?"

"Playing" the Game

The initial requirements placed on the players of the M.I.T. Marketing Game are similar to those present in other management games. The students inherit a company that has been operating for a period of time and are given histories consisting of standard financial statements and elementary sales analyses. They must analyze these histories, evaluate their present position, and decide how they wish to operate the company in the future. In addition to these common attributes, the simulation-based game has important features that add to the realism of the situation facing the new management team. The company has been operating with decision rules that cover pricing, production, allocation of funds to various operations, etc. The design of the game does not force the new management to begin immediately making decisions by filling in input forms governing operations in each area. They may accept all or any part of past management's policies. Even if they elect to do absolutely nothing, the company will continue to operate using existing (past management's) decision rules implemented by the simulated manufacturer sector. This facility permits the new student managers to begin their business experience with the complex and realistic problem of deciding which areas are important enough to warrant management consideration.

The players rapidly find out that before they can answer the question of what is important they must answer more fundamental questions, such as "What do we want to accomplish? What are our resources?" and "What is the relationship between the factors we control and the objectives we wish to accomplish?" Answers to the first two questions are usually reached rather quickly (at least on a first-try superficial level), but answers to the third question are in the realm of the unknown and only hypotheses are possible at this point. This is a realistic situation in which action must be taken — the managers must decide what they want to accomplish, and how they will expend their resources to achieve desired results even though they have little or no concrete knowledge about the effect of particular actions.

Because the environment is not a simple one in which the form and amount of information are predetermined and relationships are easily discerned, the students soon conclude that they must organize and plan their activities if they are to make significant progress toward understanding their environment. Thus they take the first step in the decision process outlined earlier completely within the structure of the game. It is important to note that the players themselves decide which problems are important, what available information is relevant, whether additional information is worth the cost of obtaining it, what analytical techniques may be used to aid decision making, and how results are to be evaluated.

Obviously the sophistication of a particular game management depends to a large extent on prior preparation and time available to devote to the course. The important point is that the structure of the game does not preclude the use of rigorous and sophisticated techniques.

The M.I.T. game emphasizes marketing problems. However, the players soon recognize that they cannot deal with any functional problem in a vacuum, for frequent product changes or multiple model variations may create production and financial problems, and both the type and level of marketing activity may be severely constrained by financial factors. This experience of encountering internal constraints and problems while attempting to implement a marketing strategy helps the student gain a more meaningful understanding of the interdependence of functional factors in management decision making.

The Impact of a Simulation-Based Game

Problem-Solving Approach

The impact of student experiences such as those discussed in the previous section on the development of desired problem structuring and solving skills should be evident.

Interpersonal Relations

The environment of a complex simulation-based game also places emphasis on the development of a working knowledge of interpersonal relations and, to a lesser degree, organization. The student quickly recognizes that the task facing the management team is too extensive and complex for one person to handle alone. Organization and coordinated action are obvious prerequisites to effective disposition of problems at hand. Planning and delegation of responsibility take on new and highly personal meanings as the student-managers attempt to allocate their scarcest resource, their time, to the various areas in which they believe action is required.

The requirements of this environment lead to a situation in which individual success is inextricably tied to group performance. Thus there is substantial pressure on the individual to contribute to a smoothly functioning and cohesive management group. However, because of the previously noted emphasis on company performance, there is also substantial pressure on the individual to implement those policies and procedures that he believes will best contribute to achievement of company objectives. The stage is then set for a realistic experience in management group interaction, organization theory in practice, and structured decision making.

Communication Skills

Development of communication skills is not an automatic by-product of game utilization. However, the game situation provides an excellent opportunity for incorporating requirements that place emphasis on effective oral and written communication. For example, new managers may be given an initial assignment to develop a two-year plan of operations including a statement of company objectives, strategies to be used in achieving them, measurement techniques to be employed in monitoring progress, and criteria for evaluating success. The plan is updated once each simulated year and modified as the player-managers gain new information and/or observed conditions in the market change. The plan is reviewed with the instructor and evaluated as a policy document suitable for communication to a higher management level.

The plan may serve as the basis for oral presentations to a board of directors consisting of faculty members and businessmen. In meetings with their board, management is expected to sell their ideas and justify actions in the course of a critical profit-oriented review of operations. In both oral and written presentations, the students are required to analyze a complex situation, focus on what they consider salient, evaluate alternative courses of action, arrive at and support a decision, and effectively sell both their decision (or recommendation) and the reasoning on which it is based.

Summary

This chapter has discussed applications of microanalytic simulation in total market environment simulations used in teaching marketing management at the M.I.T. Sloan School of Management. Results achieved through the use of these systems have been evaluated in terms of objectives proposed as appropriate goals for management education.

The structure and operating characteristics of the system now in use have been related to the system design and behavioral sector models discussed in preceding chapters. Characteristics of courses in which the game serves as an integrating element have been noted.

It has been proposed that the use of a realistically complex artificial environment motivates students to seek out relevant information, gain an improved understanding of management processes, and develop skills important to effective management.

The major disadvantage of this application is the problem of resources required. A large-scale computer is a necessity, and time demands on students, instructors, and supporting staff are substantial. However, experience to date indicates that gains realized in student ability to structure, analyze, and solve complex management problems, develop communication and organization skills, and attain functional knowledge fully justify the requisite expenditures.

Chapter 15

MANAGEMENT APPLICATIONS OF MICROANALYTIC BEHAVIORAL SIMULATIONS

This chapter examines the problems and benefits realized when applying microanalytic simulation-based systems to problems of concern to corporate management. It is concerned largely with matters of implementation. The objective is to outline an approach that reduces implementation problems and establishes an environment in which operating and policy management may be introduced to the decision-oriented use of microanalytic simulation with relative ease.

The Importance of Management Involvement

On the basis of experience working with the managements of small and large companies, the author has concluded that factors in the corporate environment which limit or prohibit management involvement in the simulation process may constitute a greater threat to the successful implementation of simulation-based systems than any technical considerations that have been identified. Lack of management understanding of the nature, implications, and limitations of basic sector models can create insurmountable obstacles to effective system implementation.

A Focus on Policy Management

The ultimate impact of the approach discussed in this book is at a corporate policy level. As such, the approach must be understood and fully accepted at a policy management level. This is not to suggest that operating management problems are unimportant. However, a special class of problems and potentialities are associated with application of microanalytic simulation at a policy level. Once these have been solved, application to problems encountered at lower levels in the organization is greatly simplified.

The Application Context

The situations to be considered are encountered when introducing microanalytic behavioral simulation to managers involved in establishing broad corporate or functional policy. Specific problems are not particularly relevant. Representative situations would include corporate diversification, new product introduction, competitive posture toward new companies entering a market, and marketing program evaluation. The common element in these situations is that microanalytic simulation has the potential to contribute substantially to policy and strategy formulation.

The managers involved are not apt to be technically oriented. In many instances, they are only vaguely familiar with even basic quantitative techniques. They may become distinctly uneasy when asked to face problems of quantitative specification or evaluation.

The Simulation Process

In situations of the type described, interaction between manager and would-be developer of a simulation-based system is often initiated as a result of management recognition or suspicion of the existence of a problem. The problem may be very specific, "We're losing market share," or nothing more than a feeling, "We've got all kinds of numbers but really don't know what's going on in our market." In either case, an approach to problem formulation and solution based on microanalytic simulation should differ from traditional analytic procedures in several subtle but important respects, as indicated in Table 15.1.

The Table 15.1 outline provides a framework within which the sources of several potential difficulties may be isolated. The first step to be considered is problem definition.

Problem Definition

In most instances, management provides the initial problem definition stated in "business terms." This initial statement will probably

TABLE 15.1. *Comparison between Traditional Analytic and Simulation Approaches*

Traditional Analytic Procedure	Proposed Simulation Approach
1. *State* the problem.	*Define* the problem.
2. Determine what data exist.	Evaluate existing data.
3.	Determine what additional data can be obtained at what cost.
4.	Determine management assumptions regarding the problem.
5. Make assumptions in absence of data.	Explicate and test assumptions.
6. Develop model(s).	Consider alternative model structures.
7.	Finalize model through function validation.
8. Establish criteria for alternative solution evaluation.	Determine management criteria for alternative solution evaluation.
9. Prepare input(s) for system run or test.	Prepare input(s) for system run or test.
10. Generate solution(s).	Generate solution(s).
11.	Check validity of solution(s).
12. Make recommendations.	Infer policy and strategy implications of solution(s).
13.	Establish plan.
14.	Establish evaluation and review procedures.
15.	Implement plan.
16.	Implement evaluation and review procedures.

be qualitative. It may be vague and ambiguous. If explicit behavioral models are to contribute to a solution, the problem must be restated in explicit terms. Factors considered relevant must be defined and differentiated from those to be excluded through procedures of the type described in Chapters 2, 3, and 4.

Management must be involved in this quantitative specification of problem boundaries. They must also understand and agree with the conceptual structuring of the problem in terms sufficiently explicit to define the measurements through which the problem environment is to be described. If this level of communication is not achieved, it is impossible for those concerned with macrospecification to be sure that they are simulating the right behavior.

But, it may be argued, this means involving top management in model building. "Management is appropriately concerned with 'the big picture.' It is unrealistic to expect them to become involved in questions of measurement." The appropriate response to this objection is to reiterate the class of problems being considered — matters of company policy that require top management involvement. It is difficult to conceive of a point in the decision-making process at which involvement is more warranted than in ensuring that management understands and accepts the initial description of the problem environment.

The process of explicit problem definition often uncovers the not altogether surprising fact that various members of management have different implicit conceptual models of the problem situation. Making these models explicit removes the ambiguities that permit vague words to mean different things to different people. This often results in alternative representations of the problem situation and necessitates the creation and validation or rejection of several behavioral representations.

Data Generation

Quantitative problem specification facilitates identification of appropriate data for analysis or model testing. However, because data are often incomplete or were developed for other purposes at some time in the past, it may be desirable to generate new data to test hypotheses and/or provide estimates of model parameters. In this context, it might be noted that, in the author's experience, once management has developed system specifications to the point where appropriate measurements become evident, they strongly support research necessary to obtain estimates for model parameters even when this involves substantial expenditures of time and money.

Assumption Formulation

In designing a model, it is usually necessary to go beyond available data by making assumptions regarding the behavior to be simulated. If management has been involved in specification development, their assumptions will have been made explicit. In the absence of such interaction, it is at best difficult to establish management's understanding of the situation. When management and model builders do not share a common conception of the problem, management perceptions may be ignored with disastrous results.

Model Development

Model formulation and programming is often the sole province of the technical specialist. In successful simulation development management is exposed to and considers the *implications* of *alternative* structures. They become familiar with and understand the conceptual impact of model formulations considered in the course of microspecification development. They gain an understanding of system scope and an appreciation for considerations affecting choices between functions at differing levels of abstraction.

Model Evaluation

Once models have been developed and tested and the simulation is functioning, system performance must be evaluated. Determination of appropriate criteria for system evaluation must involve joint management-specialist action.

Criteria development requires a reasonable knowledge of the simulation to be evaluated. Management must be familiar with models being used. This is not to suggest that management needs to understand the computer instructions associated with each equation in the model. They should, however, understand the conceptual structure and relationships governing behavior within each sector of the simulation. They should, for example, be familiar with the assumptions underlying the consumer purchase and selective response functions as developed in Chapter 8.

In order to achieve this level of understanding, those concerned with model design and programming may be forced to communicate their ideas in simpler, less esoteric, language than they are in the habit of employing. Although this may require some imagination and a good deal of patience, the advantages that accrue from management's understanding of the potentialities and limitations of the system more than justify whatever effort is expended.

Policy Inference

Once criteria are established, solutions may be generated, checked for consistency, and evaluated in terms of agreed upon standards. At this point, the management who have been involved in the system development process will be prepared to use the simulation as a basis for policy formulation and evaluation. The management who have abdicated all system development to "the experts who understand models" while retaining "policy prerogatives" for themselves are in real trouble. Such functional bifurcation creates a major obstacle to intelligent discussion of simulation output and produces misunderstandings of the type discussed earlier in context of problem definition. Absence of informed interaction throughout system design, development, and implementation is the primary cause of misinterpretations, invalid conclusions, and improper applications.

Policy Implementation

Lack of continuity, from policy analysis and evaluation to implementation, can produce situations in which the action taken in implementing policy is contrary to the recommendations that initiated the action. Simulated results are based on assumed conditions. If policy is not implemented using strategies that produce these conditions, desired results will not be achieved. Effective involvement of those familiar with the simulation in the implementation program can ensure that actions taken and criteria applied are reasonably consistent with those established in analysis. Misinterpretation of policy directives can be minimized and mistakes based on lack of understanding reduced.

Review Procedures

Review procedures should be established during the implementation phase to ensure that the established course of action is reviewed at appropriate intervals. These procedures should be designed to detect significant changes in relevant conditions and to initiate management reconsideration of the problem. A management that understands a simulation structure and recognizes its limitations will not expect a decision based on one series of runs incorporating data available at one point in time to represent a final solution valid for all time. They will recognize the desirability, if not the necessity, for continuing policy review.

Unless appropriate review procedures are established in advance and management recognizes the need to reconsider policy decisions based on a simulation when factors to which the simulation is sensitive change, a shift in underlying environmental conditions may result in application of a wholly outdated policy.

A Four-Phase Approach

If basic agreement regarding the desirability of management involvement in the system development process is assumed, the relevant question becomes "What approach to the implementation of quantitative techniques will provide for this type of involvement and lead to the orderly development of an operating system?" In working with policy managements to design and implement microanalytic simulations, the author and his associates have established a four-phase approach which has proved effective in achieving the noted objectives.

Provision for Evaluation and Review

A basic tenet of this approach is that system design, development, and implementation should be undertaken in an orderly, cautious fashion, with adequate provision for management review at preplanned points. This assures that all concerned understand what is being done and are convinced of its utility before resources are commited on a large scale.

The Four Phases

The four phases of the program may be described as (1) macrospecification development, (2) microspecification development, (3) testing and evaluation, and (4) implementation.

Macrospecification Development

The macrospecification development phase is designed to achieve two interrelated objectives. First, to acquaint management with the microanalytic simulation technique and associated model building procedures. Second, to provide an opportunity for management and advisers to establish a conceptual framework and to define objectives and theories in measurable terms.

During the macrospecification phase, major emphasis is placed on making explicit that which management knows, assumes, and hopes. Underlying assumptions about the nature of the environment are given close scrutiny.

As noted earlier, there is a danger that in discussing policy problems one may reach apparent conclusions as a result of different people using the same words to describe different ideas. If words are ambiguous enough, it is possible to achieve agreement in form without facing fundamental disagreements as to facts. During the first stages of phase 1, every effort is made to minimize the potentialities of future problems based on such communication failures.

On the basis of conclusions reached during phase 1, boundary conditions determining the scope and detail of behavior to be encompassed by sector models are established. The conceptual framework developed in this phase (comparable to that established in Chapter 3) provides the structure for detailed representations formulated in later phases.

At the completion of phase 1 interactions between managers and model builders are summarized in a set of macrospecifications detailing conclusions reached regarding the nature of the problem environment. These specifications provide a broad but definite description of the facts and assumptions to be encompassed by later models and delineate criteria to be employed in evaluating simulation runs. Criteria development is particularly valuable in that it focuses management attention on objectives. In order to specify criteria to be used in evaluating model performance management must establish the basis for choice between alternatives.

Microspecification Development

The microspecification phase may be conveniently considered in terms of the two related but functionally separate subsections pertaining to (*a*) sector model design and formulation and (*b*) system programming and testing.

The first activity in this phase is the formulation of detailed sector models based on management hypotheses regarding the behavior to be simulated, verified where possible with reference to existing data. Working within the structure supplied by the macrospecifications, microspecifications detailing the characteristics of sector models are developed. The microspecifications contain detailed descriptions of each functional relationship (comparable to those presented in Chapters 7 through 11) and complete instructions for system design and programming.

Most behavioral simulations involve the development of relatively complex computer programs. For this reason, program coding and testing are major activities in phase 2.

Testing and Evaluation

At the beginning of phase 3 the simulation must be tested for consistency and used to generate output under specified conditions. When one or more alternative representations are proposed, criteria developed in the macrospecification stage are applied to evaluate alternative models. At the conclusion of the third phase, test results are summarized in a validation report evaluating system performance in terms of measures comparable to those discussed in Chapter 13.

Implementation

Initiation of activity in the fourth phase is contingent upon full management acceptance of phase 3 results. Phase 4 involves those previously associated with simulation design and development in an educational role working with operating personnel to implement the operating system. During this phase, review procedures, designed to ensure that representative functions in the simulation models will be monitored, and that significant changes in environmental conditions will initiate reconsideration of concepts and related policies, are established.

Organizational Considerations

When operating under a program of the type just outlined it is often useful to establish a formal organizational tie between project group members. At various times, such groups have been designated as "task force," "project group," and "steering committee." In most instances they have consisted of the major simulation system adviser and one staff man from the advising organization or department along with one member of management and one staff representative from each department or division involved in the project. This steering committee, normally chaired by the top ranking adviser or senior corporate executive, is the coordinating and planning entity for the project. Ad hoc subgroups made up of interested members of the steering committee coordinate specific activities within each project phase.

The steering committee may perform the additional functions of lending prestige to the project group's activity and assuring effective communication. This organization also facilitates consideration of alternative approaches from several different perspectives and detection of best sources of information in addition to the more obvious functions associated with achievement of the objectives outlined previously.

A Qualification

An important qualification should be noted with respect to the suggested approach. It will work only with certain types of managers. It requires a specific management orientation and personality.

The managers involved in the steering committee must be interested in making better decisions. They must be sufficiently confident and mature to consider contradictory model structures and to choose between alternatives on the basis of rational evaluation. They must be willing to give up implicit models with which they have worked for many years if, when made explicit and tested, these models are found lacking.

Over and above the personalities of individual managers, the environment within the company must support a free interchange of ideas. If managers are unable to separate ideas from men — if they evaluate the worth of a concept in terms of the title of the individual proposing it — steering committee sessions will quickly give way to corporate infighting.

Obviously no company has a management that is perfectly objective or an organization devoid of all negative attributes. In final analysis, successful implementation is dependent on the ability of proponents of the microanalytic simulation approach to communicate this concept and of management's willingness to engage in this type of activity, recognizing the commitment required for success.

Management Uses of Simulation

At the conclusion of phase 3, management must assess system performance in terms of intended applications. If, in their opinion, performance is sufficiently good to warrant use of the simulation as a representation of the real-world environment, applications of the type outlined below may be appropriate. However, if, in their opinion, the simulation fails to duplicate salient attributes of the real-world environment, further development leading to a more refined system must be undertaken or the use of the technique rejected.

Testing Implicit Models

One of the first benefits to accrue from the development of a simulation system is the systematic testing of management conceptions of the environment in which they operate. In reviewing alternative formulations and evaluating functions, cell model behavior, and total population performance, management must make explicit the often implicit models on which their decision making is based.

The "What If" Question

Given that management accepts simulation performance as indicative of real-world response under comparable conditions, the simulation becomes a test market without a memory in which management may examine with impunity the implications of alternative policies and strategies. Whether introducing new products or considering modification of a marketing program, management may apply alternative strategies in the simulated environment and evaluate their implications under various assumed competitive conditions.

The effectiveness of such pretesting is dependent on management's ability to predict probable competitive responses to proposed actions as well as the accuracy of the simulation system. Management may find it profitable to examine the impact of best and worst case competitive response patterns. In most instances the best case assumes that competition will continue with programs developed prior to initiation of company actions, while the worst case assumes full competitor knowledge of the proposed company program and combined action to thwart company efforts.

Performance References

The simulated environment provides the references against which the progress of operations in the real world may be measured. Given a simulation pretest, management can determine by monitoring appropriate variables whether or not a program is progressing as planned. If conditions producing satisfactory performance in the simulated environment are encountered in the real world, it is assumed that final results will be comparable.

Simulation-Based Management Information Systems

Management uses of microanalytic simulation may be summarized with reference to a simulation-based management information system of the type illustrated in Figure 15.1. Data-gathering procedures are established to generate inputs describing the current state of the market in terms of measures referenced in the simulation structure. These inputs are reviewed and the format set by a preprocessor system before being transferred to the master data file. The data file serves as the reference source for the information system and provides the historical data base for simulation model initialization.

Management has the ability to interrogate the data file to obtain information regarding the current state of the market. This basic retrieval function is described by the set of interactions noted by A in Figure 15.1. Management's use of the simulation model as a basis for testing proposed programs is illustrated by the interaction set indicated by B. Proposed plans are input to the information system, which establishes hypothetical

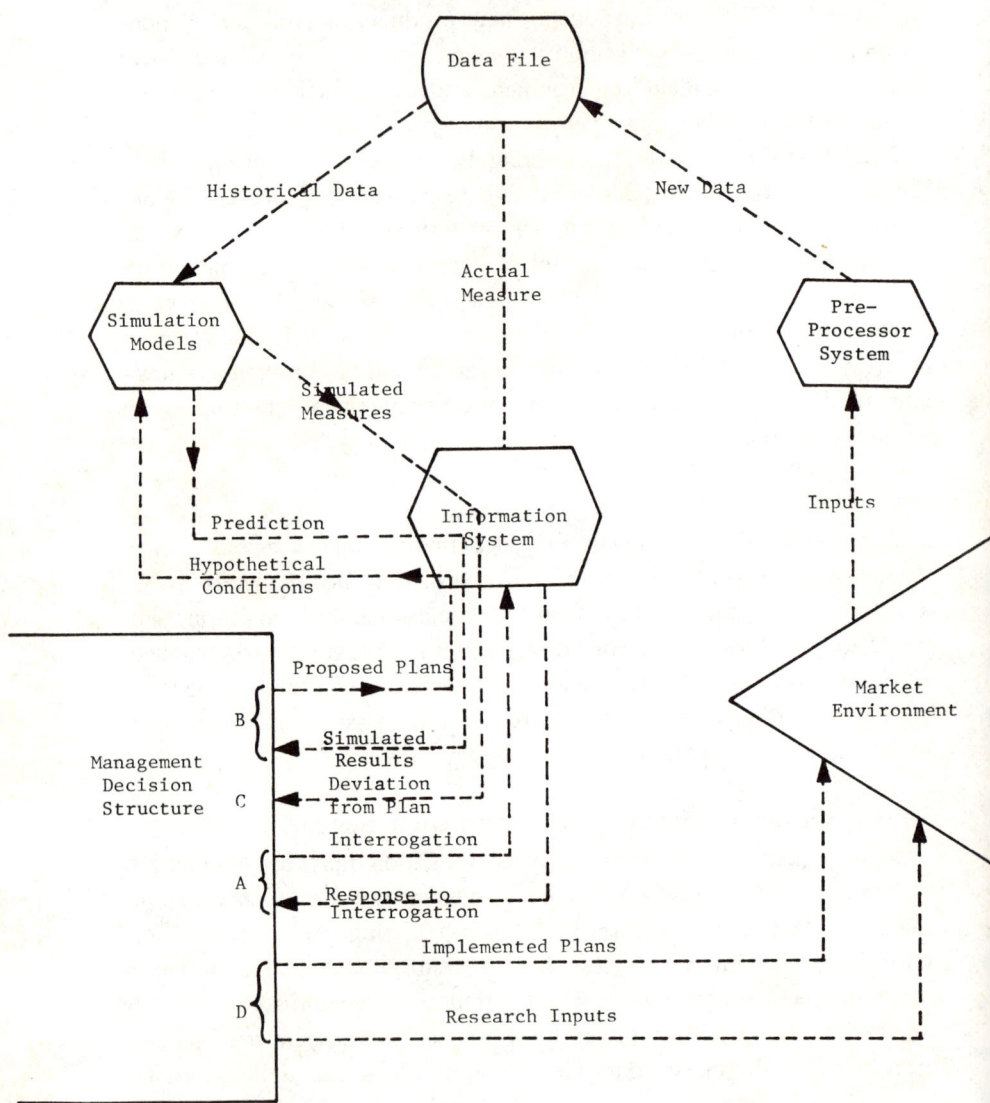

Figure 15.1. Simulation-based management information system structure.

conditions for runs of the simulation model. Results obtained in the simulated environment are then transferred to the information system, which formats them for presentation to management. Following this process, management is able to evaluate the conditional results of proposed programs using the same procedures and equipment employed to assess the current state of the market through interrogation.

Once policy and strategy have been finalized, the proposed plan is established as a reference, and simulated measures based on the plan are generated for use by a monitor program. As plans are implemented in the market environment, the monitor program compares actual measures of market performance with simulated measures indicating the expected results of planned implementation. Significant deviation from plan becomes the criterion for monitor referral to management as indicated by C in Figure 15.1. The information system may be used to evaluate the results of research activities as well as operating plans, as indicated by D.

Summary

This chapter has focused on factors influencing the successful implementation of microanalytic behavioral simulations in operating companies. It has been suggested that the probability of successful implementation at a policy management level may be substantially increased through careful organization, high management involvement, orderly development, and preplanned review and evaluation. A four-phase development and implementation procedure was described.

It has been argued that management involvement in system design, development, and evaluation may be the single most important determinant of successful application. Involvement of the type proposed is believed to challenge management to state hypotheses about the nature of the business environment unambiguously. This emphasis on converting implicit assumptions to explicit statements has been credited with creating an environment conducive to the continued and expanded use of microanalytic simulation.

Three major areas of simulation application were noted: (1) testing implicit models, (2) evaluating proposed policies and strategies, and (3) establishing performance references.

INDEX